At
Freedom's
Door

At Freedom's Door

AFRICAN AMERICAN FOUNDING FATHERS AND LAWYERS IN RECONSTRUCTION SOUTH CAROLINA

EDITED BY

JAMES LOWELL UNDERWOOD AND W. LEWIS BURKE JR.

WITH AN INTRODUCTION BY ERIC FONER

University of South Carolina Press

© 2000 University of South Carolina

Published in Columbia, South Carolina, by the
University of South Carolina Press

Manufactured in the United States of America

04   03   02   01   00   5   4   3   2   1

Library of Congress Cataloging-in-Publication Data

At freedom's door : African American founding fathers and lawyers in
   Reconstruction South Carolina / edited by James Lowell Underwood and
   W. Lewis Burke, Jr.
      p.   cm.
   Includes bibliographical references and index.
   ISBN 1-57003-357-9 (cloth)
      1. Afro-Americans—South Carolina—Politics and government—19th
century.   2. Reconstruction—South Carolina.   3. Afro-American
leadership—South Carolina—History—19th century.   4. Afro-American
judges—South Carolina—History—19th century.   5. Afro-American
lawyers—South Carolina—History—19th century.   6. South Carolina—
Politics and government—1865–1950.   7. South Carolina—Race relations.
I. Underwood, James L.   II. Burke, William Lewis.   III. Title.
E185.93.S7 A8   2000
975.7004'96073'0922—dc21   00-008951

Contents

Illustrations

Preface

The history of the role of the African American founding fathers, lawyers, and judges in Reconstruction South Carolina has never been completely told. In fact, many of these men were virtually unknown until the monumental works of Eric Foner, J. Clay Smith Jr., and John Oldfield began to shed some light on these important figures in South Carolina history. This book includes additional contributions by those three fine historians plus those by Richard Gergel and Belinda Gergel, Michael Robert Mounter, and the editors.

The inspiration for this book really began with the discovery by Richard and Belinda Gergel of a photograph of Jonathan Jasper Wright. Their discovery led to the South Carolina Supreme Court's commissioning of a portrait of Justice Wright and formation of the South Carolina Supreme Court Historical Society. The founding committee was chaired by Richard Gergel and included Justice Jean Toal, Joseph D. Shine, James A. Stuckey Jr., and Robert S. Wells. The founders of the society then developed the idea of sponsoring an annual conference in which leading academics would be invited to present papers related to the legal history of South Carolina. After obtaining financial support from the South Carolina Bar Association, the South Carolina Bar Foundation, and the University of South Carolina School of Law, Richard Gergel organized the inaugural seminar for February 1998. This seminar was preceded by the unveiling of the supreme court's portrait of Justice Wright and the first annual meeting of the Supreme Court Historical Society.

The seminar was entitled "Jonathan Jasper Wright and the Early African-American Bar in South Carolina." At the seminar, papers were presented by Eric Foner of Columbia University, J. Clay Smith Jr. of Howard University, James Lowell Underwood of the University of South Carolina Law School, John Oldfield of Southampton University, W. Lewis Burke Jr. of the University of South Carolina Law School, and Randall Kennedy of Harvard Law School. I. S. Leevy Johnson moderated a discussion by some of the African American judges in South Carolina who reflected upon the challenges that faced them as minority lawyers attempting to carve out a career during the tempest of the early civil rights movement. These judges were Chief Justice Ernest A. Finney Jr., U.S.

District Judge Matthew J. Perry, Circuit Judge Richard E. Fields, and Family Court Judge Willie T. Smith.

After the seminar, Professor Burke proposed to all of the contributors that the papers should be published as a collection. Almost all of the contributors were able to prepare their papers for publication, and Richard and Belinda Gergel and Michael Mounter were recruited to author papers related to the seminar.

This book grows out of a need to more thoroughly explore the African American role in government and law during Reconstruction in South Carolina. The founding fathers, judges, and lawyers discussed in this book left a legacy that has not been fully recognized. The Underwood chapter demonstrates that the contribution of African Americans to the Constitutional Convention of 1868 was critical in the drafting of the first true democratic constitution in the history of the state. These men saw to it that South Carolina had a modern constitution whose reforms in areas such as public education have persisted to this day. In other areas, such as voting rights and local government, the reforms were abandoned after Reconstruction; but similar measures returned in the late twentieth century under federal civil rights legislation and the state government modernization movement. Contrary to the stereotype, the leading African American delegates to the Constitutional Convention of 1868 displayed considerable debating skill and intellectual firepower in developing political, legal, philosophical, and comparative government arguments in framing a new fundamental law for the state during tumultuous times. Charts and an appendix illustrate the varied voting patterns of the African American delegates on key issues.

The Smith and Gergel articles on Justice Jonathan Jasper Wright reveal much new biographical information about the first African American to sit on a state supreme court and reveal much about Justice Wright's jurisprudence and his role in the turbulent times of Reconstruction. The Smith chapter examines Wright's approach to judicial decision making, and the Gergel chapter probes his entire life with emphasis on his role in the Dual Government Controversy and events leading to his resignation from the state supreme court under pressure. Lewis Burke's chapter on the "radical" period in the history of the law school exposes a long lost history and highlights the careers of the first African American lawyers educated in the South. John Oldfield's chapter focuses attention on the fact that there were African American lawyers and an African American–run law school in post-Reconstruction South Carolina. For the first time, Oldfield and Burke's appendix provides as complete as possible data on who all of the African American lawyers were in South Carolina in the nineteenth century. Michael Mounter captures the story of Richard T. Greener, the first African American graduate of Harvard, the first African American professor at the University of South Carolina, a lawyer, and a diplomat. And finally, in his introduction and his chapter Eric Foner places both South Carolina and Reconstruction in a national context. Just as Professor Foner subtitled his book, *Reconstruction*, "America's Unfinished Revolution," in this present volume of essays we again see that, while South Carolina's African Americans stood at freedom's door, their revolution cannot be complete until all of their story is told.

Acknowledgments

Many people and institutions deserve praise for their assistance on this project. In fact, we feel honored to have been able to work with many outstanding scholars. So first we want to thank Eric Foner, J. Clay Smith Jr., John Oldfield, Richard Gergel, Belinda Gergel, and Michael Robert Mounter not only for their chapters but for their cooperation. The sage advice of Clay Smith is really appreciated. While Randall Kennedy's schedule prevented him from participating, we want to thank him for his participation in the seminar and invaluable help in obtaining research materials.

We also have to thank the South Carolina Supreme Court Historical Society and the South Carolina Bar for their help. Special thanks is owed to Karen Taylor, Michael Mounter, Joe Cross, Rebekah Maxwell, Pamela Melton, Rob Jacobi, and Shirley Williams of the University of South Carolina Law Library. Pamela Robinson of the USC Law School's Legal History Collection is owed a special thanks. South Caroliniana Library and its staff deserve praise not only for their help but for their endeavors to preserve so much history with so few monetary resources. Appreciation needs to be expressed to Allen Stokes, Roberta Copp, Thelma Hayes, and Mark Herro of South Caroliniana. The staff of the South Carolina Department of Archives and History was most helpful, and the advice of Marion Chandler was especially useful.

We must thank the University of South Carolina School of Law for its financial support for the seminar and this book and Dean John E. Montgomery for his collegial support throughout. We had great support by our student research assistants. Of especial help were Tracey Mitchell, Justin Werner, James Lai, Stephanie Nye, Romona Keith, and Ariane Deutz. The staff of the Law School's Information Processing Center were our constant allies. We have to say thank you to Deanna Sugrue, Frances Molten, Doris Cooper, Janice Face, Nancy Shealy, and Vanessa Byars.

We also have to thank the staffs of the many institutions and libraries that helped with interlibrary loans and research questions. Because of our desire to include many photographs and pictures of the African American leaders discussed in this book, we owe an especial thanks to a number of people and institutions. First, we have to say thank you to artist Larry Francis Lebby for graciously allowing us to use the portraits of Jonathan Jasper Wright, Samuel J. Lee, and Robert Brown Elliott. The South Carolina Supreme Court, the South Carolina House of Representatives, and the University of South Carolina allowed us special access to the works of Mr. Lebby, and to them we are grateful. Special thanks is due South Caroliniana Library for allowing us to use numerous photographs from their collection. We also must thank the Library of Congress, the South Carolina Department of Archives and History, the Denver Public Library, Western History Collection, the Chattanooga-Hamilton County Bicentennial Library, Allen University, Oberlin College Archives, Charles Sumner Brown, J. Clay Smith Jr., O. V. Burton and C. B. Bailey Jr. for the use of other prints and photographs in this volume. We are also appreciative to the Amistad Center at Tulane University, the University of Georgia Library, College of Charleston, University of Florida, Emory University, Atlanta-Fulton Public Library, Kent State University, University of Wyoming, Arizona State University, Detroit Public Library, Georgetown University, Western Carolina University, Jacksonville State University, Harvard University, and SUNY at Buffalo for their granting access to their materials. We also need to acknowledge Keith McGraw and Phil Sawyer for their camera work.

We also must thank the University of South Carolina Press for all of their help. We want to especially thank Alexander Moore for his patience and assistance. We want to thank Richard Gergel for his vision in creating the South Carolina Supreme Court Historical Society and for his enthusiasm for this book. Finally, we appreciate the help of our wives, Joan Underwood and Anne Johnson Burke, for both their editorial suggestions and their patience.

Introduction

ERIC FONER

The papers collected in this volume form part of the ongoing reevaluation of one of the most crucial periods of American history—the era of Reconstruction that followed the Civil War. The task of rewriting Reconstruction's history and dispelling many of the myths that surrounded it has occupied scholars of the period for the better part of the past half century. The papers that follow shed new light on Reconstruction in South Carolina, the state where African Americans probably achieved the greatest political power after the Civil War. In recounting and honoring the career of Jonathan J. Wright, the first African American to serve on a state supreme court in American history, and in viewing Wright's career from the perspective of South Carolina's history after the Civil War, the essays make a notable contribution to our understanding of Reconstruction. It is worthwhile, however, to recount briefly some of Reconstruction's national significance, in order to place the South Carolina experience in a broader historical context.

Reconstruction was a period of profound change in all aspects of American life. The Civil War, as we all know, not only preserved the Union but destroyed the institution of slavery. And the fundamental question that agitated American life in the period after the Civil War was precisely how our society would respond to emancipation. What system of labor would replace slave labor? What system of race relations would replace the race relations of slavery? What would be the role of former slaves in American civic life? These questions became the focus of a tremendous political struggle in which African Americans themselves played a central role by demanding that the nation give substantive meaning to the freedom they had acquired.

This introduction is primarily drawn from two of the author's other works, *Reconstruction: America's Unfinished Revolution 1863–1877* (New York: Harper & Row, 1988) and *Freedom's Lawmakers: A Directory of Black Officeholders during Reconstruction* (Baton Rouge: Louisiana State University Press, 1996).

As a result of this political crisis, a series of laws was passed that for the first time in American history established the principle of equal rights before the law for all citizens regardless of race. The Civil Rights Act of 1866, passed by Congress over the veto of President Andrew Johnson, the Fourteenth and Fifteenth Amendments, the Civil Rights Act of 1875—these and other measures declared that black Americans were citizens of the United States and would have the same legal rights as other citizens, that is to say the same laws and punishments would apply to them as to whites, and neither the government nor places of public accommodation could discriminate against them because of race. In addition, black men, although not women, received the right to vote in the South in 1867, and later throughout the nation via the Fifteenth Amendment.

It is important to recognize how revolutionary a change in American society these measures represented. Today it is a part of the very nature of our society to assume that all Americans will be equal before the law. This is not to say that African Americans are in fact treated equally, but legal distinctions between American citizens no longer exist. In the Reconstruction era, this was a completely new idea in American society—there was no precedent for it. Slavery had been an intrinsic part of the original Constitution. Before the Civil War, both northern and southern states practiced widespread discrimination against black Americans, whether free or slave. In 1857, in the *Dred Scott* decision, the Supreme Court ruled that no black person could be a citizen of the United States. The Constitution begins with the words "We the People of the United States." The "people," the Court declared in *Dred Scott*, meant the white people. Thus, the establishment in Reconstruction of civil and political equality represented a radical change in the nature of American public life. Indeed, it was precisely because of this that Reconstruction aroused such bitter opposition. "We are not of the same race," declared Indiana senator Thomas Hendricks. "We are so different that we ought not be compose one political community." Reconstruction represented a remarkable repudiation of the prewar tradition that defined America as a "white man's government," and it created for the first time an interracial democracy in which rights attached to persons not in their capacity as members of racially defined groups but as members of the American people. The implementation of this principle in the South during the period of Radical Reconstruction (1867–77) witnessed the establishment of new state governments that sought to reform fundamentally the legal, social, educational, and political structure of the region—as the papers in this volume describe.

This departure was intimately related to a second profound change—the establishment of the federal government as the main protector of citizens' rights. The laws and amendments of Reconstruction gave the national government the authority to intervene in local and state affairs to protect the basic rights of all American citizens. As with equal civil and political rights, this is a principle that we generally take for granted, although it has been challenged of late. Certainly, during the civil rights era it was widely accepted that the ultimate guardian of citizens' rights was the federal government. This principle was established during the first Reconstruction, and again it represented a repudiation of the previous traditions of American history. Before the Civil War, most Americans (most free Americans at any rate) believed that a powerful national government posed a danger to their liberties, that local and state authorities could best protect the rights of citizens. The Bill of Rights, added to the Constitution in 1791, rested on the idea that the federal government needed to be restrained from abusing its power. The Bill of Rights does not apply to the states at all. It prohibits Congress from restricting the freedom of speech or the press and from taking away your freedom of worship. States before the Civil War had the power, and frequently exercised it, to deprive people of freedom of speech, or to support religion with public funds. So long as this was done by state governments and not the federal government, it did not violate the Constitution.

The Civil War and Reconstruction reversed this pattern, thus redefining the nature of American federalism. With the Fourteenth Amendment, the Bill of Rights was now applied to the states. Indeed, the amendment made the federal government responsible for ensuring that the states abide by the Constitution in this respect. The Fourteenth Amendment prohibited states from denying any American the "equal protection of the laws" or abridging the "privileges and immunities" of citizens. This broad language opened the door for future Congresses and the federal courts to define and redefine the guarantee of legal equality, a process that has occupied the courts for the better part of the last half century. Perhaps I can illustrate this point most clearly by contrasting the language of the Bill of Rights with that of the Thirteenth, Fourteenth, and Fifteenth Amendments. The Bill of Rights restrains federal power—"Congress shall pass no law," it begins. The three Civil War–era amendments all end with a section empowering Congress to pass appropriate legislation for enforcement. The federal government, not the states, had become, in Charles Sumner's words, "the custodian of freedom."

Let me turn briefly to the economic realm, since the problems of former slaves were not, of course, simply related to their civil and political status. Most blacks came out of slavery impoverished and propertyless. The believed that freedom meant more than simply not being a slave. Along with emancipation should come equal standing in the polity, access to education, autonomy for their families, and ownership of land. Slavery, said black minister Garrison Frazier, was "receiving . . . the work of another man, and not by his consent." Freedom meant "placing us where we could reap the fruit of our own labor." Genuine economic freedom, Frazier insisted, could only be attained through ownership of land, for without land, blacks' labor would continue to be exploited by their former owners. Former slaves believed that they had earned, through their 250 years of unrequited labor, a claim to land in the South. There were some in the North, most prominent among them Thaddeus Stevens, the Radical Republican congressman from Pennsylvania, who urged the federal government to confiscate land belonging to former slave owners and give it, in forty-acre plots, to the former slaves.

Of course, this did not happen. Most northerners probably believed it would not be a bad idea if former slaves obtained some land. But they did not think that it was the role of the federal government to *give* them land belonging to someone else. According to the prevailing free labor ideology, individuals should work for wages, save their money, and slowly acquire the wherewithal to purchase land for themselves. The government's role was to remove artificial barriers to social mobility, such as the Black Codes enacted by southern legislatures during Presidential Reconstruction, codes which required most blacks to sign yearly contracts to labor on white-owned plantations. The Civil Rights Act of 1866 voided the Black Codes and insisted that the rights of free labor—to sign contracts freely, acquire and own property, sue and be sued, enjoy equal treatment before the laws and courts—were essential ingredients of citizenship. But beyond this, Congress would not go. And the idea that blacks would slowly work their way up the agricultural ladder proved completely unrealistic in the postwar South. The wages that former slaves could earn were very low, and most whites were not willing to sell land to blacks. Those African Americans who did acquire land often became special targets of the Ku Klux Klan.

By itself, land ownership would not have offered a panacea for the economic plight of former slaves. After all, millions of white farmers were losing their land in the last third of the nineteenth century. But land distribution would have sharply altered the balance of power in the rural South and given the freedpeople far more choice as to when, where, and under what circumstances to enter the wage labor market. In the end, most former slaves were consigned to the situation of being propertyless laborers on land owned by whites, often their own former slave owners. So there was a vast dichotomy between the very real and dramatic political gains and the failure of Reconstruction to address significantly the economic plight of the mass of black Americans. What happened in Reconstruction, one might say, is that the political revolution went forward on the basis of equality, but the economic revolution, the transition from slavery to freedom, produced an extremely unequal system of class relations.

Even the political changes of the first Reconstruction, of course, proved to be temporary. The final abandonment of Reconstruction came in 1877; there followed a long period in which the laws and Constitutional amendments, although remaining on the books, had no bearing on the actual conditions of life of blacks in the South. Why did political Reconstruction fail? Why did white southerners rally against their new governments and the North progressively abandon its commitment to equal citizenship? First, there were charges of corruption by the southern governments, in which black Americans for the first time held public offices. The Democratic Party charged, and northerners increasingly came to believe, that alleged southern misgovernment arose not from a general decline of public morality (after all, the depredations of the Tweed Ring in New York City and the scandals of the Grant administration involved far more money than anything seen in the Reconstruction South) but from the inherent incapacity of African Americans. As social Darwinism gained increasing acceptance among intellectuals, journalists, and politicians in the North, the Reconstruction ideal of racial equality came to seem a remnant of a romantic, unscientific era. Only a restoration of white supremacy could bring good government to the South.

During the 1870s, the cry of reverse discrimination was raised by Reconstruction's opponents, who charged that black Americans had become special favorites of the law. Somehow, the efforts of the federal government to uplift and protect former slaves came to be seen by many white Americans as a form of favoritism, which in effect discriminated against the white population. President Andrew Johnson played upon this sentiment in his veto messages; the Reconstruction measures, he insisted, were efforts to aid the black race, as he called it, but nothing was being done for whites. Of course blacks responded that it was ludicrous to call efforts to counteract the effects of 250 years of slavery special privilege or, in the language of the day, "class legislation." "The white race," replied black political leader William Whipper in the 1870s, "have had the benefit of class legislation ever since the foundation of our government." But Johnson's argument, echoed in the 1870s by increasing numbers of northern Republicans, proved to be a potent weapon in the hands of Reconstruction's opponents. The idea of reverse discrimination dovetailed with a resurgence of localist and laissez-faire ideology, a sense that the federal government had become too powerful and intrusive, and that power needed to devolve back to the states.

At the state level, too, Reconstruction's opponents charged that public authorities were assuming too many new responsibilities. The Reconstruction governments in the South established the region's first public school systems, provided medical care for the poor, built asylums, and sought to promote economic development. These programs cost money, a great deal of money. The states were now serving a much larger population, since before the Civil War southern governments provided services only for whites. After the war, property values in the South were sharply lower. The result of all this was that taxes went up. The cry of excessive taxation was a potent weapon against the Reconstruction governments. Southern Democrats insisted that the region must reduce the level of government expenditures and cut taxes, even if it meant gutting social expenditures like education.

Finally, of course, there was rampant violence in the South, by criminal organizations like the Ku Klux Klan. The inability of local governments to put down violence and the federal government's unwillingness, after the early 1870s, to intervene to protect the rights of black citizens helped to doom the Reconstruction experiment.

In this retreat, the Supreme Court played a crucial role, a fact that must have been especially galling to accomplished black jurists like Jonathan J. Wright. In 1873, in the *Slaughter-House* decision, the Court severely restricted the scope of rights the federal government could protect under the Fourteenth Amendment. Soon afterwards, in *United States v. Reese*, the court emasculated federal power to prosecute those who used violence to deprive individuals of the right to vote, insisting that law enforcement was almost always a state concern. In 1883, in the Civil Rights Cases, the Court declared unconstitutional the Civil Rights Act of 1875, which had prohibited racial discrimination in public accommodations. Invoking the specter of reverse discrimination, Justice Joseph P. Bradley declared that henceforth, blacks must no longer think of themselves as "the special favorite of the laws." The decision made it impossible for the federal government to protect blacks from day-to-day discrimination, even had the will to do so survived.

By 1896, when the Court gave the green light, in *Plessy v. Ferguson*, to white southerners to construct whatever racial system they desired without fear of federal intervention, the Fourteenth Amendment had already become a dead letter in much of the South. The decision was important not only for what it said, but for what it symbolized about American politics, social thought, and race relations at the close of the nineteenth century. The 1890s, after all, witnessed the resurgence of a racialist outlook that united patriotism, xenophobia, and an ethnocultural definition of nationhood in a renewed rhetoric of racial exclusiveness. Two years after *Plessy*, America's triumphant entry onto the world stage as an imperial power in the Spanish-American War tied nationalism ever more closely to notions of Anglo-Saxon superiority. In speaking for the Court in *Plessy*, Justice Henry B. Brown declared that the Fourteenth Amendment could hardly have been intended to abolish all distinctions based on color, since what he called "racial instincts" were inborn, unreachable by law. If blacks construed forced segregation as demeaning, they had only their own excessive sensitivities to blame. Yet Brown also referred to whites as the "dominant race," suggesting that blacks had some ground for feeling that they were being accorded inferior treatment.

In this context, the alleged "failure" of Reconstruction strongly reinforced racialist thought, fueling the conviction that nonwhites were unfit for self-government. Historians at Columbia University and elsewhere would soon be giving scholarly legitimacy to a view of Reconstruction premised on the idea that granting blacks the right to vote had been a terrible mistake, and that white southerners knew better than meddling outsiders how to deal with their region's "race problem."

The *Plessy* case, of course, applied specifically to a Louisiana law mandating separate cars for railroad passengers. But as Justice John Marshall Harlan predicted in his lone dissent, segregation, which had already developed informally in many sectors of southern life, now became a pillar of the region's racial system. *Plessy* unleashed a flood of legislation affecting institutions from schools to hospitals, waiting rooms to toilets, pay windows to cemeteries. Despite what Harlan called the "thin disguise" of equality mandated by the "separate but equal" doctrine, separate facilities were always unequal, and always demeaning.

It is worth noting that while the South's post-Reconstruction racial system was far more severe than race relations in the rest of the country, segregation was a national, not a regional, phenomenon. Although most northern states did not require it by law, the practice was pervasive. Nor would it be accurate to describe the federal government as simply abandoning civil rights enforcement. Rather, for much of this century Washington actively promoted segregation and racial inequality. Woodrow Wilson ordered federal offices in Washington segregated. New Deal programs like Social Security intentionally omitted from coverage domestic and agricultural laborers—the largest job categories for blacks—at the insistence of powerful southern congressmen chosen by lily-white electorates. Federal housing authorities reinforced residential segregation by refusing to allow blacks and whites into the same public housing projects and channeling mortgage loans almost exclusively to whites. Thus, when the civil rights movement reached its peak in the 1950s and 1960s, its task was not simply to dismantle legalized segregation, but to combat the legacy of decades of discriminatory actions by federal and state authorities, private employers, real estate agents, educators, and a host of others.

I think it was the historian C. Vann Woodward who coined the phrase "the Second Reconstruction" to refer to the period from 1954 to the late 1960s. Although history never really repeats itself, the parallels between the two eras are certainly evident. On the political and legal ground, the second Reconstruction was an effort to reinvigorate, to breathe new life into the principles established during the first. The Fourteenth and Fifteenth Amendments were still parts of the Constitution. The Civil Rights Act of 1866 was still on the books, as were laws to suppress the Ku Klux Klan. It took the greatest mass movement of the century to force the national government and federal courts, after seventy or eighty years of looking the other way, to enforce the laws which had been enacted during Reconstruction, and to pass new ones. The political gains of the second Reconstruction have proved to be more permanent than those of the first. The right to vote is now guaranteed. The edifice of legal segregation has been dismantled and many areas of our society—from workplaces to universities to the mass media—are far more integrated than was conceivable a few decades ago.

On the other hand, numerous and disturbing parallels exist between the retreat from the first Reconstruction and the events of the past generation. One is the role of the Supreme Court. Just as the judicial retreat did not happen overnight in the nineteenth century, so we have seen, over the past twenty years, a slow but steady repudiation by the Court of the idea of aggressive enforcement of civil rights laws, and a narrowing of the definition of racial equality. I am less concerned here with the specifics of individual cases than the general pattern by which the Court today interprets civil rights laws in the narrowest possible manner without actually overturning them. Lately, the Court has also begun aggressively to reassert the powers of the states and move away from the broad definition of federal power embodied in the constitutional amendments of the first Reconstruction and the legislation of the second.

As during the first retreat, the Court's recent decisions reflect a growing skepticism in society at large about efforts to undo the legacy of 250 years of slavery, now exacerbated by nearly a century of segregation. Blatant appeals to racism are not, to be sure, nearly as prominent as a century ago, and the Ku Klux Klan is nowhere near the force it was in the 1870s. But taken together, much of our public discourse on race, taxation, state rights, and laissez-faire, and on the wastefulness of public spending and the intractability of poverty, is eerily reminiscent of the political dialogue of a century ago.

Another key parallel between the first and second Reconstructions lies in the economic realm. Even though the second Reconstruction achieved a much more permanent guarantee of the basic political and civil rights of African Americans than the first, it likewise failed to confront effectively the economic plight of most African Americans. One has only to look at statistics of unemployment, health, housing, and family wealth and income to appreciate this failure. It is important to note, however, that one result of the second Reconstruction has been a widening of class differentiation among African Americans, making the problem of assessing economic progress that much more complex. We have witnessed the rise of a large, impoverished "underclass" as well as severe economic problems for the much larger black working class, hard hit by recessions and the flight of manufacturing jobs from urban centers to rural areas or low-wage areas abroad. But at the same time, thanks in large measure to the civil rights revolution and to the affirmative action programs of the 1970s and 1980s, the number of black professionals and of blacks in business has grown apace, as has the proportion of black families earning, say, fifty thousand dollars per year. This widening gap within the black community makes the task of addressing the economic plight of the underclass or the working class much more problematic.

Drawing lessons from the past is a hazardous enterprise. But one lesson of both Reconstructions is that rights need to be defended after they are won. As Thomas Wentworth Higginson, who commanded a black regiment in the Civil War, said at that time, "Revolutions may go backward." The first Reconstruction went backward after being a revolution. The second Reconstruction has begun to go backward as well. Anyone who grew up, as I did, in the 1940s and 1950s knows that American society has changed in profound ways, and for the better, as a result of the second Reconstruction. But the struggle to protect these gains continues long after they have been won. Meanwhile, it is worth recalling again, as the essays in this volume so eloquently do, the heroic struggles of black South Carolinians and their white allies to construct on the ashes of slavery a society that truly lived up to the dream of liberty and equality for all.

At Freedom's Door

1

African American Founding Fathers

The Making of the South Carolina
Constitution of 1868

JAMES LOWELL UNDERWOOD

INTRODUCTION

The South Carolina Constitution of 1868 was a wrenching departure from the state's past wrought by the Civil War and Reconstruction. The political world was turned upside down. For the first time African Americans exercised a strong voice in framing South Carolina's fundamental law.[1] They produced a modern constitution. It contained a balanced tripartite form of government that bore more resemblance to the United States Constitution than it did to its legislatively dominated South Carolina antecedents.[2] Comprehensive local governments replaced the patchwork of specialized commissions that had governed everything from road construction to welfare throughout much of pre–Civil War South Carolina.[3] A detailed Declaration of Rights mandated political equality regardless of race and required the separation of church and state while inconsistently stipulating that no person could be governor who denied the existence of a "Supreme Being."[4] Statewide public education traces its roots to the constitution of 1868.[5] A welfare program for the aid of the poor, aged, and disabled was channeled through the county governments.[6] The constitution did not contain precise limits on public spending. The delegates trusted that restraint would be imposed by separation of powers and the political process, chiefly through a requirement that increases in state debt must be approved by a two-thirds vote of both houses of the legislature.[7] That constitution lasted for twenty-seven years. The South Carolina Constitution of 1895 dismembered many of its innovations as the product of Reconstruction and other outside forces. But a few continued with hardy persistence.

This chapter will focus on the significant role played by leading African American delegates to the constitutional convention in framing the South Carolina Constitution of 1868. Emphasis will be placed on the debates concerning the provisions relating to voting rights, education, the judicial system, local government, and religious qualifications for public office, because these discussions deal with subjects that recur in South Carolina constitutional history, and they best illustrate the forensic skills and varied views of the black delegates. Each topic will be placed in a historical setting illustrating the extent to which the 1868 document changed its predecessors or was changed by its successor, the constitution of 1895. Analysis of the debates shows an important, often pivotal role being played by the black delegates. It will be seen that any stereotype that brands the black delegates as a ragtag collection of hustlers and political naifs does not accurately reflect the actual nature of the debates. Some of the leading black delegates displayed considerable skill in dissecting the verbal refinements of the proposals, presciently reading their political implications and placing them in the context of comparative government and history.[8] Although such skills may not have been possessed by the less active majority of the black delegates, they certainly were possessed and effectively utilized by their leaders. The thoroughness with which they approached their task is exemplified by the efforts of Francis L. Cardozo, through correspondence with the American Missionary Association, to obtain copies of the constitutions of all other states prior to the convention.[9]

Blacks composed a majority of the convention delegates. The estimates of historians vary but generally place black membership at 71 to 76 out of 124 members.[10] It was once fashionable to condemn the convention members in sweeping terms.[11] One prominent early-twentieth-century Reconstruction scholar, William Dunning, referred to the southern state constitutional conventions of the late 1860s as "a group of constituent assemblies whose unfitness for their task was pitiful."[12] He admitted that there were some able members, "but the mass of the delegates consisted of whites and blacks whose ignorance and inexperience in respect to political methods were equaled only by the crudeness and distortion of their ideas as to political and social ends."[13] A more favorable view of the black delegates was expressed by the *New York Times* correspondent at the South Carolina Convention who stated, "[T]he colored men in the Convention possess by long odds the largest share of mental calibre. They are the best debaters; some of them are peculiarly apt in raising and sustaining points of order; there is a homely but strong grasp of common sense in what they say, and although the mistakes made are frequent and ludicrous, the South Carolinians are not slow to acknowledge that their destinies really appear to be safer in the hands of these unlettered Ethiopians than they would be if confided to the more unscrupulous care of the white men in the body."[14] By contrast, the *Charleston*

Mercury produced a stream of invectives questioning the qualifications, and even the humanity, of the black delegates.[15]

The South Carolina Convention has been criticized as lacking in fiscal responsibility because many delegates had insufficient wealth to incur substantial tax responsibilities.[16] But one noted twentieth-century black commentator considered this a positive trait; it gave the delegates a greater understanding of the rights and needs of those who did not come from the traditionally powerful segments of society.[17] Many of the black delegates were former slaves who had had few opportunities to gain an education; but recent commentaries have concluded, contrary to earlier assumptions, that although the level of education among the ex-slave delegates was not high, most had achieved basic literacy.[18] After studying the backgrounds of the black delegates to the ten southern state constitutional conventions that met during 1867 through 1869, Richard Hume concluded that the traditional view of the group as being "ignorant" and "propertyless" was misleading.[19] Some ex-slaves, like Robert Smalls, had managed to overcome the odds and diligently educate themselves until they "had mastered the rudiments."[20] But Eric Foner has noted that "the educated, articulate, and politically experienced freeborn delegates" dominated the debate "often outmaneuvering white participants."[21] For example, Francis Cardozo, a freeborn South Carolina native who was educated in Scottish universities, was a leading figure throughout the debates, as was Benjamin Randolph, a freeborn minister educated at Oberlin College, who came to South Carolina as a chaplain with federal black troops and returned as a representative of the American Missionary Association.[22]

Why was the work of these delegates needed at all? A new constitution had been adopted less than three years earlier. The 1865 constitution, the product of Presidential Reconstruction, during which the old white power structure still exercised sway, was timid in moving toward a broader electorate and a better balance of power among the branches of government; its grant of civil rights to the newly freed slaves was narrow, grudging, and resentful.[23]

The 1865 document recognized the abolition of slavery and dispensed with most property-holding qualifications for voting.[24] Article 1, section 4, of the 1790 constitution had contained substantial property owning–tax paying qualifications for voters, qualifications which were ameliorated by an 1810 amendment, approved after scrutiny by a legislative committee led by John C. Calhoun. The amendment provided that a citizen could be qualified to vote in a district by either owning property in it or residing there.[25] An 1808 message by Governor Charles Pinckney to the legislature had paved the way for the change by arguing "that in the future *no pecuniary qualifications* should be required from an elector of the Legislature" because the sense of responsibility needed for a voter could be demonstrated by means other than owning property, means such as performing civic duties related to residence, such as service in the militia.[26] The governor contended that widening the electoral base was an effective means for a republic to gain the loyalty of the people.[27]

This amendment was a significant movement toward universal white male suffrage in that one could vote by proving residence alone. However, by also continuing to allow nonresident property holders to vote, the 1810 amendment still gave the larger role to the propertied elements, who sometimes voted both where they resided and where they owned property until an 1833 resolution attempted to limit each person to voting in only one district in legislative elections.[28] Furthermore, voter choice continued to be limited by substantial property qualifications for house and senate membership as well as for governor.[29] The Civil War–era constitution of 1861 continued the alternative property holder–residency qualifications for voters and the property-holding qualifications for house and senate members and governor.[30] The 1865 constitution insisted that a voter not be a pauper, but it removed the property-holding alternative to residency used in the 1810 amendment.[31] The 1865 constitution provided that the governor be elected by the people rather than the legislature and moved toward a greater balance of power by restoring a weak version of the long-dormant executive veto power which was strengthened in 1868.[32] Thus it deserves credit for being a more populist document than its 1790 predecessor since it eliminated references to property in the voter qualification provisions and eliminated property qualifications for house and senate members and the governor.[33] The inequitable parish system, which gave undue weight to the Low Country in the senate, was abolished.[34] But the house of representatives apportionment method, adopted in 1808, that gave equal weight to property and white population was not abolished until the 1868 constitution provided for representation in the lower house solely on the basis of population without regard to race.[35] Thus, the 1865 fundamental law was a creature of measured, incremental change at a time when the once distant thunder of radical innovation grew louder.

Of most significance was the fact that the 1865 constitution did not grant African Americans the right to vote and retained racial qualification for house and senate membership.[36] Thus, it did not meet the requirements of the Reconstruction Act of 1867.[37] The tone was set by Governor B. F. Perry in an address to the 1865 convention. He argued, "To extend this universal suffrage to the 'freedmen' in their present ignorant and degraded condition, would be little less than folly and madness . . . [because] this is a white man's government, and intended for white men only."[38]

African Americans had difficulty getting a hearing at the 1865 convention. The *Charleston Daily Courier* observed, "It is understood that a number of negroes in Charleston city have prepared a memorial, which they have requested to be presented to the Convention by a delegate from that place, in which they claim it to be the duty of the State to extend to them equal political rights and privileges. The Charleston delegate has not seen fit to present the memorial, and we trust for the future safety and welfare of the State that the document will not be placed on the records of the proceedings."[39] Black citizens did not take the convention's failure to act on equal rights, especially voting rights, silently. In late November 1865 the Colored People's Convention met in Charleston and passed a resolution vehemently pointing out the internal contradiction in the 1865 constitution. It stated: "*Resolved*, that we endorse that portion of the State Constitution of South Carolina that declares that 'all power is vested in the *people*, and all free governments are founded upon *their authority*, and are instituted for their peace, safety and happiness,' and that we reject the construction that has been placed upon it vesting the right of suffrage in only one portion of the people; and that while we accept qualifications, we reject discriminations because of color."[40] Once the logic of broad-based suffrage had been set in motion by documents such as the 1810 amendment and the populist rhetoric of the constitution of 1865, inertia developed for following the road to the end. The 1865 constitution stopped well short of the end and clung to the past in other ways that did not bode well for African Americans.

The 1865 fundamental law created a favorable constitutional climate for the repressive Black Codes. These late 1865 statutes sought to recapture much of the power the master enjoyed during slavery while granting blacks minimal rights "to acquire, own and dispose of property; to make contracts; to enjoy the fruits of their labor; to sue and be sued; and to receive protection under the law in their persons or property" while denying them "social and political equality."[41] Article 3, section 1, of the 1865 constitution, directed the legislature to create a judicial apartheid in the form of a system of district courts, "which Court shall have jurisdiction of all civil causes wherein one or both of the parties are persons of color, and of all criminal cases wherein the accused is a person of color."[42] Under the dual court system, a white person accused of a capital crime against a "person of color" would be brought before the regular superior courts; but if the case were a civil action in which one or both parties were "persons of color," the case would be shunted into the judicial ghetto of the district courts or comparable magistrates' courts.[43] Another provision restricted the competency of black witnesses to "civil and criminal [cases], in which a person of color is a party, or which affects the person or property of a person of color."[44]

Even though the 1865 constitution recognized the abolition of slavery, many oppressive practices survived during its three-year reign. One of the harshest incidents of slavery was restriction on freedom of movement. Although the Black Codes, did not resuscitate the full range of these limits, the restrictions which they imposed did significantly curb the freedom of blacks to travel. One provision mandated that "[n]o person of color shall migrate into and reside in this State, unless, within twenty days after his arrival within the same, he shall enter into a bond with two freeholders as sureties."[45] Another feature of this labyrinthine tangle of regulations controlling the lives of "persons of color" dealt with the relationship of master and servant. A provision regulating farm workers mandated that "[s]ervants shall not be absent from the premises without the permission of the master."[46] Anyone who enticed a servant away from his master was penalized.[47] Responsibilities far exceeding those of modern day employees were imposed upon the servants, including the duty to assist the master "in the defense of his own person, family, premises or property."[48]

The economic freedom of blacks was sharply circumscribed by a provision restricting their entry into skilled trades and profitable businesses. It stipulated that no person of color could become an artisan, mechanic or shopkeeper unless he obtained a license from the judge of the district court.[49] Since the licenses were expensive (one hundred dollars per year to be a shopkeeper), the barriers blocking the economic self-improvement of blacks were formidable.[50] Such provisions insulated white artisans and shopkeepers from competition from the newly freed slave.

Even though the Black Codes were abrogated on January 1, 1866, by order of General Daniel Sickles, the federal military commander of South Carolina, and the legislature enacted new laws making blacks competent witnesses in all cases, granting them equal property rights and personal liberty, and stipulating that they should not be subjected to harsher punishment than whites, the outlook for genuine freedom, particularly the right to vote, remained bleak under the constitution of 1865.[51] Sickles's order with its strong guarantees of equal treatment under the law, including equal access to the courts, prohibition of corporal punishment of adults, ban of discriminatory taxes, and its guarantee of equal access to all occupations, had some of the qualities of a constitutional bill of rights for the post-slavery era; but a military fiat cannot do the work needed to be done by a broad-based constituent assembly.[52] The grudging approach of the 1865 constitution to the rights of blacks, among other deficiencies, necessitated the calling of the 1868 convention to comply with requirements set by the Reconstruction Act for the state to regain representation in Congress.[53]

In addition to issues concerning government structure, civil liberties, and the balance of power, the 1868 convention was also needed so that the state could address a number of economic relief issues that had not been resolved by the 1865 conclave. Many African American delegates to the 1868 convention believed that meaningful freedom required a secure economic base, such as land ownership, as well as political freedoms such as the right to vote.[54] But the 1868 convention avoided adopting radical land-reform measures such as confiscation. Instead, it passed a resolution offered by black delegate R. H. Cain to ask the president and Congress for a million dollar loan to the state to be used to buy land for the newly freed slaves and other landless citizens.[55] When this request met with a cool reception, the convention adopted an ordinance creating a land commission which would use funds raised by sale of state obligations to purchase land for resale on reasonable terms.[56] The effectiveness of the commission was hindered by fraud, speculation, and corruption, with officials responsible for the purchase and sale of land personally profiting from the transactions.[57] Even though the success of the commission was significantly impaired by venal conduct, many black families did obtain land through its operations from 1869 to 1890.[58]

To protect families who had gained an economic foothold from losing it, the convention adopted a constitutional provision creating a homestead exemption from legal process of one thousand dollars in real property and five hundred dollars in personal property for each family head.[59] A highly controversial economic issue before the convention concerned attempts to stay the legal process of debt collection. A resolution requesting the military commander to suspend debt collection was adopted by the convention on a close vote after a heated debate in which several black delegates argued that such action would illegally impair the obligation of contracts and would save the planter class from having to sell their plantations, one of the means by which redistribution of land to the landless might have been achieved.[60] One type of contract received special treatment from the convention. In implementation of the abolition of slavery, the convention included in the judicial article of the new constitution a provision declaring that contracts for the purchase of slaves were void and no suits to enforce them could be entertained in the state courts.[61]

As significant as adoption of economic relief measures and a more balanced system of government power were, the greatest focus of the 1868 convention was on civil rights. As representatives of a theretofore disenfranchised class, the African American delegates lent a unique perspective to the voting rights discussions.

THE DEBATES ON THE RIGHT TO VOTE

It is in the area of political equality that the South Carolina Constitution of 1868 stands in sharpest contrast to its immediate predecessor, the constitution of 1865, which failed to grant blacks the right to vote, and its successor, the 1895 constitution, which erected high barriers to black political participation.[62] Several black delegates to the 1868 Constitutional Convention made especially distinguished contributions to the debate on voting rights. As will be demonstrated below, they favored equal voting rights but did not have a monolithic, stereotypical view as to how this was to be accomplished.

The 1868 constitution granted the right of suffrage without any racial restrictions or property-holding requirements to all male citizens of the United States who had resided in the state one year prior to the election but with provisos that no one of unsound mind, a prison or asylum inmate, or anyone disqualified by the Constitution of the United States be allowed to vote.[63] The convention fought back attempts to restrict the franchise that would have destroyed black political influence. The Committee on the Franchise and Elections proposed that all persons coming of age after 1875 had to prove that they could read and write before they would be permitted to vote.[64] This proposal was greeted with strong but not universal opposition by the black delegates. Francis L. Cardozo, of Charleston, argued that the timetable was too short. The system of statewide public schools, necessary to educate the black population after long neglect, would not be able to accomplish its task by 1875. He pointedly observed, "I think it would come with bad grace from any individual in the State, who has helped deprive men for two centuries of the means of education to demand that in seven years all unable to read should not be allowed to vote."[65]

Robert B. Elliott was one of the convention's most politically astute black delegates. Elliott later served as a member of Congress and Speaker of the South Carolina House of Representatives.[66] He argued that a literacy test would violate the federal Reconstruction Act's mandate that all males meeting age and residency requirements, and not laboring under specified disabilities, be given the right to vote.[67] Alonzo J. Ransier opposed the literacy test on broad philosophical grounds. The right to vote is an inalienable right, possessed by all men regardless of educational attainment. It is an attribute of manhood, a basic right that is essential to protect other rights.[68] Richard H. Cain refuted arguments that a literacy test should be adopted as a means of encouraging the new public school system. Like Elliott, Cain considered a literacy test to be a violation of the Reconstruction Act.[69] Robert C. DeLarge combined theological and constitutional arguments: the power to vote was an inherent right of all men since they were created in God's image; equality with regard to the right to vote ensures equality with regard to all rights.[70]

But not all black delegates were opposed to the literacy test. W. J. McKinlay, a conservative, affluent black delegate, voiced approval of the test but wanted to postpone effectiveness until 1878.[71] Benjamin F. Randolph initially favored the literacy test as a means of encouraging use of the new public school system that would be mandated by the new constitution.[72] However, when widespread use of the public school system was guaranteed by a compulsory attendance rule,

TABLE 1.1 : Voting Results on Amendment to Remove the Literacy Test
from Proposed Voter Qualifications

	AYES	NAYS	ABSENT
Black Delegates	92.65%	1.47%	5.88%
White Delegates	87.76%	2.04%	10.20%
Total Delegates	90.60%	1.71%	7.69%

he switched his position to oppose the literacy test.[73] In a key vote, almost 100 percent of the black delegates voted to remove the literacy test (see table 1.1).[74]

The mood of the convention was probably influenced by the pending adoption of the Fourteenth Amendment to the United States Constitution, which completed the ratification process later the same year.[75] That amendment provided for reduction in a state's representation in Congress in proportion to the male inhabitants at least twenty-one years of age who were denied the franchise.[76]

The 1868 convention also passed up other opportunities to create an exclusive electorate. Voters were disqualified for criminal convictions only if the offense was a major one involving violence or a serious threat to the government structure, such as treason, murder, robbery, or dueling.[77] An annual poll tax of one dollar was adopted, but the proceeds were to go to the public school system and a proviso prevented failure to pay the tax to be used to disqualify voters.[78] The convention vigorously debated the issue of whether defaulting on payment of the poll tax should bar one from voting. There were black delegates on both sides. R. B. Elliott addressed the issue on several occasions. He first argued that making payment of the tax a voter qualification would be unfair to many poor but hardworking people.[79] He then observed with a politician's astute eye that such a requirement would lead to massive vote buying and an exodus of the common citizen away from the Republican Party because opponents would pay the taxes for the voters.[80] F. L. Cardozo contended that payment of the tax could be enforced by means other than voter disqualification. Cardozo, who was later state treasurer as well as secretary of state, argued that defaulters could be forced to work on the public roads.[81] By contrast, another black delegate, B. F. Randolph, concluded that making the poll tax a prerequisite to voting was the only effective way to enforce it.[82] Jonathan J. Wright agreed. He argued that fiscal support of the new school system was vital. Many people did not own property that would be subject to the other tax supporting the schools. Black citizens were committed to the schools and would do their part. He noted: "I have the utmost confidence in my people. I have been among them sufficiently to know that there is no person among them but who, if he has been taught the sacredness of the use of the ballot, if he has been taught the duty he owes to himself and his

TABLE 1.2: Voting Results on Proposal to Adopt the Poll Tax with Proviso that No Voters Be Disqualified for Nonpayment

	AYES	NAYS	ABSENT
Black Delegates	73.53%	13.24%	13.24%
White Delegates	62.00%	22.00%	16.00%
Total Delegates	68.64%	16.95%	14.41%

country, will have a dollar when the time comes to pay into the Treasury of the State."[83] When passing the poll tax, a strong majority of the black delegates voted not to disqualify voters for nonpayment of the tax.[84] Table 1.2 shows the results of this.[85]

As liberal as the suffrage provisions were, they did not include voting rights for women. Black delegate William J. Whipper argued that women should have the right to vote; until then there would be a large segment of society to whom the law applied but who had no power to help shape it. He observed: "Governments will continue to totter and fall until the rights of all parties are respected—womankind as well as mankind. We have seen the uprising and downfall of Republics everywhere, and the great secret of revolution has been, that governments have not extended the rights of the people to this sex. The systems of legislation have been laid upon insecure foundations, and they never will be permanent until women are recognized as the equal of men, and with him permitted to enjoy the privileges which appertain to the citizen."[86]

Whipper's remarks were all the more notable because they came as a rift was growing in the ranks of those favoring an expanded franchise. During 1868 and 1869, Frederick Douglass spoke in favor of woman suffrage but argued that priority be given to obtaining the vote for black men since the right to vote was needed to preserve their hard-won freedom and protect them against violence. He believed that the country was not yet ready to grant women the vote and that simultaneously pushing for eliminating race and gender limits on the right to vote would doom black male suffrage. Women's rights advocates, such as Susan B. Anthony and Elizabeth Cady Stanton, argued that priority should be given to obtaining woman suffrage as an essential measure for limiting the dependence of women upon men.[87]

Whipper's proposal was rejected by the convention.[88] However, the convention did pass another important advance in women's rights: the separate property-holding rights of married women.[89] B. F. Randolph, who was a strong advocate of this measure, gave a trenchant description of its purpose when he noted that "it is a common thing for men to talk about marrying rich wives; and to marry them for no other purpose than to squander their property. To protect this class of women, and to prevent them from falling into the hands of scoundrels, is the object of this section, and I confidently look to this Convention to pass it."[90] The convention also addressed other issues of interest to women. Divorce through the court system was provided for.[91]

The liberal suffrage rules of the constitution of 1868 were dismantled by its 1895 successor. But the demise of black voter influence began earlier. Shortly after Reconstruction ended, devices were enacted to confuse the illiterate and inexperienced voter, but poll officials aided white voters to navigate through the electoral rocks while leaving the African American citizen unassisted.[92] The system reached its most Byzantine complexity in an 1882 law that required voters to place the ballots for each category of office in a separate box (eight in all) with the result that ballots placed in the wrong box would be disqualified.[93] Registration books were kept open only a short time each month and reregistration was required every time the voter moved, even a short distance within the same precinct.[94] An 1894 law, enacted to implement the call for a new constitutional convention, added to the paperwork barrier to voting by requiring that registrants not only submit detailed personal information but also affidavits from two reputable citizens attesting to the applicant's good character.[95]

The 1895 Constitutional Convention completed the crippling of black voting rights by requiring a literacy test for registrants, disqualifying voters for crimes that blacks were stereotypically expected to commit, and requiring the payment of the poll tax six months prior to the election.[96] Robert Smalls had been a delegate to the 1868 convention and was one of the small number of black delegates in the 1895 conclave. He unsuccessfully tried to convince the 1895 convention to continue the liberal universal male suffrage system of the 1868 constitution.[97]

The heart of the 1895 system for disfranchising blacks was the literacy test, coupled with alternatives that would make it possible for illiterate whites to continue to vote. All persons registering prior to January 1, 1898, had to be able to read any section of the Constitution submitted to them by the registration officer *or understand and explain* the provision when it was read to them by the official.[98] After January 1, 1898, a registrant had to be able to read *and* write any section of the constitution submitted by the registration officer *or* show that he owned and had paid taxes during the previous year on property in the state valued at three hundred dollars or more.[99]

These provisions were neutral on their face but susceptible to discriminatory application by registration officials. This was especially true of the "understand and explain" alternative to the literacy test. This alternative, which was to remain in effect for three years, was susceptible to manipulation by registration officials, who could read difficult constitutional provisions for explanation by illiterate blacks and then be hypercritical of the registrant's explanation while submitting easier provisions to illiterate whites and grading the explanations more indulgently. Indeed, Senator Ben Tillman, the moving force behind the provisions, admitted on the convention floor that it was his intent that the "understand and explain" alternative would be applied in a discriminatory manner. He said: "Some have said there is fraud in this understanding clause. Some poisons in small doses are very salutary and valuable medicines. If you put it in here that a man must understand, and you vest the right to judge whether he understands in an officer, it is a constitutional act. That officer is responsible to his conscience and his God, he is responsible to nobody else. There is no particle of fraud or illegality in it. It is just simply showing partiality, perhaps, [laughter] or discriminating."[100]

Black delegates in the 1895 convention opposed the restrictive suffrage plans and presented more moderate alternatives. Thomas E. Miller observed: "Mr. President, the conservative force in our State, is the common people, the burden-bearing people, and, sir, when you say that $300 and the capacity to read and write are the requirements to be possessed by voters, you are striking at the root of the tree of universal government."[101]

James Wigg, a black delegate from Beaufort, presented an alternate suffrage plan to the 1895 convention which required the registrant to either read a section of the constitution or prove that he owned a freehold, or taxable personal property worth at least one hundred dollars. The Wigg plan was less susceptible to manipulation than Tillman's proposals since it contained no "understand and explain" provision.[102] Wigg's proposal would have prohibited devices such as the eight-box balloting system and would have protected voters from having to travel more than eight miles to register or vote.[103] W. J. Whipper, who had also been a delegate to the 1868 convention, offered a voter qualification plan which required delegates to be able to read and write but contained no "understand and explain" or property-owning alternative.[104] Thus there was acquiescence by black delegates to the 1895 convention to the straight literacy requirements but strong opposition to devices such as the "understand and explain" provision.

The small band of black delegates in the 1895 convention could not prevail against the white supremacist tide.[105] The constitution produced by the 1895 convention included not only the literacy test with the temporary "understand and explain" alternative and the permanent property ownership–taxing alternative, but also a provision that disqualified registrants if they had been convicted of certain crimes that blacks were stereotypically considered more likely to commit.[106] The array of crimes for which the 1895 constitution disqualified a voter was odd both in what it included and what it excluded. A registrant was not disqualified for committing murder but was for adultery and bigamy and some other relatively minor crimes.[107]

Thus the straightforward universal male suffrage approach successfully advocated by most black delegates in 1868 was replaced by an intricate maze of requirements designed to stifle African American political participation.

DEBATES ON PUBLIC EDUCATION

Even though the work of the 1868 convention in establishing the right of blacks to vote was undone by its 1895 successor, many of its contributions to the establishment of public education had greater staying power, but they did not escape unscathed in the 1895 constitution. To the 1868 convention, a broadly accessible system of public education was essential to effective black participation in the political process, even if a literacy test were never adopted.[108] The emphasis given to education in the 1868 Constitutional Convention was foreshadowed by a resolution passed in the 1865 Colored People's Convention of the State of South Carolina. The resolution called for the establishment of a public school system open to their race because "an educated and intelligent people can neither be held in, nor reduced to slavery."[109] These sentiments echoed the comments made by Frederick Douglass in 1845 when he observed that just as forced ignorance was essential to maintaining slavery, education was "the pathway from slavery to freedom."[110]

Vestiges of public education could be found in antebellum South Carolina.[111] For example, an 1811 statute gave each election district the same number of free schools as it had representatives in the general assembly.[112] However, since according to an 1808 amendment to the constitution of 1790, representation was apportioned by a complex formula giving equal weight to population and taxable property, the schools were not always established where there were the heaviest concentrations of children.[113] Furthermore, availability of the school to the general population was limited by a provision requiring that if there were more applicants than there were spaces, preference was to be given to poor children or orphans.[114] A report issued in 1839 by South Carolina College professors Stephen Elliott Jr. and J. H. Thornwell concluded that the free schools lacked uniformity and central direction.[115] To provide coordination, they recommended creation of the post of State Superintendent of Education.[116] It was not until the adoption of the constitution of 1868 that these recommendations were implemented. That document provided for the election of a state superintendent of education to supervise the schools under standards set by the general assembly.[117] The constitution required the general assembly to establish "a liberal and uniform system of free public schools throughout the State."[118] Attendance at a public or private school was to be compulsory for all children between the ages of six and sixteen who were not physically or mentally disabled, and they were to attend school for a total time of at least twenty-four months.[119] The most controversial provision required that "all the public schools, colleges and universities of this State, supported in whole or in part by public funds, shall be free and open to all the children and youths of the State, without regard to race or color."[120] Black delegates played a prominent role in the passage of the educational provisions. Early in the convention, Robert Smalls introduced a resolution calling for compulsory education and "a system of common schools of different grades to be open without charge to all classes of persons."[121] Smalls's struggle, against great odds to gain an education probably made him sensitive to the need to make the path easier for others.[122]

A sharp debate swirled around the educational provision: did it require racial integration in the pubic schools or only grant access to a free education to all children, regardless of race, somewhere in the public school system? The latter interpretation would permit segregated schools so long as both black and white students gained entry to the system at large. But the phrase "without regard to race or color" could be construed to prohibit segregated schools because, by definition, such schools give "regard to race or color" as a preeminent principle.[123] B. O. Duncan, a white delegate, interpreted the measure as mandating racial integration and viewed this as a disastrous policy likely to drive white children out of the public school system, thus sapping it of support needed for its survival.[124] J. J. Wright sought to assuage these fears. He stated: "I did not suppose that this section would elicit any discussion whatever. The gentleman who last resumed his seat [Duncan] has referred to the impropriety of allowing the children of the two races to attend school together. If I read the section aright it contemplates no such thing."[125]

Wright sought to assure white citizens that the school system was not the opening wedge of a movement toward forced social integration. He noted: "One thing I would have understood, the colored people do not want to force what is called social equality; that is a matter that will regulate itself. No law we can pass can compel associations that are distasteful to anybody."[126]

One of the most powerful arguments in favor of making the schools open to all children regardless of race, and making education in either public or private schools compulsory for children between six and sixteen, was made by F. L. Cardozo.[127] He argued that although compulsory education did impinge upon parental freedom, it was necessary to build a more civilized society.[128] He contended that the compulsory attendance rule was not an artifice to bring about racially integrated schools. The education article did not require that the public schools be racially integrated or racially separate. It merely required that the school be open to all children regardless of race and this meant that if a black child wanted to attend a school that was predominantly white, he had a right to do so.[129] Ultimately, the black delegates overwhelmingly advocated the opening of state-supported schools to all children without regard to race (see table 1.3).[130]

TABLE 1.3: Voting Results on Proposal to Make State-Supported Schools Open to All Children Regardless of Race

	AYES	NAYS	ABSENT
Black Delegates	92.86%	0.00%	7.14%
White Delegates	64.71%	7.84%	27.45%
Total Delegates	80.99%	3.31%	15.70%

Despite the adoption of the "open to all" provision, segregation was a deeply entrenched custom. In 1874, a correspondent for the *New York Times* found that generally the common schools were segregated, and that while facilities were provided for both races in the larger towns that some smaller communities could afford only one school and it was exclusively for use by white students.[131] The 1895 constitution made segregation the clear policy for public school children. Article 11, section 7, stated that "Separate schools shall be provided for children of the white and colored races, and no child of either race shall ever be permitted to attend a school provided for children of the other race."

The statewide uniform school system provision of the 1868 constitution did not exist only on paper. It was implemented, but progress was slow with setbacks occurring because of corruption, inefficiency, and political wrangling.[132] In an 1875 address to the legislature, Governor D. H. Chamberlain observed that less than 50 percent of the school-age population attended school, the average school was open only five months per year, many teachers were incompetent, and schools at the high school level needed to be provided.[133] The beginning of statewide public education was shaky, but progress was still significant.[134]

DEBATES ON THE JUDICIAL SYSTEM

Even though the 1868 constitution departed markedly from South Carolina tradition with regard to voting rights and public education, its approach to the judicial system was a mixture of tradition and mild innovation. Nowhere is this more clearly seen than in the convention debates on the method for selecting judges. These debates illustrate that the black delegates espoused a variety of views rather than a monolithic position. The arguments also demonstrate the considerable ability of several black delegates in making sophisticated comparative government arguments. The provisions that were adopted perpetuated the South Carolina tradition of selection of judges by the legislature but departed from the tradition granting judges tenure during good behavior for a new system that gave judges a set term.[135] The constitutions of 1776, 1778, 1790, 1861, and 1865 all provided for legislative election of the judges of the principal courts of record and service during good behavior.[136]

Both the tradition of legislative selection of judges and that of judicial tenure during good behavior spring from a colonial dispute in which the South Carolina Commons House of Assembly developed increasing resentment of the royal practices of using South Carolina judicial positions as the dumping ground for unqualified office seekers and keeping the judges subservient by giving them tenure only during the pleasure of the king.[137] The controversy reached its height in 1768 and 1769 when the South Carolina Commons House of Assembly sought to reform the judicial system by establishing courts in the backcountry and ensuring judges tenure during good behavior like their English counterparts. The South Carolina Commons House passed a 1768 law providing for tenure during good behavior, but it was disallowed by the British Privy Council and then replaced by the South Carolina Commons House with a new statute restoring judicial service during the pleasure of the king.[138] But these royal pressure tactics so increased the colonists' resentment of executive involvement in the judicial selection process that legislative dominance of that process became a fixed star in the South Carolina constitutional firmament.[139]

The debates in the 1868 convention focused on whether the tradition of selecting judges by joint vote of both houses of the general assembly should be retained or replaced by another method, such as federal-style executive appointment with the advice and consent of the senate or popular election. Black delegates spoke for and against each of these methods. B. F. Randolph argued that legislative selection made the judges too dependent on the legislature and dispersed responsibility for the appointments over too numerous a body. It was too hard to hold such a large group accountable for bad appointments. The involvement of both houses of the legislature was a cumbersome method that would lead to protracted contests.[140] J. D. Bell, a white delegate, augmented Randolph's arguments. He contended that because the executive appointment method focused responsibility on the governor, it would lead to "cool and deliberate" decisions, whereas legislative selection involved "a numerous body of men" that would act in a more excitable manner, often blindly following party lines rather than inquiring into the candidate's merits. Gubernatorial appointment, although it centered responsibility on the governor, would not become dictatorial because the consent of the senate must be obtained.[141] J. J. Wright swooped down on the proponents of the federal model with scathing rhetoric. The federal model granted judges tenure during good behavior.[142] Wright argued that you could not get rid of such lifetime appointees except by extreme measures. He preferred a ten-year term, which was long enough to create a stable judiciary but not so long as to produce judges who were arrogant and out of touch with reality. The federal model did produce such judges. The prime example to Wright was Chief Justice Roger Brooke Taney, author of the infamous *Scott v. Sandford* (Dred Scott case) opinion holding that descendants of slaves could not be citizens, that slaves were constitutionally protected property, that the federal government could not prohibit the spread of slavery to the territories, and that states could decide whether a freed slave could revert to slavery.[143] Wright supported legislative selection of supreme court judges because the general assembly was the distillation of the statewide voice of the people. It was not the unwieldy, inchoate voice of the people expressed through direct election but a voice channeled responsibly through elected representatives.[144] For judges below the supreme court level, Wright preferred popular election.[145] It is interesting to note that Wright became a state supreme court justice in 1870, having been elected under the legislative selection system while a state senator.[146]

D. H. Chamberlain, a white delegate who later became governor, was the leading advocate for the popular election method.[147] His theory was that the more directly responsible the judges were to the people, the more likely the state was to have equitable justice. Presumably, he meant that popularly elected judges would be less beholden to special interest groups because their return to office would be in the hands of the people at large. He admitted that some popularly elected judges in some states had become corrupt, but that was not attributable to the selection method but because the political systems of those states were generally corrupt. Clean judges could not swim in a filthy political pool no matter what system was used to select them. Chamberlain was a negotiator. Although he preferred popular elections, he compromised and agreed to support legislative election as a system that was still influenced by the popular will but would be effective in fending off one-man rule by the governor, who would become a kingmaker under an executive appointment system.[148]

Black delegate A. J. Ransier took an approach similar to that of Chamberlain. He argued that judges, like most officials, should be "directly responsible to the people."[149] But he agreed to legislative selection as a "wise middle course" in which judges would be one step "removed from direct responsibility" to the people.[150] Ransier believed that generally "the people are the best judges of who shall make their laws in any department of government" but that "the masses of the people of this State are not, perhaps, at present in a position to use their power wisely and judiciously."[151] A large majority of the black delegates voted to retain general assembly election of circuit judges (see table 1.4).[152]

TABLE 1.4: Voting Results on Continuing to Elect Circuit Judges by the General Assembly

	AYES	NAYS	ABSENT
Black Delegates	64.29%	12.86%	22.86%
White Delegates	39.22%	29.41%	31.37%
Total Delegates	53.72%	19.83%	26.45%

Because of his populist sentiments, Ransier was against the historic practice of giving judges tenure during good behavior as this amounted to lifetime tenure in practice. His remarks showed an interest in history, contemporary developments, and comparative government. He observed, "As regards the term of office, I find in the original Constitutions of most of the States, it was fixed during good behavior; but, in most of the present Constitutions, the terms are variously limited to five, six, and ten years. I am disposed to keep up with the march of events."[153] Ransier later served as lieutenant governor and as a member of Congress.[154]

The black delegates also actively participated in the debate over whether an age limit, such as seventy, should be placed on eligibility for election as judge. Their predominant view was in opposition to such a limit since it tended to stereotype candidates on the basis of age rather than assess them as individuals.[155] No upper age limit was adopted.[156]

The 1868 convention's debate of the judicial article also involved one of the most persistently controversial questions in American constitutional law: whether courts can render constitutional decisions when asked by the government for advice or whether they must decide such matters only when necessary to resolve concrete cases presented to the courts by adversary parties. The federal constitutional convention of 1787 chose the latter route when it limited federal court jurisdiction to cases of a "Judiciary Nature."[157] This conclusion is reflected in the language of the U.S. Constitution, which permits the federal courts to consider issues involving the Constitution, laws, and treaties of the United States but only if presented as concrete "cases" or "controversies."[158] When court decisions are not confined to narrow cases, the judiciary power increases at the expense of the other branches and the people. Advisory opinions would be rendered without the benefit of adversary arguments that sharply define the issues in a way that avoids sweeping uninformed decisions.[159]

A proposal was made, to the South Carolina Constitutional Convention of 1868, that the state supreme court be permitted to render advisory opinions on constitutional issues.[160] Although advisory opinions were not permitted under the federal Constitution, some states had well-established procedures for such opinions. For example, Massachusetts made provision for the governor, the council, and the branches of the legislature to obtain opinions from the Massachusetts Supreme Judicial Court "upon important questions of law and upon 'solemn occasions.'"[161] J. J. Wright attacked the proposal that South Carolina adopt an advisory opinion procedure as granting the judiciary improperly broad powers. The procedure was defeated after Wright pointedly suggested that government officers needing advisory opinions could consult the attorney general.[162]

The 1868 convention produced one of the most significant court reforms in South Carolina history. Rather than maintaining separate courts for issues of law and equity, the constitution of 1868 granted the Court of Common Pleas the jurisdiction to resolve both types of issues, thus eliminating the delay caused by jurisdictional disputes and making possible a more complete resolution when legal and equitable issues were intertwined.[163] On this issue J. J. Wright took a conservative position, arguing that the "Courts of Equity in this State are indispensable."[164]

Closely related to the nature of the judicial system is the manner in which a defendant is formally accused of a crime and brought to trial. The Fifth Amendment to the U.S. Constitution guarantees that "no person shall be held to answer for a capital, or otherwise infamous crime, unless on a presentment or indictment of a Grand Jury, except in cases arising in time of war or public danger." This system has ancient roots with some commentators tracing it "back to Athens, pre-Norman England, and the Assize of Clarendon promulgated by Henry II."[165] In this country the system is traceable to the New York Colonial Charter of Liberties and Privileges of 1683, which required "That in all Cases Capitall or Criminall there shall be a grand Inquest who shall first present the offence."[166] In describing the role of the grand jury, the Supreme Court of the United States noted that "in this country as in England of old the grand jury has convened as a body of laymen, free from technical rules, acting in secret, pledged to indict no one because of prejudice and to free no one because of special favor."[167]

The grand jury system came under fire in the 1868 constitutional convention. An argument was made that the grand jury system of indictments should be deleted from the proposed Declaration of Rights on the grounds that its secret nature made it easy to put people in jail on the basis of trumped-up evidence, while letting others against whom strong evidence could be assembled go free.[168] Most black delegates who spoke on the issue supported the traditional Anglo-American grand jury role. W. J. Whipper contended, "[I]t is one of the principal means by which the liberties of the people have been protected for years."[169] J. J. Wright concurred. He noted, "It protects the people being proceeded against, except through regular indictment." The provision finally adopted permitted summary trial before a justice of the peace, by information, without grand jury indictment of offenses "less than a felony" when punishment did not exceed a hundred dollar fine or thirty days in jail; but it further stipulated that "no person shall be held to answer for any higher crime or offence unless on presentment of a Grand Jury, except in cases arising in the land and naval service, or in the militia when in actual service in time of war or public danger."[170]

LOCAL GOVERNMENT

Even though the 1868 convention adopted judicial system provisions that were a relatively moderate mixture of tradition and innovation, its action with regard to local government represented a more significant break with the past and a movement toward home rule. Article 4, section 19, provided for an elected board of county commissioners with comprehensive power over roads, highways, and ferries. It granted these bodies such taxing and spending powers as were "necessary to the internal improvement and local concerns of the respective counties."[171] When this provision is viewed in conjunction with a constitutional requirement that counties provide for "inhabitants who, by reason of age and infirmities or misfortunes, may have a claim upon the sympathy and aid of society," it is clear that the 1868 fundamental law called for local governments that intervened to solve society's problems. This approach contrasted sharply with the pre–Civil War system that relied heavily upon special commissions created by the legislature to address particular problems or narrow categories of problems, such as building roads or bridges. This system made it difficult for government to comprehensively address problems that crossed jurisdictional lines of several narrowly focused commissions, and made it difficult to address new problems outside the specific mandates of local commissions until the laborious process of legislative amendment had been accomplished.[172]

Not all black delegates approved of this activist approach. William McKinlay, a conservative black delegate who possessed considerable property and paid a hefty tax bill, was so alarmed at the powers proposed to be given to county government that he told the convention, "In my opinion this section, as it reads, confers unlimited and dangerous powers upon the boards it proposes to create; powers capable of great abuse, and, if injudiciously exercised, calculated to entail ruin not only upon the district, but the entire State."[173]

McKinlay was concerned that the broad powers given to county commissions would lead to the building of unneeded roads and bridges and a consequent increase in taxes. To guard against this, he suggested that more general assembly oversight be given to local government.[174] Although such legislative controls were not imposed directly by the constitution, an 1868 statute dealing with local government power to build roads and bridges and levy taxes for the project required that "no tax shall be levied and collected by county commissioners until the same has been authorized by the General Assembly."[175]

The broad county government authority soon led to allegations of abuse of power and high taxes. It is ironic that some of these comments resemble William McKinlay's observations to the 1868 convention. For example, testimony given in 1871 to a congressional committee investigating state and local government in the South heard charges that spending on roads, buildings, and bridges was out of control, that the state had shifted much of the financial burden of the court system from the state to local government, and that county commissioners were impervious to complaints about the tax burden since they were only interested in personal gain.[176] Attempts to place the entire responsibility for the tax burden on the broad powers given local government under the constitution of 1868 were unconvincing since much influence over the taxes was wielded by state officials such as the legislators and governor.[177] In addition, the local government structure provided by the constitution of 1868 did not have a fair chance to succeed in some areas because of violent interference by the Ku Klux Klan, which attempted to force local officials to resign.[178]

In addition to the racial power struggle and white citizens' complaints about increased spending and taxes, the legal elite charged that strong county governments led to increased local legislation with the result that the law became a discordant patchwork that changed as one moved from county to county.[179] After Reconstruction, the pressure for a reduction in local government power increased. In 1886, Governor J. C. Sheppard argued, "[I]t is unquestionable that the present system is not suited to our condition and is the cause of many of the evils of which the people complain."[180] Pursuant to his recommendation, a constitutional amendment, adopted in 1890, abolished the elective county councils.[181] Dismantling of the 1868 local government system was completed when the constitution of 1895 included a provision limiting county taxing and bonding power to a narrow list of county purposes.[182] The 1895 document contained a provision on counties, but it focused on county boundaries and the creation of new and merged counties; it provided no local government structure.[183] This power vacuum was filled by county legislative delegations who controlled county fiscal power through bills passed at their behest by the general assembly.[184] A complex network of special-purpose districts was created to discharge vital functions, such as providing recreation, fire fighting, and water and sewer services outside of city boundaries, because counties were not empowered to perform these functions.[185] This highly fragmented local government system was an unwieldy and ineffective means of addressing local problems. This condition continued until a constitutional amendment passed in 1973, implemented by legislation in 1975, gave counties powers similar to those envisioned in 1868.[186] Thus the 1868 provisions were more harbingers of the future than a contemporary success.

GOD AND THE GOVERNOR

The debates on voting rights, education, the judiciary, and local government demonstrate the variety of opinions espoused by, and the considerable ability of, the leading black delegates. However, no part of the convention records paints a richer portrait of the varied oratorical styles of the black delegates than the controversy surrounding the convention's adoption of a requirement that "no person shall be eligible to the office of Governor who denies the existence of the Supreme Being."[187] Before sketching these debates, however, it will be useful to consider the position of the constitution of 1868 in the evolution of the freedom and establishment of religion in South Carolina, especially with regard to religious qualifications for office.

In many respects, the constitution of 1868 constitutes another advance toward greater religious tolerance because it is the first of the South Carolina constitutions that contains the equivalent of the federal First Amendment's prohibition on government establishment of religion.[188] In colonial South Carolina, the Church of England was the established religion, receiving financial support from the state and having the details of its governance prescribed by law.[189] This system was replaced in the constitution of 1778 by a general Protestant establishment which was not a regime of state financial support but a provision for Protestant churches to be incorporated if they adhered to specified beliefs.[190] The constitution of 1790, and its 1861 and 1865 successors, contained no language establishing any religion and broadly guaranteed religious freedom "without discrimination or preference."[191] Thus it remained for the constitution of 1868 to include specific antiestablishment language.[192] Despite its language prohibiting the establishment of religion, the constitution of 1868 was itself a religious document in one respect. It began by noting that the people of South Carolina were "Grateful to Almighty God" for the opportunity peacefully to enter into a new constitutional compact, and it asked "the Great Legislator of the Universe" for direction.[193] However, this general monotheistic language was a long distance from the complex and explicit establishment of the Protestant religion found in the constitution of 1778.[194]

Religious qualifications for office were the rule in colonial South Carolina. For example, a 1759 statute made adherence to Protestant Christianity a qualification for voting for, or serving in, the general assembly.[195] The constitution of 1778 required major officials to be "of the Protestant religion."[196] The constitution of 1790 contained no religious qualifications, perhaps due to the influence of Charles Pinckney of South Carolina, who was the leading proponent in the federal constitutional convention in 1787 of the proposal that led to the adoption in the U.S. Constitution of a prohibition of religious tests for officials of the federal government.[197] But an 1834 amendment to the South Carolina Constitution of 1790, and provisions in the 1861 and 1865 constitutions, returned the customary "So help me God" to the oath to be taken by officeholders.[198]

Thus the debates in the 1868 convention took place against a rich and contentious history concerning religious qualifications for office, with the tide flowing away from requiring such qualifications except for the formalistic "so help me God" recited by officeholders. A return to religious qualifications by the 1868 convention, even in the general form of belief in a Supreme Being, would be a major step that could lead to more active probing of the religious beliefs of officeholders. The black delegates arguing in behalf of precluding from the governorship those who denied the existence of a Supreme Being considered that it was essential to a civilized society that its leaders believe in God. R. H. Cain, a minister, used colorful hyperbole to support his arguments. He contended, "Take God out of the Government, and we shall have anarchy, bloodshed, and crime of every kind stalking abroad at noon-day and at midnight. There will be no security for society, no security for the sacred relationship of life, no security of law, no security anywhere. We shall have midnight assassinations. An individual who disbelieves in the existence of a Supreme Being is a dangerous man in the community, and into whose hands the people should not intrust their interests. If a man fear not God, he cares little for mankind. . . . I think this idea of the existence of God was before there ever was any Constitution. The existence of God seems to take priority."[199]

B. F. Randolph, also a minister, argued in favor of the requirement as an endorsement of Christian doctrine. He observed, "I believe we are a Christian people. We all, as a people, believe in the existence of a Supreme Being."[200]

R. C. DeLarge made a sophisticated distinction between personal beliefs and constitutional principles. He observed, "I am not disposed, however, to have an infidel hold the position of Governor of this State. But whilst that is my individual opinion, I am not prepared to say a religious test should be incorporated into the Constitution of the State."[201]

The most interesting legal arguments in opposition to the religious test were made by J. J. Wright, who contended that the proposal would violate the mandate in Article 6, section 3, of the U.S. Constitution, stating that "no religious test shall ever be required as a qualification to any office or public trust under the United States."[202] At first glance the argument seems unsupported by the text of Article 6, section 3, since the religious tests prohibition does not explicitly refer to state officers. However, the words "under the United States" could be construed to cover both federal and state officers since both categories are bound by the federal Constitution, which the same section requires all state and federal officials to vow to obey.

Even though Wright's arguments did not prevail in the convention, they proved to be prophetic. In the 1997 case of *Silverman v. Campbell*, the Supreme Court of South Carolina struck down similar provisions that stipulated that "no person who denies the existence of the Supreme Being shall hold any office under this Constitution."[203] The court held that the provisions violated two parts of the U.S. Constitution, the First Amendment, which prohibits government establishment of religion or infringement on its free exercise, and the Article 6, section 3, prohibition of religious tests for officers. The case dealt with an applicant for notary public credentials and did not directly address the similarly

TABLE 1.5: Voting Results on the Religious Test for the Governor

	AYES	NAYS	ABSENT
Black Delegates	81.43%	7.14%	11.43%
White Delegates	70.59%	3.92%	25.49%
Total Delegates	76.86%	5.79%	17.36%

Note: This vote passed the provision to a third reading.

worded provision that disqualifies anyone for the governorship who denies the existence of the Supreme Being.[204] However, the logic of the ruling would seem to apply equally well to the gubernatorial provision. The outcome was foreordained by a 1961 U.S. Supreme Court decision, *Torcaso v. Watkins*, which invalidated as violative of the First Amendment a Maryland provision that made belief in God a prerequisite for holding state office.[205] A strong majority of black delegates supported the religious test (see table 1.5).[206]

Even though they produced a provision that ultimately proved to be unconstitutional, the 1868 convention debates on the Supreme Being clause were characterized by a thorough airing of a variety of constitutional perspectives, with black delegates taking prominent roles on both sides.

CONCLUSION

The convention of 1868 was no more a meeting of constitutional gods on Olympus than most state constituent assemblies, past or present, North or South. The debates showed a mixture of self-interest, partisan maneuvering, idealism, and patriotism, a mixture that is characteristic of most such conclaves. But they also showed that the leading African American delegates were nobody's pawns. Their intellectual firepower matched that of anyone in the convention. They did not follow a herd instinct; their views cannot be stereotyped. Some were for a literacy test and a poll tax as voter qualifications while others, the majority, were against them. Some were for strong local government and some were opposed. Some preferred executive appointment for judges, some legislative selection, while others preferred a popular vote. Some preferred retaining the traditional role of the grand jury while others favored jettisoning it. The reasoning was sometimes impressive, such as that of Jonathan Jasper Wright in opposition to granting the courts the power to render advisory opinions. The arguments were sometimes hyperbolic, such as those of R. H. Cain in favor of disqualifying for the governorship anyone who denied the existence of a Supreme Being; they were sometimes subtle, such as the argument of R. C. DeLarge against the same requirement. Perhaps the debates were sometimes politically naive, but at other times they were politically astute, such as the comments of Robert Elliott concerning the consequences to the Republican Party of making poll tax payments a voter qualification.

Was the constitution produced by the convention a radical destruction of tradition? In some provisions tradition was rudely elbowed aside; in others it was guardedly embraced, then spurned again. The suffrage provisions departed substantially from South Carolina tradition. This was mandated by the Reconstruction Act, which required universal male suffrage regardless of race.[207] Viewed in a longer perspective, however, the suffrage provisions were an extension of earlier measures popularizing the political process, such as the 1810 amendment removing property-holding barriers to voting and the 1865 constitution's removal of such barriers to holding key offices. The 1868 constitution's attempt to provide an even broader electorate was viewed by many as radical at the time. But any political system (such as that prevailing prior to 1868) which excludes from participation a major portion of the population, especially the group upon which the law has its harshest impact, is riddled with fault lines that can destabilize the government. The 1868 constitution attempted to repair those fault lines by removing racial restrictions on voting. If its suffrage scheme had been kept in force long enough to allow the new public education system to have a positive impact on the quality of the electorate, it might have produced a fair and stable government.

The 1868 constitution also departed from South Carolina tradition in the mode of its adoption. Unlike its predecessors and its successor, the constitution of 1895, it was submitted to the people for ratification.[208] But the convention was also surprisingly traditional in some respects, such as retaining the selection of judges by the general assembly. The provision for a statewide system of uniform public schools was an innovation, but important elements of this structure were retained, even though racial segregation was imposed, by the 1895 constitution.[209] The comprehensive county government powers of the constitution of 1868 were eliminated by its 1895 successor, but the current constitution, after the home rule movement of the 1970s, has restored a broader role for county government.[210] The 1868 convention's creation of a better balance of power between the executive and legislative branches by the restoration of a strong veto power followed the approach of the federal Constitution and was not as drastic as the first South Carolina State Constitution, that of 1776, which provided for an absolute executive veto.[211] It was the 1868 document's voting rights provisions that were most drastically decimated by its 1895 successor.[212] The pendulum swung back toward the position of the 1868 convention, but it was a long time in doing so. South Carolina repealed the poll tax in 1951.[213] In the Voting Rights Act of 1965 the Congress suspended in states with low voter participation (including South Carolina) the use of literacy tests and other devices that had been used discriminatorily.[214] The ban on literacy tests was made nation-wide in 1970.[215]

During the time that it was in effect, the constitution of 1868 provided African American lawyers with the tools of liberty. For example, S. J. Lee was able to invoke the constitution to obtain reversal of a conviction obtained in violation of the rule against double jeopardy and to obtain modification of a criminal case sentence that exceeded constitutional limits.[216]

The constitution of 1868 has been described as possessing many admirable features of a model frame of government but one that was not suited to the needs and traditions of the people since it was constructed by delegates who had little practical familiarity with conditions in the state.[217] There is much truth in these assertions. But since the slaves were free and "the people" would now have an expanded meaning, including all races, incremental changes, such as those of the constitution of 1865, were no longer enough. The 1868 convention made an earnest effort to make the needed revisions. Perhaps it overestimated the speed at which significant innovations could be accomplished, but it was prophetic in anticipating standards that would become the norm a hundred years later. The African American founding fathers, representing a constituency that previously had been ignored, crafted a document with a deeper insight into the meaning of freedom, an insight possessed only by the freedmen who had known slavery and the freeborn who knew how precarious freedom could be without constitutional protection.

Appendix
SELECTED ROLL-CALL VOTES

DELEGATE LISTS

Black Delegates

The following is a conservatively constructed list of the black delegates who attended the South Carolina Constitutional Convention of 1868. This list represents only the seventy delegates who are listed in all of the following sources: *Proceedings of the Constitutional Convention of South Carolina* (1868, see pages 6–7); Eric Foner's *Freedom's Lawmakers: A Directory of Black Officeholders during Reconstruction* (1993); and Thomas Holt's *Black over White: Negro Leadership in South Carolina during Reconstruction* (1977, specifically table 5, Summary of Biographical Data for Negro Legislators, 1868–76).

The seventy delegates are as follows: Purvis Alexander, Martin F. Becker, John Bonum, Isaac P. Brockenton, Barney Burton, Benjamin Byas, Edward J. Cain, Richard H. Cain, Francis L. Cardozo, John A. Chestnut, Frederick Albert

Clinton, Wilson Cooke, Nelson Davis, Robert C. DeLarge, Abram Dogan, William A. Driffle, Harvey D. Edwards, Robert B. Elliott, Rice Foster, William H. W. Gray, David Harris, Charles D. Hayne, Henry E. Haynes, James N. Hayne, James A. Henderson, Richard H. Humbert (Humbird), Henry Jacobs, William R. Jervay (Jervey), John W. Johnson, Samuel Johnson, William E. Johnston [Johnson], W. Nelson Joiner, Charles Jones, Henry W. Jones, Jordan Lang, Landon S. Langley, George H. Lee, Samuel Lee, Hutson J. Lomax, Julius Mayer, Harry McDaniels, W. J. McKinlay, William McKinlay, John W. Meade (Mead), Abram Middleton, Lee A. Nance, William Beverly Nash, William Nelson, Samuel Nuckles, Joseph H. Rainey, Benjamin F. Randolph, Alonzo J. Ransier, Prince R. Rivers, Thaddeus Sasportas, Sancho Saunders (Sanders), Henry L. Shrewsbury, Robert Smalls, Calvin T. Stubbs, Stephen A. Swails, William M. Thomas, Augustus R. Thompson, Benjamin A. Thompson, Samuel B. Thompson, William M. Viney, William James Whipper, John H. White, Charles M. Wilder, Thomas Williamson, Coy Wingo, and Jonathan J. Wright.

Note that names given in parentheses indicate the spelling used in *Proceedings of the Constitutional Convention of South Carolina;* names given in brackets indicate the spelling used in *Freedom's Lawmakers: A Directory of Black Officeholders during Reconstruction.*

White Delegates

The following is a list of the white delegates who attended the South Carolina Constitutional Convention of 1868. This list represents the fifty-four delegates who are listed in *Proceedings of the Constitutional Convention of South Carolina* and are not classified as black in the list provided above.

The fifty-four delegates are as follows: James M. Allen, Frank Arnim, James D. Bell, Lemuel Boozer, C. C. Bowen, Alexander Bryce, J. P. F. Camp, D. H. Chamberlain, T. J. Coghlan, William S. Collins, Simeon Corley, Jesse S. Craig, Joseph Crews, William Darrington, George DeMeddis, Elias Dickson, S. G. W. Dill, R. J. Donaldson, B. Odell Duncan, John S. Gentry, James H. Goss, R. G. Holmes, Jno. A. Hunter, Timothy Hurley, George Jackson, Joseph H. Jenks, J. K. Jillson, Dr. L. B. Johnson, William B. Johnson, Charles P. Leslie, A. G. Mackey (President), E. W. M. Mackey, M. Mauldin, Bailey Milford, Franklin F. Miller, F. J. Moses Jr., Dr. J. C. Neagle, Dr. N. J. Newell, C. M. Olsen, Y. J. P. Owens, Niles G. Parker, William Perry, Gilbert Pillsbury, A. C. Richmond, Thomas J. Robertson, W. E. Rose, James M. Runion, James M. Rutland, F. A. Sawyer, John K. Terry, Henry W. Webb, B. F. Whittemore, Francis E. Wilder, and John Wooley.

Note that in Eric Foner's *Freedom's Lawmakers: A Directory of Black Officeholders during Reconstruction* (see page 115), George Jackson's biography indicates that some sources classified him as white; however, Jackson is referred to as black in the complaint of the South Carolina Democrats against the 1868 constitution. Furthermore, Jackson is not included in Thomas Holt's *Black over White: Negro Leadership in South Carolina during Reconstruction* (see specifically table 5, Summary of Biographical Data for Negro Legislators, 1868–76). Due to the lack of consensus, George Jackson is classified as a white delegate for the purposes of this work.

PREFACE: VOTING RESULTS

Calculations were not made as to all issues discussed within the text. Many issues debated in the convention were decided by a vote that did not involve a roll call or involved a vote which merged several issues, or in which the nature of the vote was obscured by parliamentary maneuvers. The votes tallied in the charts involved roll-call votes in which the issue voted upon was reasonably clear. In some instances, the second ballot rather than the third ballot was used because there was a roll-call vote on the former but not the latter.

Moreover, it is important to note that vote totals do not always equal 124, the total number of black and white delegates attending the convention. Frequently, some delegates did not vote or an ambiguous vote was recorded. As a result, all percentages are based on the total number of delegates for whom a vote was recorded.

METHODOLOGY

The percentages appearing in tables 1.1 through 1.5 represent the number of votes in a given category (ayes, nays, or absent), as determined by the author of this work, over the total number of votes recorded across that segment (black, white, or total delegates). That result is then multiplied by 100 to ascertain the percentage. All results are rounded to the nearest hundredth. In order to illustrate this methodology, the calculations for black delegates in table 1.1 will be shown.

Total number of ayes = 63
Total number of nays = 1
Total number of absents = 4
Total number of voting black delegates = 68

Ayes percentage for black delegates = (63/68) x 100 = 92.65%
Nays percentage for black delegates = (1/68) x 100 = 1.47%
Absent percentage for black delegates = (4/68) x 100 = 5.88%

TABLE 1.1: ROLL-CALL VOTE RESULTS

Black Delegates

Ayes: Purvis Alexander, Martin F. Becker, Isaac P. Brockenton, Barney Burton, Benjamin Byas, Edward J. Cain, Richard H. Cain, Francis L. Cardozo, John A. Chestnut, Frederick Albert Clinton, Wilson Cooke, Nelson Davis, Robert C. DeLarge, Abram Dogan, William A. Driffle, Harvey D. Edwards, Robert B. Elliott, Rice Foster, William H. W. Gray, David Harris, Charles D. Hayne, Henry E. Hayne, James N. Hayne, James A. Henderson, Richard H. Humbert (Humbird), Henry Jacobs, William R. Jervay (Jervey), John W. Johnson, Samuel Johnson, William E. Johnston [Johnson], W. Nelson Joiner, (no first name) Jones, Jordan Lang, Landon S. Langley, George H. Lee, Samuel Lee, Hutson J. Lomax, Julius Mayer, Harry McDaniels, John W. Meade (Mead), Lee A. Nance, William Beverly Nash, William Nelson, Samuel Nuckles, Joseph H. Rainey, Benjamin F. Randolph, Alonzo J. Ransier, Prince R. Rivers, Thaddeus K. Sasportas, Sancho Saunders (Sanders), Henry L. Shrewsbury, Robert Smalls, Calvin T. Stubbs, Stephen A. Swails, William M. Thomas, Augustus R. Thompson, Benjamin A. Thompson, Samuel B. Thompson, William James Whipper, John H. White, Charles M. Wilder, Coy Wingo, Jonathan J. Wright (total of 63). (No first name was provided for the Jones who voted aye. Nevertheless, because both delegates with the last name Jones are black, the vote is appropriately included with the black delegates even though the vote cannot be attributed to the specific delegate. The Convention Proceedings list a vote for S. H. Thompson. Since no such delegate attended the Convention, the vote has been attributed here to Samuel B. Thompson.)

Nays: Thomas M. Williamson (1).

Absent: W. J. McKinlay, William McKinlay, Abram Middleton, William M. Viney (4).

No vote was recorded for John Bonum or the other Jones delegate.

White Delegates

Ayes: James M. Allen, Frank Arnim, James D. Bell, Lemuel Boozer, C. C. Bowen, Alexander Bryce, J. P. F. Camp, D. H. Chamberlain, T. J. Coghlan, William S. Collins, Simeon Corley, Jesse S. Craig, William Darrington, Elias Dickson, S. G. W. Dill, B. Odell Duncan, John S. Gentry, James H. Goss, R. G. Holmes, Timothy Hurley, Joseph H. Jenks, Dr. L. B. Johnson, William B. Johnson, Charles P. Leslie, A. G. Mackey (President), E. W. M. Mackey, M. Mauldin, Bailey Milford, Franklin F. Miller, F. J. Moses Jr., Dr. J. C. Neagle, Dr. N. J. Newell, C. M. Olsen, Y. J. P. Owens, Niles G. Parker, Gilbert Pillsbury, A. C. Richmond, W. E. Rose, James M. Runion, James M. Rutland, B. F. Whittemore, Francis E. Wilder, John Wooley (total of 43). (Four Johnsons attended the convention. The vote for three of the Johnsons is clear; however, the record contains an aye vote for W. A. Johnson. Because there was no W. A. Johnson who was a delegate to the convention, it is presumed that the vote is a typographical error and should have been recorded for W. B. Johnson. Therefore, the vote has been attributed to W. B. Johnson.)

Nays: Henry W. Webb (1).

Absent: Joseph Crews, Jno. A. Hunter, George Jackson, J. K. Jillson, William Perry (5).

No vote was recorded for George DeMeddis, Thomas J. Robertson, F. A. Sawyer, or John K. Terry. Because an aye and an absent vote were recorded for R. J. Donaldson, both votes were disregarded, thus he is not included in the roll-call results.

TABLE 1.2: ROLL-CALL VOTE RESULTS

Black Delegates

Ayes: Purvis Alexander, Martin F. Becker, John Bonum, Isaac P. Brockenton, Barney Burton, Benjamin Byas, Edward J. Cain, Francis L. Cardozo, John A. Chestnut, Frederick Albert Clinton, Wilson Cooke, Nelson Davis, Robert C. DeLarge, William A. Driffle, Harvey D. Edwards, Robert B. Elliott, William H. W. Gray, David Harris, Charles D. Hayne, James N. Hayne, James A. Henderson, Richard H. Humbert (Humbird), Henry Jacobs, William R. Jervay (Jervey), John W. Johnson, William E. Johnston [Johnson], Charles Jones, Henry W. Jones, Jordan Lang, George H. Lee, Hutson J. Lomax, Julius Mayer, John W. Meade (Mead), Abram Middleton, Lee A. Nance, William Nelson, Samuel Nuckles, Alonzo J. Ransier, Prince R. Rivers, Sancho Saunders (Sanders), Henry L. Shrewsbury, Calvin T. Stubbs, Stephen A. Swails, William M. Thomas, Augustus R. Thompson, Samuel B. Thompson, William M. Viney, John H. White, Thomas M. Williamson, Coy Wingo (total of 50). (Three Haynes attended the convention. The vote for two of the Haynes is clear; however, the record contains an aye vote for James H. Hayne. Because there was no James H. Hayne who was a delegate to the convention, it is presumed the vote is a typographical error and should have been recorded for James N. Hayne. Therefore, the vote has been attributed to James N. Hayne. Three Thompsons attended the convention. The vote for two of the Thompsons is clear; however, the record contains an aye vote for S. A. Thompson. Because there was no S. A. Thompson who was a delegate to the convention, it is presumed the vote is a typographical error and should have been recorded for A. R. Thompson. Therefore, the vote has been attributed to A. R. Thompson.)

Nays: Henry E. Hayne, Landon S. Langley, W. J. McKinlay, William McKinlay, William Beverly Nash, Joseph H. Rainey, Benjamin F. Randolph, Benjamin A. Thompson, Jonathan J. Wright (9).

Absent: Richard H. Cain, Abram Dogan, Rice Foster, Samuel Johnson, W. Nelson Joiner, Harry McDaniels, Thaddeus K. Sasportas, Robert Smalls, William James Whipper (9).

No vote was recorded for Samuel Lee. A nay vote was recorded for Wilder; however, it cannot be ascertained if that vote was for Charles M. Wilder (black delegate) or Francis E. Wilder (white delegate). Therefore, no vote has been recorded for Charles M. Wilder.

White Delegates

Ayes: Frank Arnim, James D. Bell, Lemuel Boozer, C. C. Bowen, Alexander Bryce, J. P. F. Camp, D. H. Chamberlain, T. J. Coghlan, William S. Collins, Simeon Corley, Jesse S. Craig, William Darrington, Elias Dickson, S. G. W. Dill, B. Odell Duncan, John S. Gentry, James H. Goss, Charles P. Leslie, A. G. Mackey (President), E. W. M. Mackey, M. Mauldin, Bailey Milford, Franklin F. Miller, F. J. Moses Jr., Dr. J. C. Neagle, Dr. N. J. Newell, Y. J. P. Owens, Niles G. Parker, Thomas J. Robertson, W. E. Rose, James M. Rutland (total of 31).

Nays: James M. Allen, R. J. Donaldson, R. G. Holmes, J. K. Jillson, Dr. L. B. Johnson, William B. Johnson, C. M. Olsen, James M. Runion, Henry W. Webb, B. F. Whittemore, John Wooley (11). (The Convention Proceedings list a vote for F. E. Wooley. Since there was no such delegate, the vote has been attributed here to John Wooley.)

Absent: Joseph Crews, Jno. A. Hunter, Timothy Hurley, George Jackson, Joseph H. Jenks, William Perry, Gilbert Pillsbury, A. C. Richmond (8).

No vote was recorded for George DeMeddis, F. A. Sawyer, or John K. Terry. A nay vote was recorded for Wilder; however, it cannot be ascertained if that vote was for Charles M. Wilder (black delegate) or Francis E. Wilder (white delegate). Therefore, no vote has been recorded for Francis E. Wilder.

TABLE 1.3: ROLL-CALL VOTE RESULTS

Black Delegates

Ayes: Purvis Alexander, Martin F. Becker, John Bonum, Isaac P. Brockenton, Barney Burton, (no first name) Cain, Francis L. Cardozo, John A. Chestnut, Frederick Albert Clinton, Wilson Cooke, Nelson Davis, Robert C. DeLarge, Abram Dogan, William A. Driffle, Robert B. Elliott, Rice Foster, William H. W. Gray, David Harris, Charles D. Hayne, Henry E. Hayne, James N. Hayne, James A. Henderson, Richard H. Humbert (Humbird), Henry Jacobs, William R. Jervay (Jervey), John W. Johnson, Samuel Johnson, William E. Johnston [Johnson], W. Nelson Joiner, (no first name) Jones, Jordan Lang, Landon S. Langley, George H. Lee, Samuel Lee, Hutson J. Lomax, Julius Mayer, Harry McDaniels, W. J. McKinlay, William McKinlay, John W. Meade (Mead), Abram Middleton, Lee A. Nance, William Beverly Nash, William Nelson, Samuel

Nuckles, Joseph H. Rainey, Alonzo J. Ransier, Prince R. Rivers, Thaddeus K. Sasportas, Sancho Saunders (Sanders), Henry L. Shrewsbury, Robert Smalls, Calvin T. Stubbs, Stephen A. Swails, William M. Thomas, Augustus R. Thompson, Benjamin A. Thompson, Samuel B. Thompson, William M. Viney, William James Whipper, John H. White, Charles M. Wilder, Thomas M. Williamson, Coy Wingo, Jonathan J. Wright (total of 65). (No first name was provided for the Cain who voted aye. Nevertheless, because both delegates with the last name Cain are black, the vote is appropriately included with the black delegates even though the vote cannot be attributed to the specific delegate. No first name was provided for the Jones who voted aye. Nevertheless, because both delegates with the last name Jones are black, the vote is appropriately included with the black delegates even though the vote cannot be attributed to the specific delegate. An aye vote is recorded for Williams. Because there was no Williams who was a delegate to the convention, it is presumed the vote is a typographical error and should have been recorded for Thomas Williamson. Therefore, the vote has been attributed to Thomas Williamson.)

Nays: (0).

Absent: Benjamin Byas, (no first name) Cain, Harvey D. Edwards, (no first name) Jones, Benjamin F. Randolph (5). (No first name was provided for the Cain who is listed as absent. Nevertheless, because both delegates with the last name Cain are black, the vote is appropriately included with the black delegates even though the vote cannot be attributed to the specific delegate. No first name was provided for the Jones who voted absent. Nevertheless, because both delegates with the last name Jones are black, the vote is appropriately included with the black delegates even though the vote cannot be attributed to the specific delegate.)

White Delegates

Ayes: Frank Arnim, James D. Bell, C. C. Bowen, D. H. Chamberlain, T. J. Coghlan, William S. Collins, Simeon Corley, Jesse S. Craig, Joseph Crews, William Darrington, Elias Dickson, S. G. W. Dill, James H. Goss, R. G. Holmes, Timothy Hurley, Joseph H. Jenks, J. K. Jillson, William B. Johnson, A. G. Mackey (President), E. W. M. Mackey, Bailey Milford, Dr. J. C. Neagle, Dr. N. J. Newell, Y. J. P. Owens, Niles G. Parker, Gilbert Pillsbury, Thomas J. Robertson, W. E. Rose, James M. Rutland, Henry W. Webb, B. F. Whittemore, Francis E. Wilder, John Wooley (33). (No first name was provided for the Mackey who voted aye; however, because A. G. Mackey was president of the convention and his vote was recorded accordingly, the vote is attributed to E. W. M. Mackey.)

Nays: Alexander Bryce, B. Odell Duncan, Dr. L. B. Johnson, James M. Runion (4).

Absent: James M. Allen, Lemuel Boozer, J. P. F. Camp, R. J. Donaldson, John S. Gentry, Jno. A. Hunter, George Jackson, Charles P. Leslie, M. Mauldin, Franklin F. Miller, F. J. Moses Jr., C. M. Olsen, William Perry, A. C. Richmond (14).

No vote was recorded for George DeMeddis, F. A. Sawyer, or John K. Terry.

TABLE 1.4: ROLL-CALL VOTE RESULTS

Black Delegates

Ayes: Martin F. Becker, Isaac P. Brockenton, Barney Burton, Benjamin Byas, Edward J. Cain, Francis L. Cardozo, John A. Chestnut, Frederick Albert Clinton, Wilson Cooke, Nelson Davis, Robert C. DeLarge, Harvey D. Edwards, William H. W. Gray, Charles D. Hayne, Henry E. Hayne, James N. Hayne, Richard H. Humbert (Humbird), William R. Jervay (Jervey), John W. Johnson, Samuel Johnson, Charles Jones, Jordan Lang, George H. Lee, Samuel Lee, Hutson J. Lomax, Julius Mayer, William McKinlay, John W. Meade (Mead), Lee A. Nance, William Beverly Nash, Samuel Nuckles, Joseph H. Rainey, Benjamin F. Randolph, Alonzo J. Ransier, Prince R. Rivers, Thaddeus K. Sasportas, Sancho Saunders (Sanders), Henry L. Shrewsbury, Calvin T. Stubbs, Augustus R. Thompson, Benjamin A. Thompson, Samuel B. Thompson, John H. White, Charles M. Wilder, Coy Wingo (total of 45). (An aye vote is recorded for F. J. Cain. Because there was no F. J. Cain who was a delegate to the convention, it is presumed the vote is a typographical error and should have been recorded for Edward J. Cain. Therefore, the vote has been attributed to Edward J. Cain.)

Nays: John Bonum, Robert B. Elliott, Rice Foster, Henry Jacobs, William E. Johnston [Johnson], Henry W. Jones, Landon S. Langley, Stephen A. Swails, Jonathan J. Wright (9).

Absent: Purvis Alexander, Richard H. Cain, Abram Dogan, William A. Driffle, David Harris, James A. Henderson, W. Nelson Joiner, Harry McDaniels, W. J. McKinlay, Abram Middleton, William Nelson, Robert Smalls, William M. Thomas, William M. Viney, William James Whipper, Thomas M. Williamson (16).

White Delegates

Ayes: James M. Allen, Lemuel Boozer, T. J. Coghlan, William S. Collins, Simeon Corley, Jesse S. Craig, B. Odell Duncan, J. K. Jillson, Charles P. Leslie, A. G. Mackey (President), E. W. M. Mackey, Bailey Milford, Dr. J. C. Neagle, Gilbert Pillsbury, Thomas J. Robertson, W. E. Rose, James M. Rutland, B. F. Whittemore, Francis E. Wilder, John Wooley (total of 20).

Nays: James D. Bell, C. C. Bowen, Alexander Bryce, J. P. F. Camp, D. H. Chamberlain, S. G. W. Dill, R. J. Donaldson, John S. Gentry, R. G. Holmes, Timothy Hurley, Dr. L. B. Johnson, William B. Johnson, M. Mauldin, Y. J. P. Owens, James M. Runion (15).

Absent: Frank Arnim, Joseph Crews, William Darrington, Elias Dickson, James H. Goss, Jno. A. Hunter, George Jackson, Joseph H. Jenks, Franklin F. Miller, F. J. Moses Jr., Dr. N. J. Newell, C. M. Olsen, Niles G. Parker, William Perry, A. C. Richmond, Henry W. Webb (16).

No vote was recorded for George DeMeddis, F. A. Sawyer, or John K. Terry.

TABLE 1.5: ROLL-CALL RESULTS

Black Delegates

Ayes: Martin F. Becker, John Bonum, Isaac P. Brockenton, Edward J. Cain, Richard H. Cain, John A. Chestnut, Frederick Albert Clinton, Wilson Cooke, Nelson Davis, Robert C. DeLarge, William A. Driffle, Harvey D. Edwards, Rice Foster, William H. W. Gray, David Harris, Charles D. Hayne, Henry E. Hayne, James N. Hayne, James A. Henderson, Richard H. Humbert (Humbird), Henry Jacobs, William R. Jervay (Jervey), John W. Johnson, Samuel Johnson, William E. Johnston [Johnson], W. Nelson Joiner, Charles Jones, Henry W. Jones, Jordan Lang, Landon S. Langley, Samuel Lee, Hutson J. Lomax, Julius Mayer, Harry McDaniels, William McKinlay, John W. Meade (Mead), Abram Middleton, Lee A. Nance, William Nelson, Samuel Nuckles, Joseph H. Rainey, Benjamin F. Randolph, Alonzo J. Ransier, Prince R. Rivers, Sancho Saunders (Sanders), Henry L. Shrewsbury, Robert Smalls, Stephen A. Swails, William M. Thomas, Augustus R. Thompson, Benjamin A. Thompson, Samuel B. Thompson, William M. Viney, John H. White, Charles M. Wilder, Thomas M. Williamson, Coy Wingo (total of 57).

Nays: Purvis Alexander, Benjamin Byas, Robert B. Elliott, George H. Lee, Jonathan J. Wright (5).

Absent: Barney Burton, Francis L. Cardozo, Abram Dogan, W. J. McKinlay, William Beverly Nash, Thaddeus K. Sasportas, Calvin T. Stubbs, William James Whipper (8).

White Delegates

Ayes: James M. Allen, Frank Arnim, James D. Bell, C. C. Bowen, Alexander Bryce, J. P. F. Camp, D. H. Chamberlain, T. J. Coghlan, William S. Collins, Simeon Corley, Jesse S. Craig, Joseph Crews, William Darrington, S. G. W. Dill, R. J. Donaldson, B. Odell Duncan, John S. Gentry, R. G. Holmes, Joseph H. Jenks, J. K. Jillson, Dr. L. B. Johnson, William B. Johnson, Charles P. Leslie,

A. G. Mackey (President), M. Mauldin, Bailey Milford, Dr. J. C. Neagle, Niles G. Parker, Gilbert Pillsbury, W. E. Rose, James M. Runion, James M. Rutland, Henry W. Webb, B. F. Whittemore, Francis E. Wilder, John Wooley (total of 36).

Nays: E. W. M. Mackey, Y. J. P. Owens (2).

Absent: Lemuel Boozer, Elias Dickson, James H. Goss, Jno. A. Hunter, Timothy Hurley, George Jackson, Franklin F. Miller, F. J. Moses Jr., Dr. N. J. Newell, C. M. Olsen, William Perry, A. C. Richmond, Thomas J. Robertson (13).

No vote was recorded for George DeMeddis, F. A. Sawyer, or John K. Terry.

2

"To Vindicate the Cause of the Downtrodden"

Associate Justice Jonathan Jasper Wright and
Reconstruction in South Carolina

RICHARD GERGEL AND BELINDA GERGEL

In the spring of 1865 a young black man, the son of a runaway slave, left his native state of Pennsylvania to venture to the captured territory of the sea islands of South Carolina to serve as a teacher to black federal troops, many of them recently liberated slaves. Brought to South Carolina under the auspices of the American Missionary Association, the most influential abolitionist organization in the country, this young man was given the duty of teaching the troops sufficient skills to read the Bible and to make basic mathematical calculations. His own education was quite extraordinary; it was acquired in the common schools of Pennsylvania, with private tutoring by a Presbyterian minister who was a leading local abolitionist, and included advanced schooling at Lancasterian Academy in Ithaca, New York, and three years of reading law.

Jonathan Jasper Wright undertook his new duties with the idealism and enthusiasm of a young man of great promise presented with an extraordinary challenge. Millions of slaves were now free, the South lay in ruins, and the old order was now dead; but the future was uncertain and the road was uncharted. Wright viewed his work as a religious mission, writing at one point to his superiors with the American Missionary Association, "I believe that as God aided David of old to slay the mighty warrior, the same is aiding these men to kill ignorance."[1] In addition to his teaching duties, Wright provided his students with legal advice as they attempted to sort out what it meant to be free and spoke at large public gatherings on the political rights of black Americans. Living in the midst of this great sea change in American history, Wright wrote in December 1865 that he was "thankful that [his] lot [was] now in this land" and stated hopefully, "I cannot help [but] think the time was not far distant when there would

be more than one colored lawyer south of the Mason and Dixon line to vindicate the cause of the downtrodden."[2]

Wright could not have conceived what was soon to come so rapidly and
dramatically—the bestowing of full political rights on the newly freed slaves; the
creating of a new state government, established with the input and votes of the
state's black majority; and the electing of blacks to seats in the general assembly,
to Congress as South Carolina representatives, to state constitutional offices;
and, finally, the electing of Wright himself as the first African American ever
elected to a state supreme court. This chapter will trace the remarkable life and
career of Jonathan Jasper Wright and give him his due as one of the most important figures of the African American bar of the nineteenth century.

THE MAKING OF A LAWYER

Jonathan Jasper Wright was born on February 11, 1840, in Luzerne County,
Pennsylvania, and was one of six children of Samuel and Jane Wright. Samuel
Wright had come North as a runaway slave from Maryland, aided by the Under-
ground Railroad that was very active in northeastern Pennsylvania. He realized
some success as a farmer, sufficient to buy a homestead in the Susquehanna
County town of Springville in April 1854 for $165. The family was apparently
already living in Springville at the time because the records of Springville Presbyterian Church indicate that on October 9, 1853, "Jonathan Wright (colored)
presented himself as a candidate for admission to the church" and was accepted.[3]
Jonathan was then thirteen years of age and was the only member of his family
to join the previously all white church. The admission was endorsed by the ruling elder of the church, Dr. William Wells Pride, a former missionary to the
Choctaw Indians of Mississippi, who was also a practicing physician, "an active
anti-slavery advocate," and young Jonathan's tutor and mentor.[4]

Wright's initial schooling was in local common schools, but his more for-
mal training began at age fifteen when he became a private pupil of Dr. Pride.
He studied with Dr. Pride for three years and then enrolled at Lancasterian
Academy near Ithaca, New York, in 1858. Wright graduated from Lancasterian
Academy in 1860 and began teaching school in the town of Montrose in Susquehanna County. In 1862, Wright began reading law in the offices of Bentley,
Fitch, and Bentley while he continued to teach school in Montrose. After two
years of reading law in Montrose, Wright assumed a teaching position with the
Wilkes–Barre, Pennsylvania, school district; he was one of only three black
teachers. Wright continued to read law after his arrival in Wilkes–Barre, now at
the chambers of Judge O. Collins.[5]

During this period, Wright also began his involvement in political affairs.
In October 1864, Wright attended the first national black convention in Syra-

cuse, New York, which was called by the legendary Frederick Douglass. Among the 145 attendees were Richard H. Cain and Francis L. Cardozo, both of whom would be close allies of Wright in Reconstruction South Carolina. Wright was also an active participant at the Pennsylvania State Equal Rights Convention for Colored People in Harrisburg on February 8–10, 1865, where he spoke passionately for the right of the franchise. He told the convention, "We have come to ask that our white fellow citizens may act as though they believed in their own Declaration of Independence, and especially in its assertion that all men are equal." He followed that appeal with a letter to the *Christian Recorder* in July 1865, where he declared that if "the blacks of the South are denied the elective franchise, the war has failed to accomplish anything except a gigantic national debt." 6

Wright made an "informal application" for admission to the Pennsylvania Bar to Judge Ulysses Mercur in 1864; this would have made him the first black attorney licensed in Pennsylvania. Judge Mercur declined to provide Wright a direct response but indicated that it was "scarcely probable the application would receive a favorable reply."7 Disheartened with his chances of being licensed to practice law in Pennsylvania, Wright accepted a position with the American Missionary Association to organize regimental schools for the black federal units enlisted on the sea islands near Beaufort, South Carolina.

As Wright was preparing to leave Pennsylvania, he was invited to deliver a major address at the Susquehanna County Courthouse in Montrose; the address was carried in full by the local Republican newspaper. Wright chastised white Northerners for having acquiesced too readily to the demands of the slaveholding South: "Whenever they asked a thing they got it. They asked of you the Missouri Compromise, and they got it. They asked of you the fugitive slave law, that gave the human bloodhounds of the South the right to hunt us like wild beasts, and gave them the right to order you to help them do it, and they got that too. You laid your faces in the dust and blindly gave them whatever they asked." Wright warned that as soon as the war was over, the South would attempt to reimpose slavery, repeal the emancipation of the slaves, and seek an amnesty for all "political offenders." He reminded his audience that the black soldier had "mingled his blood" with his fellow white soldier on the battlefield and was entitled to those rights "the Creator intended we should have." Wright asked, "[L]et us own ourselves and our own labor and we can work out our fortune." He concluded by stating that the "prayers of four million . . . will thank you for delivering them from bondage."8

Wright arrived in South Carolina in April 1865 and set about to organize regimental schools for black soldiers, about a third of whom could read and spell. He opened schools at Camp Stanton in Beaufort County and on Parris

Island. He ran a Sabbath school on Sunday and a night school one evening a week. Wright encountered many obstacles, including an absence of books and other appropriate reading materials, inadequate compensation, and poor health. He was, however, enthusiastic about his work, reporting to his superiors at the American Missionary Association, "[T]here is a great field of labor here" and "I feel elevated every day." He reported excitedly in December 1865, "God has given [my students] minds just as great as he has white men and now they are cultivating them very rapidly." By February 1866 he certified that "every man in the regiment [could] read the New Testament."[9]

Wright became increasingly engaged in civic and political affairs and began acquiring a large following among the newly liberated black citizens of Beaufort County. He began lecturing every Thursday evening at a local African Methodist Episcopal church and at other civic forums on legal and political matters. Wright was a delegate from Beaufort County to the first organized political gathering of black citizens of South Carolina, the Colored People's Convention, held at Zion Church in Charleston in November 1865. On January 1, 1866, already becoming an important holiday on the anniversary of emancipation, Wright spoke to a gathering of five thousand people, including two regiments of soldiers. His work often involved the provision of legal advice to recently emancipated slaves regarding the terms of their employment with their former masters.[10]

Wright's civic activities, many of which were outside his assigned duties as a regimental teacher, became a source of some conflict and jealousy with his primarily white coworkers in the American Missionary Association. The major criticism of Wright appeared to be that he was devoting increasing amounts of time to his legal work and correspondingly less time to teaching, a charge that was undoubtedly true. In defending his actions to his superiors in Philadelphia, Wright responded sarcastically to his critics: "Had I been contented to settle down and been what the masses of white persons desired of me (a boot-black, a barber or a hotel waiter), I would have been heard of less."[11]

After a year in Beaufort County, Wright was ready to come home. He reported that due to his continuing health problems, his physician had recommended that he "come North for a while." Wright's yearning to return to Pennsylvania came from another source as well, a report that the judge who had blocked his admission to the bar, Ulysses Mercur, had left the bench after being elected to Congress. A new judge, B. F. Streeter, was now the presiding judge for Susquehanna County, and it was thought that he might be more sympathetic to Wright's application. The supposition proved to be true and on August 13, 1866, Wright's application for admission to the Pennsylvania Bar was approved by Judge Skinner after "sustaining a good examination," making Wright the first black attorney licensed in Pennsylvania. Wright's admission was not without controversy, with the local *Montrose Democrat* criticizing his "impudence" in seeking admission to the bar and the "modern radical doctrine of equality" which permitted his acceptance.[12]

Having achieved his goal of admission to the Pennsylvania Bar, Wright received a heavy dose of reality when he attempted to open a law practice. Wright later noted, "[The] practice came in so slow I thought sure I would be famished for want of money to buy food." Wright began exploring options for practice outside of Pennsylvania. In October 1866, he made application for admission to the District of Columbia Bar, and a committee of three was appointed to examine his qualifications. Apparently, before the District of Columbia application process could be completed, Wright was offered an opportunity to return to Beaufort County, South Carolina, as an employee of the Freedmen's Bureau. His new job was officially described as "agent assisting free people in legal affairs."[13]

THE MAKING OF A PUBLIC LIFE

Wright's return to Beaufort County in January 1867, now officially serving as an attorney employed by the federal government, could not have been better timed. Radical Republicans had thoroughly defeated the Democratic Party allies of President Andrew Johnson in the November 1866 elections and were now poised to implement more aggressive terms for the reconstruction of the South. The previously rebellious states were compelled by the Reconstruction Acts of March 1867, to adopt new state constitutions that provided for universal male suffrage, and delegates to the state constitutional conventions were to be elected by all male citizens twenty-one years of age and older. In South Carolina, with its 60 percent black majority, a new era had arrived. As Wright would later explain, he found upon his return to the state "a field of opportunity spread wide to ambition."[14]

Wright assumed an increasingly high profile from both his political and legal work. In February 1867, Wright, along with another black attorney, William Whipper, formally petitioned the commanding general of troops in South Carolina, D. E. Sickles, to prosecute a white man, William T. Bennett, for allegedly assaulting a black man, Pompey Coaxum, with the intent to kill him. The attorneys argued that intervention by military authorities was necessary because local officials were refusing to protect the civil rights of the black citizen. This proceeding, *United States v. William T. Bennett*, is the first recorded instance in which a black attorney practiced before a legal tribunal in South Carolina.[15]

In July 1867, Wright emerged onto the political stage in South Carolina at the first meeting of the South Carolina Union Republican Party. In response to press reports that the new political party was organized exclusively for blacks, Wright offered a resolution welcoming "all citizens of South Carolina loyal to the nation and the principles of the national Republican Party." The resolution was adopted unanimously by the convention and received a positive response in the press. Wright was elected by the convention to the party's twenty-one-member State Central Committee, and the seeds of his reputation for moderation and reason were planted.[16]

Wright was elected as a delegate to the state constitutional convention in November 1867 and was forced to resign his position with the Freedmen's Bureau upon the opening of the convention on January 14, 1868. He immediately established himself as a major force at the convention, being named one of the five vice chairs and appointed to one of the early critical committees. Wright spoke passionately and frequently on a wide range of subjects. Indeed, there appeared to be few topics that Wright was hesitant to address.[17]

Wright spoke with great authority on the benefits of public education, having been both a student and teacher in the Pennsylvania public school system. South Carolina had little tradition of public education, something the convention from its beginning appeared determined to do something about. Wright pointed to New England as an example of what South Carolina could be, noting that the northeastern states' commitment to public education was the "glory of the land" because of the "knowledge and zeal which they have given to their children." Wright warned the delegates that "where there is no education, vice thrives and the people sink deeper and deeper into misery." Moreover, he reminded the convention of the "great cry throughout the state" to send men and women who "will teach us to read and write."[18]

Wright addressed directly the issue of school integration, which white opponents claimed was the natural consequence of establishing a public education system. Wright stated that he did not believe "that the colored children [would] want to go to white schools, or vice versa," but vigorously and successfully opposed any constitutional provision that would mandate segregation. He insisted that the matter would regulate itself. In this, Wright was essentially correct because throughout Reconstruction, even at a time when black citizens constituted a majority of the house of representatives and of South Carolina's delegation in Congress, few, if any, public schools in the state below the college level were ever integrated.[19]

Wright encouraged the convention to provide a means to fund the system of public education because the people were "hungry and thirsty after knowledge." In an effort to provide a stable funding source for the schools, Wright unsuccessfully supported a poll tax of one dollar per year to be used exclusively for the schools. Wright rejected the argument that such a poll tax could disenfranchise poor blacks, contending that they could simply "smoke less cigars or chew less tobacco." Instead, Wright contended that it was important for every citizen to contribute "his share to the education of the people of South Carolina." The convention ultimately created the state's first public school system, perhaps its greatest accomplishment, although the lack of an adequate funding source would prove to be an drag on South Carolina's schools for nearly the next century.[20]

Wright brought equal passion to the fight for a homestead exemption, which was something needed by small farmers, both black and white. He argued that South Carolina needed to build a foundation "broad enough for all to flourish upon it" and that no people could succeed without protecting the homestead. Wright proposed a resolution asking the commanding general for South Carolina to halt all levies on the sale of homesteads of one hundred acres or less for four months to allow the legislature to be organized and to adopt appropriate homestead protections.[21]

The issue of enforcing slave contracts was also of great interest to Wright. He argued that any contract for the sale of slaves could not be enforced because there was no consideration since no man could be property. Wright urged his fellow delegates to "destroy all institutions of slavery" and not let it be said that "we refuse[d] to do our duty." Interestingly, Wright took a different view once he joined the South Carolina Supreme Court, upholding various contracts involving the sale or lease of slaves.[22]

Wright served on the convention's judiciary committee and was intimately involved in the development of the judicial section of the new constitution. He argued against life tenure for judges, noting with disdain that life tenure in the federal system had produced the likes of Chief Justice Taney and the *Dred Scott* decision. Wright's proposal of election by the general assembly for limited terms was ultimately adopted by the convention.[23]

Wright spoke on a broad array of subjects; in some he proved to be most insightful and in others he may have been wiser simply to have kept his seat. He opposed a religious test for holding public office as unconstitutional, something that would not be firmly established in the law until a century later, but also supported the shortsighted efforts of some delegates to ban the reporter from the *Charleston Mercury* from the convention floor because of the newspaper's blatantly biased reporting. He complained that the delegates were not working hard enough each day and proposed that the convention adopt an afternoon session. Wright vigorously opposed any limits on indebtedness, explaining that "portions of the State in which the people are poor will require aid in the erection of schools, poor houses or other public works." Proving that he was not universally farsighted, Wright also opposed compulsory school attendance, responding to fellow delegate Francis Cardozo's point that this was being tested in Germany with the searing question, "Will you inform us what State in the Union compels parents to send their children to school?"[24]

In all of his some eighty speeches on the floor of the convention, Wright spoke with clarity and force and often displayed moderation and a spirit of reconciliation that won him many admirers. The *Charleston Daily News*, a paper not known for its fair treatment of black political leaders, observed that Wright "could out talk any man on the floor of the convention and had the assurance to attack any subject." The paper went on to note that Wright was "clear headed, quick as a flash, [and] by no means a bitter Radical."[25]

As the constitutional convention was winding down in March 1868, party caucuses met to nominate candidates for statewide and legislative races, with elections scheduled along with a vote on the new constitution on April 14, 1868. The Republican caucus unanimously nominated the assistant commissioner of the Freedmen's Bureau in South Carolina, Major General Robert K. Scott, as governor. A hotly contested race emerged in the lieutenant governor's contest, with three prominent black convention delegates—Jonathan Jasper Wright, Robert Brown Elliott, and William J. Whipper—seeking the office as well as a white man, Lemeul Boozer. When Elliott, later a United States congressman and Speaker of the South Carolina House, realized he did not have the votes to win, he threw his support behind Wright to assure that a black candidate would hold one of the major state officers. Whipper, who was destined to be Wright's rival in future battles, also withdrew but endorsed Boozer over Wright. This tipped the balance in Boozer's favor, and he captured the Republican nomination and was elected the following month as the state's first Reconstruction lieutenant governor.[26]

Having narrowly lost the nomination for lieutenant governor, Wright was selected as the Republican candidate for the senate from Beaufort County. With the county's overwhelming black majority, Wright was almost assured of victory. His election in April 1868 made him, along with nine others, the first black senators in the state's history.

Wright was now emerging as one of the most respected elected officials of the new Reconstruction legislature. The *New York Times* reported that the "most notable negro in the legislature [was] Senator Wright" and described him as "intelligent, fluent and facile." In the pattern established during the constitutional convention, Wright "spoke perhaps more than any other senator and generally very clearly." He was considered hard working and industrious and was respected for his passionate support for a broad homestead exemption, which helped equally long-suffering white farmers as well as recently landed former slaves.[27]

DONNING THE ROBES

Wright's legislative career was destined to be short-lived because less than two years following his election to the state senate a seat on the state supreme court opened with the election of Associate Justice Solomon Hoge to Congress. Hoge had distinguished himself in his eighteen months on the court by not producing even one written order. The election was set for February 1, 1870. A general consensus was quickly reached in the general assembly that Hoge's replacement would be an African American. This set up the race between Wright and his old nemesis, Representative William J. Whipper; they were both legislators from Beaufort County. Their styles could not have been more different, however, with Wright having the reputation as a consensus builder and a moderate and Whipper as flamboyant and a member of the Republican Party's "Radical" wing. If this choice had been made by the Republican Party caucus, there is little doubt that Whipper would have prevailed over the more cautious and circumspect Wright. Speaker of the House Franklin J. Moses Jr., who would later serve as one of the most corrupt governors in the nation's history, endorsed Whipper, noting that while Wright might be better educated, "men had frequently been placed in the position Whipper sought . . . who could lay no claim whatever to legal ability."[28]

Wright appreciated the importance of building a coalition of his fellow senators along with Democrats who feared Whipper's ascendancy to the supreme court. Faced with a choice of Wright and Whipper, Democrats viewed Wright as "much better fitted for the place." Moreover, Wright showed considerable political savvy by agreeing to have his supporters vote for a white Democratic candidate for a circuit judgeship in return for Democratic support for his candidacy. These various voting blocks were more than enough to overcome Whipper's decided advantage in the larger house of representatives and among Republican loyalists.

Wright's name was placed in nomination by legendary Charleston state senator Richard "Daddy" Cain, a renowned orator who described Wright as an "indefatigable laborer for the rights and interests of the colored race." Cain highlighted Wright's impressive resume, including graduation from college in New York, admission to the Pennsylvania Bar, legal adviser to the freedmen, and senator from Beaufort County.[29]

The proceedings were cloaked with a sense of history in the making. One reporter noted that even "the most careless observer" knew that this election was for no "ordinary purpose." Wright and Whipper sat at the same desk in the center of the house chamber during the proceedings, with a mutual friend sitting between them. Wright was noted to have "looked uneasy," but "spoke freely" with Whipper and "to such friends as came up to impart words of cheer." As the vote was called, a sense of tension and anxiety gripped the joint session of the general assembly. "Great beads of perspiration stood on the foreheads" of several legislators, and, as the presiding officer readied to announce the vote, "all rose with him and bent eagerly forward" to hear the result.[30]

Drawing upon his overwhelming support in the senate and among the Democratic members of the house, Wright captured seventy-two votes, with fifty-seven for Whipper and five for the remaining candidates. The presiding officer then announced that the "Honorable J. J. Wright, having received a majority of the whole number of votes given, was duly elected as associate justice of the Supreme Court for the unfinished term ending 30 July, A.D. 1870." Wright's supporters "immediately commenced to applaud him" but promptly ceased when it was announced that the joint session would then proceed to fill the six-year term commencing August 1, 1870. This announcement produced "great disorder," which the presiding officer's "repeated rappings of the . . . gavel failed to subdue." The joint session ultimately dissolved without a vote on the full six-year term.[31]

Despite the short term setback, with the joint session failing to proceed with Wright's election to a full six-year term, Wright's supporters were "jubilant" and were telegraphing the result all over the country. The Union League of Charleston passed a resolution praising the general assembly for its historic decision: "The (W)right man in the (W)right place." Newspapers and magazines widely reported Wright's election, with the *Nation* observing, "He is said to be the best educated negro in the state and enjoys the reputation of being the ablest man of his race." The Charleston *News* noted that Wright held "the highest position held by a colored man in the United States."[32]

Wright wasted no time in assuming his new position, promptly resigning from the senate upon his election and receiving his commission as associate justice. The morning following his election, February 2, 1870, Wright appeared at the supreme court chambers to assume his new position. In the rush of events of the previous twenty-four hours, Wright had no opportunity to obtain judicial robes and appeared on the bench in his business suit. As Wright ascended the bench, Chief Justice Franklin Moses Sr. "turned in his seat, bowed and shook hands with Wright," but, as newspapers reported, the other associate justice, A. J. Willard, made "no sign of recognition whatever."[33]

After the initial fanfare over the election of America's first black state supreme court justice, Wright quickly settled into the relative obscurity of an appellate court judge. His salary allowed him to live in "great style" in Recon-struction-era Columbia, with his own carriage and driver. Within months of his elevation to the court, Wright's relations with Associate Justice Willard were sufficiently collegial that Reverend John Cornish would record in his diary on April 14, 1870, that he was introduced to Justice Wright by Willard. On December 9, 1870, Wright was elected by the general assembly to a full six-year term with only token opposition.[34]

Shortly after Wright's election to the court, on a visit to his family in Susquehanna County, he had a chance encounter with Congressman Ulysses Mercur, the former trial judge who five years earlier had blocked his admission to the Pennsylvania Bar. Mercur congratulated Wright on his new position, at which time Wright replied that he hoped one day to be able to congratulate Mercur "on attaining as high a position in Pennsylvania as he had attained in South Carolina." Wright's "assumption of superior dignity" was apparently not "very highly appreciated" by Mercur.[35]

The three-member supreme court that Wright joined was certainly able. Chief Justice Moses was a highly respected antebellum state senator from Sumter County and a former circuit judge and was one of the most productive justices in the court's history. He was also, in this period of diversity and equal-ity, the first Jewish chief justice ever elected by any state. Associate Justice Willard, a native of New York, was a law school graduate, a rather uncommon distinction in a state where most lawyers were trained in the offices of other attorneys. In a backhanded compliment, earlier historians noted that "in spite of the fact that the Supreme Court was composed of a scalawag, a carpetbagger and a Negro, its administration was fair and its decisions equitable."[36]

Wright was, throughout his seven-year tenure on the South Carolina Supreme Court, an active member. He authored some ninety reported decisions and clearly influenced the court's direction in a number of important cases, most notably those appeals involving legal issues and relationships arising out of the abolition of slavery. In Wright's first written order, *Burgess v. Carpenter*, a farmer who contracted with a farm laborer for his services sought to assert a claim against a defendant who allegedly shot the laborer, thereby reducing his pro-ductivity and causing damage to the farmer.[37] Wright rejected the plaintiff's claim, noting that the laborer, "being a free man, and competent to make a con-tract, [was] responsible for his own actions" and could assert a claim against the wrongdoer for his personal injuries. The farmer, unlike the slave owner in for-mer days, did not own the laborer and could not assert a claim for damages to his property.

In *Redding v. South Carolina Railroad Company*, Wright rejected an effort by the railroad to avoid liability for the act of its agent in violently removing a black woman from the ladies' parlor at the Charleston depot because of her race.[38] The railroad claimed that it could not be held responsible for the tortious acts of its employee, acts in which it had no notice, and that the appropriate claim was individually against the employee. Wright reversed a lower court order dismissing the case, noting that under the doctrine of respondeat superior the employer is liable for the torts of the employee so long as they are committed in the course of employment. Wright explained the court's holding: "On what principle of fairness could it be contended that either the error or folly of employing an incompetent or careless servant should bring damage to a stranger, while the master, who put him in the position where he might commit the wrong, should be free from all obligations to respond to the injury? . . . When the community deal with a corporation of the character of this defendant, with diversified departments and various branches . . . , 'public policy and convenience' require that they should be responsible for the acts of commission or omission by their agents while in the course of their employment."[39]

Wright certainly identified personally with the plaintiff in *Redding* because while serving as a state senator, he was removed from the first-class compartment on the Richmond and Danville Railroad. Wright responded by seeking to have the general assembly revoke the railroad's charter to do business in South Carolina. When that failed, Wright instituted suit in U.S. District Court in Richmond under the new Reconstruction Acts for damages arising from his ejectment from the first-class compartment due to his race. The case came to trial on April 12, 1871, in Richmond, with Wright now the preeminent black judicial figure in America. The railroad settled after the first day of trial with the payment of twelve hundred dollars, a significant sum during this era.[40]

Wright was invited in early 1872 by a group of black leaders in Charleston to deliver a major address to the community. He accepted and promised to get back with his hosts once he had composed the speech. After meticulously preparing his address, he advised the community leaders that he was ready and the speech was scheduled for May 31, 1872, at Liberty Hall. The speech, which emphasized the need for racial and political reconciliation, was pure Wright and was very well received. He urged the black community "not to cherish any malice or hatred in our hearts against any man because he has been a slaveholder, or because he differs with us in politics. Let us labor for the peace, union and prosperity of all our fellow-citizens of whatever race or color." Wright concluded the speech with a ringing call for a color-blind society: "[L]et us with a fixed, firm, hearty, earnest and unswerving determination move steadily on and on, fanning the flame of true liberty until the last vestige of oppression shall be destroyed, and when that eventful period shall arrive, when, in the selection of rulers, both State and Federal, we shall know no North, no East, no South, no West, no white nor colored, no Democrat nor Republican, but shall choose men because of their moral and intrinsic value, their honesty and integrity, their love of unmixed liberty, and their ability to perform well the duties to be committed to their charge."[41]

While Wright's vision of racial fairness, reflected in cases such as *Redding* and *Burgess*, clearly influenced his colleagues on the South Carolina Supreme Court, it might be said that the traditions and the responsibilities of the position of associate justice influenced Wright as well. As a member of the constitutional convention, Wright frequently and vigorously spoke out against slave contracts and argued that they should be deemed void against public policy. Dealing with these issues as an appellate justice, however was a lot more complicated. In *Grier v. Wallace*, a surety on a long-standing note sought to escape liability on the basis that the contract guaranteed by the surety originally involved the sale of slaves.[42] The trial court agreed, holding that "the collection of negro bonds was bad and unfortunate, and would not likely be law long." The problem with this approach is that, by disregarding the contract, the court ultimately favored one party to a slave transaction over another and allowed an undeserving party to prevail simply because the debt he incurred arose out of a slave transaction. Wright, writing for an unanimous court, held that his court, as well as the U.S. Supreme Court, had upheld the validity of slave contracts and that it was improper for the trial judge to instruct a jury to return a verdict contrary to law.

Wright faced a similar situation in *Bailey v. Greenville and Columbia Railroad Company*, which involved a refusal by the defendant railroad to pay for certain slave labor contracted for and received because the services were rendered after the Emancipation Proclamation was issued.[43] Wright rejected the railroad's argument, noting that "whether the . . . laborers were or were not slaves" was irrelevant since the railroad received the laborers' services and must compensate the party which provided the services. Again, Wright refused to provide one party to a transaction with slaves with a windfall simply on the principle that slave contracts were per se void.

Perhaps no case tested Wright more than *Russell v. Cantwell*, which involved an action by a former slave for malicious prosecution arising out of false allegations made against the plaintiff while he was a slave.[44] Although this was not an action by a former slave against his former master, the implications of this case were tremendous because if the plaintiff could assert a legal claim from injuries suffered while he was a slave, what would prevent the same former slave or others similarly situated from asserting claims against their former masters for wrongs inflicted against them while in bondage? Wright clearly understood the incendiary potential of this claim, noting: "To permit those who were slaves . . . to bring actions . . . for wrongs and injuries committed against them during the existence of slavery, would open the door to a flood of litigation that would prove disastrous to all classes of persons in the State."[45] Rather than set off this "flood of litigation," which would have established the right of the victims of slavery to seek reparations from those that had held them in bondage, Wright affirmed the long-held legal precedent that persons who were slaves had no right to assert legal claims and all rights relating to slaves were owned by their masters.

Wright felt strongly about the illegality of the rebellion, secession, and the Confederacy and did not hesitate to apply harsh remedies and principles against those who had been loyal to the Lost Cause. No case more dramatically demonstrates this point than *Chicora Company v. Crews*, which initially arose as an ordinary contract dispute brought by the Chicora Company over the sale of cotton.[46] The Chicora Company, however, was no ordinary corporation. Indeed, Chicora's charter indicated that the company was incorporated during the war as a blockade runner for the importation of arms and munitions; Wright characterized this "as an act of hostility to the United States authority, an act against public policy, an act contributing to and aiding the rebellion." Such a charter was "void," making any contract of Chicora "void against public policy." Wright reasoned that "[t]o recognize such legislative authority [chartering Chicora] would be to recognize the right of the Legislature to give aid and comfort to an enemy to overthrow the government of the United States."[47] Thus, Chicora's routine efforts to enforce its rights under a contract for the sale of cotton resulted in the effective dissolution of the company due to its origins and conduct during the war.

A similarly harsh result was visited, in *Creighton v. Pringle*, upon trustees who accepted payment on prewar debt instruments with Confederate currency, which was then invested in Confederate bonds.[48] Wright concluded that to accept payment in "a depreciated currency" or to purchase Confederate bonds "was a breach of trust by the trustees, for which they [were] responsible."[49] The fact that the trustees accepted payment in the then lawful currency was no defense because the acceptance of the Confederate currency was a windfall to the debtor at the expense of the beneficiaries of the trust.

During Wright's tenure on the supreme court, South Carolina's profound economic decline following the devastation of the Civil War produced many foreclosure actions and suits to enforce payments due on notes. Debtors sought to employ creative defenses to avoid judgments, but perhaps none were as imaginative as the defendant in *Brewster v. Williams*.[50] The note in question provided that payment was due "six months after peace is declared between the United States and the Confederate States of America." Since the war had ended in surrender, without a peace treaty, the debtor claimed that the note was not yet due.

Wright was unimpressed, noting that since the Confederate States were never "recognized by any government on earth" and were never a lawful entity, it was not possible that such a construction was ever contemplated.[51]

In another debtor–related matter, *Detheridge v. Earle*, the trial judge charged the jury that while the total debt was due the plaintiff, the jury could in its discretion return a verdict for one-half of the amount due.[52] This is exactly what the jury did, and the plaintiff appealed. Wright interpreted the judge's charge to be based on a sympathy for the debtor for obligations incurred in the midst of the war, which Wright characterized as "unjust, erroneous and unwarranted." In reversing the verdict, Wright asserted that to allow a discount of the contractual obligation under these circumstances was "no more nor less than offering a premium for rebellion."[53]

An area of debtor rights dear to Wright was the homestead exemption, which he championed as a member of the constitutional convention and as a state senator. As an associate justice, Wright was confronted with issues regarding the reach of the homestead exemption. In *Ex Parte Hewett*, a debtor sought to invoke the protections of the homestead exemption despite the fact that the obligation was incurred before the exemption was adopted.[54] Wright rejected the defense, holding that the application of the homestead exemption under such circumstances would impair the obligation of contracts, in violation of the U.S. Constitution. Similarly, in *Kibler v. Bridges*, Wright held that the homestead exemption was inapplicable to mortgaged property since the mortgaged real estate was an essential element of the obligation.[55] While these decisions likely produced a result not desired by Wright, they reflect good examples of the limitations on even the most sympathetic and kindhearted appellate justices, who must be guided by the rule of law and controlling legal precedent.

The body of case law authored by Wright in his seven-year tenure on the South Carolina Supreme Court is reflective of the type of legal matters generally addressed by the state courts during this era, with a heavy emphasis on debtor-creditor, real property, and estate-related issues. Many of these cases address rather mundane legal questions, yet one sees Wright's personality and experiences in a number of them. This is most obviously true in the civil rights cases and those matters which touched directly or indirectly on the legal legitimacy of the Confederacy. There might be complaints that he simply did not go far enough, such as the decision, in *Russell v. Cantwell*, rejecting the right of a former slave to assert a claim arising from the period of his bondage. But these criticisms ignore the fact that Wright was but one of three justices, and any effort to give former slaves the right to sue their former masters for damages arising from their period of bondage would have likely produced a powerful and violent backlash from the heavily armed rifle clubs and other white citizen groups. This potential for massive and systematic violence, always just below the surface, was ultimately unleashed in the election campaign of 1876, resulting first in the debasement of the political process and then in the politicization, manipulation, and intimidation of the judicial process, the likes of which the state had never before seen.

THE REDSHIRT CAMPAIGN OF 1876, ELECTION FRAUD, AND THE SOUTH CAROLINA SUPREME COURT

By 1876, Republican Party fortunes in most southern states were in serious decline, as southern white Democrats reasserted their control over state and local governments. South Carolina and Mississippi seemed destined for a different course, however, since these states had significant black voting majorities, strong black political networks, and unquestioned Republican Party control over most state and local elective offices. These assumptions were certainly questioned when Mississippi Democrats seized control of statewide offices in 1875 after engaging in a systematic campaign of voter intimidation, disruption of Republican Party campaign activities, and massive voter fraud.

The Mississippi experience certainly caught the eye of former Confederate general Martin Witherspoon Gary of Edgefield County, an energetic firebrand who had never given up the dream of the restoration of white Democratic hegemony in South Carolina. At a time when some Democrats were so demoralized that they were proposing a fusionist effort with reformist Republican governor Daniel Chamberlain, Gary began developing a campaign plan to overcome the state's 60 percent black voting majority by the use of violence, intimidation, and fraud. It was known variously as the "Mississippi Plan" and the "Edgefield Plan." Gary proposed the creation of Democratic rifle clubs in each community, to provide the armed force necessary to overcome the Republican Party advantage. Gary's plan required each white voter to control the vote of at least one black by "intimidation, purchase [or] keeping him away"; established a system of disrupting Republican Party meetings by appearing in large numbers unannounced, armed, and with a demand for a "division of time"; and organized systematic ballot-box stuffing to correct the numerical imbalance of the Democrats.[56] To provide both an inspiration to the Democratic effort and a cover for his illicit activities, Gary persuaded the state's most distinguished Confederate hero, Wade Hampton III, to return to South Carolina from Mississippi to run for governor.

The Democrats' 1876 campaign effort was waged on two distinct levels— one directed by Hampton, who crossed the state with great dignity and pageantry and invited blacks and whites to support his candidacy, and the other implemented by Gary, who directed a force of nearly three hundred rifle clubs in a military-type assault on the political rights of black South Carolinians. One

Democratic observer called the party's campaign "one of the grandest farces ever seen." Gary's hand could be seen in a July 1876 gun battle between Edgefield County whites and members of the state's virtually all-black militia at Hamburg, South Carolina; the battle ended with local rifle club members selecting six captured black militiamen for execution because one white man had died in earlier gunfire. Murder and related charges were brought against over eighty Edgefield whites in what became widely known nationally as the "Hamburg massacre." Gary personally secured bail for all of the defendants.[57]

Another armed confrontation occurred in September 1876 between the militiamen and the rifle clubs near the town of Ellenton, on the border of Barnwell and Aiken Counties. Over thirty state militiamen were killed, as well as black state representative Simon Coker, who was shot at point-blank range while on his knees praying. The rifle club–inspired violence continued after Ellenton, forcing President Grant on October 17, 1876, to send federal troops to South Carolina in response to the "insurrection" and "domestic violence."[58]

Election day, November 7, 1876, brought reports of black voter intimidation, ballot-box stuffing, and disruption of traditionally Republican boxes, although the presence of the federal troops probably averted open warfare by the rifle clubs. As the votes began rolling in, it became clear that the Democrats had overcome the Republicans' traditional majority of 25,000 to 30,000 votes, and the various candidates for state and legislative offices were in virtual dead heats. Hampton led Chamberlain by approximately 1,300 out of over 180,000 votes, but this had been accomplished by Edgefield and Laurens Counties, where four thousand more males than resided there had voted. In the legislative races, Democrats held a lead, sixty-five to fifty-nine votes, in the state house of representatives, but this included the election of eight Democrats from the obviously fraudulent Edgefield and Laurens returns. Republicans continued to control the state senate, eighteen to fifteen, on the face of the returns. Moreover, in the South Carolina returns for the presidential race, Republican candidate Rutherford Hayes appeared to have a lead of approximately 1,000 votes over Democratic candidate Samuel Tilden, with a number of votes challenged by both parties. As the dust settled nationally on the presidential returns, Tilden was only one electoral vote shy of being elected president, with three states, including South Carolina, under challenge. It appeared that control of the state house, the South Carolina governorship, and possibly even the presidency might turn on election challenges from Edgefield and Laurens Counties.[59]

Three days following the election, on November 10, 1876, the State Board of Canvassers convened to review and calculate the election results. The board consisted of five members, all elected officials, who had the duty to tabulate the votes and decide all cases under contest. The board had existed since 1870 and had heard election protests without challenge for local and legislative elections. The Board of Canvassers did not hear any election challenge involving the governor's race, since this responsibility was explicitly given to the general assembly. Another provision of the state constitution provided that "each House shall judge of the election returns and qualifications of its own members."[60]

Because the Board of Canvassers consisted entirely of Republican elected officials, Democrats began complaining loudly that the board's review of legislative races was improper and was the exclusive responsibility of each legislative body. This was no small dispute since the Board of Canvassers might declare the Edgefield and Laurens votes invalid, refuse to seat the challenged legislators from those counties, and give control of the general assembly to the Republicans. This would, in turn, allow a Republican majority in a joint session to declare Chamberlain the governor. Additionally, the Board of Canvassers could review and affirm the state's presidential vote for Hayes, possibly determining the outcome of the national election.[61]

On November 14, 1876, the Democrats filed an action for original jurisdiction with the South Carolina Supreme Court to have the court prohibit the board from performing any duty regarding the legislative races other than tabulating the returns and issuing election certificates to those with the largest number of votes on the face of the returns. In short, the Democrats sought a court order prohibiting any board inquiry into the facially fraudulent results from Edgefield and Laurens Counties.[62]

In pursuing this course, the Democrats seemed to have the upper hand. Chief Justice Moses and Associate Justice Willard were known to be Hampton men. Moses deeply resented Governor Chamberlain's controversial efforts to keep his son, former governor Franklin Moses Jr., off the circuit court bench; this had been praised a year earlier by prominent Democrats as an act of honesty and courage by Chamberlain. Willard, although nominally a Republican, was reported to have a brother in New York who was closely allied with the Tilden campaign and the Tammany machine. Wright, as the third member of the court, was thought to favor Chamberlain and the Republicans but was considered to be powerless with the bloc of Moses and Willard.[63]

The supreme court promptly granted the Democrats' request to hear the matter in its original jurisdiction and scheduled the case for oral argument two days hence, on November 16, 1876. While this was certainly an expeditious schedule, time was of the essence since by law the Board of Canvassers would cease to exist on November 22, 1876. On November 17, the court issued an order requiring the board to proceed at that time with only its ministerial function of tabulating the vote and to deliver to the supreme court the then unreported election results for the justices' review. Wright dissented from the portion of the order requiring reporting of the election results to the court, explaining that the question before the court, the jurisdiction of the Board of Canvassers, was "purely a legal one" and that consideration of the consequences of the decision might "turn the court into a political machine to elect parties."[64] Wright further elaborated his views in a court proceeding shortly thereafter on this matter: "I did not consider it necessary that the court should know whether A, B or C was elected, and the only question before the court was whether the board had the power to hear and determine protests and contests."[65]

The Democrats were represented by a team of the ablest lawyers of the state, while the Republicans had far fewer resources, relying primarily on U.S. attorney David T. Corbin and the Republican candidate for attorney general, Robert Brown Elliott. On November 19, reflecting the high stakes of the litigation, former U.S. attorney general Amos Akerman arrived to take charge of the Republican legal effort. Further, U.S. Circuit Judge Hugh L. Bond arrived in Columbia for the federal civil rights prosecution of the Ellenton rioters and word soon spread that he might involve himself in the electoral controversy in some manner.[66]

Matters came to a dramatic head on November 22. The supreme court convened in the morning to render a decision on the authority of the board to hear protests in state legislative races. As the court prepared to issue its decision, the Board of Canvassers convened, threw out the Edgefield and Laurens results, and adjourned sine die. The court, unaware of the board's actions, issued an order permitting the board only the authority to report election results and requiring the board to issue election certificates to the highest vote-getters in each legislative race. Wright again dissented from the decision. By the time the court could deliver its order, the board was no longer in legal existence to accept service or honor the terms of the decision.[67]

The Board of Canvassers' audacious actions shocked the Democrats and brought them out of their recent complacency that they were only days from having their election victory affirmed by the supreme court. Hampton issued a statement calling the board's actions "daring and revolutionary" and in contempt of the supreme court. He urged his followers to "maintain, even under that provocation, your character as an orderly and law-abiding people." The Democrats' lawyers responded by filing a motion to hold the Board of Canvassers in contempt and to jail them until the required election certificates were issued.[68]

The Board of Canvassers' strategy, while effective in the short term in avoiding the supreme court's directive that would have sealed the defeat for Republicans in the house and for Chamberlain, was legally risky and in open defiance of the court. The court immediately set a hearing on the contempt motion for November 24, and the board found the justices in a very angry disposition. Moses' and Willard's demeanor was described by one reporter as "savage in the extreme," with Willard's vehement denunciation of the board receiving the most attention: "As the case now stands, an incident has occurred, rare in the history of civilized society; men clothed with civil authority of limited character, subject to the courts of the land, have placed themselves in defiance of the highest court in the State of South Carolina, and are now jeopardizing the security of justice and the security of peace. . . . This court is clothed with majesty. We do not speak the voice of men; we speak in judgment and judgment is the voice of God."[69]

Wright sought to calm the dark temper of the court and to find some solution around this crisis, yet even he realized that the Board of Canvassers had placed the court in a corner. He explained from the bench his view of the matter: "I am not ready to sign the order [of contempt], but will be if the Board does not make the return according to the order. While it is true I do not agree with my associates in this order, this order was passed by a majority of this Court, and inasmuch as the Board are to report to the Court whether they have or not complied with the order, and if they desire to report I think they should have the time, and now is the time. If they do not report, I must join in the order for them to show cause why they should not be attached for contempt."[70]

Wright's call for restraint confronted a reality of the calendar. The general assembly was scheduled to convene on November 28, just four days hence, and it was necessary for the board to issue the required election certificates for the house and senate to organize. At this point, election certificates had been issued for all representatives and senators save the eight from Laurens and Edgefield Counties, the eight which represented the balance of control between the Democrats and the Republicans. In an apparent concession to Wright, the court delayed until the following day, Saturday, November 25, the jailing of the board, to allow twenty-four hours to facilitate compliance.

All eyes appeared to be on Columbia as this extraordinary test of political wills unfolded. The mood on the street was becoming increasingly ominous. Democrats reported that there would be ten thousand armed men in Columbia when the legislature convened on November 28. President Grant, apparently in response to this threatened armed force, issued an order on November 26 directing federal troops to Columbia "to sustain Gov. Chamberlain in his authority against domestic violence." As the jailing of Board of Canvassers appeared an increasingly more likely event, it was widely reported that Judge Bond would schedule an immediate hearing in federal court to hear the board's writ of habeas corpus. Further, the *New York Times* reported that Associate Justice Willard's brother, a New York bond trader with close ties to the National Democratic Party and the Tammany Hall machine, had arrived in Columbia "in the interest of Tilden."[71]

The South Carolina Supreme Court reconvened in an unusual Saturday session on the morning of November 25, 1876, on the issue of the Board of

Canvassers' contempt in failing to issue the required election certificates of the Democratic house candidates from Laurens and Edgefield Counties. Democratic partisans crowded into the courtroom within minutes of the doors opening and "every foot of standing room . . . was occupied." The court delayed the proceeding one hour, apparently in the hope of obtaining the board's compliance. Finally, at 11:30 A.M. the court commenced the proceeding and promptly announced the orders of contempt against all five members of the board: State Treasurer F. L. Cardozo, Controller General T. C. Dunn, Secretary of State H. E. Hayne, Attorney General W. Stone, and Adjutant General H. W. Purvis. Each was fined fifteen hundred dollars and ordered into the custody and confinement of the sheriff of Richland County. The room burst into "great applause" after the court announced the extraordinary arrest and jailing of the Board of Canvassers.[72]

The court then turned its attention to the highly explosive issue of the presidential electors, knowing that a Tilden victory in South Carolina would put him over the top in the electoral college. The Hayes-Tilden dispute was a more difficult matter for the court, however, since Hayes had a slight majority in the official returns, notwithstanding the massive fraud in Laurens and Edgefield Counties. To rule with Tilden, the court would have to overturn the election results with little support in the record. Indeed, the Republicans' attorney, David Corbin, appeared to anger the court's majority when he reminded them that "they were bound by the record as it was." Associate Justice Willard seemingly acknowledged that there were substantial questions about the South Carolina Supreme Court's jurisdiction over the presidential election results but assumed that there was no court to review the state court's decision in this matter. The state supreme court agreed to hear further argument concerning whether it could review and throw out ballots in the presidential race.[73]

By 5:00 P.M. on November 25 all members of the board were in the custody of the Richland County sheriff and were reported by the highly partisan *Charleston News and Courier* to be "refreshing themselves in jail after their labors." The board was confined in two small rooms at the Richland County jail since the cells were then occupied by a large number of criminal defendants scheduled to go on trial before Judge Bond for federal civil rights violations in association with the Ellenton riot. This strange convergence of criminal defendants in the Richland County jail, Republican elected officials attempting to preserve the party of Lincoln and rifle club members seeking to restore white hegemony by armed force, was noted in the national press, and a drawing of the imprisoned board members was carried in the widely read national magazine *Leslie's*.[74]

The imprisoned members of the Board of Canvassers received an unexpected visitor on the second day of their incarceration, Associate Justice Wright.

While Wright would publicly explain his visit of Sunday, November 26, as a personal mission to relay a message from Secretary of State Hayne to a dying mutual friend, the far more likely purpose of the visit was to find some resolution to this potentially incendiary confrontation between the Republican-controlled Board of Canvassers, potentially backed by the U.S. Army, and the state supreme court, which had the support of thousands of armed rifle club members who were descending on Columbia. Whatever Wright's purpose in visiting the jailed board members, the matter remained unresolved and the tensions rose in Columbia as "white men in red shirts swaggered in the streets of the town, displaying their revolvers."[75]

On Monday, November 27, 1876, the members of the Board of Canvassers appeared before U.S. Circuit Judge Hugh L. Bond on a writ of habeas corpus. They asserted that the federal court had jurisdiction over the matter because their duties included certifying the vote of the presidential electors and that the South Carolina Supreme Court had acted unlawfully in jailing the board. Judge Bond immediately directed the Richland County sheriff to transfer the prisoners to the custody of the U.S. marshal, who released the board members pending the court's review of the matter. Judge Bond agreed to hear further argument on the case later in that week, but his prompt overriding of the state supreme court's arrest order heightened the Democrats' fears that the Republicans would use their control over the federal government to facilitate electoral victories for Hayes, Chamberlain, and the Republican candidates for the state house of representatives from Edgefield and Laurens Counties.[76]

The Democrats' worse fears regarding the Republicans use (or abuse) of federal power appeared to be realized the following morning, November 28, 1876, when the general assembly convened to organize and take up any election protests. The legislators found the statehouse surrounded by armed federal troops and the entrances guarded and controlled by the soldiers. Access to the statehouse was granted only to persons with electoral certificates issued by the Board of Canvassers; this excluded the eight legislators from Laurens and Edgefield Counties. When the Democrats presented an order from the South Carolina Supreme Court indicating that the Board of Canvassers had been directed to issue certificates of election to the eight Laurens and Edgefield legislators and had unlawfully failed to do so, the federal troops were unmoved. Their orders were no election certificate, no admission.[77]

The Democrats, now represented by literally thousands of armed men in and around the center of town and the statehouse, were outraged by the intervention of federal troops. Many of the rifle club members converged on the statehouse when word spread of the refusal of the federal troops to allow the Laurens and Edgefield representatives to enter; this was characterized as "barefaced usurpation" in "defiance of the highest tribunal of the State." Some of the federal troops, intimidated by the temper and number of the rifle club members, retreated into the statehouse, and there was genuine concern that armed conflict might ensue between the Democratic partisans and the troops of the U.S. Army. At the request of the commander of the federal troops, General Thomas Ruger, Wade Hampton came to the steps of the statehouse and urged his supporters "to disperse, to leave the grounds of the Capitol . . . and do nothing to provoke a riot." In response to Hampton's plea, the rifle club members left the grounds of the statehouse, and what would have been for the Democrats a catastrophic confrontation with the federal troops was averted.[78]

The following day, November 29, 1876, the Board of Canvassers members were back before Judge Bond arguing that the state supreme court had acted unlawfully in presuming to order the board to do anything since the court had no jurisdiction under the state constitution to oversee the actions of the board. In recognition of the importance of the legal issues in dispute here, the national Republican Party brought into the state attorneys from Indiana and North Carolina to argue the motions. Judge Bond took the matter under advisement, but the threat of federal court intervention on behalf of the Republicans remained an active concern of the Democrats in this battle for legal legitimacy, a battle which was being fought out in the courts, in the statehouse, and in the streets.[79]

The Democrats seized the initiative over the next several days to support their claims of victory in the presidential, gubernatorial, and legislative races. On November 30, 1876, on the third day of the legislative session, the Democratic house members, with the Laurens and Edgefield aspirants with them, slipped into the statehouse an hour before the scheduled legislative session and began conducting the business of the house. When the Republicans arrived, they found William Henry Wallace, the Democratic claimant, as Speaker, in the Speaker's chair. The Republicans promptly arranged for another chair for their speaker, E. W. M. Mackey, and he began conducting the business of the house. Each presumed speaker recognized only members of his party and dual speakers with dual houses functioned literally side by side. The *New York Times* reported that the "scene in the House at this moment is disgraceful, and portends a serious riot within the hall."[80]

General Ruger advised the Democrats that the Laurens and Edgefield representatives would not be permitted to enter the following day; this precipitated a strongly worded telegram from Wade Hampton to President Grant indicating that the challenged legislators would remain "until expelled by force." Both houses remained in session, day and night, for four consecutive days in this test of wills. Ultimately, President Grant and Secretary of War James B. Cameron countermanded Ruger's order and directed that Governor Chamberlain must initially attempt to use his own authority to remove the challenged legislators. On December 4, 1876, the Democratic house members suddenly left the statehouse en masse and reconvened at Carolina Hall.[81]

In conjunction with their move to the statehouse and creation of the dual houses, the Democrats filed a series of motions with the South Carolina Supreme Court to cement their electoral victory. First, they asked the court to order the secretary of state to deliver the official electoral returns for the house to the Democratic speaker, effectively asking the court to recognize Wallace as the official Speaker of the house and the Laurens and Edgefield legislators as properly serving members. Second, the Democrats requested that the Republican presidential electors, presently scheduled to meet as part of the electoral college on December 6, 1876, be enjoined from convening. Third, they asked the court to enjoin all of the statewide Republican candidates with the highest number of votes in the official returns from assuming their positions.[82]

The supreme court initially took up the matter of the legal status of the Wallace house, hearing a day of legal argument on the question on December 4. The Republicans initially sought to argue that the court had no jurisdiction over the Board of Canvassers, but this was greeted unenthusiastically by the justices. Indeed, Justice Wright, who, prior to the sine die adjournment by the Board of Canvassers, had been a supporter of the Republican position, told the Republicans' counsel during oral argument that "the only thing that ought to be before the Court is the legal question [of] which is the legal House."[83] Two days later, on December 6, 1876, an unanimous supreme court, in *Wallace v. Hayne*, ruled that Wallace was the lawful Speaker and that the Edgefield and Laurens Democratic candidates, having the largest number of votes in the official returns, had the prima facie right to sit in the body.[84] The court further held that the house, and not the Board of Canvassers, had the right under the constitution to be the final arbiters of the membership of the body. In a concurring opinion, Justice Wright observed: "I presume the object of the government is, or should be, the protection and representation of the people. If a body of men, acting as a Board of State Canvassers, have the right to throw out one county and thus defeat its representation, they can throw out one-half or all of the counties in the State and defeat an entire election. Consequently, I take it that those eight men had a right to participate in the organization of the House of Representatives. That being the fact, it was impossible for the other so-called House to have the requisite constitutional majority."[85]

The supreme court's decision in *Wallace v. Hayne* was given little weight by Governor Chamberlain or President Grant. After the Democratic house members left the statehouse on December 4, the remaining Republicans in the house met in joint session with the senate, threw out the results from Laurens and Edgefield Counties, and declared Chamberlain reelected as governor. He was officially sworn in on December 6, the very day of the *Wallace v. Hayne* decision. The Democrats shortly thereafter swore Hampton in as governor. Federal troops continued to surround the statehouse and maintained their orders that without election certificates the Laurens and Edgefield representatives would not be admitted. President Grant, in a newspaper interview, defended his continued support for the Chamberlain government on the basis that Laurens and Edgefield County votes were obviously fraudulent.[86]

The state supreme court's decision in *Wallace v. Hayne* was further undermined on December 11, 1876, by the decision of U.S. Circuit Judge Hugh Bond, a decision granting the writ of habeas corpus on behalf of the Board of Canvassers. Judge Bond held that the South Carolina Supreme Court had no jurisdiction over discretionary decisions of executive department officials and had no right to order the Board of Canvassers to do anything. This very argument had been made before the South Carolina Supreme Court in the *Wallace* case by the Republicans and had been summarily rejected by a unanimous court. Judge Bond invited the losing party to appeal his order to the U.S. Supreme Court; this was apparently never done.[87]

Although the South Carolina Supreme Court had rapidly and enthusiastically taken the Democrats' position on the question of the legal status of the Wallace house, the justices were far more reluctant to enter the fray regarding the presidential electors. From a practical standpoint, ruling in favor of the Tilden electors was difficult since on the face of the state returns the Hayes electors were the winners and the court had not developed a record upon which to set aside challenged ballots. Furthermore, the Democrats were seeking truly extraordinary relief, an injunction preventing the South Carolina electors from participating on December 6, 1876, in the electoral college, with the South Carolina votes possibly determining the outcome of the presidential race. If the state supreme court were to issue such an injunction, there was little doubt that the Republican electors would defy the order and force the court to issue another arrest warrant. This would then trigger still another writ of habeas corpus to U.S. Circuit Judge Bond, whose position on the supreme court's legal authority over the various election matters was well known. Faced with significant legal and practical obstacles to granting the Democrats the relief requested on the presidential elector issue, the South Carolina Supreme Court simply allowed the date for the meeting of the electoral college to pass without holding a hearing or responding to the motion for a temporary injunction. The electors convened on November 6, as scheduled, and cast the state's electoral votes for Rutherford B. Hayes. Wright, who had apparently counseled caution to his colleagues on the issue, explained that the presidential elector case raised a "very important and grave question and should be fully argued by counsel" before a decision was rendered by the court.[88]

After nearly a month of intense litigation in the state and federal courts, the movement of thousands of armed rifle club members into Columbia to intimidate the opposition, and the placement of federal troops around and within the statehouse to preserve the authority of Governor Chamberlain, the Democrats and the Republicans were in a standoff. Neither party could muster sufficient legal or political authority to establish itself as the winner. Hampton clearly commanded great strength within traditional power centers within the state, and his ability to control what amounted to a massive armed militia was unquestioned. Chamberlain possessed little real power as governor but had for the moment the power and authority of the federal government standing behind him. Recognizing that this was now a war of attrition, Hampton and the Democrats began attacking the Republicans at every point of vulnerability, confident that their uncompromising determination to restore white hegemony would ultimately prevail.

The Democrats moved forcefully to cut off the revenues of the Chamberlain government. Hampton publicly urged citizens not to pay their taxes to Chamberlain's government and to remit one-tenth of their prior year's taxes to his regime. Utilizing the battle cry of "starve out the thieves," white taxpayers complied with Hampton's request and dramatically reduced revenue to the Chamberlain government. Democrats also persuaded state circuit judge Robert B. Carpenter, a political enemy of Chamberlain, to issue a temporary injunction against two banks from releasing funds from the state's accounts to Republican treasurer F. L. Cardozo on the basis that his prior term had expired and results from the present election were under challenge. These efforts essentially dried up the financial resources of the Chamberlain regime. Meanwhile, the Democrats were able to persuade local banks to take their drafts and were thus able to pay Democratic legislators their salaries for the session. The Democrats also assumed responsibility for paying for other functions and operations of the state, including, interestingly, the salaries of the justices of the Supreme Court.[89]

The success of the Democrats' tax boycott campaign did not go unnoticed in Washington. President Grant, in the final days of his term, candidly stated to a reporter that "the whole army of the United States would be inadequate to enforce the authority of Governor Chamberlain." He further observed, "Unless Governor Chamberlain can compel the collection of taxes, it will be utterly useless for him to expect to maintain his authority for any length of time."[90]

As the tax boycott sapped the vitality out of the Chamberlain regime, the Democrats planned one last grand gesture on the legal front, a declaration by the South Carolina Supreme Court that Hampton was the duly elected governor. They apparently sought to time this decision to the assumption of office of the new president, who, despite the ongoing election dispute, appeared to be

Republican Rutherford B. Hayes. The message was to be clear—support of Chamberlain was futile and all legal, military, and political authority within the state rested with Hampton.

The ability of Hampton to win before the state supreme court was considered a foregone conclusion by the Democrats. Chief Justice Moses and Associate Justice Willard were strongly, vocally in Hampton's corner; and since the effort by the Board of Canvassers to defy the court, even Justice Wright seemed sympathetic. Moreover, the supreme court justices were receiving their salaries from the Hampton regime; this the Democrats took as an implicit recognition of his status as governor.

The Hampton claim of the governorship was not without its difficulties, however. While Hampton did maintain a narrow lead in the official election results, his slight majority rested on the clearly fraudulent returns from Edgefield and Laurens Counties. Further, the state constitution required that any disputed election result be resolved by a joint session of the general assembly. Hampton's election had been ratified by the Wallace house without the benefit of the senate meeting with it in joint session. Beyond this formality, state circuit judge Robert Carpenter, on the petition of a prisoner (Peter Smith) pardoned by Chamberlain, ruled, on January 28, 1877, that Chamberlain remained governor because neither candidate had satisfied the constitutional formalities to validate their election. Smith was thus ordered released from prison. To further cloud the picture, another state circuit judge, T. J. Mackey, a vocal Hampton partisan, ordered the release of a prisoner, Amzi Rosbourough, on the basis of a pardon granted by Hampton. Since both decisions were by state trial judges, they had no binding effect statewide.[91]

To set the stage for a binding state supreme court decision, Hampton issued another pardon to a woman prisoner, Tilda Norris, on February 9, 1877. The request for a writ of habeas corpus by Norris was accepted by the court in its original jurisdiction with a referee appointed to develop a record. While the matter was pending, Chief Justice Moses suffered a devastating stroke that completely incapacitated him. The court apparently had no practice to appoint interim justices in such circumstances, even for individual cases, and all eyes now turned to Justice Wright. In the absence of his concurrence, the writ would fail.[92]

The Democrats soon discovered that Wright was prepared to rule against Hampton's claim for governor and "extraordinary efforts" were made by Willard and the Democrats to persuade him to change his views. Rumors that the case would soon be decided resulted in large crowds which "densely packed" the courtroom, primarily Democrats whose purpose may have been both to hear the decision and to send Wright a message about the consequences of nonconcurrence.[93]

On February 27, 1877, the court convened at 11:00 A.M. to a packed court-room "in anticipation of a decision" in the *Norris* case. No decision was forth-coming and the court announced it would reconvene at 1:00 P.M. Wright and Willard then retired to the court's consultation room, and Willard informed Wright that "the Democrats could no longer be restrained." If Wright's position became known to the crowd in the courtroom, Willard informed Wright, "their full fury would be visited" upon him. Willard then arranged to bring Hampton's attorney, James Conner, into the court's private consultation room, and Conner stated to Wright that if the Democrats did not prevail "many lives would be sac-rificed." Wright then agreed to concur in a one-sentence order releasing Tilda Norris from prison so long as this was not filed until Friday, March 2. When the court reconvened that afternoon, again to a crowded courtroom, it was announced no decision had been made but there might be one in a few days.[94]

Wright immediately regretted his decision to concur and set upon a course to revoke his order. Reportedly in close consultation with Robert Brown Elliott, Chamberlain's attorney, Wright prepared an order finding that Hamp-ton had not satisfied the formalities of the constitution to be governor and, thus, had no authority to pardon the prisoner.[95] He concluded his order with the fol-lowing defense of his actions: "I have most strenuously endeavored to arrive at the correct conclusions in the present case, for I am deeply impressed with its gravity in its relations to all our public affairs. But the Constitution is the supreme guide, and I must follow it heresoever it leads. If I have erred, I shall greatly regret it; but I shall have the consolation of knowing that I have endeav-ored to honor my judicial trust by a faithful regard to my official oath and the Constitution of South Carolina."[96]

Wright delivered his opinion to the clerk of the supreme court on March 1, 1877, and requested that it be filed. He also delivered a brief memorandum opinion formally revoking the yet unfiled order releasing Tilda Norris. Wright explained that after "mature deliberation" he determined that the order "should not have been made" and substituted his opinion for his former concurrence.[97]

Willard appeared at the court on March 2, 1877, with the expectation that the court would convene and the decision releasing Norris would be orally announced. Wright, however, was nowhere to be found. With a packed court-room waiting, Willard sent the sheriff to Wright's home and received a report back that he was not there. Despite the fact that Willard was informed by the court's clerk that Wright's opinion of March 1, 1877, and memorandum revok-ing the prior concurrence had already been filed, Willard filed the earlier order releasing Norris, the order which contained Wright's signature and the state-ment "I concur in the above." Tilda Norris was directed to be released from prison on the strength of the Hampton pardon and the dubious order filed by Judge Willard.[98]

The Democrats' response to Wright's actions was immediate and vociferous. The *Columbia Register* declared that Wright had made an "ass of himself . . . Condemn him!" The major complaint against Wright appeared to be that, having "drawn his pay from the moneys contributed by taxpayers to sustain the Hampton government," he owed his allegiance to Hampton. As the *Columbia Register* asked, "[W]as it right, Wright, for you to take your salary with your left hand while you denied the Governor's right with your right?"[99]

On the same day as the Tilda Norris debacle, the Electoral Commission, responsible for determining the contested presidential race, formally voted eight to seven to recognize Rutherford B. Hayes as the next president of the United States. This decision was reportedly made amid a deal, among southern Democrats and northern Republicans, that the price for the Hayes presidency would be the removal of federal troops from the South; this removal would, among other things, lead to the recognition of Hampton as governor of South Carolina.[100]

Hayes was sworn in as president on March 4, 1877, and on March 9 a delegation of black South Carolinians presented themselves to the White House to see the president. In addition to Congressmen J. H. Rainey, R. H. "Daddy" Cain, and Robert Smalls, the delegation included Justice Wright and several other black state officials. Hayes met with the South Carolinians for forty minutes and explained that he sought "to remove the antagonism existing between the races . . . so that the colored men and Republicans might not need the protection of the Army." While he recognized that the Democrats did not have a respect for the political rights of their opponents, he found the "use of military force in civil affairs repugnant to the genius of American institutions." Although he pledged a careful review of the South Carolina situation before a final decision was made on the federal troops, Hayes sentiments could not have been encouraging to his visitors. Indeed, within the month, after having separate private meetings with Hampton and Chamberlain, Hayes announced that federal troops would leave South Carolina on April 10, 1877. On that day, Chamberlain abandoned all claims to the governorship and Hampton became the unchallenged victor of the election of 1876. Reconstruction had ended in South Carolina.[101]

THE BITTER END

Shortly after the Democrats seized the governorship and control of the South Carolina House, a move was afoot to remove Wright from his position as associate justice. The initial resolution adopted by the house was couched in the vaguest of language, seeking an inquiry into "all matters pertaining to the proper discharge of the official conduct of Hon. J. J. Wright." Three days following the adoption of the resolution, on May 1, 1877, a committee of five was appointed to conduct the investigation of Wright, an investigation which historian George Tindall described as being organized "with the obvious purpose of seeking some pretext for removing him." Ten days later, after conducting hearings in secret, the committee, in a secret session of the house of representatives, presented a resolution to the body to impeach Wright for "drunkenness." Wright denied the allegations and described the impeachment effort as a "persecution." His supporters also attempted to lift the veil of secrecy and to conduct all proceedings in public, but this was defeated.[102]

The impeachment effort seemingly stumbled in its initial stages. The house voted on May 19, 1877, to continue the matter until the next legislative session. On May 23, 1877, Rep. Thomas Miller, a Republican supporter of Wright and later a U.S. congressmen, accused the chair of the investigative committee, Rep. Charles S. Minot, of bribing a witness. The house appointed still another committee to investigate that allegation. Several days later, the committee recommended a resolution requesting that Wright resign because "after the charge of drunkenness ha[d] been made and established against him," it brought "discredit upon the administration of justice" to allow him to continue in office.[103]

Finally, on June 6, 1877, when it was clear that Wright would not simply abandon his position, the house voted seventy-five to twenty-three to impeach Wright and to send the matter to the senate for a trial. Several legislators entered into the House Journal their bases for voting against the measure, including their assertion that the facts were not sufficient to convict and that the process had moved in too "hasty" a fashion.[104]

Hampton and the Democrats were then in full control of the levers of power, and the result in the senate trial was not in doubt. Other Republican judges and elected officials were being forced out of their positions and Wright had few options. In August 1877, Wright submitted his letter of resignation as associate justice of the South Carolina Supreme Court, effective December 1, 1877. Hampton, in formally accepting Wright's resignation, stated, "[This is a] tribute on your part to the quietude of the State, and . . . in no sense an acknowledgement of the truth of the charges which have been made against you." Wright later stated that when he submitted his resignation, Governor Hampton indicated that "he placed no belief in the charges, and that as a jurist [Wright] was one of the purist."[105]

An assessment of the validity of such a vague charge as "drunkenness" against Wright, now more than 120 years after the impeachment effort, is most difficult, but the greater weight of the evidence points in the direction that there was not a sufficient basis to support removal from office. Upon assuming power, the Democrats were most anxious to expose the defects of their Republican predecessors and held numerous public hearings and issued detailed reports exposing prior misconduct. The insistence upon secrecy in the Wright impeachment investigation, both in taking the evidence and in failing ever to issue any report of the findings, bears, according to historian Thomas Holt, "all the marks of [the charges] being fabricated." In addition to the absence of any evidence in the public record to support the charges against Wright, the actions of the Hamptonians in unilaterally removing dozens of validly elected and appointed Republican officials in the early months following the end of Reconstruction give little credibility to the Democrats' impeachment effort against Wright.[106]

Wright's name also surfaced in a legislative investigation of an alleged bribery scheme involving former governors Daniel Chamberlain and Franklin Moses Jr. Shortly after the Democrats took control of the general assembly, they created the Joint Investigative Committee on Public Frauds and held public hearings on corruption by their Republican predecessors. These hearings appeared designed to permanently tarnish the image of the South Carolina Republicans, both within the state and with their defenders in the North. No target was more inviting to the Joint Investigative Committee than Daniel Chamberlain, the former Republican governor and student at Yale and Harvard Law School, who had earned a national reputation as a reformer and advocate of clean government.

The primary charge of corruption against Chamberlain was made by his avowed enemy and predecessor as governor, Franklin Moses Jr., whose rapacious plunder of the state while governor was even then legendary. While the Joint Investigative Committee was conducting its work, Moses was a resident of the Richland County Jail, then being held on charges of forgery. Moses was most anxious to cooperate with the Democrats and was prepared to testify about an alleged bribe made in April 1874 involving Chamberlain, then a practicing attorney, and Associate Justice Wright. Moses claimed that while he was occupying the office of governor he was the middle man in a scheme to bribe Wright to fix a case pending before the supreme court. This was the same court his father served on as chief justice.[107]

Moses testified that he was approached by Chamberlain, who was acting as counsel for an estate involved in an appeal against the Bank of Charleston concerning a claim of alleged mismanagement of between sixty and seventy thousand dollars, an enormous sum in that day. The estate had prevailed at the trial level and the supreme court unanimously affirmed the decision in *Whaley v. Bank of Charleston*.[108] Wright did not participate in the oral argument of the case or in the decision of the court. The bank moved to reconsider and, reportedly, Justice Willard and Chief Justice Moses differed on this motion, with Wright holding the deciding vote.

In Moses' original statement on the matter, he claimed that Chamberlain came to him at the governor's office and asked that he determine what price

Wright would charge to vote with his client on the motion for rehearing. Moses stated that he then made contact with Wright, who allegedly demanded twenty-five hundred dollars, which had to be paid before the vote. Moses stated that he passed this on to Chamberlain, who immediately drew up two notes "in his own handwriting" promising to pay to Wright twenty-five hundred dollars over the ensuing sixty days. According to Moses, Wright then sold the notes at a discount to two named persons and then cast the deciding vote for the estate in denying the motion for a rehearing.[109]

This original account, if true, was presumably subject to verification since there should have been two notes made payable to Wright and the testimony of two persons to whom Wright negotiated the notes at a discount. The independent evidence revealed, however, that there were two notes totaling twenty-five hundred dollars executed by Chamberlain, but these were made payable to Moses and not Wright. Moreover, the two persons who negotiated the notes dealt only with Moses and had no contact with Wright. Faced with this conflicting evidence, Moses then changed his statement to claim that he obtained the notes from Chamberlain made payable himself, negotiated them immediately at a discount, and took the proceeds to Wright, who then agreed to loan the bribe money to Moses.[110]

This account was simply too fantastic even for the Joint Investigative Committee. The committee concluded in its final report that while they believed that Chamberlain had intended to bribe Wright by utilizing Governor Moses as a presumed middle man, they were unable to determine whether Justice Wright was ever aware of this scheme or received any part of the bribe proceeds.[111] For his part, Wright emphatically denied Moses' allegations and made the following dramatic public challenge in a letter to the general assembly: "Although I am no longer a judge of the Supreme Court, I hold myself responsible to the law for any violation of it while I held that distinguished position . . . , and I therefore pray your honorable bodies to take such action as will the cause [the charges] . . . to be laid before the proper law officers of the state, to the end that, if sufficient evidence be found to warrant it, legal proceedings may be taken at once against me, or if no such evidence be found that I be relieved of the scandalous imputations sought to be put against me."[112]

The general assembly forwarded Wright's letter to the attorney general and no prosecution was ever initiated on Moses' dubious and inconsistent allegations. Indeed, it might be said that Wright's public invitation to the highly partisan Democrats, who were then actively pursuing corrupt Republican office holders at every opportunity, to prosecute him if they had a case was the very best evidence of his innocence.[113]

Shortly after resigning the court, Wright briefly took a position traveling in the North raising funds for black Sunday schools. In August 1878, Wright was in Philadelphia on a fund-raising mission and told a reporter that his efforts were "fairly successful." In response to the question of whether he intended to return to South Carolina, Wright stated, "[South Carolina is] where sir . . . I propose to reside the residue of my life span and there be buried."[114]

Wright kept his word, returning soon to his adoptive state to practice law and to work with Claflin College in building a Law Department to provide formal training for aspiring black attorneys. Shortly after Wright's return to the state, he found himself involved incidentally in a controversy which reverberated across the state during Wade Hampton's reelection campaign of 1878. In the course of a campaign swing through Orangeburg, Hampton and the candidate for state superintendent of education, Hugh S. Thompson, arranged to dine at the home of the president of Claflin College, Rev. Edward Cooke, who was white. When Hampton and Thompson arrived, they discovered to their surprise that also in attendance were Jonathan Jasper Wright and another black professor at the college. While interracial dining was commonplace during Reconstruction, the newly emerging racial orthodoxy, soon to be known as Jim Crow, made such social contacts taboo. To his credit, Hampton, after "a moment's hesitation," sat down and dined with Wright and the professor. Word rapidly spread among the more rabid of the Democratic Party supporters that Hampton had violated this essential social custom, and the first rumblings against Hampton among white conservatives had begun. They would subsequently go public, attacking Hampton for his practice of "din[ing] with Negroes."[115]

Wright made no public comment regarding his dinner with Governor Hampton but vocally supported his reelection in 1878, noting, "[Hampton has] "kept every pledge he has made. He will get nine-tenths of the colored vote. . . . There is not a decent Negro in the state that will vote against him." Indeed, the Republican Party, terribly dispirited by the their abandonment by the national government and the domination of the levers of power by the Democrats, fielded no opponent in the governor's race, allowing Hampton to be reelected without opposition.[116]

In this era when many attorneys were still trained by "reading law" in the offices of a licensed attorney, Wright attempted to formalize the process by setting up law offices at 84 Queen Street in Charleston and opening his chambers to students who were officially registered with the Law Department at Claflin College. As a former associate justice, Wright had a good law library, an essential resource for conducting a training program. Wright was officially designated Claflin College's Chair in Law and took in at least seven students. Little is known of the specifics of the curriculum, but Wright's students were intensely loyal and devoted to him.[117]

Wright also practiced law from his Queen Street office, with apparently mixed success. In the criminal courts, Wright handled matters ranging from bigamy to murder, but this area of practice in Charleston County was dominated by another black attorney, former house Speaker Samuel J. Lee.[118] Part of Wright's difficulty was undoubtedly poor health, primarily progressive tuberculosis. There was no known treatment for this common and dreaded disease in the 1880s, and Wright experienced increasingly greater difficulties.[119]

Despite his health problems, Wright did have the opportunity to try cases in the Charleston County criminal courts. In *State v. August Gibbes*, Wright's client was acquitted of larceny of livestock.[120] His client in *State v. Bill Brown* was charged with murder and went to trial five days after being arraigned.[121] The jury spared the client's life, finding him guilty of manslaughter. The judge promptly sentenced the defendant to twenty years in the state penitentiary.[122]

Wright's most notable case was probably among his last, a murder trial involving a dispute over a debt that ended with one of the disputants, Merriman DeVeaux, stabbing the other in the back of the head. The blow did not initially kill the victim, but the knife injury resulted in the development of traumatic meningitis, which ultimately proved fatal. The surviving case file reveals surprisingly thorough police and investigative work, including an autopsy confirming the role of the knife attack in the death of the patient and sworn statements from a number of the eyewitnesses. Wright apparently had little to work with since his client had elected to do the deed after a loud argument which attracted an ample number of independent and reliable eyewitnesses to the event. Not surprisingly, the jury convicted DeVeaux and the judge sentenced him to hang. Fortunately for DeVeaux, Wright had friends in high places. Shortly before the sentence was to be carried out, Governor Hugh S. Thompson, who years before had been Wright's dinner companion with Wade Hampton at the controversial dinner at Claflin College, commuted the sentence to life at hard labor.[123]

By early 1885, Wright's health was becoming increasingly precarious, with the tuberculosis rendering him essentially an invalid. Then only forty-five years old, he found himself cared for by his students, who included a physician, William F. Holmes. On February 17, 1885, as death approached, Wright prepared a will with the assistance of Dr. Holmes. He appointed a former student, George Marshall, as his personal representative and devised his law library to Robert L. Smith, his first law graduate. The balance of his estate, which included a home in Columbia and real estate in Beaufort County, was left to his siblings, Campfield Wright, Stephen Wright, and Nancy Wright Howard, all of Springfield, Pennsylvania.[124]

Wright died two days following the execution of his will, on February 19, 1885. The black members of the Charleston County Bar took solemn note of his passing, giving him tribute during a ceremony in the court of general sessions on the morning of February 20, 1885. Former Speaker of the house Samuel J. Lee made reference to Wright's actions in 1876 and 1877 during the dual government litigation and stated that his "sacrifices [were] sufficient to entitle the deceased to the grateful memory of the citizens of the State." Lee concluded by calling Wright "a true and constant friend to his people." On the motion of Lee, W. J. Bowen, and J. W. Polite, all African American members of the Charleston County Bar, court was adjourned for the day as a tribute to Wright.[125]

The local paper, the *Charleston News and Courier,* prominently featured Wright's death on the front page with the headline "one more relic of Reconstruction disappears." Showing the danger of having one's enemies write an obituary, the article highlighted the unproven allegations of accepting bribes, referred to his service on the bench as a "curious career," and stated that after leaving office he "sank into obscurity."[126] This image of Wright, and really of all black public officials during Reconstruction, advanced by the Democrats would dominate the historical record for over a century.

Wright was buried at the Calvary Episcopal Church cemetery at 106 Line Street in the city of Charleston on February 21, 1885, a block down the street from his residence at 69 Line Street. Since the intention was to move his body North for permanent burial in the future, a simple marker stating "Wright" designated the grave site. The family apparently never had the resources to move the body home and no headstone was placed on the grave until a granite marker was placed in the cemetery in February 2000 by the South Carolina Supreme Court and Bar. Like his grave site, Wright, America's first black appellate judge and arguably the most important black legal figure of the nineteenth century, was seemingly lost to history.[127]

Recent scholarship on Reconstruction has led to a reexamination of the era, particularly of the lives and service of the black public figures of the day. Rather than emphasizing allegations of corruption and incompetence advanced by the Democrats to justify the disenfranchisement of the state's black majority, this new work has focused on this noble experiment in equality, what one author has called the "glorious failure" of Reconstruction.[128]

In recognition of the reassessment of this most extraordinary era, the South Carolina Supreme Court on February 20,1997, in conjunction with Black History Month, held a formal ceremony in its courtroom in honor of Justice Wright. The "rediscovery" of Wright was prominently featured on the front pages of many of the state's major newspapers the day following the ceremony. A year later, the supreme court unveiled an oil portrait of Wright; it now hangs prominently in the supreme court's lobby. A day-long conference titled "Jonathan Jasper Wright and the Early African American Bar in South Carolina" was held in conjunction with the unveiling of the portrait at the University of South Carolina School of Law and was keynoted by Eric Foner, America's preeminent scholar of Reconstruction. That same year the Black Law Students Association at the University of South Carolina School of Law renamed its annual award to a distinguished member of the bar the "Jonathan Jasper Wright Award." In Susquehanna County, Pennsylvania, where Wright was sworn in as the first black lawyer in that state, local historians and the county bar association on February 11, 1999, hung a portrait of Wright in the very courthouse where he took his oath as an attorney. The Wright homestead, which still stands in the town of Springfield, Pennsylvania, is now being assessed for potential historic designation.[129]

The life of Jonathan Jasper Wright was written on the canvas of the great events of the nineteenth century. The son of a runaway slave, he was among the first African Americans to enjoy professionally the fruits of the liberation of his people and the adoption of the Civil War amendments to the U.S. Constitution. His dream of "vindicat[ing] the cause of the downtrodden" was at least partially realized as a teacher, attorney, vice chair of the state's constitutional convention, state senator, and as American's first black appellate judge. He could say with confidence as Reconstruction came to a close, "My own race has advanced . . . in a way that has no parallel in the history of the progress of civilization."[130] That progress was partially reversed over the ensuing years, as Jim Crow laws reinstituted a new form of servitude on the South's black citizens, but the life of Jonathan Jasper Wright offers a striking example of the talent lost to the state, region, and nation by suppressing the educational opportunities and political rights of black citizens. Wright's "rediscovery," now over a century following his death, offers the hope that his dream that "we shall know no North, no East, no South, no West, no white nor colored, no Democrat nor Republican, but choose men because of their intrinsic value [and] their honesty and integrity" still lives.[131]

LAWRENCE CAIN, senator and
USC Law School class of 1876.
Courtesy South Caroliniana Library,
USC Columbia.

R. H. CAIN, delegate to the 1868
Constitutional Convention. Simmons's
Men of Mark (1887).

FRANCIS LEWIS CARDOZO,
state treasurer, secretary of state,
delegate to the 1868 Constitutional
Convention, USC Law School class of
1876. Courtesy South Caroliniana
Library, USC Columbia.

ROBERT C. DELARGE,
congressman, delegate to the 1868
Constitutional Convention. Courtesy
South Caroliniana Library, USC
Columbia.

ROBERT BROWN ELLIOTT,
Speaker of the house and attorney
general. Courtesy South Caroliniana
Library, USC Columbia.

RICHARD T. GREENER, USC
professor and diplomat, USC Law
School class of 1876. Used with
permission of Larry Francis Lebby,
artist.

STYLES LINTON HUTCHINS,
USC Law School class of 1876.
Courtesy Chattanooga-Hamilton
County Bicentennial Library.

SAMUEL J. LEE, Speaker of the
house. Used with permission of Larry
Francis Lebby, artist.

THEOPHILUS J. MINTON, USC Law School class of 1876. *Colored American Magazine*, 1903.

JOSEPH W. MORRIS, president of Allen University, USC Law School class of 1876. Used with permission of Allen University.

B. F. RANDOLPH, delegate to the 1868 Constitutional Convention. Courtesy Oberlin University.

A. J. RANSIER, lieutenant governor, delegate to the 1868 Constitutional Convention. Courtesy South Carolina Department of Archives and History.

RADICAL MEMBERS of the South Carolina legislature, 1868. Courtesy South Caroliniana Library, USC Columbia.

Benjamin A. Boseman (row 2, 7th from left)
William J. Brodie (row 3, 2d from left)
Barney Burton, delegate to the 1868 Convention (row 5, 3d from left)
Lawrence Cain, graduate USC Law School, Class of 1876 (row 3, 4th from left)
John A. Chestnut, delegate to the 1868 Convention (row 6, 6th from left)
Wilson Cooke, delegate to the 1868 Convention (row 3, 7th from left)
Hiram W. Duncan (row 4, 2d from left)
Simeon Farr (row 7, 7th from left)
John Gardner (row 6, 9th from left)
David Harris, delegate to the 1868 Convention (row 1, 7th from left)
Eben Hayes (row 3, 3d from left)
Henry E. Hayne, delegate to the 1868 Convention, South Carolina Secretary of State, first black student to attend USC (row 5, 9th from left)
James A. Henderson, delegate to the 1868 Convention (row 5, 7th from left)

James Hutson (row 5, 11th from left)
Burrell James (row 7, 3d from left)
William E. Johnson, delegate to the 1868 Convention (row 7, 4th from left)
Samuel J. Lee, Speaker of the House (row 6, 4th from left)
Hutson J. Lomax, delegate to the 1868 Convention (row 2, 3d from left)
Henry J. Maxwell (row 3, 5th from left)
James P. Mays (row 2, far left)
Harry McDaniels, delegate to the 1868 Convention (row 6, 7th from left)
Whitefield J. McKinlay, delegate to the 1868 Convention (row 1, 2d from left)
John W. Meade, delegate to the 1868 Convention (row 7, 8th from left)
Edward C. Mickey (row 5, 6th from left)
Junius S. Mobley (row 5, 10th from left)
William B. Nash, delegate to the 1868 Convention (row 5, 12th from left)
Samuel Nuckles, delegate to the 1868 Convention (row 4, 8th from left)
Wade Perrin (row 7, 2d from left)
Joseph H. Rainey, delegate to the 1868 Convention, first black seated in the U.S. House of
    Representatives (row 7, 10th from left)
Benjamin Randolph, delegate to the 1868 Convention (row 1, 6th from left)
Prince R. Rivers, delegate to the 1868 Convention (row 4, 1st from left)
Sancho Saunders, delegate to the 1868 Convention (row 4, 7th from left)
Henry L. Shrewsbury, delegate to the 1868 Convention (row 5, 5th from left)
William M. Simons (row 6, 5th from left)
Abraham W. Smith (row 6, far left)
Powell Smythe (row 4, 4th from left)
Stephen A. Swails, delegate to the 1868 Convention (row 7, far left)
William M. Thomas, delegate to the 1868 Convention (row 2, 5th from left)
Benjamin A. Thompson, delegate to the 1868 Convention (row 7, 9th from left)
John H. White, delegate to the 1868 Convention (row 5, 2d from left)
Charles M. Wilder, delegate to the 1868 Convention (row 1, 4th from left)
Lucius W. Wimbush (row 7, 5th from left)
John B. Wright (row 4, 5th from left)
Jonathan J. Wright, selegate to the 1868 Convention, associate justice of the South
Carolina Supreme Court (row 2, 9th from left)

J. H. RAINEY, congressman, delegate to the
1868 Constitutional Convention. Courtesy
Library of Congress.

3

The Reconstruction of
Justice Jonathan Jasper Wright

J. CLAY SMITH JR.

> [I am] one who is a laborer in the cause of human
> freedom and progress . . . particularly among my
> own class.
>
> Jonathan Jasper Wright

I. INTRODUCTION

Justice Jonathan Jasper Wright was the first African American justice to sit on
the Supreme Court of South Carolina, making him the first black lawyer in the
nation to serve on the highest court of a state.[1] From 1870 to 1877, Justice
Wright served on the highest court of a former slave state, a feat which deserves
great and honorable mention. During his tenure on the bench, Justice Wright
was dedicated to his judicial duties and was present for nearly all of the 441 cases
decided by the South Carolina Supreme Court from the time he took his seat on
the bench until the time of his resignation.

It may sound strange to Americans that black lawyers in southern states
were the architects of state constitutions in the nineteenth century. In South

---

This paper was presented at the first annual meeting of the South Carolina Supreme
Court Historical Society, Feb. 26–27, 1998. The assistance of my able research assistant, Aquanetta Addie Lee Knight, is acknowledged. This paper is dedicated to the
black lawyers of the Reconstruction era and Ernest Finney, the presiding chief justice of the South Carolina Supreme Court. The chief justice was elected to the court
in 1985, becoming the first black to serve on the court since 1877, the year that Justice Wright retired. Finney was elected chief justice of the South Carolina Supreme
Court by the general assembly on May 11, 1994. *The American Bench: Judges of the
Nation* (Sacramento, Cal.: Forster-Long, 1997), 2152.

Carolina, at least four African American members of the 1868 Constitutional Convention were or would soon become lawyers.[2] On September 23, 1868, Robert Brown Elliott (Edgefield County), Jonathan Jasper Wright (Beaufort County), William J. Whipper (Beaufort County), and F. L. Cardozo (Charleston) were members of the 1868 Constitutional Convention of the State of South Carolina.[3] Wright was chosen as one of five vice presidents of the constitutional convention; after the convention, Wright was elected to represent Beaufort County at the state senate of South Carolina.[4]

These lawyers were unlike the lawyers in South Carolina who had dominated the legal and political landscape of the state for a century and a half before, men such as John Julius Pringle, who served as attorney general of South Carolina for sixteen years and would in 1779 receive from "[George] Washington the appointment of District Attorney in the United States Court of South Carolina."[5] They were unlike James Ervin, a graduate of Brown University, who was admitted to the Constitutional Court of 1800 and became solicitor of the Northern Circuit in 1802 and was elected as a trustee of the University of South Carolina in 1809.[6] They were unlike Thomas Smith Grimké, educated at Yale College in the early 1800s, who became a respected scholar, jurist, and legislator on the basis of class and wealth.[7]

In reading the proceedings one is struck by the cordial nature of its black members, who years before were defined as chattel property in the state or, if freedmen, mere sojourners in the land.[8] From all accounts, the black members of the convention, eager to perfect a document of freedom for all people, were gracious to their former slave masters. However, some of the convention's white members appeared to cling to the trappings of the old regime and were against civic republicanism.[9]

These black lawyers stepped into the arena of nation building with a fervor of democratic ideas, which were no less expressive than the founders of the nation. The record of the proceedings appears devoid of blame or hatred of the white supremacist, who seceded from the Union and threatened the survival of the nation.

The proceedings reveal a commitment by black lawyers to draft a constitution based on "humanity" and "mercy" so that a poor man and his family, in postwar debt, would not lose all of their land to creditors.[10] Thus Wright argued in favor of an homestead exemption that would protect a percentage of a landowner's land from foreclosure by creditors.[11] Wright believed that "[members of the convention] owe[d] it to the prosperity of the State to secure to every man a home, and in doing this we shall invite capital to the State, identify every man, woman and child with the soil, and create in his heart a stronger love of country. . . . If we fail to do it, we shall be overrun by legalized robbers."[12]

Since there is no available verbatim transcript of arguments before Justice

Wright or expressions about his demeanor as a justice, we are left to unearth the measure of his personality and his political beliefs as a delegate to the constitutional convention. A fair reading of the proceedings determines undeniably that Jonathan Jasper Wright was among the most influential and intellectual members of the convention. He was a person who frequently called upon the convention to act in a dignified manner, a standard which he openly applied to himself.[13] Wright urged that "dignity . . . should be sustained in this body, and as long as I am in this house I shall raise my voice to maintain that dignity."[14]

Wright was also a taskmaster. On the thirty-sixth day of the constitutional convention, Wright gently urged his colleagues to exert more industry in completing their tasks. Wright spoke eloquently as to why due diligence was required. On February 16, 1868, he said, "In facilitating this business it may be the salvation of the entire people. . . . We cannot give too much of our time to this work. The more we are together, the more we talk matters over; the more we exchange opinions with each other, the better we are prepared to mature our work."[15]

He was a man who believed in hearing the opinions of others. In fact, during the debate on the homestead exemption, he stated, "If we differ in our views of what [our duty is], it is no reason why we should attempt to crush one another."[16] Wright, the consummate statesman, chided the members against "malice or hatred toward any person, [for after all], [we] are about to lay a new foundation."[17]

As a member of the Committee on the Judiciary, Jonathan Jasper Wright had great influence on the structure that the South Carolina Supreme Court would take in both courts of law and equity.[18] During the period of time that Justice Wright served on the court, it consisted of three members. That number was influenced by Wright during the constitutional convention. It was on a motion to amend that Wright moved to create "'The Supreme Court . . . of a Chief Justice and two Associate Judges, any two of whom shall constitute a quorum.'"[19] It was Wright who pressed for the election of justices by the legislature so that the people of every section of the state "shall have a voice in saying who shall or shall not be the persons who shall hold this great . . . office."[20] He opposed a proposal for life terms for justices.[21] He also waged a vigorous effort for the election of inferior court judges believing that "every Judge shall be directly responsible to the people. . . . They are a safer tribunal than [appointment by] the Legislature."[22]

This essay offers an exposition of Justice Wright's tenure on the Supreme Court of South Carolina. It will discuss his historical approach to deciding law, his method of interpreting and analyzing relevant statutory law, and the impact of the decisions he authored. In essence, this essay seeks to reconstruct one of South Carolina's finest: Justice Jonathan Jasper Wright.

II. Cases Authored, 1871–1877

My count is that the Supreme Court of South Carolina published 441 opinions during Justice Wright's tenure on the bench; of these, 426 were signed by a justice; ninety, or roughly 21 percent, of these opinions were authored by Justice Wright.[23] It cannot be determined with any certainty how cases were assigned between the three sitting judges, however, an examination of the breakdown of cases creates the presumption that, despite the exceptional qualifications of Justice Wright, he was assigned fewer cases per term than either Chief Justice Moses or Associate Justice Willard. Table 3.1 represents the number of opinions (volumes 2 through 8) written during Justice Wright's term on the court.[24]

With three justices sitting on the bench, one could assume that each justice would be assigned one-third of the cases per term; however, this chart indicates that this was not the case during any term for which Justice Wright was on the court. The true impact of the assignment process on the number of cases authored by Justice Wright becomes clear in table 3.2, showing the total number of cases decided by each justice.[25]

In all, Justice Wright authored only 21 percent of the cases and controversies before the court during his tenure on the bench. In my view, Justice Wright's ability to influence legal history and create binding precedential authority was severely limited by the small number of cases that he was assigned. This does not, however, in any way minimize or diminish his standing as one of the finest legal minds that emerged during the era that we now know as Reconstruction.[26]

The opinions authored by Justice Wright are everlasting evidence of his aptitude for legal analysis and statutory interpretation. The disparity in the number of cases assigned to him, coupled with the social and political tension which existed in the former slave states during the Reconstruction era to

TABLE 3.1: Cases per Term

	VOL. 2	VOL. 3	VOL. 4	VOL. 5	VOL. 6	VOL. 7	VOL. 8
Moses	31	25	27	31	27	16	18
Willard	23	30	20	29	23	25	12
Wright	12	13	11	16	13	15	10
Total Signed Opinions	66	68	58	75	63	56	40
Per Curiam and other unsigned opinions	0	3	4	3	3	2	0
Total Opinions	66	71	62	78	66	58	40

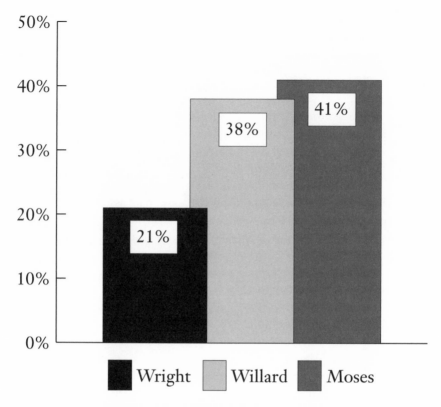

TABLE 3.2: Percentage of Signed Opinions

reestablish white supremacy, contributed to Justice Wright's untimely departure from the bench in 1877.[27]

III. Justice Wright's Legal Method

A. Jurisprudential Method: Formalism

Justice Wright authored his opinions with strict adherence to the law. His dedication to the law and his desire to see laws enforced equally across the board forced him to put aside his own personal feelings and ignore past existing social disabilities or political pressures. Moreover, the period of Reconstruction saw instances of litigation involving former slaves as well as the institution of slavery itself; all cases and controversies had to be decided in accordance with the law. This strict adherence to the law has historically been known as legal formalism.

1. What Is Formalism?

Various schools of jurisprudential thought arose during the early years of the nineteenth century. In the work titled *Foundations of Law*,[28] Bailey Kuklin and Jeffrey Stempel examine many of the different schools of thought; one school of thought discussed at length in the work is legal formalism.

Formalism usually requires a two-step approach to adjudication of legal issues. First, there are a series of laws of general applicability, laid down by society, to be applied to various cases and controversies as they arise. Second, lawyers and judges—those individuals who define what the law is—are expected to reason deductively, drawing fact-specific conclusions based on the general rules of law.[29] Under classical formalism it was not within the purview of the judge to make any moral or policy decisions. In theory, this strict adherence to rules was expected to create and sustain an unbiased system of law which indiscriminately applied to everyone.[30]

Formalism moved to the forefront of the American legal community in 1870, the very year that Justice Wright became a member of the bench and Professor Christopher Langdell assumed the position of dean at Harvard Law School.[31] From this pinnacle of legal affluence, Professor Langdell greatly influenced formalism. This method involved the study and application of appellate decisions. Judges were required to "read the case; distill the rule; apply the rule to future cases."[32] While widely accepted, formalism was criticized because it often benefited only the elite of society at the expense of the masses and was in no wise "completely neutral, detached, fair, and just."[33]

2. JUSTICE WRIGHT'S USE OF FORMALISM

Justice Wright's adherence to formalism as a jurisprudential method, and perhaps his proclivity not to offend the white establishment, may have influenced him to decide cases before him without emphasizing race, class, or community disability or personal standing.[34] His ability to maintain his judicial integrity in the face of sensitive, socially and politically divisive issues is evidence of his strength of character, as well as his pledge to uphold the law.

One case which clearly illuminates Justice Wright's formalistic approach to judicial decision-making is that of *Russell v. Cantwell*.[35] Russell was charged with theft; the charges were dismissed for lack of evidence against him. He subsequently brought suit against Cantwell for malicious prosecution, the controversy which was before the supreme court.

Writing for a unanimous court, Justice Wright held that the action for malicious prosecution would have to be dismissed.[36] Justice Wright reasoned that because Russell was a slave at the time the injury was incurred, he could not bring the cause of action. Slaves were considered chattel which had no legal rights that could be judicially enforced. It was of no moment that Russell was at the time of the action a freeman; it was his status at the time of the injury which was determinative. In dictum, Justice Wright stated that to allow former slaves to bring causes of action which had accrued during slavery would wreak havoc on the legal system.[37]

Justice Wright's personal feelings concerning the institution of slavery could have colored his opinion in favor of the plaintiff; however, one sees no personal feelings or judgments concerning the institution of slavery, but an explanation of a general rule of law applied to a specific set of facts. However sympathetic Justice Wright might have been to a former slave seeking to recover for a damaged reputation, his sympathy or lack thereof cannot be detected from his judicial opinion, which contains only an exposition of the law and its application to the facts of the case. This opinion quite possibly made Justice Wright socially unpopular in the black community because it could be read as acknowledging that slaves had no legal existence and were entitled to no protection under common or natural law during slavery.[38] Even an inference of such a view coming from Justice Wright appears to be absurd, making him in this instance no better or worse than southern judges who believed in the doctrine of racial supremacy.[39] Perhaps, it is cases such as this that caused one writer to describe Justice Wright as "a Negro of some ability, but of little or no moral courage."[40]

Another controversy surrounding the institution of slavery was that of *Chicora Co. v. Crews*.[41] The plaintiff corporation was incorporated under the laws of the state of South Carolina. In its bylaws, the corporation's stated purpose was to frustrate the blockade being enforced by the federal government against the southern states which had seceded from the Union.

Pursuant to this corporate charter and bylaws, the plaintiff corporation purchased 250 bales of cotton and contracted with the defendant to store the cotton. The defendant sold the cotton for a profit of $45,600.75 and refused to return the proceeds to plaintiff—thus, the controversy. Writing for a majority of the court, Justice Wright reversed a lower court decision in favor of the plaintiff, explaining that no state has the authority to act, or empower another entity to act, in a manner detrimental to the federal Union.[42]

The contract between the parties was void because it was formed pursuant to a certificate of incorporation issued during, and in furtherance of, the rebellion; therefore, the certificate of incorporation and any contracts made pursuant thereto were against public policy and void.[43] Justice Wright and the method of formalism itself may today be criticized for its uncaring application and seeming disregard for matters of intrinsic fairness. While he is not above criticism, his dedication to the law and his unbiased approach to judicial review, notwithstanding the parties involved, are characteristics which dominated the precedents that Justice Wright, legally trained in an era of unabashed formalism, was constrained to follow.

B. Justice Wright and the Power of Precedent

In addition to being a legal formalist, Justice Wright displayed an unwavering deference to the binding authority of precedent.[44] This is not surprising; in fact, it could be no other way. Theoretically, a true formalist must honor the rules of law established in former cases and apply those rules accordingly to each case and controversy. As a true formalist, this is what Justice Wright did.

Roof v. Railroad Co., an early opinion authored by Justice Wright, shows his adherence to precedent.[45] The plaintiff owned cattle that were permitted to wander and graze freely. One of the cattle was killed by the defendant railroad through no apparent fault of the railroad. The defendant sought to have a decision for the plaintiff overturned.

Justice Wright refused to overturn what was known as the rule in Danner's Case; this rule stated that if cattle were killed by a railroad company, this was rebuttable prima facie evidence of negligence on the part of the railroad.[46] Citing a string of cases which had followed the principle of Danner's Case, Justice Wright opined that the precedential value of the case far outweighed the possibility that it was no longer a valid decision and that it should not be disturbed unless there existed a compelling reason to do so.[47] This opinion itself became precedential authority in a subsequent railroad case, *Rowe v. Railroad Co.*[48]

Legal scholars today might cringe at the theory undergirding the rule in Danner's Case, as did Associate Justice Willard.[49] However, because the rule had been relied upon without question for many years, Justice Wright felt disinclined to abandon this legal principle and set in place a new standard by which railroad companies would be judged under similar facts.

A second case relying heavily on precedent to decide an issue of substantive law is *Grier v. Wallace*.[50] This contract case involved the purchase of several slaves. The defendant made partial payment on the slaves and later presented a note for the remaining amount due. When the plaintiff sought to act on the note, the defendant alleged that the slaves were unsound at the time of purchase, which precluded the plaintiff from recovering the amount still due.[51]

Justice Wright overturned a lower court decision holding that the defendant was now estopped from inquiring into the soundness of the slaves at the time of purchase. He reasoned that the second note issued for the amount due on the purchase constituted a new contract, and thus the terms of the previous contract were no longer relevant. In his reasoning, Justice Wright provided several cases supporting the applicable rule of law.[52]

Justice Wright's use of precedent includes not only substantive questions of law but procedural matters as well. In *Gilliland, Howell, and Co. v. Gasque*, the court was called on to determine what matters may be examined when a case is appealed by a losing party.[53] The dispute between the parties had been submitted to a referee, whose factual findings were adopted by the trial judge.

Justice Wright affirmed the trial court's finding for the plaintiff, holding that an appellate court may not interfere with findings of fact in a case at law.[54] Justice Wright limited his reasoning to several cases previously decided by the court, cases which supported this holding, stating that this procedural rule of law was so well established in the jurisdiction that further discussion of the issue was unnecessary.[55]

Justice Wright always cited some precedential authority for his opinions; this deference to precedent illuminates his enduring faith and belief in the ability of the judicial system to provide solutions to society's problems. Furthermore, his use of precedential authority makes clear his ability to correctly determine the applicability of past appellate decisions to cases and controversies then before the court. Finally, his use of precedent makes it virtually impossible to attack his opinions as legally unsound; his use of authority gives his opinions validity and sustenance which cannot be denigrated on the basis of his race or his status as the first African American state supreme court justice since the founding of the nation.

C. Statutory Analysis

During his tenure on the bench, Justice Wright authored many opinions in which he was called on to interpret various statutes and their applicability to specific factual scenarios.[56] Essentially, he believed that the canons of statutory construction required a plain meaning interpretation in the absence of ambiguity. This necessitated that he show deference to the intent of the legislature when they adopted the statute.

In *Boykin v. Watts*, Justice Wright was called on to interpret a provision of the state code dealing with actions against persons acting as executors.[57] The provision in question, section 415, precluded a party from testifying to issues in dispute when an action was being brought against the executor of an estate in his official capacity. The plaintiffs had been given the notes by the decedent prior to his death, payable to the decedent by a third party. They left the notes in the decedent's possession; upon his death, the defendant-executor refused to release the notes to the plaintiffs. At trial, the plaintiffs sought to testify to the matter in question, i.e., the notes owed to decedent by a third party.[58]

Justice Wright affirmed a lower court decision in favor of the defendant. In their complaint, the plaintiffs did not name the defendant as executor of the estate but brought the action against him in his personal capacity. Justice Wright reasoned that the purpose and facial intent of section 415, to protect executors in their official capacity, could not be circumvented by the mere word choice of plaintiffs when structuring their complaint. Because the defendant alleged and proved that the notes in question were not in his own name but in the name of decedent, the plaintiffs could not be permitted to sue him in his personal capacity and, thus, were precluded from testifying to the matter in question.[59]

A second case concerning a provision of the state code is *Sullivan v. Hellams*.[60] The plaintiff sought to recover on a note payable to a third party by the defendant; the defendant demurred on the ground that the plaintiff did not have the legal capacity to bring the action because he was not the real party in interest.[61] Justice Wright reversed a lower court decision for the plaintiff, holding that the code required that any party bringing an action must be the real party in interest.[62]

Plaintiffs were essentially relying on a provision of the state code that predated the 1868 Constitutional Convention, and that code, if operative, would have allowed the action to proceed. The provision of the state code relied on by Justice Wright to invalidate the lower court decision, section 136, was adopted in 1870 and was inconsistent with this previous provision, causing said provision to be effectively repealed. Section 136 required that any person bringing an action must be the real party of interest unless they are an executor, administrator, express trustee, or other person authorized by statute.[63] The former rule was invalid with respect to the issue then before the court because the new provision was adopted prior to commencement of the action.[64] Justice Wright held that a claim must be adjudicated in conformity with the law which exists at the time the action is litigated.

These cases are clear and convincing evidence that Justice Wright was familiar with, and adept at using, the various canons of statutory interpretation. In *Boykin*, Justice Wright applied a canon of interpretation that required that a statute be given its plain meaning in the absence of ambiguity. By using this canon, Justice Wright gave meaning to the provision in question by recognizing the purpose and intent of the legislature when it adopted the provision.

The second case involved the use of a different but equally important canon of interpretation. In *Sullivan*, Justice Wright relied on the canon which states that no language in a statute should be deemed surplusage. To rule in favor of the plaintiff would have required Justice Wright to ignore the import of the language in section 136 of the code in favor of the previous provision. To do so would have been to strip section 136 of any meaning, thus reducing the section to mere verbiage. Without question, Justice Wright realized that the language would have been excluded had the legislature not intended for it to have meaning.

1. THE POLITICAL CASES

Justice Wright's belief in limited judicial review of administrative matters and protecting the integrity of court orders is revealed in the political cases.[65] These cases were before the court near the end of Justice Wright's tenure on the court and the Reconstruction era.

In 1876 the presidential and state elections were held. These would be the last elections before the post-Reconstruction era and the decline of significant black leadership and influence in southern politics.[66] Much was at stake for both the Republican and Democratic parties vying to retain and to capture the White House, electoral votes from the state of South Carolina, and the executive and legislative majority in the state legislature. The election in South Carolina and other states captured the daily attention of major northern newspapers.

Reports indicate that voter fraud was rampant in South Carolina during the election of 1876.[67] In some districts, black voters were denied the right to vote by force and intimidation.[68] This conduct created one of the bases used by the Republicans to protest such actions before the Board of the State Canvassers.

The power of the state canvassers, as provided by law, was threefold: The state board was, first, to "make a statement of whole number of votes given [as reported by the county boards of canvassers] at such election for the various officers," second, to declare "what persons have been, by the greatest number of votes, duly elected," and, finally, to decide all cases under protest and contest.[69]

Evidence of voter fraud was contested by the Republicans. The Democrats, hoping to block any negative outcome by the board, filed suit in the South Carolina Supreme Court, contesting the power of the Board of State Canvassers to act on their duties, perhaps because the Democrats were in the board's minority.[70] The Democrats by "the mandamus asked that the Board of Canvassers should be compelled to . . . aggregat[e] the returns as received by the County Commissioners."[71] There was no objection to this request by the Republicans because they believed that the request was within their existing power. However, the court ordered the board to report its findings to the court. This action was contested as beyond the power of judicial review because the matter was committed to the discretion of the board.

The order to present was signed by Chief Justice Moses and Justice Willard. Justice Wright dissented on the grounds that the law did not require presentment to the court.[72]

Justice Wright's dissent may have had an indirect effect of favoring black voters in counties where they had been intimidated, a matter that could be corrected by the board. These black citizens, who were essentially all Republicans, would surely favor the annulment of fraudulent votes cast by the Democrats. They would also have wanted a tally that counted their votes. They would have wanted a hearing before the board to argue that "no man shall be deprived of any privilege enjoyed by any other man on account of 'race, color, or previous condition of servitude.'"[73] The heightened interest of blacks in the outcome of the proceedings was manifested by the number of black people present at the court for the hearing.[74]

The *New York Times* characterized the opinions of Chief Justice Moses and Justice Willard as political in nature. It praised the "colored Judge Wright" as making "the clearest statement that has yet come from any member of the court."[75] Even those using racial epithets toward Wright praised his decision. For example, one correspondent to the *New York Times* wrote, "The Supreme Court of the State, composed of one scallawag, one carpet-bagger, (the worst in the lot) and one nigger, has been on this egg ever since the 11th inst. And all that has been hatched out yet is the fact that this Supreme Court is supreme even over the Constitution. . . . The black man on the Supreme Court, however, seems to have at least a 'level head,' and, during the controversy, appears not to have lost his equilibrium."[76]

The impact of the court's ruling and Justice Wright's dissent ultimately had little effect. To avoid the court order to present the aggregation of returns by a certain date, the "Board of State Canvassers . . . performed its duty and terminated its legal existence while yet uninformed of the ultimate decision of the perplexed and procrastinating Court."[77] This action was intended to rob the Democrats of an adequate remedy at law.

Prior to voting itself out of existence, the Board of State Canvassers threw out the votes of the citizens of Edgefield and Laurens Counties. These counties had a large population of black citizens. Justice Wright, possibly caught between his prior dissent barring judicial review and arguments before the court that the expired Board of State Canvassers had pulled a fast one to oust the court of its stated power, modified his position. In *State ex rel. Wallace v. Hayne and Mackey*, Justice Wright joined the majority opinion of the court.[78] He said that the court had power to inquire into and determine the matters subject to its original order: to present the aggregation of votes in the state to the court.[79]

However, Justice Wright framed his concurrence on the ground that the action of the Board of State Canvassers both violated the law and was undemocratic in effect. The following portion of Justice Wright's opinion best explains his turnaround:

> I fully concur with my associates in all that they have said. . . . The whole point in this case is whether or not five persons from Edgefield and three from Laurens had a prima facie right to take their seats and participate in the organization of the General Assembly of South Carolina. In looking, a moment ago, at the statutes under which the state Board of Canvassers are directed to act, I find the 24th Section, which is one of the Sections which defines their powers and duties, reads thus:

"The Board, when thus formed, shall, upon the certified copies of the statements made by the Board of County Canvassers, proceed to make a statement of the whole number of votes given at such election for the various officers and for each of them voted for [and] certify such statement to be correct, and subscribe the same with their proper names." That was an indisputable duty . . . that they did not perform . . . I regard that as a wise provision of the law. . . . I presume the object of the government is, or would be, the protection and representation of the people. If a body of men, acting as a Board of state Canvassers, have the right to throw out one County and thus defeat its representation, they can throw out one-half or all of the Counties in the State and defeat an entire election.[80]

These cases buttress the contention that Justice Wright possessed exemplary skill and acumen when analyzing and interpreting statutory law. Justice Wright was capable of giving meaning and definition to the newly enacted code, adopted the year he became a member of the bench, a code history which he played a vital role in shaping and formulating. Justice Wright's consistent use of well- and not-so-well-established canons of statutory interpretation, like his use of precedent, gives credence and credibility to his decisions; Justice Wright's analytical ability cannot easily be called into question or reasonably doubted, even if some may not be as sound.

IV. The Long-Term Effect of Justice Wright's Decisions

Justice Wright stood in a powerful and influential position. As a justice on the supreme court, he had the authority to decide the direction the law of the state would take in years to come. His opinions were not only binding on the supreme court with respect to cases on appeal, but they were binding on the inferior courts of the state as well. In order to have any impact, however, the cases would have to be cited as authoritative in later opinions. Two factors are necessarily relevant in determining the true effect of Justice Wright's tenure on the bench. First, an examination of the number of decisions cited as authoritative in later opinions will illuminate the level of importance attached to his opinions by his successors. Next, it is helpful to determine which opinions have been modified, distinguished, or overruled by later cases.

A. Justice Wright's Cases in Later Opinions
Shephard's Citations for the state of South Carolina show that the majority opinions authored by Justice Wright—eighty-five of ninety (90 percent)—were

cited in later opinions by the court. Of these, eight opinions not only were cited as authoritative on the issue at bar, but were directly followed by the citing court. Only nine of his ninety-four total opinions have never been cited in a later opinion.

While nine of the ninety majority opinions authored by Justice Wright were distinguished by later courts, and the reasoning of two of the opinions has been questioned, none of the cases have been overruled by a later decision. After more than 110 years and an undetermined number of South Carolina Supreme Court justices, all opinions authored by Justice Wright remain on the books.

V. CONCLUSION

Against any odds that may have presented themselves, Justice Wright assumed the position and responsibilities of a supreme court justice for the state of South Carolina.[81] His adherence to formalism is evidence of his dedication to the institution of law and the pursuit of justice. However, it is also evidence that Justice Wright was aware of his strained and precarious social and political position. It was clear that liberalism or radical social change might not be tolerated by a society critical of—and hostile to—the period of Reconstruction and many of the great African American legal minds that emerged.[82]

It is my hunch that Justice Wright, eager to demonstrate that a black man could give the law to white and black people in the state, was more conservative than he needed to be. In fact, some of his decisions can be criticized as borderline heartless, which, based on his empathy during the constitutional convention, appears inconsistent. So a question lingers as to why Justice Wright's method of judicial review was at odds with his prior "course of human freedom" for people of his class.[83] There may be several answers to these questions. He may have tried to prove that the first black justice in South Carolina and the nation was not a radical or pro-black. Surely, Wright was aware that the eyes of South Carolina were on him. He could have been influenced by his two colleagues to stay within the bounds of existing case law as they observed. It is not likely that Wright lost sight of his status in the South prior to the Civil War, but he may have been given a special place in the white community, given his position on the court, blurring southern blacks' past status.

On the other hand, Justice Wright may have been a justice of the time and a real believer that the law, if applied with blinders on, would eventually be fairly applied to all, regardless of race or class.

We may never know the answers to these inquiries. However, one thing is certain; by the mid 1870s, Justice Wright begin to feel the sting of the white backlash against the Reconstruction that he had brilliantly engineered during the 1868 Constitutional Convention. This backlash would taint his proven integrity and allegedly force him to resign from the court based on unproven allegations that he took a twenty–five–hundred dollar bribe to swing the decision in *Whaley v. Bank of Charleston*, a case involving a bank in which former governor Daniel H. Chamberlain had an interest, and allegations in the press that he was a drunkard.[84] The charges made by Justice Wright's political enemy, Franklin J. Moses Jr., were never adjudicated even upon demand for due process by Wright. These claims against the black and white leadership during Reconstruction were routine.[85]

I have previously written, "The allegations against Justice Wright appear to be groundless, since he did not participate in the initial decision in *Whaley v. Bank of Charleston*, the so-called bribe case. Justice Wright's participation in this case was limited to hearing the petition for rehearing [in which] [h]e concurred with [an opinion written by] Chief Justice Moses denying the bank's motion, a decision reasonably supported by law."[86]

History has not been totally one-sided with respect to Justice Wright's character and fitness for the bench. On January 15, 1868, the *Charleston Daily News* commended Justice Wright's work for the Freedmen's Bureau; the same newspaper on March 9, 1868, called Wright a "very intelligent, well-spoken colored attorney."[87] Moreover, the press and the general public recognized "the proven good character of Wright," and while they did not approve of the election of a Negro to the Supreme Court, they were perfectly aware of the fact that the legislature had acted with much moderation and good sense in electing Wright rather than some less fit person."[88]

History has a way of creating and vesting allegations as truth. The allegations that Justice Wright violated his oath of office by taking a bribe and that he was a drunkard remain very much a part of the history of South Carolina. Given Wright's extraordinary performance as a leading member of the 1868 South Carolina Constitution and his distinguished service as a justice, it is time to reconstruct Justice Jonathan Jasper Wright to his rightful place in the political and judicial history of the state of South Carolina and the nation.

From 1870 to 1877 Justice Wright authored insightful and thought-provoking opinions, influencing not only the state of the law in South Carolina but the state of American history. While the quantity of opinions by his hand is less than that of his judicial counterparts, the quality is by far comparable to any opinion written by either of the two justices who shared the bench with him. This is evidenced by the fact that no opinion authored by Justice Wright has ever been overruled, and the majority have been cited as authoritative in either ensuing majority or dissenting opinions. While his time on the bench was short in length, it can never be erased or forgotten; his opinions stand as a monument to one of the finest legal minds that the Reconstruction era, or any other, has produced.

Appendix
OPINIONS BY JUSTICE JONATHAN JASPER WRIGHT, SOUTH CAROLINA SUPREME COURT, 1870–1877

Majority Opinions: 90
Concurring Opinions: 3
Dissenting Opinions: 1
Burgess v. Carpenter, 2 SC 7 (1870)
Cooke v. Moore, 2 SC 52 (1870)
Mobley v. Cureton, 2 SC 140 (1870)
Reilly v. Whipple, 2 SC 277 (1870)
Bailey v. Greenville and Columbia R.R. Co., 2 SC 312 (1871)
Reister v. Hemphill, 2 SC 325 (1871)
Mellichamp v. Seabrook, 2 SC 366 (1871)
Byrd v. Small, 2 SC 388 (1871)
McMillan v. McCall, 2 SC 390 (1871)
Gilliam v. McJunkin, 2 SC 442 (1871)
Blackwood v. Clawson, 2 SC 452 (1871)
Brewster v. Williams, 2 SC 455 (1871)
Redding v. South Carolina R.R. Co., 3 SC 1 (1871)
Kibler v. Bridges, 3 SC 44 (1871)
Cureton v. Gilmore, 3 SC 46 (1871)
Creighton v. Pringle, 3 SC 77 (1871)
Fleming v. Robertson, 3 SC 118 (1871)
State v. London, 3 SC 230 (1872)
Parker v. Wilson, 3 SC 296 (1872)
Robertson v. Evans, 3 SC 330 (1870)
Byrd v. Charles, 3 SC 352 (1872)
Cambell v. Bank of Charleston, 3 SC 384 (1872)
Detheridge v. Earle, 3 SC 396 (1872)
Allen v. Harley, 3 SC 412 (1872)
McCants v. Wells, 3 SC 570 (1872)
State v. Hamblin, 4 SC 1 (1872)
Roof v. Railroad Co., 4 SC 61 (1872)
Patterson v. Railroad Co., 4 SC 153 (1873)
Halfacre v. Whaley, 4 SC 173 (1873)
Means v. Feaster, 4 SC 249 (1873)
Sumter v. Deschamps, 4 SC 297 (1873)
Earle v. Stokes, 4 SC 309 (1873)
Detheridge v. Earle, 4 SC 310 (1873)
Guignard v. Kinsler, 4 SC 330 (1874)

State v. Chairman City Canvassers, 4 SC 485 (1873)

Fox v. Railroad Co., 4 SC 543 (1873)

Nettles v. McGown, 5 SC 43 (1873)

Brothers v. Railroad, 5 SC 55 (1873)

Moore v. Richardson, 5 SC 143 (1874)

Burge v. Willis, 5 SC 212 (1874)

Horde v. Landrum, 5 SC 213 (1874)

Pope v. Frazee, 5 SC 269 (1874)

Pickett v. Lyles, 5 SC 275 (1874)

Chalk v. Patterson, 5 SC 290 (1874) (concurring)

Wilson v. Harper, 5 SC 294 (1874)

Davis v. Winsmith, 5 SC 332 (1874)

Kibler v. Bridges, 5 SC 335 (1874)

Welsh v. Kibler, 5 SC 405 (1874)

Ex parte Hewlett, 5 SC 409 (1874)

Thew v. Porcelain Mfg. Co., 5 SC 415 (1874)

McCullough v. Kibler, 5 SC 468 (1874)

Winsmith v. Walker, 5 SC 473 (1875)

Russell v. Cantwell, 5 SC 477 (1875)

Hunter v. Wardlaw and Edwards, 6 SC 74 (1875)

Boykin v. Watts, 6 SC 76 (1875)

Billings v. Williamson, 6 SC 119 (1875)

Hammond v. Northeastern R.R. Co., 6 SC 131 (1875)

Dewitt v. Atkinson, 6 SC 140 (1875)

Lynch v. Goodwin, 6 SC 144 (1875)

Monaghan v. Small, 6 SC 177 (1875)

Sullivan v. Hellams, 6 SC 184 (1875)

Chicora Co. v. Crews, 6 SC 243 (1875)

Perry v. Sullivan Mfg. Co., 6 SC 310 (1875)

Gower v. Thomson, 6 SC 313 (1875)

State v. Dent, 6 SC 383 (1875)

Gilliland Howell, and Co. v. Gasque, 6 SC 408 (1875)

State v. Watson, 7 SC 66 (1876)

State v. Watson, 7 SC 67 (1876)

Loyns v. Tedder, 7 SC 69 (1876)

Ex parte Williams, 7 SC 71 (1876)

Abrams v. Moseley, 7 SC 150 (1876)

Rowe v. Railroad Co., 7 SC 167 (1976)

Grier v. Wallace, 7 SC 182 (1876)

McCelvey v. Thomson, 7 SC 185 (1876)

Cherry v. McCants, 7 SC 224 (1875)

McElway v. Jeffreys, 7 SC 232 (1875)

State v. Nerland, 7 SC 241 (1876) (concurring)

Davis v. Vaughn, 7 SC 342 (1876)

Rosenberg v. Lewi, 7 SC 344 (1876)

Prince v. Nance, 7 SC 351 (1876)

Gibson v. Gibson, 7 SC 356 (1876)

Edwards, Admin. v. Creditors of King, 7 SC 370 (1876)

Hair v. Blease, 8 SC 63 (1876)

Wolf v. Hamberg, 8 SC 82 (1873)

Mordecai v. City of Charleston, 8 SC 100 (1876)

Jacobs v. Earle, 8 SC 105 (1877)

Tinsley v. Kirby, 8 SC 113 (1877)

Henneman v. Thomson, 8 SC 115 (1877)

Gates v. Whetstone, 8 SC 244 (1876)

Clarke v. Harper, 8 SC 256 (1876)

Thew v. Porcelain Mfg. Co., 8 SC 286 (1876)

State ex rel Wallace v. Hayne and Mackey, 8 SC 367 (1876) (concurring)

In re Corbin, 8 SC 389 (1877)

Ex parte Norris, 8 SC 409 (1877) (dissenting)

4

The Radical Law School

The University of South Carolina School of Law and Its African American Graduates, 1873–1877

W. LEWIS BURKE JR.

Neglect and misrepresentation have obscured the early history of the University of South Carolina School of Law. Although the school was begun in 1867, one modern historical sketch asserts that the "real beginning" of the law school came in 1883.[1] Edwin Green's history of the university intentionally relegates part of the first decade to an appendix in the back of the book titled "The Negro in Possession, 1873–1877."[2] As the title and placement of Green's appendix suggest, the early history of the law school has been the victim of racism.

In 1873 the University of South Carolina became the first institution of higher education in the South to admit African American students. With those admissions, the law school became the first state-supported law school to integrate. The admission of these African Americans outraged conservative, white South Carolinians. One newspaper, the *Charleston News and Courier* pronounced, "[T]he University is dead."[3] The *Edgefield Advertiser* described the university as "only a dreary and dirty sham."[4] The *Georgetown Times* issued this diatribe: "Let the sons of carpetbaggers, scalawags, and African citizens go there and have a homogenous genetic mixture of elements in perfect accord."[5] The Charleston newspaper as late as 1875 was asserting that "the South Carolina University has been broken up by the admission of colored students and except in the matter of cost, has only a nominal existence."[6] But in fact, before integration in 1872 and 1873 the university had only 65 students,[7] while in 1874 and

I want to express my appreciation for the work of my research assistants, Romona Keith and Justin Werner. Without their help many of the men and their photographs would have remained hidden in history. Werner also is entitled to most of the credit for the appendix to this chapter and for identifying at least two men who had attended the law school and whom I had missed.

1875, the university had at least 156 students.[8] To counter the belief that integration would not work, in 1875 some Carolina students wrote to the local newspaper that "white and colored students are now pursuing their studies amicably together, and there is no war of races."[9]

Other derogatory claims were made about the university during Reconstruction. One of these was that the African American students were all Republican politicians who entered the school on pretense "to show the white people of South Carolina that the negroes intended to dominate in the state university and there enforce the social equality of the black with the white race."[10] Another newspaper described the university as "a political nursery."[11] While it is true that many students were Republicans, there is little to suggest that they entered simply to integrate the university, and much evidence to suggest that they were serious about obtaining an education. Of the nineteen African Americans who enrolled in the law school from 1873 to 1877, eleven got their degrees. Lawrence Cain and Paris Simkins persisted in their studies for over three years to obtain their degrees. Political favoritism does not seem to have been a major influence, since J. D. Boston, G. T. McIntyre, and W. F. Myers, all Republican legislators, never were awarded degrees, and S. L. Hutchins, a well-known Democratic African American, was awarded his degree.

Another prevalent claim against the university was that the "student body was composed almost entirely of boys and men of the black race."[12] This assertion is inaccurate. In his two-volume history of the university, Daniel Hollis says that in June 1874 the student body was equally divided between the races.[13] When asked about the integration at the university, Professor Richard Greener replied that a third of the students were white and that students of both races "recite together in recitation rooms and play together."[14] A white professor observed that the white and black students "do not see why, if a black man and a white man can ride on the same seat in the market wagon or in the railroad car for the sake of convenience or economy without impropriety, why they may not sit on the same seat to hear about medicine and law and science and literature."[15] And it is certainly true that all of the law school's graduating classes in this era were integrated.[16]

Between 1868 and 1876 the law school had thirty-nine graduates, of whom eleven were African American men.[17] The first two graduates of the law school were Arthur C. Moore and John Trimmier Sloan in 1868. Moore and Sloan were white natives who became successful Columbia lawyers. Sloan was very active in Democratic Party politics and ultimately served as South Carolina's lieutenant governor from 1903 to 1907.[18] The first professor was A. C. Haskell, a Confederate veteran and a leader in the Democratic Party, and later in his career, a state supreme court justice. From 1868 to 1873, the law school had five graduating classes and a total of twenty graduates. All of these graduates were white and most were probably natives of the state. Only three of this group were ever admitted to the bar by the South Carolina Supreme Court, but at least twelve of these early graduates practiced law in Columbia;[19] apparently this was through admission to practice before the circuit courts.[20]

The "Radical" Law School

In 1873 the students and the school began to change.[21] On October 7, 1873, the University of South Carolina admitted its first African American student with the admission of Henry E. Hayne to the school of medicine. Before the end of that October, five African American men had enrolled in the school of law. These men were Walter Raleigh Jones from Charleston, Joseph D. Boston from Newberry, C. M. Wilder from Columbia, and Laurence Cain and Paris Simkins from Edgefield. According to a Reconstruction-era student, C. C. Scott, there were seventeen African Americans enrolled in the law school between 1873 and 1877.[22] Using Scott's letter and other sources, I have identified at least nineteen African American law students during the period.[23]

Following the integration of the university, Francis L. Cardozo, state treasurer, former principal of Avery Normal Institute in Charleston,[24] and later himself one of these law students, encouraged many of his former Avery students to return to the state and attend the university. One such student was Thomas McCants Stewart, who left Howard University and enrolled at the University of South Carolina in January of 1874.[25] Three months later Stewart wrote, "The institution is calculated to do much good for South Carolina and the Negro race. If the time ever comes when the descendants of the Rutledges and the Marions shall believe in the unlimited brotherhood of man, the University of South Carolina will have a dwelling place in the breast of every Africo-American."[26] Stewart's hope for the future was not to be. The end of Reconstruction in the spring of 1877 signaled the end for the integrated school. Following the removal of federal troops from South Carolina, the Democrats "quickly acted to close down the Republican-dominated school" because it "represented everything its loyal native supporters detested."[27] When the university reopened in 1881 it was all white and remained so until the 1960s.

In 1873, the University of South Carolina School of Law resembled similar schools around the country.[28] There was one professor of law and a two-year curriculum that many students completed within a year. And its faculty complained about law students who came to class unprepared![29] The professor of law in 1873 was C. D. Melton, a native Republican. Before the integration of the school Melton had served as defense counsel for one of the Klansmen convicted in the Ku Klux Klan Trials of 1871 and 1872.[30] Melton had graduated from South Carolina College in 1840.[31] He had practiced law since admission to the bar in 1844 and after the Civil War had been in partnership in Columbia with

Washington A. Clark.[32] He was appointed professor of law in 1869. In addition to Melton, university professors T. N. Roberts, Henry J. Fox, and Richard T. Greener also taught in the law school.[33] Greener, the first African American on the university faculty, will be discussed below. Roberts, an M.D., was the professor of history, political philosophy, and political economy. Fox was a minister who taught rhetoric, criticism, elocution, and English language and literature.[34] The academic program was intended "to acquaint the student with the principles, and prepare him for the practice of his profession."[35] The first-year curriculum consisted of common and statute law, history, English language, declamation and composition, contracts, and mercantile law. The second year included pleadings, code practice, evidence, political philosophy, elocution and composition, constitutional and international law, equity, rhetoric, logic, political economy, orations in the chapel, and moot courts twice a month.[36]

Professor Melton died in the summer of 1875. He was succeeded by Franklin J. Moses Jr., chief justice of the South Carolina Supreme Court. Moses had been admitted to the bar in 1825 after reading law under James Louis Petigru. Petigru was considered the leading lawyer in South Carolina.[37] Moses was a native, a Jew, and an ex-slave-owner.[38] Under Moses the curriculum of the law school was modified to place a heavy emphasis on Blackstone's *Commentaries* and Kent's *Lectures*. In addition to moot courts, the students were expected to write essays on legal topics. Lectures were on Mondays, Wednesdays, and Fridays at 5 P.M. in Judge Moses' chambers at the supreme court.[39]

THE CLASS OF 1874

Walter Raleigh Jones

Who were these men who came to law school with such hopes for the future? And what became of them? On October 13, 1873, Walter Raleigh Jones became the first African American to enroll in the University of South Carolina law school. Jones's enrollment did not attract the attention that Hayne's enrollment in the medical school did, but his passage of the admission examination was an historic moment.[40] Jones apparently was the first person of his race to enroll in a state-supported law school in the history of the United States.[41] He was born about 1850 in Charleston. His mother, Septima A. Jones of Charleston, was a free person of color,[42] and according to a classmate his father was a prominent white Charlestonian.[43] As his mother was free, Jones was born free, and it is highly likely that he attended the schools organized by the free community in Charleston. After the Civil War Jones attended Avery Normal Institute in Charleston, and through the assistance of Francis L. Cardozo he obtained a scholarship to attend Oberlin College in Ohio. He was enrolled in Oberlin's preparatory department from 1867 to 1868 and then attended the college from 1868 to 1870.[44] Upon returning home, he worked for Secretary of State Francis

L. Cardozo, who described his work as a clerk as "important and invaluable."[45] During this employment he prepared "a mammoth report for the legislature" on corruption at the South Carolina Land Commission.[46] He also prepared an index of state laws.[47] As a law student he was elected librarian of the Clariosophic Society, the major intellectual student organization on campus, and gave a valedictory address at a university event.[48] One contemporary described him as one of "the brightest young men Charleston has ever produced."[49]

Before he graduated from the law school, in April of 1874, Jones was elected Columbia city clerk, treasurer, and assessor. A newspaper of the time described him as "a young man whose mental and moral fitness are unquestioned."[50] Jones graduated with his LL.B. on June 30, 1874.[51] He was admitted to the South Carolina Bar in November 1874.[52] By December of 1874 he was employed as the private secretary to Governor D. H. Chamberlain.[53] Jones was active in state and local politics.[54] He served as secretary to the state financial board,[55] as treasurer of a fire engine company,[56] and as director of the state penitentiary.[57] He was the featured orator of the city for Columbia's July 4, 1876, celebration.

Walter Raleigh Jones seemed destined for a future of achievement and public service. However, his life was cut tragically short when he died of meningitis on November 29, 1876, in Columbia, less than a month after he had been elected probate judge for Richland County.[58] Jones did not die penniless. His estate was valued at more than three thousand dollars and apparently was sufficient to help support his mother and siblings until 1884.[59] Eric Foner says that Jones was "[c]onsidered the 'most brilliant young colored man' in South Carolina."[60] In many ways the early death of Jones symbolizes what was to become of Reconstruction.

Of the other African Americans who entered law school with Jones, two graduated later and one dropped out. The dropout was Joseph Boston, a member of the legislature from Newberry, who subsequently did practice law.[61] Of Jones's four white classmates, the most well-known was Niles Gardner Parker.[62] Parker had been one of the white Union officers assigned to the Thirty-third U.S. Colored Infantry, but he became infamous as a corrupt state treasurer. Some of his African American law school classmates testified against him in a corruption trial.[63] It is thought that Parker returned to his home state of Massachusetts after his legal troubles.

THE CLASS OF 1875

Henry Barton Johnson

In 1874, three more African Americans entered the law school. Henry Barton Johnson was probably born a free person of color in Charleston around 1850.[64]

He entered the University of South Carolina School of Law on October 10, 1874, and graduated in December 1875. He served as chief clerk to Secretary of State Henry E. Hayne. Hayne was his brother-in-law and had been the first African American to enter the University of South Carolina.[65] Johnson was active in Republican Party politics and drew the ire of the Democratic press for his activities.[66] He served on the Richland County election commission, having been appointed twice by Governor D. H. Chamberlain,[67] and he was called to testify in the election disputes arising from the election of 1876.[68] Johnson was admitted to the South Carolina Bar in November of 1877, while residing in Charleston. A classmate reported that Johnson left the state with his brother-in-law after Reconstruction. Hayne was reported residing in Cook County, Illinois, in 1885.[69] There is no record of Johnson ever becoming a member of the bar of Illinois. Of course, Johnson could have moved anywhere. Many South Carolinians moved to Washington, D.C., after 1877 and obtained employment with the U.S. Treasury Department. A "Henry Johnson" was employed by Treasury in 1879 and 1880.[70] However, of all eleven law school graduates discussed in this article, Johnson is the only one who really seems to have disappeared with the fall of Reconstruction.

T. McCants Stewart

Another member of the class of 1874 did not so quickly fade from view. In 1874, a Columbia newspaper, reporting on a speech by a South Carolina student, remarked, "[If this student] does not write his name upon the annals of his country, it will be because justice is not done to the race which he represents."[71] The student was Thomas McCants Stewart,[72] born in Charleston on December 28, 1852.[73] His parents, George Gilchrist Stewart and Anna Morris Stewart, were free persons of color who supported their three children by the father's labor as a blacksmith.[74]

Stewart started to school at age five in one of the schools of the free community of African Americans in Charleston, and during the Civil War he was tutored by a minister who boarded with his family.[75] After the Civil War he attended Avery Normal Institute and received a scholarship to Howard University, which he attended from 1869 to 1873. He enrolled at the University of South Carolina in January of 1874 and on October 9, 1874, enrolled in the law school.

As a student Stewart was ever on the move. One month he would be lecturing students in a rural school on geography and history, while the next he would be delivering the July 4 oration in Sumter or addressing a debating club in Charleston or debating in the Clariosophic Society.[76] He was so active in politics that he was once admonished by the faculty for "his gross neglect of his college duties for the past week." Stewart's response, supported by a letter from state treasurer F. L. Cardozo, was that he had the permission of the chairman of the faculty to be campaigning with Cardozo and Attorney General Robert Brown Elliott.[77] But Stewart normally drew high praise for his work as a student and was chosen to give the valedictory address at his graduation.[78]

He received his A.B. and LL.B. in law on December 21, 1875. He was admitted to the practice by the supreme court in November of 1875. He practiced law briefly in Sumter, South Carolina, and was in partnership with Robert Brown Elliott and D. A. Straker. His reputation as a lawyer was such that he was appointed by the supreme court to serve on a committee to examine a candidate for admission to the bar.[79] He was very active in the campaign of 1876, delivering speeches around the state for D. H. Chamberlain and other Republicans. A speech at Liberty Hill was reported to have been three hours long.[80]

Stewart married Charlotte P. Harris of Columbia on December 28, 1876, and immediately moved to Orangeburg to serve on the faculty of the State Agricultural and Mechanical College.[81] In 1877, their first child was born and Stewart was ordained a minister by the African Methodist Episcopal Church in Orangeburg.[82] But with the fall of Reconstruction, he resigned from the faculty of the agricultural college on July 22, 1878,[83] and he moved to New Jersey to accept a pastorate.[84] In September 1878 he entered Princeton Theological Seminary.[85] After two years, he left Princeton to become pastor of the Bethel African Methodist Episcopal Church in New York City. In 1883 he left Bethel A.M.E. Church to assume a professorship at Liberia College in Monrovia, but he returned from Monrovia in 1885 because Liberia College was a college in name only.[86] When he returned to New York he began a law practice that gave him substantial recognition.[87] He also became a corresponding editor for the *New York Freeman*. In this position he returned to South Carolina, ever hoping that his home state might be welcoming, but while he reported promise in the state he could not bring himself to move home. As late as 1890 he was still visiting Charleston and reminiscing about his boyhood days before the Civil War, and even then he was optimistic that the "rule of the people" would bring rights and liberties to his people.[88] But 1895 saw South Carolina adopt a constitution that effectively eliminated African Americans from participating as voters or candidates for public office.[89]

Until the late 1890s Stewart lectured, wrote, and practiced law in New York. He tried politics and served on the school board for Brooklyn and was instrumental in the integration of the city's schools.[90] By 1887 he had grown disillusioned with the Republican Party and had become active in the Democratic Party.[91] His activities for the Democrats drew a sharp rebuke from Frederick Douglass.[92] After Stewart's active role in the Grover Cleveland campaign of 1892, the African American press speculated that he would be appointed recorder of deeds in Washington or even given a foreign mission.[93] The recorder of deeds had been the position long held by Fredrick Douglass and was considered the premier presidential appointment for an African American. In May of 1893 he met with Grover Cleveland, but Stewart was disappointed and came away empty-handed.[94] However, as late as 1895 there were reports that he still might be rewarded with some appointment.[95] His flirtation with the Democrats led to an open and bitter dispute with his old professor, Richard Greener.[96] As the century closed, Stewart had certainly grown disillusioned with politics, his native state, his old friends, and his native country. With the rendering of *Plessy v. Ferguson* Stewart again looked for a new promised land.[97]

In 1898, he moved to Hawaii, becoming the first African American admitted to the bar of the newly acquired territory.[98] He was active in Hawaiian politics and the practice of law until he moved to London in 1905 and then on in 1906 to Liberia, where he renounced his United States citizenship and became a Liberian citizen. As a Liberian, he represented the country in diplomatic disputes, served as a deputy attorney general, and was charged with reforming the judicial and customs systems of the country.[99] As a reward for his invaluable service he was appointed an associate justice of the Liberia Supreme Court.[100] But Stewart's stalwart commitment to reform led to conflict with corruption at the highest levels of the country, and President Daniel H. Howard removed Stewart from the court when Stewart tried to expose the bribery of the country's secretary of treasury.[101] Despite some local protest as well as some American protestations, Stewart could not regain his seat.[102] Although never relinquishing his title as associate justice, Stewart left Liberia and returned to England in 1914. In 1921 he moved to the Virgin Islands and practiced law. He died in the Virgin Islands in 1923. He had two sons, Gilchrist and McCants; both became attorneys. His daughter, Carlotta Stewart Lai, became a teacher and principal in Hawaii.

Professor Charles Wynes once described Stewart as "peripatetic."[103] This he certainly was, but perhaps a better way to sum up Stewart's life would be to look back at that prophetic newspaper reporter who heard Stewart's remarkable undergraduate address. Stewart's life was indeed remarkable because of the breadth of his accomplishments. However, he remains virtually unknown in the "annals of his country" because, as the reporter had feared, justice was not done to his race. In 1907 when Stewart renounced his United States citizenship, he concluded that the struggle for equality in the United States was "hopeless."[104]

Joseph Henry Stuart

Joseph Henry Stuart was born in 1849. He was admitted to the University of South Carolina School of Law on October 2, 1874, and graduated in December 1875, having been admitted to the bar by the supreme court the month before.[105] Stuart was an activist as a student and as a lawyer. During his time at the University of South Carolina he was thrown off a train in the middle of the night for refusing to leave a first-class car that the conductor claimed was for whites only.[106] Stuart's protestation led to the arrest of the conductor. Stuart was an excellent law student, scoring a 100 percent on at least one of his final examinations.[107] He developed his forensic skill as a student in the Clariosophic Society,[108] and he was selected to deliver one of the two student addresses at his law school graduation.[109]

On the roll of attorneys of the South Carolina Supreme Court, Stuart listed Camden as his hometown. Following his admission to the bar, he served briefly as principal of the Sumter Graded School,[110] but by February of 1879 he was practicing law in Camden. He appeared as an attorney in one of the so-called political corruption trials that followed the end of Reconstruction.[111] His client was Probate Judge Samuel Lee of Sumter, who had been charged with "official misconduct" for closing his office. Stuart called witnesses who testified that Lee had closed his office and was in hiding because of threats on his life by whites; nevertheless, Lee was convicted.

Stuart moved from Kershaw County after the Lee trial and was admitted to the Kansas Bar on June 7, 1883. His law practice there included an unsuccessful suit to integrate the public schools.[112] He then moved to Denver and was admitted on motion to the Colorado Bar on December 1, 1891. He was elected to the Colorado House of Representatives from Arapahoe County and served from 1893 until 1897. Apparently Stuart was involved in some national politics and had contact with Booker T. Washington. Through Washington he sought but did not secure an appointment as justice of the peace in Washington, D.C., in 1902.[113] He practiced law in Denver until his death on April 4, 1910.[114]

Graduating with Johnson, Stewart, and Stuart were two white men: Henry Austin Fox was the son of faculty member Rev. Henry J. Fox.[115] Fox was admitted to the bar in 1875. He served for a time as assistant principal of the preparatory school at the university.[116] Mortimer Alanson Warren had been principal of Avery Normal Institute, principal of the university preparatory department, and principal of the state normal school. He was never admitted to the bar in South Carolina but remained an educator and moved to Connecticut after Reconstruction.[117]

THE CLASS OF 1876

The law school class of 1876 had nine graduates and the school probably had another five students enrolled in that academic year. Seven of the graduates were African American. One of the two white graduates was the son of a university faculty member. C. J. Babbitt served as Governor Chamberlain's private secretary after the death of Walter Jones,[118] and he was practicing law in Columbia in

1879 and 1880.[119] Thomas Meredith Canton, the other white graduate, was apparently a Republican. He had been appointed as a trial justice in Columbia by Governor Chamberlain.[120] The African American graduates included three elected officials, a university professor, and one of the few African American Democrats in the state.

Lawrence Cain

One of those elected officials, Lawrence Cain, was born a slave in Edgefield, South Carolina, in 1845. After the Civil War, Cain tried both farming and teaching. As a teacher he drew the praise of local whites, but when he entered politics, the praise ended.[121] In 1868, he was elected to represent Edgefield County in the South Carolina House of Representatives. He won reelection in 1870 and then was elected Edgefield's senator in 1872. Cain was an active senator whose speeches and legislative proposals often drew comment by the press.[122] Cain's ability to turn a phrase is demonstrated by this excerpt from one of his letters published in a local newspaper: "If the straws can indicate the wind's course, it seems to me that facts, undeniable and undenied, of so grave importance as these should throw some light upon the 'mutual distrust' entertained in my county between the races."[123]

His senatorial career ended with the election of 1876. This election was unlike any in the country other than in Reconstruction Mississippi. The conservative whites were determined to regain control. One historian describes it this way: "[A]nd war it was. The Democratic campaign resembled a military operation. Led by former captains of the South's struggle for independence, the Democrats fought the election of 1876. Wade Hampton, the Democratic candidate for Governor, had been the state's highest-ranking Confederate officer. Lieutenant General Hampton's chief aides in 1876 were South Carolina's other major war leaders: Major Generals Matthew C. Butler and Joseph B. Kershaw and Brigadier Generals Martin W. Gary, John D. Kennedy, Johnson Hagood, James Conner, John Bratton, and Samuel McGowan."[124]

Cain's home county of Edgefield was one of the major battlegrounds. In fact, the campaign plan came to be known as the "Edgefield plan" under the leadership of Edgefield's Martin Gary.[125] Although the majority of Edgefield's voters were African American, Cain lost his senate seat to none other than Martin Gary by a margin of over two to one.[126] In fact, Gary received 6,268 votes, just slightly less than the entire voter-eligible male population in the county.[127] Cain testified that after oral, written, and gun barrel threats he feared to campaign and knew of hundreds of his supporters who were not allowed to vote.[128]

Lawrence Cain entered the law school in 1873 with the first class to include African Americans. Earning his degree took three years; consequently, he was also in the last nineteenth-century class to include African Americans, with his graduation in December of 1876. He was never admitted to the bar by the supreme court, but he remained active in public life, attending Republican conventions and serving as deputy director of the Internal Revenue Department. Senator Cain died of tuberculosis on March 28, 1884.[129]

Francis Lewis Cardozo

In October 7, 1874, Francis L. Cardozo enrolled in the law school.[130] At that time he was thirty-eight years old and treasurer of the state of South Carolina. Cardozo had been one of the founding fathers of Reconstruction. He had begun his political career with attendance at the National Convention of Colored Men held in Syracuse, New York, in 1864.[131] He had attended the Colored People's Convention held in Charleston to protest the 1865 constitution, which had failed to grant suffrage to African Americans.[132] He was one of the leading and most influential delegates to the Constitutional Convention of 1868.[133] Upon his election as secretary of state in April 1868,[134] he became the first African American elected to statewide office in South Carolina.[135] Many thought him the most powerful African American in South Carolina. He was president of the Union League state council, which some considered the most powerful influence on the African American voters.[136] Governor D. H. Chamberlain considered Cardozo his "ablest and wisest adviser."[137] Moreover, Cardozo had been mentor to most of the African American law students at the university.

So why would a man of his station in life have enrolled in law school? Critics of this early period of integration would claim that Cardozo entered just to inflate enrollment numbers. But by 1874, the university's enrollment was at its highest since before the Civil War. Could Cardozo have simply been interested in obtaining a law degree because he wanted the education? A brief review of his life may offer an answer to such a question.

Francis L. Cardozo was born January 1, 1836, in Charleston, South Carolina.[138] His mother was a free woman of color, and his father was from a prominent Jewish family. His father was Isaac Nunez Cardozo, an official in the Customs House in Charleston.[139] A family tree identifies his mother as Lydia Williams.[140] He attended the schools of the free African American community in Charleston. He was trained as a carpenter and shipbuilder. In 1858 he traveled to Scotland and attended the University of Glasgow until 1861 and then studied at seminaries in Edinburgh and London.[141] In 1864 he returned to the United States and was soon ordained a Congregational minister in Connecticut.

In 1865 Cardozo was called to Charleston to teach for the American Missionary Association and to replace his brother, Thomas, who had been dismissed for alleged improprieties.[142] He helped found Avery Normal Institute and became its first superintendent. As a delegate to the 1868 Constitutional Convention he was chairman of the education committee and a strong advocate for economic reform.[143] In the fall of 1868, he was elected South Carolina's secretary of state, becoming the state's first African American ever elected to statewide office.[144] On October 31, 1871, he resigned as secretary of state to take a professorship at Howard University where he served one year.[145] Thereafter he returned to South Carolina and was elected state treasurer, serving from 1872 until 1877. He enrolled in the University of South Carolina School of Law while treasurer and graduated in December of 1876. He was admitted to the bar by the supreme court in April of 1876.

Cardozo had achieved both financial success and a leadership role in public life.[146] However, under the threat of violence his career in elected office came to an end in 1877. Following the 1876 election, the Democratic gubernatorial candidate, Wade Hampton, assumed office only after the removal of federal troops from around the statehouse. Hampton's claim to election required the inclusion of returns from Edgefield and Laurens Counties; these, however, had been thrown out by the state Board of Canvassers.[147] But even with the stuffed ballot boxes from Edgefield and Laurens Counties, Cardozo had still won reelection as state treasurer. Nevertheless, on April 14, 1877, Governor Hampton's private secretary sent Cardozo and other elected African American officials threatening letters demanding that they vacate their offices.[148] Cardozo and the others did so but continued to insist that they had been reelected. After the Democrats instituted litigation, Cardozo and the others finally relented on May 1, 1877.[149]

Soon Cardozo was indicted for corruption in what Walter Edgar describes as a systematic attempt by the Democrats to "blacken the reputation of those who governed the state from 1868 to 1877."[150] Another historian quotes Democratic attorney general James Conner as saying that the corruption investigation and indictments "would politically guillotine" the Republican Party.[151] Cardozo was the highest-ranking target of the Democrats and his prosecution was clearly tinged by political purposes.

Throughout his political career he had had a reputation for honesty. When a white-dominated reform party was organized in 1870, it nominated Cardozo as its candidate for lieutenant governor because he was an "honest, capable colored man."[152] Early in his political career he had resigned from the advisory board of the state land commission to protest corruption in the agency.[153] As secretary of state, he had reorganized the land commission and is credited with eliminating the corruption and thievery that had been rampant there.[154] In 1872 Cardozo found himself nominated by the Republicans for state treasurer on the ticket headed by Franklin J. Moses Jr. for governor. Historians seem unanimous in believing that the junior Moses was one of the most corrupt politicians during Reconstruction.[155] But as state treasurer, Cardozo's performance drew praise from both Republican and Democratic newspapers.[156] In one instance, as treasurer he foiled an attempt by Governor Moses to steal twenty-five hundred dollars.[157] With the election of D. H. Chamberlain in 1874, the Republican Party was determined to rid itself of corruption.[158] As state treasurer Cardozo faced the major burden of keeping the state's purse strings safe, and those legislators aggrieved by his tight money management soon brought impeachment proceedings against Cardozo.[159] The impeachment failed when a coalition of reform Republicans and Democrats in the general assembly defeated the effort.[160] In an 1888 history, Governor Chamberlain is quoted as saying that "to my knowledge [Cardozo] has not done a dishonest act."[161]

So when the charges of corruption were renewed in 1877, it is not surprising that Cardozo demanded a trial. Before the trial began seven of the charges against him were dropped,[162] and he was tried on a charge that he conspired to issue fraudulent pay certificates. The trial began on November 1, 1877.[163] Cardozo was defended by S. W. Melton, brother of the late law school professor, and prosecuted by Attorney General James Conner, who had been a general in the Confederate army.[164] Conner began his case with his star witness, former Speaker of the House Samuel J. Lee, who testified that Cardozo had conspired with him and other legislative leaders to issue the fraudulent pay certificates. Lee had most recently been solicitor in Aiken. He had resigned from office and agreed to testify against Cardozo, apparently in exchange for not being prosecuted.[165] Other witnesses testified that the fraudulent pay certificates were made payable to fictitious people with the initials of public officials in reverse order. The initials of the fictitious payee in Cardozo's case were "C.L.F." One of these witnesses was Josephus Woodruff, who had been clerk of the senate. Woodruff had been indicted with Cardozo and the others but turned state's evidence and supported Lee's testimony. After the close of the state's case, Cardozo testified and vehemently denied the charges. Law school classmate T. J. Minton testified that as clerk for the office he had actually redeemed the certificates. Minton said that the certificates bore the genuine signatures of Richard H. Gleaves, Samuel J. Lee, A. O. Jones, and Josephus Woodruff and that since these were appropriate signatories for the general assembly, he had presumed the certificates were genuine. Despite the genuine signatures, the pay certificates were fraudulent because the payee was fictitious. Minton and Cardozo testified that they had rejected numerous fraudulent certificates and had kept a file of them. After this claim was challenged by Conner, Melton requested that a court clerk be sent to the state treasurer's office to retrieve the supposedly rejected certificates. The clerk returned with a file containing over twenty-seven thousand dollars in certificates that Cardozo and his staff had refused to honor. But the tide was against Cardozo and he was convicted.[166]

Many historians assume that Cardozo was soon pardoned after an agreement was reached between Governor Wade Hampton and President Rutherford

B. Hayes, whereby the federal government dropped prosecutions against Democrats for election fraud.[167] But for Cardozo, the benefits of the agreement were slow in coming. Cardozo was not, in fact, pardoned until April 23, 1879, by Governor William D. Simpson, Wade Hampton having moved on to the U.S. Senate. This came only after Cardozo had spent a month or more on two occasions in the Richland County jail, and only after the Rev. Henry Cardozo, his brother, had obtained petitions supporting the pardon signed by many prominent citizens from Charleston and Columbia and from ten of the twelve jurors who had convicted him.[168] In a letter to Governor Simpson, a letter which accompanied the petitions, Reverend Cardozo urged consideration of the fact that Cardozo's wife was an invalid with five living children under the age of twelve.

After his release from jail, Cardozo moved to Washington, D.C., and by one account had "lost every dollar of an estate of about $10,000 and [was] now living here, poor and with a family."[169] Secretary of Treasury John Sherman soon employed Cardozo in the U.S. Treasury for six years. After the move to Washington, D.C., Cardozo seems not to have pursued an active role in politics, other than to use his political connections in pursuit of advancement in government service.[170] Prior to 1868 Cardozo had been a leading national figure in Republican and African American politics, but when national conventions of African Americans were held in 1879 and 1883, Cardozo did not participate.[171] And it is also clear that he had no further use for the South.[172] After a speaker at the Bethel Literary Society cited the growing population of African Americans in the South as a harbinger of a political future for the African American in the South, Cardozo described the idea as a chimera.[173] Ultimately, he even grew so embittered by the status of his people in the United States that he advocated emigration to Haiti or Liberia.[174]

When Democrat Grover Cleveland was elected to the presidency in 1884, Cardozo lost his job with the Treasury Department.[175] When Cardozo had resigned as South Carolina's secretary of state in 1871 to teach at Howard University, he had written, "I did this under a profound conviction that I can be of more service in the great work of reconstruction in the South by occupying such a position, where I can prepare the rising generation, of my own race especially, for the honorable discharge of the important duties resting upon them as American Citizens."[176] In 1884 Cardozo was to return to the classroom for good. Calvin Chase, the editor of the *Washington Bee*, was soon a perennial critic of Cardozo and his work in the District of Columbia schools. In 1888 Chase suggested that Cardozo was currying favor with the Democrats in search of some reward.[177] From July of 1888 until 1896, Chase campaigned to have Cardozo removed from his position as principal of the high school.[178] However, other newspapers praised Cardozo's role in the schools. For example, the *Colored*

American said that "under his management the school seemed to take on a new life, and in a few years it had grown beyond the limits of the building."[179] He taught in the public schools of Washington, D.C., until one month before his death. In one high school he introduced vocational and industrial courses and started a business department, while at the same time striving to maintain the academic standards of the college preparatory curriculum.[180] He resigned from his teaching position because of ill health on June 10, 1903, and died on July 22, 1903. He has been remembered and honored in Washington, D.C., for his many years of service as a high school principal. Francis L. Cardozo High School was named in his honor in 1928 and remains a high school in the city today.[181]

Did Cardozo simply attend the law school to make a social and political statement? In part, he probably did. But he probably also went to law school to further his own education and his ability to prepare future generations for public service.

Richard Theodore Greener

Richard Greener was born January 30, 1844, in Philadelphia to Mary Ann and Richard Wesley Greener.[182] He attended Oberlin College Preparatory School and Phillips Academy at Andover and taught school one term in Highland County, Ohio.[183] In 1870 he became the first African American to graduate from Harvard College.[184] After his graduation, Greener became vice principal of the male department of the Institute for Colored Youth in Philadelphia, and then principal of Preparatory High School for Colored Youth in Washington, D.C. (now known as Dunbar High School). In 1873 he was appointed professor of mental and moral philosophy at the University of South Carolina. In addition to his professorship he also taught in the law school and served as university librarian.[185] While an undergraduate student at Harvard, Greener had expressed a desire to enter the legal profession,[186] so it is not surprising that on October 7, 1874, he enrolled in the law school at the University of South Carolina and graduated in December 1876.

While at the university, Greener was in great demand. The community sought his attention, and the local press noted his activities. He spoke to a teachers' meeting in Chester;[187] he delivered an address marking the anniversary of Charles Sumner's death;[188] he served as a speaker at a local church's lecture series;[189] he spoke to the Masons in Savannah;[190] he was elected to a learned society;[191] and he wrecked his carriage in Washington, D.C.[192] Greener was also active in politics. He served on the city's Board of Health.[193] Once he was even invited to address a Democratic meeting,[194] and he presided over a bipartisan meeting to nominate the mayor of the city.[195] But he was very active in Republican Party politics, serving as a state representative to Union League of America National Executive Committee, and was even assigned what he described as the worst district in the state to campaign for the reelection of Governor Chamberlain in 1876.[196] His experiences in the campaign resulted in his being called as a witness for the Republicans before the congressional investigative committee hearings on the election violence of 1876.[197]

Greener was admitted to the South Carolina Bar by the South Carolina Supreme Court on December 20, 1876. He resigned from the University of South Carolina on June 29, 1877.[198] In early 1877 he moved to Washington, D.C., where he, like Francis Cardozo, worked at the Department of Treasury. He was admitted to the bar in the District of Columbia on April 14, 1877,[199] and from 1878 to 1880 he served on the faculty of Howard University School of Law. He was dean of Howard Law School from 1879 to 1880. While on the Howard faculty, he had a private law practice;[200] in one case he defended a black cadet from South Carolina who was being court-martialed by the U.S. Military Academy.[201]

After 1880 Greener served in various government positions. At one point he was considered for the prestigious position of recorder of deeds in Washington, D.C.[202] In 1898 he was appointed as the first United States consul and commercial agent to Vladivostock, Russia, where he served from 1898 to November 20, 1905. This was a period of armed conflicts in Asia, including the Boxer Rebellion and the Russo-Japanese War. During the Russo-Japanese War, Greener represented the Japanese government's interest in Vladivostock.[203] During the war he faced many trials but provided great service to war refugees. Many of his duties involved shipping and commercial matters, but he once appeared in a Russian court to represent some Japanese and Americans accused of seal poaching.[204] A modern biographical sketch suggests that Greener was forced out of his State Department position because of race. Allison Blakely concluded that "his optimism about individualism and American society was permanently shaken when he was ultimately unable to attain a status he believed commensurate with his talents and education."[205] After 1906 he lived in Chicago where he practiced law.[206] He also wrote and lectured until his death on May 2, 1922.[207]

Styless Linton Hutchins

In 1904, a book was published extolling Chattanooga, Tennessee's, prominent African American citizens. Included in this book was a biographical sketch of Styless Linton Hutchins, describing him as "one of the most unique characters of the Negro race, and . . . a many sided man."[208] According to this sketch Hutchins was born on November 21, 1852, in Lawrenceville, Georgia. His father was an artist who had accumulated sufficient money to send his son to college. Hutchins apparently graduated from Atlanta University and became a teacher and principal at Knox Institute, a Congregational Church school for

African Americans in Athens, Georgia.[209] According to the sketch, Hutchins moved to South Carolina in 1873. However, in testimony before two different congressional committees he gave conflicting stories about his background. Before a U.S. House of Representatives committee, he said that he had moved to the state in October 1875 and that he had taught in Laurens, South Carolina.[210] He also testified that he had lived in Georgia about one or two years; that he had been in Alabama, Mississippi, Arkansas, and Texas; and that he had been in the southern states and had traveled around for the last eight years. In a hearing before a U.S. Senate committee the next day, he started by claiming to be a native of Indiana but then expressed confusion and proceeded to give a more detailed rendering of his life.[211] Hutchins said he was twenty-four years old and had been born in Georgia, had moved to Tennessee at age ten, after three years had moved to Arkansas, and after four or five years had moved on to Indiana and had returned to Tennessee after four years. When asked how long he had lived in Tennessee he answered that he had lived there six years ago and then moved to Paris, Texas; Galveston, Texas; Delphi, Louisiana; Vicksburg, Mississippi; Jackson, Mississippi; Montgomery, Alabama; Atlanta, Georgia; Athens, Georgia; and then to South Carolina. During one year in South Carolina, Hutchins had lived in Greenville, Laurensville, Tumbling Shoals, and then Columbia after visits to Augusta, Atlanta, and Athens, Georgia. When asked what he had been doing he first asserted that he did nothing, but his account included references to having attended school in Nashville and graduated college in Atlanta. When pressed as to how he had supported himself, he said that he had capital of two to three thousand dollars and that his father in Atlanta had forty to fifty thousand dollars in capital. He also said that he had taught public school in Montgomery, preparatory school in Athens, and school in Tumbling Shoals. When asked his profession, he said he was a lawyer, having read law under a lawyer Goss in Nashville, John A. Wempey in Atlanta, and Chief Justice Moses in Columbia. As with many men of his era it is difficult to determine his background with certitude.[212]

However, University of South Carolina records establish that Hutchins entered the School of Law in the academic year 1875–76 and graduated in December 1876.[213] The only grade report on Hutchins suggests that he was an average student. He was admitted to the South Carolina Bar by the South Carolina Supreme Court in November 1876.

Despite political differences with his fellow students, Hutchins was elected class secretary.[214] The political differences were caused by the fact that Hutchins was a Democrat. This status drew him substantial notoriety. Unlike most of his classmates, he campaigned all over the state for General Wade Hampton and other Democrats in the fall 1876 campaign.[215] He may have given hundreds of speeches for Hampton. Press accounts of his efforts on behalf of

Hampton report one confrontation between Republicans and Democrats when Hutchins tried to speak at a rally. After this confrontation, in Hopkins in Richland County, Hutchins was allowed to speak and then to debate classmate Richard Greener.[216] When the U.S. Congress held hearings on the issue of 1876 election violence, Hutchins was called as a witness by the Democrats,[217] and his classmate Greener was called as a witness by the Republicans.

After the election, Governor Hampton appointed Hutchins a trial justice.[218] But the legislature abolished his judgeship and he was forced to resign after only five weeks on the bench. A letter from Governor Hampton's private secretary expresses satisfaction with Hutchins's service as a trial justice and regret that he was forced to relinquish the position.[219] According to his biographical sketch, Hutchins returned to Georgia and became the first African American admitted to the Georgia Bar.[220]

In 1881 he moved on to Chattanooga, Tennessee, where he started a newspaper, entered Republican Party politics, and practiced law. He was elected as a Republican to the Tennessee House of Representatives in 1886 and served two terms. While in the Tennessee legislature he introduced legislation to ban convict leasing, but the bill was not enacted. In 1909 Hutchins represented a client who was lynched while his appeal was pending before the U.S. Supreme Court. Because the lynch mob had violated a stay of execution, the U.S. Supreme Court held those who could be identified in contempt and jailed them. The jailing so angered the local whites that Hutchins and his family were forced to flee to Oklahoma.[221]

Theophilus J. Minton

Theophilus J. Minton was born in Philadelphia and graduated from the Institute for Colored Youth in Philadelphia.[222] He appears to have been the son of prominent Philadelphia caterer Henry Minton.[223] His wife, Virginia McKee, was also from a prominent African American family in Philadelphia.[224] They moved to South Carolina after the Civil War. He was admitted to the South Carolina Bar in November of 1871. For several years he worked as a bookkeeper in the office of the state treasurer. In 1875, while employed in the treasurer's office, he enrolled in the University of South Carolina. He received his LL.B in law in December of 1876.

Minton was active in Republican politics. Once he traveled to Laurens to join Richard Greener on the campaign trail. Laurens was, at that time, a town notorious for the recent killing of Joe Crews, a Republican leader.[225] Greener feared there would be violence in Laurens and asked Minton to assist him there. In another campaign stop, Minton was quoted as saying that "every colored man who loved freedom would walk up to the polls and vote for Chamberlain and reform."[226] Minton drew attention from the press when he and fellow law student T. McCants Stewart testified against another former classmate, Niles Parker, in his corruption trial.[227] Minton also testified for the defense in the corruption trial of his former employer, Francis L. Cardozo.[228]

With the end of Reconstruction, Minton first moved to Indiana to serve as secretary to the governor, then to Washington, D.C., to work in the Treasury Department, and finally to Philadelphia.[229] While in Washington, Minton was active in the local intellectual life. He was very active in the Bethel Literary group founded by Frederick Douglass. He presented papers and frequently participated in the group's activities.[230] His progress in the Treasury Department was noted with interest by one local newspaper.[231] But when Minton lost his appointment after the election of Grover Cleveland and tried to secure a position in the Washington schools, another newspaper attacked Minton as a South Carolina politician and urged his rejection.[232] After the loss of his Treasury post he returned to Philadelphia. Having been admitted to the Pennsylvania Bar in 1880, he began the practice of law in Philadelphia. He was one of the most well-known African American lawyers in Philadelphia. His clients included such prominent African Americans as Whitefield McKinlay, Robert Harlan, and Mrs. J. H. Rainey.[233] He served as counsel to a building and loan association and to the African Colonial Enterprise.[234] He also helped organize the Frederick Douglass Memorial Hospital and Training School and the American Negro Historical Society.[235] His interest in history led him to write a biographical sketch of Robert Brown Elliott; it was published by the *African Methodist Episcopal Church Review* in 1892.[236] He remained active in Republican politics until his death in 1909.[237] His son, Henry McKee Minton, briefly attended law school at the University of Pennsylvania and ultimately became a physician. Henry Minton was one of the founders of Mercy Hospital in Philadelphia.

Joseph White Morris

Joseph White Morris was born a slave in Charleston on August 26, 1850. His parents, John B. Morris and Grace Morris, had two daughters and two sons. John Morris was a wheelwright and the owner of real estate valued at seventeen hundred dollars.[238] He purchased his wife, Grace, and his son Joseph in 1851 from William Bee.[239] Though technically a slave, Joseph Morris was raised as a free person of color. His father even appears to have represented to the census takers that his wife and children were free.[240] In reality, however, John Morris could not free his wife and son because the South Carolina General Assembly in 1820 had prohibited the manumission of slaves except by act of the legislature.[241]

Joseph Morris attended Simeon Beard's school in Charleston and then Avery Normal Institute.[242] While at Avery he worked for Robert Brown Elliott's newspaper, *The Leader*, and came under the tutelage of F. L. Cardozo, who helped procure a scholarship for Morris to attend Howard University in 1868.[243]

After graduating from Howard in 1875, he enrolled in the University of South Carolina School of Law, graduating in December 1876. He was admitted to the bar by the supreme court in November of 1876. He practiced law briefly and then became the principal of Payne Institute. When Payne Institute merged with Allen University in Columbia, Morris became professor and later president of the university. He served two tenures as president of Allen University from 1881 to 1885 and from 1895 to 1897.[244] During his first term he oversaw the early years of the first law school in the South at a predominantly black college.[245] D. A. Straker served as dean of this law school from 1882 to 1887, and Morris served as a professor of law. Under Morris's leadership Allen University awarded at least thirty law degrees.[246] He continued to teach at Allen and was on the faculty, teaching Greek, in 1912,[247] and he was vice president of the university in 1913.[248] Morris must have died in 1913 or 1914.[249]

Paris Simkins

Paris Simkins was born a slave on February 18, 1849, in Edgefield, South Carolina. His mother was Charlotte Simkins, a slave. His father was his owner, Arthur Augustus Simkins, publisher of the local newspaper.[250] A fellow slave, his father's coachman, taught the boy Simkins to read and write. Although it was illegal to teach slaves to read and write, the coachman and Simkins persisted with the lessons while hiding in the woods. In his early adolescence, Simkins went with his master to serve as a barber with the Confederate army. He witnessed a number of battles, including Gettysburg. After the war he returned home and opened a barbershop. Simkins used his spare time to educate himself. Sometimes he was tutored by a local minister. He became involved in politics, religion, and civic affairs. He helped found Macedonia Baptist Church in 1868. He was head of the local militia, served on the jury commission, and was a trial justice.[251] He was elected to the House of Representatives of South Carolina in 1872. As a legislator, Simkins was described by even the opposition press as a "colored man of more than average intelligence,"[252] and he was elected chairman of the House Ways and Means Committee.[253] His legislative proposals attracted national attention.[254] As chairman of Ways and Means he helped bring embezzlement charges against Niles Parker.[255] While in the legislature he attended the University of South Carolina School of Law and graduated in 1876. Like many of his fellow students, Simkins was active in the campaign of 1876. He and Laurence Cain posed such a threat to the Democratic plans for the 1876 election in Edgefield that local Democrats trumped up charges of conspiracy to commit murder against them.[256] These charges disappeared in the heat of the campaign.

Only thirteen days after Simkins graduated from law school he was called to testify before a congressional committee about intimidation of voters.[257]

Simkins testified that threats of violence had been widespread and that of the Republicans who came out to vote many were physically prevented from voting. Before another congressional committee he testified that he did not campaign for reelection because there was a one thousand dollar bounty on his head and that he himself had been stopped from voting for his own reelection.[258] The final tally had him defeated by a margin of two to one.[259]

After Reconstruction, Simkins remained active in church, civic, and political affairs. Simkins was not admitted to the bar until 1886. He did not have a substantial law practice and never tried cases in the courthouse, but he did draw up the legal papers for the Mutual Aid and Burial Society and served as its president. His grandson, C. B. Bailey, reported that Simkins served as secretary to Governor John C. Sheppard.[260] Sheppard was one of the Democrats who had "defeated" Simkins in the election for the House of Representatives in 1876.[261] While he may have served in some capacity for Governor Sheppard, he was not the governor's private secretary.[262] But Sheppard served as governor from July 1886 to December 1886, and it was during this period that Simkins finally became a member of the bar. He also served as postmaster in Edgefield, the position from which he retired. Simkins, the father of sixteen children, died on September 26, 1930.

Conclusion

Chief Justice Moses died in June 1877. Of the students then enrolled in the law school, at least two were African Americans, Joseph D. Boston and William F. Myers. Myers had been admitted to the bar in December of 1875. There is no record of Boston's ever becoming a lawyer. The university and the law school were closed in 1877,[263] and the law school opened again in 1884 as an all-white institution. The university had ceased having "a dwelling place in the breast of every Africo-American."

The critics of the "radical" university and law school were right in predicting destruction. That destruction, however, did not come from the fact that African Americans studied in the halls of the university. That destruction came at the hands of the white conservative South Carolinians who used violence and fraud to overthrow the Republican government in South Carolina.[264] These white Democrats closed the school in 1877 to prevent African Americans from being educated at the university. Their excuses for the closing and their malicious criticisms for the "Radical University" are mostly answered now.

The careers of the African American men who graduated from the University of South Carolina in the 1870s add no weight to the claim that they enrolled only to produce some "homogenous genetic mixture." No doubt, these men were advocates for civil rights and equal treatment. But these men were serious students; and probably more so than any other men of their age in South Carolina, they saw the value of a legal education. It is true that these men sought equality and expected to be leaders. Having been deprived of education, they craved this route to equality. A legal education offered much simply because of the promise of the law. The great American experiment in democracy was being opened up to their race for the first time. The law through the Thirteenth and Fourteenth Amendments to the U.S. Constitution and the South Carolina Constitution of 1868 clearly provided for equality under the law for all men.

These men believed in these promises and used their legal training from the University of South Carolina to further the cause of civil rights. Joseph H. Stuart fought valiantly to prevent the fraudulent attempt to remove an African American judge in the dying hours of Reconstruction and brought one of the earliest lawsuits to integrate the schools in the country when he filed such a suit in Kansas. Richard Greener used his skills to try to undo the injustice done to an African American cadet at West Point. T. McCants Stewart used the legal system to challenge civil rights violations from the saloons of New York City to Hawaii and Africa. Styless Linton Hutchins fought for civil rights in the legislature of Tennessee and saw his legal career and his family's lives threatened because of his advocacy for a client.

Just as lawyers had done for centuries, these men entered public service. They served as judges, lawyers, legislators, constitutional officers, diplomats, civil servants, ministers, college presidents, teachers, and in other positions in service to their communities. Their leadership was recognized throughout the African American community. For example, four of these graduates were included in William Simmons's *Men of Mark* as leading men of their race in America in 1887.[265]

One of the criticisms of the radical law school was that all of these men were Republicans who were just exerting their political power by attending the university. It is true that if the Republicans had not been elected by a majority of the voters of the state there would have been no radical law school. It is also true that most of these men were Republicans, but in fact, as the one Democrat among them, Styles Linton Hutchins, soon found out, no other political party would allow an African American to achieve any position of power or influence in the South. In the eyes of many whites in South Carolina, a Republican was black and a Democrat was white.[266] As the nineteenth century faded, and the memories of Reconstruction dimmed, the desire for political acceptance for African Americans did not. Both T. McCants Stewart and F. L. Cardozo sought influence in the Democratic Party. Their sojourns were short-lived as they discovered their race prevented any real future in American politics, Republican or Democrat.

Despite the dire predictions of the conservatives, between 1873 and 1877 the law school lived up to its mission of preparing students for their profession. Most of the graduates practiced law. Thomas McCants Stewart, Richard Greener, Styless Linton Hutchins, T. J. Minton, and Joseph Henry Stuart remained active in their profession until the turn of the century and beyond. Paris Simkins must have found little opportunity for practice in Edgefield. As John Oldfield has noted, black lawyers in South Carolina during this period "were consistently frustrated by impoverished clients, local prejudice and . . . lack of business."[267] Joseph White Morris practiced law only briefly, but he made his impact by becoming a college president and helping found a law school. The law school at Allen University and the increasing number of African Americans being admitted to the South Carolina Bar in the last two decades of the century suggest that the hope and promise of a law school education did not die easily. As the Oldfield-Burke appendix (following chapter 5) demonstrates, nearly eighty African Americans were admitted to the South Carolina Bar in the nineteenth century, including forty-two admitted between 1877 and 1900. After 1900, the promise was gone. In his study of the African American bar, Clay Smith could find only a handful of African American lawyers in South Carolina in the first half of the twentieth century.[268]

The lives of Francis Lewis Cardozo and Walter Raleigh Jones provide poignant examples of the promise, the failure, and the aftermath of Reconstruction. The lives of Cardozo and Reconstruction are similar. Cardozo achieved the height of power and influence in the nation and the state during Reconstruction. Like Reconstruction, he demonstrated that African Americans could do much with freedom, from running a government to providing education to the newly freed people. But Cardozo and Reconstruction were defeated. Cardozo had been a leader in both his nation and state, but for the last twenty years of his life he had to settle for being a school principal. It is clear that Cardozo's position as a principal was one of great honor and prestige in his community. But because of Reconstruction's defeat, Cardozo could have no higher ambition and seems to have given up hope for justice for his race. And like Cardozo, the nation gave up hope when it let Reconstruction die. Walter Raleigh Jones's life is also similar to Reconstruction. Jones and Reconstruction were thought to have great promise. Jones's family must have had great hopes in his future, as so many African American families must have had hope for Reconstruction. Jones achieved much in his short life. He attended college and obtained a legal education. He worked in the offices of the highest officials of the state and achieved some financial success. He was even elected to the judiciary. Reconstruction achieved much in its short life in South Carolina. From the constitution of 1868 came the revolutionary advance of public education, voting rights, and a promise of a better economic future for the working people of the state. Reconstruction gave the opportunity for African Americans to attend the state's university and law school. African Americans were elected to some of the highest offices in the state. Reconstruction gave the state and the nation the first African American to sit on a supreme court. But both Jones and Reconstruction died young. Both left legacies that faded quickly but that now at the close of the twentieth century are at last being recognized in South Carolina.

What is the legacy of these eleven men? If one assumes that at the December 1876 law school graduation, the graduates received their degrees in alphabetical order, then Paris Simkins was the last African American graduate of the University of South Carolina School of Law in the nineteenth century. The first African American who tried to attend the law school in the twentieth century was C. B. Bailey, grandson of Paris Simkins. Bailey applied for admission in August of 1938.[269] The editorial reactions of the South Carolina newspapers were not unlike those of the 1870s. The *News and Courier* of Charleston opined that "Northern negro societies" were behind Bailey's application and that "our people will insist on separate white colleges and will have them at any cost."[270] The chairman of the special admission committee, Solomon Blatt, a powerful legislator, declared in advance of a decision on the application that "the white people of South Carolina need not have any fear as to what the outcome of this application is going to be."[271] Bailey was soon denied admission.[272] The first African American admitted to the law school in the twentieth century was Paul Cash in 1964. The first African American graduate from the law school after Simkins was Jasper Cureton in 1967, now a member of the South Carolina Court of Appeals. Today the law school has two tenured African American professors. Over the past thirty years the school has prepared hundreds of African American men and women for the practice of law. The state bar association has had an African American president, I. S. Leevy Johnson. Ernest J. Finney, an African American, became the second person of his race to serve on the South Carolina Supreme Court and retired in the year 2000 as the chief justice of the South Carolina Supreme Court.

Bernard E. Powers quotes Francis Lewis Cardozo as saying, "Slavery has produced such corrupting and degrading influences, that it requires a generation to remedy."[273]In retrospect, the idea that the corruption and degradation of slavery could be remedied in only one generation seems quaint and naive. But how different things might have been if Cardozo, Stewart, Greener, Morris, and the others had been given the chance to live out the promise of their generation.

Appendix

University of South Carolina School of Law Students, 1868–1877

These names were compiled from a number of University of South Carolina records, including the *Catalogue, University of South Carolina* for 1868, 1869, 1870, 1871, 1872, the reorganization of the university in 1873 and 1876 (South Caroliniana Library); the *Register of the South Carolina College* for the reorganization of the university in 1873, 1874, 1875, and 1876, USC Archives; the *Report of the Chairman of the Faculty of the University of South Carolina*, 1875, SCL; and the *Roll of Students, 1805–1905, South Carolina College*, USC Archives. Racial identification of the students for the period between the reorganization of the university in 1873 and its closing in 1877 was done using outside sources, such as city directories, census records, newspaper articles, and various other primary and secondary sources. Class designation indicates that the student was awarded a degree.

African American Students of the Law School, 1873–1877

Joseph Boston
Lawrence Cain, class of 1876
Francis L. Cardozo, class of 1876
Richard T. Greener, class of 1876
Styless Linton Hutchins, class of 1876
Henry Barton Johnson, class of 1875
Walter Raleigh Jones, class of 1874
Thomas E. Miller
Theophilus J. Minton, class of 1876
Paul J. Mishow
Joseph White Morris, class of 1876
William F. Myers
Arthur O'Hear
Edward James Sawyer*
Paris Simkins, class of 1876
Charles H. Sperry
Thomas McCants Stewart, class of 1875
Joseph Henry Stuart, class of 1875
C. M. Wilder

---

*Edward James Sawyer stated in a letter to John P. Green dated August 18, 1887 that he received his LL.B. in law from U.S.C. But Sawyer's graduation is not found in any university records (John P. Green Papers, Western Historical Society, Cleveland, Ohio).

WHITE STUDENTS OF THE LAW SCHOOL, FROM THE REORGANIZATION OF 1873 TO 1877

Charles L. Anderson, class of 1874
Charles J. Babbitt, class of 1876
Thomas M. Canton, class of 1876
Edgar Caypless, class of 1874
H. C. Corwin
Charles W. Cummings, class of 1874
Erastus W. Everson
Gil Dixon Fox
Henry A. Fox, class of 1875
Barnett B. Goins
William Jackson
James O. Ladd
George T. McIntyre
Niles Gardner Parker, class of 1874
Mortimer A. Warren, class of 1875
T. M. Wilkes
John Wingate

Racial Composition of the Graduating Classes of the Law School, 1868–1876

YEAR	WHITE	BLACK
1868	2	0
1869	0	0
1870	5	0
1871	3	0
1872	6	0
1873	4	0
1874	4	1
1875	2	3
1876	2	7

PARIS SIMKINS, state legislator, USC Law School class of 1876. Courtesy O. V. Burton and used with permission of C. B. Bailey Jr.

DIPLOMA of Paris Simkins, state legislator, USC Law School class of 1876. Courtesy O. V. Burton and used with permission of C. B. Bailey Jr.

ROBERT SMALLS, congressman, delegate to the Constitutional Conventions of 1868 and 1895. Courtesy South Caroliniana Library, USC Columbia.

THOMAS MCCANTS STEWART, USC Law School class of 1875. Courtesy
Moorland-Spingarn Research Center, Howard University.

JOSEPH HENRY STUART, USC Law School class of 1875. Used with permission of the Denver Public Library, Western History Collection.

W. J. WHIPPER, delegate to the Constitutional Conventions of 1868 and 1895. Courtesy Charles Sumner Brown and J. Clay Smith, Jr.

JONATHAN J. WRIGHT, justice, Supreme Court of South Carolina. Used with permission of Larry Francis Lebby, artist.

"The Board of Canvassers Jailed for Contempt," *Frank Leslie's Illustrated Weekly.* Courtesy Richard and Belinda Gergel.

"The Mackey and Wallace Houses Simultaneously Occupying the House Chambers," *Frank Leslie's Illustrirte Zeitung.* Courtesy Richard and Belinda Gergel.

5

The African American Bar
in South Carolina, 1877–1915

JOHN OLDFIELD

The history of the African American bar in South Carolina dates from the Reconstruction period. During these turbulent years black lawyers established a foothold in the state's courts and one of their number, Jonathan J. Wright, was even elected a justice of the South Carolina Supreme Court. Wright and his colleagues have understandably received a great deal of critical attention.[1] Less well documented is the expansion of the black legal profession, an expansion that occurred between the conservative victory of 1876 and the adoption of a new, white supremacist constitution in 1895. By century's end there were reported to be twenty-nine black lawyers in South Carolina.[2] This is probably an exaggeration. Nevertheless, the numbers were certainly large enough to suggest rapid consolidation of the African American bar and, in Charleston at least, the makings of a black legal community.

The first blacks admitted to the South Carolina Bar in 1868 were northerners attracted to the South after the Civil War. Jonathan J. Wright, a native of Pennsylvania, came to South Carolina as a legal adviser with the Freedmen's Bureau; William Whipper, for his part, hailed from Michigan and had received his legal training in Detroit. The early life of Robert Brown Elliott is shrouded in mystery, but he, too, was a carpetbagger and, like Whipper, came South with the Union army. These men were the pioneers. Over the next eight years another twenty-eight blacks were admitted to the South Carolina Bar, among them Samuel J. Lee, Daniel L. Straker, Francis L. Cardozo, Macon B. Allen, and

This chapter is a revised version of an earlier article by the author, "A High and Honorable Calling: Black Lawyers in South Carolina, 1868–1915," *Journal of American Studies* 23 (1989): 395; reprinted with permission.

Richard T. Greener, who for five torrid years (1873–1877) was the only black faculty member at the University of South Carolina.[3]

Contrary to what one might expect, the end of Reconstruction did not signal the demise of black lawyers. One important indicator is the record of admissions. During the 1880s approximately twenty-five blacks were admitted to the South Carolina Bar and another eighteen were admitted during the 1890s, including a cohort of four in 1897. Thereafter, numbers slowed down to a trickle, but in all some seventy-seven black lawyers were admitted to the South Carolina Bar between 1877 and 1915.[4] Of course, these figures relate only to admissions. The number who went on to become practicing lawyers was significantly lower, and the number who became full-time professionals, for whom the law was their chief source of income, was lower still.

We can also identify another trend. By 1877 the black bar in South Carolina was already predominantly native born, and by the end of the century almost exclusively so. Not surprisingly, most of these men came from the Low Country, where the bulk of the black population was concentrated. The incompleteness of the biographical data makes further analysis difficult, but it seems likely that mulattoes outnumbered blacks by perhaps as much as two to one, while a similar proportion could claim freeborn ancestry stretching back several generations. The unmistakable impression is that most prospective black lawyers came from well-established, middle-class families which historically attached a great deal of importance to the professions and, more important, could afford to give their sons the right sort of training.

How did these men get started? One obvious way was to read law with a practicing lawyer. While perhaps 40 percent of black lawyers acquired their training in this way, specific examples are tantalizingly difficult to document. Whipper and Wright both trained young men in their offices, and Samuel J. Lee in Charleston trained his future partner, William J. Bowen, as well as Robert C. Browne and Thaddeus St. Mark Sasportas.[5] Others may well have worked with northern white lawyers, and some, like George C. Clyde, who was Lee's first partner, seem to have acquired all the knowledge they required while working as clerks of court.[6]

The alternative to such practical education was to go to law school. Over 50 percent of black lawyers in South Carolina were probably educated in this way. A small number of young men were always sent out of state to colleges like Howard and Atlanta Universities. During Reconstruction as many as nineteen were also fortunate enough to be admitted to the University of South Carolina School of Law.[7] One of the most remarkable of these figures was T. McCants Stewart, who graduated from the University of South Carolina in 1875 and later went on to become an associate justice of the Liberian Supreme Court.[8]

Then there was Allen University, a Methodist institution which moved to Columbia from Cokesbury in 1880. Like neighboring Benedict Institute, Allen University was a multilevel private school that trained teachers, taught industrial trades, and provided preparatory and college courses. As the university's catalogue explained, "Allen aims for, and is destined to be, a great factor in the intellectual training and highest Christian education of the youths of the South, that they may be disciplined and inspired as leaders and teachers in the vitally important work that must be done by and for the race in this country, and in the continent of Africa."⁹ Unique among early black colleges in the South, Allen also had its own law school. Modeled on the University of South Carolina, Allen offered prospective students a two-year course leading to the LL.B. degree. In their junior year students were guided through Robinson's *Elementary Law*, Blackstone's *Commentaries*, Kent's *Commentaries*, Greenleaf on evidence, Smith on contracts, and Daniel on negotiable instruments. In their senior year they then went on to study Bishop's *Criminal Law* and *Criminal Procedure* and the *General Statues of South Carolina*. Students were granted access to the "valuable collections" of the state library—an important privilege in these pioneering years—and, in addition, there were moot courts and lectures once a month from distinguished members of the South Carolina Bar, white as well as black.¹⁰

Overseeing this ambitious enterprise was Daniel A. Straker, who was dean of the law school from 1882 to 1887. Born and educated in Barbados, Straker had arrived in Charleston in 1875 as an inspector in the customs service, having previously taught in a freedmen's school in Louisville, Kentucky, and having spent two years at Howard University Law School. Straker subsequently moved to Orangeburg, where he practiced law with Robert Elliott and T. McCants Stewart, and then to Columbia. A brilliant and dynamic figure, he was a natural choice as dean of Allen's law school and during his short term of office he had a profound and lasting effect on the black legal profession in South Carolina.¹¹

Allen's law school graduated its first class of four students in 1884. The second class graduated in 1886 and a third—which included Straker's successor as dean, Thomas A. Saxon—in 1887. The school was apparently still open to students in 1912, but by this date the endeavor had been more or less abandoned, with the last class graduating in 1898. Nevertheless, what Straker and Saxon achieved was hugely impressive. Between 1882 and 1898 thirty young men passed through Allen's law school, seventeen of whom were subsequently admitted to the South Carolina Bar. Again, most of these students were native South Carolinians, but Allen also attracted applicants from Georgia and West Virginia.¹²

The men who ran Allen University had no doubt that the law school had an important mission. "The profession of the lawyer is a necessity to our civilization," the 1890 prospectus informed prospective students. "It is a high and honorable calling, and those who enter it have opportunities second to no class of professional men of being great benefactors to the human race."[13] But training of this kind was expensive and for many prohibitively so. Allen charged its students $70 a year, exclusive of room and board, which could be anything from $3 to $6 a month. In addition, students were expected to buy their own text books and, in the words of the prospectus, "to secure them promptly when advised to." It does not seem unreasonable to surmise that the total outlay, spread over two years, would have amounted to between $150 and $200.[14] This was a lot of money for a black family to spend on education in the late nineteenth century, and despite credit arrangements the wonder is that Allen managed to attract (and keep) as many students as it did.

The final hurdle for all prospective lawyers was an examination before the supreme court. Traditionally, this ordeal took the form of a sometimes perfunctory oral examination before several of the justices. In 1887, however, South Carolina introduced a written examination as part of a general effort to professionalize the bar.[15] If anything, this reform may have worked to the advantage of black applicants, but there were undoubtedly failures. As a result, some simply gave up. Even those who were successful did not always pursue a legal career. Of Allen's thirty graduates only eight (25 percent) became professional lawyers and not all of those in South Carolina. Some taught school or edited newspapers, often combining these careers with sporadic appearances in local courts. Others worked as clerks for the state government or moved to Washington, D.C., to work for the federal government. A few, like Dock J. Jordan, who was admitted to the bar in 1892, ended their careers as presidents of black colleges.[16]

Of course, there was an element of free choice in all this, but the hazards involved in becoming a full-time professional were all too obvious. The main problem was the poverty of the black population. Typically, black lawyers in the South dealt with small property deals and criminal cases involving black clients who were usually too poor to be able to afford legal assistance. Opportunities to work for black business enterprises and, much later, organizations like the NAACP on the whole were limited. There were also some ingrained local prejudices to contend with. Very few black lawyers attracted white clients, and by choice many blacks themselves preferred to employ the services of a white lawyer. As one local newspaper noted, "the colored people have not the same confidence in a colored man's abilities."[17]

Even talented black lawyers struggled to make a career for themselves. Despite the undoubted brilliance of at least two of the partners, the firm of (Robert) Elliott, (Daniel) Straker and (T. McCants) Stewart, based in Orangeburg, finally went bankrupt in 1879 owing to lack of business.[18] As we have seen, Straker subsequently moved to Columbia, but his decision to leave South Carolina in 1887 was influenced, in part, by the failure of his legal practice. As the

Columbia Daily Register was at pains to point out, "[W]hile he (Straker) has been engaged in many important cases in which the personal and property rights of his colored clients have been faithfully and in most cases successfully represented, their poverty as a class has left his labor in their behalf unremunerated."[19]

A similar picture emerges in Sumter. John B. Edwards, an Allen graduate, started a law firm here in 1886 with his partner, Johnson C. Whittaker, who in 1881 had been expelled from West Point under controversial circumstances.[20] Within a year the two men were reported to be monopolizing nearly all the business in Sumter's busy court of sessions. Even so, neither of them was financially secure. In 1895 Edwards relocated to Charleston. Whittaker, who doubled as principal of the local black public school, clung on a little longer; but around 1900 he, too, abandoned Sumter and moved to Orangeburg.[21] His departure coincided with the arrival of another Allen graduate, William T. Andrews. A restless and ambitious man, Andrews became increasingly disillusioned. Writing to a friend in 1903, he complained that conditions in Sumter were "growing damned near intolerable and [he was] tired of it." Ever alert to the possibility of a move to Washington, D.C., Andrews survived only by teaching school and working part-time as an agent for the Pennsylvania Mutual Insurance Company.[22]

Given these difficulties, it is hardly surprising that many young men gravitated toward the Low Country where prospects were considerably brighter. Large black enclaves in Georgetown and Beaufort held out the promise of brisker business, while more alluring still was Charleston. As many as sixteen black lawyers had offices in Charleston between 1868 and 1915, although not all of them were active at the same time. The carpetbaggers had quickly grasped the potential of this area. Robert Elliott opened his first law office in Charleston in partnership with William Whipper and Macon B. Allen, and Jonathan J. Wright worked there from the late 1870s until his death in 1885.[23] By 1895 the number of black lawyers in the city had risen to seven. This busy group of men was the nearest thing to a black legal community in South Carolina. Partnerships sprang up and certain addresses became instantly recognizable as the offices of black lawyers. For years, 35 Chalmers Street was the office of John Gaillard and Martin A. Williams, while 104 Church Street was successively occupied by Robert C. Browne (1897–99), John B. Edwards (1901–13), and Thaddeus St. Mark Sasportas (1916–19).[24]

Easily the most influential figure in Charleston's black legal community was Samuel J. Lee. Born a slave on the plantation of Samuel McGowan, an upcountry planter, Lee followed his master into the Civil War and was wounded at the second battle of Manassas and again near Hanover Junction on the retreat to Richmond. After the war Lee returned to Abbeville, where he took up farming, and later moved to Hamburg, then in Edgefield County. In 1868 he was elected a member of the South Carolina House of Representatives for Edgefield and was subsequently twice elected representative for Aiken (1872–74). By the time he was admitted to the bar in 1872 Lee had emerged as one of the most able members of the house, and in recognition of the fact was elected Speaker. Then in 1874 he resigned his seat, making way for Robert Brown Elliott, and left politics to concentrate on his law practice in Aiken.[25]

Lee's meteoric rise undoubtedly had something to do with McGowan, who was probably his natural father, and Senator Frank Arnim, with whom Lee worked as a county commissioner during the late 1860s. Poorly educated, he nevertheless possessed a lively and inquiring mind. "Lee is certainly a remarkable man," wrote a correspondent in the *Charleston News and Courier* in 1873. "By dint of industry and application he has made himself one of the most creditable lawyers in the state for his age. I heard him argue a case at Chambers the other day, and he displayed a tact and ability that would have done credit to one longer engaged in the practice."[26] It was these same qualities that Lee brought to his responsibilities as Speaker. "Even the opposition party and press have repeatedly expressed admiration at Speaker Lee's graceful and yet firm discharge of his duties," noted the Republican *Aiken Tribune*. "His record is a proud one, and his people may well indulge in pride at the devotion to their interests he has evinced, and the prominent position among his fellows which he has assumed and so gracefully fills."[27]

Returning to Aiken in 1874, Lee went into partnership with George C. Clyde and set about building up a successful law practice.[28] Then things started to go badly wrong. In 1875 Lee was convicted of fraudulently issuing checks while he was a county commissioner, and in 1877 he was again charged with misconduct, this time in a larger political scandal involving some of the key black office holders in the state.[29] Wisely, he chose this moment to escape to Alabama where he worked as a special federal agent for the detection of fraudulent entries on public lands. By 1878 he was back in South Carolina—this time in Charleston. Very much the outsider, Lee started out by taking cases for a white lawyer, Robert Seymour, from whom he appears to have received a percentage of the fees. By 1882 he was the leading black lawyer in the state with a young partner and an office of his own in Court House Square.[30]

Most of Lee's work was in the busy municipal and county courts. He was particularly active in the court of general sessions, which became something of a black preserve during the 1880s.[31] Within four years of his arrival in Charleston Lee had ousted many of his rivals and was involved in nearly two-thirds of all criminal litigation handled by black lawyers. By 1885 his ascendancy was complete. Of twenty-eight cases defended by black lawyers in the court of general sessions that year, Lee and his partner, William J. Bowen, were involved in twenty-one, while Lee was personally involved in another two. Lee continued to dominate proceedings in Charleston until his death in 1895. In 1890, for example, he handled twenty out of twenty-three cases defended by black lawyers in the court of sessions and worked with Robert Browne, one of his former clerks, on two of the other three.[32]

Lee's caseload split almost evenly between crimes against property (larceny, grand larceny, burglary, receiving stolen goods) and crimes against the person (assault, murder, assault and battery). He showed considerable skill in defending accused murderers, and between 1882 and 1893 was involved in five rape cases, all of them attacks by blacks on blacks.[33] By contrast, Lee acted in only a handful of cases a year in Charleston's court of common pleas, not merely because of fierce competition from white lawyers, but because very few blacks were in a position to contest wills or make claims for damages. Black crime was of an altogether more desperate and violent nature.[34]

Lee was also a familiar face in neighboring Berkeley County, where there was a paucity of black legal talent, although in Beaufort he seems to have been willing to give way to William Whipper, by this date well established again in the Low Country.[35] Then there were his appearances before the supreme court, twenty-seven between 1880 and 1894 and far in excess of any other black lawyer in the state.[36] By and large these appearances were connected with criminal cases that Lee had personally brought up from the lower courts in Charleston, but there were some notable exceptions. It was Lee, for instance, who acted for William Whipper in *Whipper v. Talbird* (1889), a civil action arising out of a contested election for the position of probate judge in Beaufort County.[37] Lee clearly relished these occasions. The sessions of the supreme court were widely reported, and they provided the ideal opportunity for Lee to display his wit and know-how. More to the point, he sometimes won.

Lee's reputation as a lawyer rested upon his "excellent" knowledge of criminal law, "his acute and clear perception, [and] his facility for grasping points, and making the most of every slip in his opponent's argument."[38] Even whites were said to have sought out his services. And with good reason. To judge from the Charleston records, Lee's clients always stood a better than even chance of being acquitted or, more likely, of having their cases dismissed. Lee was admittedly less successful before the supreme court, but very few lawyers, black or white, could lay claim to such a record. James W. Polite and Robert C. Browne, two of Lee's nearest black rivals, won only about a third of the cases they handled in the court of sessions.[39]

Despite his success in the courtroom, Lee was never a wealthy man. What little property he owned in Charleston was heavily mortgaged, sometimes two or three times over, and on at least one occasion he was forced to sell in order to repay his creditors.[40] From all that we can gather, Lee was not a particularly extravagant man. On the contrary, his home life was described as being "quiet and unpretentious." Lee was rather the victim of a debt-ridden clientele and his own generosity of spirit. "He no doubt would have been well-to-do if his clients had all been able to pay him," the *Charleston News and Courier* concluded in 1895, "but he was not of a nature to refuse to do a poor man service and much of his time was given with no expectation of a fee."[41]

Remarkable as it was, Lee's preeminence in Charleston undoubtedly made life difficult for his competitors, and it is no accident that his sudden death from a heart attack in 1895 coincided with an influx of new talent into the city. One of these men was John B. Edwards, who until recently had been based in Sumter. Edwards subsequently went into partnership with one of Lee's clerks, Thaddeus St. Mark Sasportas, and by 1913 was one of the leading black lawyers in the state.[42] In the meantime, a new generation of lawyers was emerging, among them John Gaillard, Eugene Hayne, and Mark A. Williams, all of whom were admitted in 1897, and Edward F. Smith, admitted in 1900.[43] But these young men grew up in a harsher climate and some, like Williams and Hayne, soon went North to seek their fortunes in New York. The Wilson years witnessed further decline. In 1910 Charleston could still boast five black lawyers; in 1916 there were just two—Smith and Sasportas.[44]

Paradoxically, in Columbia prospects began to improve after 1900. Despite being the state capital, Columbia had never been a promising area for black lawyers, and even talented men like Daniel A. Straker had struggled. But black migration and the work of organizations like the NAACP opened up new possibilities. By 1918 there were three black lawyers listed in the Columbia city directory: Butler W. Nance, an Allen graduate and former railway postal clerk; Green Jackson, another Allen graduate; and Nathaniel J. Frederick, an Orangeburg native educated at Claflin and the University of Wisconsin.[45] Nevertheless, it would be stretching a point to say that any of these men were full-time professionals. Frederick was for many years (1904–1922) principal of Howard School, and when he gave that up in 1922 he became secretary-treasurer of the Regal Drug Store. Among his other business ventures was a newspaper, the *Palmetto Leader*, which first appeared in January 1925 and quickly became the "voice of black Columbia."[46]

Frederick and Jackson were still active in the late 1920s, Frederick especially so. But the twenties generally were a testing period for black lawyers. Admissions to the bar slowed down to a trickle—very few, if any, blacks appear to have been admitted to the South Carolina Bar after 1919—while opportunities to gain a legal training, particularly with a practicing lawyer, grew fewer and fewer. Stagnation quickly set in. By 1930 there were only two black lawyers of any note in the whole state: Nathaniel Frederick in Columbia and Thaddeus St. Mark Sasportas in Charleston.

Throughout this period black lawyers constituted a very small elite among

South Carolina's black population. Probably as few as 50 percent of those admitted to the bar between 1877 and 1915 went on to become practicing lawyers, and fewer still enjoyed any measure of professional success. Despite a spirit of healthy competition, the size and vulnerability of the black bar encouraged familiarity and close cooperation. This was particularly true in Charleston where at different times John B. Edwards, Thaddeus St. Mark Sasportas, Robert C. Browne, and Edward Smith were all business partners.[47] Understandably, ties with colleagues working elsewhere in the state became more and more important as time went on. When Butler W. Nance died in 1923 his pallbearers included Nathaniel Frederick, Green Jackson, and Thaddeus Sasportas.[48]

Small in numbers, black lawyers in South Carolina also did not enjoy the same professional freedom as their white colleagues. Specialization, by 1900 increasingly common in larger white firms, was almost unheard of for black lawyers. Most black lawyers could not afford to specialize and, in any case, would have found the notion absurd. Relations with white lawyers on the whole were distant. For some the social and political revolution that Reconstruction had set in motion proved too much to stomach. As one disgruntled South Carolinian put it, writing from Rio Vista, California, in 1870, "Well—you have a charming Supreme Court in S.C. now.—a contemptible scallywag occupying the seat once adorned by O'Neall and Dunkin, and two carpetbaggers (and one of them a negro) in the seats once graced by Wardlaw and Withers. How do you feel before such a Bench? When you address such creatures as 'Your Honors,' don't the blood either boil or grow chill in your veins?"[49]

As one might expect, there were similar misgivings about appearing against black lawyers, just as there were misgivings about appearing before black juries. But resistance eventually gave way to grudging acceptance. Many white lawyers found they had little cause to get involved with their black colleagues, particularly if specialized in civil litigation, while others undoubtedly saw them as a necessary evil. Nevertheless, a certain degree of professional contact was inevitable: Samuel Lee, to take an obvious example, worked with and against white lawyers throughout his career.[50] But there was never any question who held the upper hand. Black lawyers were never admitted to the South Carolina Bar Association, for instance, and to this extent they remained very much a separate (and unequal) branch of the legal profession.

Survival as a black lawyer demanded intelligence and tact. Most were quick to assess the power and influence of the white legal community and act accordingly. In Lee's case, surely instructive, his success undeniably owed something to his willingness to accept the status quo. His obituary in the *Charleston News and Courier* pointedly drew attention to his manners in the courtroom, which it applauded as being "beyond criticism, extremely courteous and never presuming."[51] Lee's public stance was equally accommodating. For a time after his arrival in Charleston Lee continued to take an active interest in politics. In 1880 he stood unsuccessfully as a Republican candidate for the First Congressional District and the following year he was included in a delegation of black leaders that met with President-elect Garfield in Ohio.[52] But increasingly after 1881 Lee channeled his energies into other interests and activities, into Zion Presbyterian Church, for instance, and the First Brigade of colored troops, which for many years he commanded.[53]

Lee's courtesy and "good sense" won him the confidence of his colleagues, black and white. It is a measure of the esteem in which he was held that on learning of his death the U.S. Circuit Court, then in sessions in Charleston, promptly adjourned, following what was described as a "high tribute" from Judge Simonton. At his funeral on April 4, 1895, Zion Church on Calhoun Street was "completely filled" and "at least 6000 people remained outside during the whole services."[54] Lee was in many respects a remarkable man, but it is worth noting that he was not an activist or a crusader for black civil rights, at least not in the modern sense of the term. Interviewed within days of the U.S. Supreme Court's decision in the Civil Rights Cases, which overturned the Civil Rights Act of 1875, Lee assured readers of the *Charleston News and Courier* that "all a colored man in South Carolina had to do was to behave himself and he would have all the civil rights he desired."[55] Comments like these had an obvious impact. What people valued and respected in Lee was clearly his "wisdom"—his sense of what was possible.

Not surprisingly, few black lawyers in South Carolina enjoyed financial security. When Samuel Lee died in 1895 his estate consisted of a small law library valued at $230 and $115 in cash. Edward F. Smith left $500; Jonathan J. Wright, who for seven years served as a justice of the supreme court, left $1,100.[56] Estimates of average yearly income are almost impossible to arrive at. W. T. Andrews in Sumter was reputedly earning $1,000 a year in 1903, but without further data there is no way of knowing whether this was an unusually high or low figure.[57] Certainly, home ownership was rare even among the elite. In Charleston, for instance, John B. Edwards lived in rented property for most of his career, as did Robert C. Browne and Edward F. Smith.[58]

It is clear that black lawyers were an integral if subordinate part of the legal profession in South Carolina well into the twentieth century. Expansion was particularly rapid during the 1880s, and, as we have seen, the black legal community in Charleston was at its peak in the 1890s. Looking back, we can now see that these decades were critical, and not only for black lawyers. In Charleston during the 1880s and 1890s blacks were also a significant presence on the local police force, and there and in other parts of South Carolina they remained a common sight on juries.[59] Put another way, the administration of justice at the turn of the century was still inclusive rather than exclusive, although this is not to deny that some blacks were losing faith in what they saw, and often experienced, as "white" justice.

What undermined the position of black lawyers in South Carolina was a combination of factors. Jim Crow or segregationist legislation undoubtedly played its part, but so, too, did economic recession, the First World War, and the narrow, coercive mood of the 1920s. Only with the increase in federal activity in the field of social security and the rise of workmen's laws during the New Deal would the situation show any signs of marked improvement, and even then progress was often slow and halting.

Black lawyers during this period (1877–1915) were consistently frustrated by impoverished clients, local prejudice, and, except for the fortunate few, lack of business. And yet in their quiet and unobtrusive way these men had an important impact on the black community in South Carolina, its progress and its future. As the *Palmetto Leader* put it in 1926, black lawyers were "invaluable to the ultimate protection of Negro people." "Very often," the paper went on, "these lawyers are doing things in defense of their people which do not comment the light of publicity. Many a humble negro's property has been saved from economic rape by the honesty and loyalty of some Negro lawyer."[60] In truth, this was a "high and honorable calling."

Appendix
AFRICAN AMERICAN LAWYERS IN SOUTH CAROLINA, 1868–1900

This appendix was originally developed by John Oldfield and has been supplemented by Lewis Burke as this book has been produced. Our source for most of the admissions to the bar is the Roll of Attorneys of the South Carolina Supreme Court. Under an 1868 statute both the supreme court and the circuit court could admit men to practice. The circuit court admission was limited to practice only before the circuit and probate courts. Admission by the supreme court allowed the attorney to practice in any court in the state. See Act No. 46, An Act to Regulate the Admission to Persons to Practice as Attorneys, Solicitors, and Counselors in the Courts of This State, *The Statutes at Large of South Carolina*, vol. 14 (1873). Therefore, this appendix may not provide a complete list of all African Americans admitted to practice law in nineteenth-century South Carolina. There are no complete circuit court records from which admissions can be gathered. However, there are newspaper accounts of lawyers being admitted by a circuit court judge. However, the authors have found no such reports that include anyone we could identify as African American.

However, we have found a few individuals who are were identified as lawyers by various sources. The specific sources for these individuals are footnoted. We are assuming that these individuals were admitted only before the circuit court. On March 12, 1878, the legislature repealed the provision that allowed admissions to practice by the circuit court. Act No. 442, *Acts and Joint Resolutions of the General Assembly of the State of South Carolina* (1876).

The racial identification of these men is not precise, nor is it practicable to provide a specific citation to racial identification for each person listed. Some major sources include the *Charleston News and Courier*, the *Columbia Daily Register*; *The State* (Columbia); the *Columbia Daily Union Herald; The People's Advocate*; the *Washington Bee*; the manuscript U.S. Censuses for 1870 and 1880 (National Archives, Washington, D.C.); *The Columbia Directory*, 1875–76; *Chas. Emerson and Co.'s Columbia, S.Ca., Directory*, 1879–80; *Directory of the City of Columbia*, 1883–84; Emily Reynolds and Joan Faunt, eds., *The Biographical Directory of the Senate of South Carolina, 1776–1964* (Columbia: South Carolina Archives Department, 1964); Thomas Holt, *Black over White: Negro Leadership in South Carolina during Reconstruction* (Urbana: University of Illinois Press, 1977); Eric Foner, *Freedom's Lawyers: A Directory of Black Officeholders during Reconstruction* (New York: Oxford University Press, 1993); and the *Catalogue of Allen University, 1911–1912* (1912). Also see the chapters by Burke and the Gergels in this volume for identification of a number of these men.

NAME	DATE	RESIDENCE
Jonathan J. Wright	Sept. 1868	Beaufort
William J. Whipper	Sept. 1868	Beaufort
Robert B. Elliott	Sept. 1868	Aiken
Theophilus J. Minton	Nov. 1871	Columbia
Robert DeLarge	Nov. 1871	Charleston
Edwin T. Belcher	Nov. 1871	Augusta, Ga.
Eugene R. B. Belcher	Nov. 1871	Augusta, Ga.
W. H. Jones Jr.	Nov. 1871	Georgetown
John F. Quarles	Nov. 1871	Augusta, Ga.
Stephen A. Swails	March 1872	Kingstree
Samuel J. Lee	March 1872	Hamburg
Henry J. Maxwell	March 1872	Bennettsville
James A. Bowley	unknown	Georgetown*
A. R. Watson	unknown	Aiken**
George C. Clyde	Nov. 1873	Aiken
Walter R. Jones	Nov. 1874	Columbia
Daniel A. Straker	July 1875	Charleston

William F. Myers	Dec. 1875	Colleton
T. McCants Stewart	Dec. 1875	Sumter
Thomas E. Miller	Dec. 1875	Lawtonville
William A. Hayne	Dec. 1875	Marion
John M. Freeman Jr.	Dec. 1875	Charleston
Samuel J. Bampfield	Dec. 1875	Beaufort
Macon B. Allen	Dec. 1875	Charleston
Joseph H. Stuart	Dec. 1875	Camden
Thomas H. Wheeler	April 1876	
Francis L. Cardozo	July 1876	Columbia
Styless L. Hutchins	Nov. 1876	Columbia
Joseph W. Morris	Nov. 1876	Columbia
William Hannibal Thomas	Nov. 1876	Newberry***
Richard T. Greener	Dec. 1876	Columbia
Henry B. Johnson	Nov. 1877	Charleston
J. Williams Polite	May 1879	Charleston
Robert O. Lee	1880	Sumter
William J. Bowen	Dec. 1881	Charleston
F. D. J. Lawrence	April 1882	Charleston
Robert L. Smith	1882	Charleston
George O. Marshall	1883	Charleston
William F. Holmes	Dec. 1883	Charleston
Talley R. Holmes	May 1884	Columbia
John B. Edwards	May 1884	Columbia
Peter Flynn Oliver	May 1884	Columbia
Robert A. Stewart	May 1884	Columbia
Major D. McFarlan	Dec. 1884	Cheraw
E. C. C. Washington	May 1885	Columia
Benjamin E. Watson	May 1885	Columbia
E. J. Sawyer	May 1885	Bennettsville
J. C. Whittaker	May 1885	Charleston
Edward J. Dickerson	Dec. 1885	Aiken
Thomas J. Reynolds	Dec. 1885	Beaufort
Robert C. Browne	May 1886	Charleston
Paris Simkins	Nov. 1886	Edgefield
A. S. Bascomb	Dec. 1886	Beaufort
Andrew E. Hampton	May 1887	Columbia
Thomas A. Saxton	May 1887	Laurens
Wm. W. Still	May 1887	Beaufort
Julius I. Washington	Dec. 1887	Beaufort
S. E. Smith	1888	Aiken

Casper G. Garrett	May 1890	Laurens
Butler W. Nance	May 1890	Newberry
Zachariah D. Greene	Dec. 1890	Georgetown
Walton W. Williams	Dec. 1890	Columbia
Dock J. Jordan	May 1892	Columbia
Isaiah R. Reed	1893	Beaufort
W. T. Andrews	Dec. 1894	Sumter
T. St. Marks Sasportas	May 1895	Charleston
Edward R. Culler	Dec. 1895	Charleston
E. Woodbury Brinkins	May 1897	Columbia
Eugene R. Hayne	May 1897	Charleston
John A. Gaillard	May 1897	Charleston
Mark A. Williams	May 1897	Charleston
Thomas T. Hilton	Dec. 1897	Marion
Green Jackson	May 1898	Columbia
S. S. Davis	1898	Darlington
Alonzo E. Twine	May 1899	Charleston
Edward F. Smith	Dec. 1900	Mount Pleasant
Nathaniel J. Frederick	May 1913	Columbia

*An advertisement for "Jas. A. Bowley, Attorney at Law, Georgetown, S.C." is found in the *Georgetown Planet*, May 31, 1873. Bowley's racial identification can be found in Thomas Holt, *Black over White: Negro Leadership in South Carolina during Reconstruction* (Urbana: University of Illinois Press, 1977), appendix A; and in the U.S. manuscript census for 1870 for South Carolina (National Archives, Washington, D.C.).

**A. R. Watson is identified as a "colored lawyer" in the *Edgefield Advertiser* on Oct. 16, 1873.

***Thomas was first admitted by the circuit court. That bar admission is noted in Theodore Jervey, *The Slave Trade* (Columbia, S.C.,1925; repr. New York: Negro Universities Press, 1969), 159. Also see William Hannibal Thomas, *The American Negro* (New York: Macmillan, 1901), xvi–xviii.

6

Richard Theodore Greener and the African American Individual in a Black and White World

MICHAEL ROBERT MOUNTER

On November 13, 1920, less than two years before Richard Theodore Greener died, Wendell P. Dabney, the editor of the Cincinnati *Union*, called Greener "one of the greatest men and grandest products of this country." Dabney recognized Greener as a "young contemporary of Fred Douglass" who "met and matched wits with the heroes of that day and emerged from that age of blood and iron an intellectual giant filled with the spirit of progress."[1] Since his death on May 2, 1922, however, Greener has been remembered simply as the first black graduate of Harvard. It is puzzling that he has received little treatment in historical studies of the period in light of the fact that he was a prominent black intellectual who was dubbed a member of the "talented tenth" by W. E. B. DuBois in 1903.[2] He held posts in both academic and public life during a fifty-year career that culminated with his appointment in 1898 to a consular post in Vladivostok, Russia. With the notable exception of Allison Blakely's 1974 article, Greener has gone relatively unnoticed by historians. Blakely analyzed his later career in the context of his membership in the talented tenth.[3] His experience at Harvard from 1865 to 1870, and as a professor of metaphysics and logic at the University of South Carolina from 1873 to 1877, provide a firmer basis for understanding Greener's troubled yet distinguished career.

As a child, Greener had no reason to expect a college education, much less one at Harvard. His grandfather, Jacob Greener, was a close associate of anti-slavery reformer Benjamin Lundy and worked with other leading black men of Baltimore to thwart the activities of the American Colonization Society. He met with William Lloyd Garrison in 1829 to urge the famous abolitionist to oppose the American Colonization Society in its efforts to send black Americans to colonies in Africa. With Garrison's help, he established a school for orphan and indigent children in Baltimore. In the 1830s Jacob Greener's sons, Richard Wesley (Richard Theodore's father) and Jacob C., worked as agents for Garrison's paper, *The Liberator.* By the time Richard Theodore was born on January 30, 1844, in Philadelphia, his father no longer worked for Garrison.[4]

Richard Theodore Greener was noted throughout his life for his light complexion. His maternal grandfather, a Spaniard from the West Indies, probably accounted for his light complexion. Struggling to make a living in Philadelphia, in the early 1850 s, his father took a job as a steward on a California packet. Soon after Richard Wesley Greener arrived, he participated in the gold rush. Successful at mining for a time, he took ill, suffered losses, and disappeared. Young Greener and his family never heard from his father again and in time presumed him dead. In the same year that his father went searching for gold, his mother, Mary Ann Le Brune Greener, moved the family to Boston so that her children could find a better opportunity for an education. Richard Greener secured his early education at Broadway Grammar School in Cambridge. When he was fourteen, he left school to help support his family. He worked in a shoe store for two years, a year with a wood engraver, a year as a porter at the Pavilion Hotel on Tremont Street in Boston, and two years as a porter for George Herbert Palmer and A. E. Batchelder.[5]

While at the Pavilion Hotel, Greener aroused the interest of a number of the guests. A Judge Russell gave him access to his library. A Mrs. Maria S. Cook instructed him in French. In 1860, he began working for Palmer and Batchelder. After two years as a porter, Batchelder suggested that he attend Oberlin College to prepare for a Harvard education. While at Oberlin, he made the "fortunate acquaintance" and experienced the "kind attentions" of black attorney John Mercer Langston and his wife, Caroline.[6] Greener left Oberlin in the spring of 1864 in disgust, believing he was unfairly denied the chance to be valedictorian of the precollegiate class.[7] Palmer, an 1864 Harvard graduate, and Batchelder arranged for his enrollment in a college preparatory program at Phillips Academy in Andover, Massachusetts. He was a member of the Philomathean Society, a literary club, and the chief editor of its publication, *The Mirror.* Greener was recognized as a keen debater, a speaker, a writer, and "a good fellow on the playground" and often joined the other students on "escapades" through the "Puritanic town of Andover."[8] He graduated in 1865 and remained active in the school's alumni association throughout his life.[9]

After graduating from Phillips Academy, Greener was accepted into Harvard through an arrangement made by Batchelder, his main benefactor, and the Harvard administration. The administration agreed to admit him in 1865 as an experiment in the education of African Americans. In February of 1866, the president of Harvard wrote to Batchelder, informing him that Greener needed to study with a private tutor. If he could improve upon his performance, he would be allowed to repeat his freshmen year at Harvard's expense.[10] Greener soon began to show the ability that Batchelder had recognized years before. He won second prize for reading as a second-year freshman. As a sophomore, he won the Boylston Prize for Oratory, which included an award of fifty dollars. In his junior year, he coached two white students in oratory, each of whom won prizes.[11] In his senior year, he received the First Bowdoin Prize for a well-researched dissertation on the tenure of land in Ireland; in it he defended the rights of Irish peasants.[12] After extensive preparatory training at Oberlin and Phillips Academy, his presence at Harvard was accepted by the overwhelmingly Republican student body. He was elected a member of various social and literary clubs and contributed articles to the *Harvard Advocate*, including one that attracted the attention of Charles Sumner, the Massachusetts senator and graduate of Harvard. Sumner sought out Greener and the two formed a friendship that lasted until Sumner's death.[13]

Greener also spent time with other African Americans while at Harvard. He befriended Frances Anne Rollin, a free black from Charleston, South Carolina, who left for Boston in 1867 while she was working on a biography of Major Martin R. Delany of South Carolina. Greener read a portion of the manuscript of her biography of Delany, but Rollin thought he was "cynical and apt to discourage instead of acting otherwise." She described Greener as living "in a grand intellectual sphere and [as] accustomed to only perfection." Nonetheless, she enjoyed his visits, at times accompanying him and "lots of her gentlemen friends" on trips to Cambridge for social events such as the "Leap Year Party" on April 13, 1868.[14] For the most part, however, Greener associated with whites while he was at Cambridge.

After winning the Boylston Prize in his sophomore year, Greener acquired a reputation for his oratorical skills. In August of 1869, he was invited to the Institute for Colored Youth in Philadelphia to give a reading that included "selections from popular authors" and an "original oration." The Philadelphia *Evening Bulletin* referred to Greener as "a young colored man of excellent character and of fine ability," noting that "his elocution [was] pronounced by Boston critics to be of no inferior character." He gave the reading in "a full mellow voice, without apparent effort, which evidently pleased his audience, judging from the frequent plaudits." The paper predicted that he would soon acquire the "title of a first-class elocutionist and rhetorician."[15] In April of 1870, just before he graduated from Harvard, Greener accepted an invitation to be the "principal speaker at the Fifteenth Amendment ratification meeting" in Troy, New York. The Troy *Whig* spoke "very highly of his effort," and quoted "freely from" Greener's speech.[16]

He graduated with honors in 1870, prepared to take advantage of new opportunities for African Americans that had arisen out of the Civil War and emancipation.[17] In debt to his white benefactors, he needed to find employment quickly. In September 1870, when Fanny Jackson Coppin, the principal of the Institute for Colored Youth in Philadelphia, and Octavius Catto, the principal of the institute's Boys' High School Department, were away from Philadelphia working with other black schools, Greener was hired as a temporary replacement.[18] Upon the return of Coppin and Catto, he accepted a position as head of the institute's English Department.[19] Coppin, a former classmate of Greener's at Oberlin, was proud to have "a graduate of Harvard College" on her staff.[20] After Catto was shot and killed in a riot on October 10, 1871, Greener was appointed as his replacement.[21] Greener, who was one of the principal speakers at a mass meeting of black Philadelphians protesting the murder of Catto, became increasingly involved in race affairs.[22] In January 1872 he headed a delegation from Philadelphia of African Americans who delivered a petition to Charles Sumner in support of his Civil Rights Bill. Sumner used examples of discrimination, recounted to him by Greener, in a Senate debate on the need for civil rights legislation.[23] The bylaws of the institute required teachers to receive permission from the board of managers to be absent from school. When Greener, who had not asked for permission to leave, returned to Philadelphia, William Evans, a member of the board of managers, informed him of the board's dissatisfaction. Although Greener took the news "in a proper spirit," he realized that his political aspirations would be stifled as long as he remained at the institute.[24]

In March, Greener asked Sumner for help in finding a position in Washington. He told Sumner that he had planned to enter the Harvard Law School in 1870 but could not afford it. He was clerking for Philadelphia attorney Edward Hopper, but did not want to "cram Blackstone and Kent in order to gain admission to the bar." Greener preferred to study "Constitutional law, Political Economy, &c." and "fit [him]self for public life." He had made several contacts in Washington, including that of Chief Justice Salmon Chase of the U.S. Supreme Court.[25] Probably due to Sumner's efforts, along with some assistance from Charlotte Forten, a fellow Philadelphia native and the future wife of Francis J. Grimké, in December 1872 Greener was appointed principal of the Preparatory School for black children in Washington. At a time when the black press regarded African American schools inferior to white schools, the Preparatory School was an exception.[26]

Greener's connections with black freemasons in Philadelphia also facilitated his move to Washington. He was initiated, passed, and raised in Philadelphia in 1872. In the late 1860s and early 1870s, the Grand Lodge of Free and Accepted Ancient Masons of the District of Columbia occupied "the most important position of any of our [black] Grand Lodges in the United States."

Blacks seeking "position and employment in Government" were usually "members of this Fraternity, and upon their arrival in Washington," sought out "their brethren in the Fraternity." In Washington, Greener served in the Knight Templars and the Ancient Accepted Scottish Rite. He worked with John F. Cook, the Grand Master of Free and Accepted Ancient Masons of the District of Columbia and a prominent black attorney in the U.S. capital, to help unify the various Masonic bodies in the District of Columbia.[27]

Charles Sumner often brought foreign dignitaries to the Preparatory School during Greener's tenure. On one such visit, Sumner brought the Marquis de Chambrun, a Frenchman who was working on a study of constitutional law in the United States, to hear recitations by some of Greener's pupils. Greener called on fourteen-year-old Clement G. Morgan, who later distinguished himself as the first black to be a class-day orator at Harvard, to recite Lincoln's Gettysburg Address. When Morgan finished, Sumner sprang to his feet and said, "My dear Professor Greener, I was at Gettysburg and heard Mr. Lincoln deliver that wonderful address, and let me assure you he did not do it better!"[28] Although Greener was "in the fullest confidence of the parents of children under his charge," for unknown reasons he was dismissed from his position as principal in July of 1873. A committee of African Americans met at the Union League hall in Washington to protest, but Greener's job could not be salvaged.[29] Greener worked briefly as an associate editor of the *New National Era*, a Washington weekly edited by Frederick Douglass and others.[30] For a speech he gave at the Celebration of the Emancipation in the District of Columbia, he was named orator of the day and compared to Sumner.[31] In September he accepted a position in the office of the district attorney and planned to enter law school.[32]

On October 10, 1873, Greener received a letter from the University of South Carolina asking if he would accept a professorship of modern languages and literature. Before Greener could reply to the query, the board of trustees elected him professor of moral and mental philosophy, sacred literature, and evidences of Christianity. James A. Bowley, a former school teacher in Baltimore who had been elected a state representative and member of the board of trustees, had known Greener for some time and had nominated him for the position. More than likely, Charles Sumner, who corresponded with Republican leaders in South Carolina, gave Greener a favorable recommendation. J. K. Jillson, the secretary of the board of trustees, sent him a letter on October 28 informing him of the decision and asking for a quick response.[33]

Greener had reservations about leaving Washington. Sumner and other prominent friends in Washington and South Carolina urged him to accept. He decided to take the offer and began his duties in late November of 1873. His reluctance to accept the professorship is understandable when seen in the light of his background. His family had been living free in the North for generations.

He was afforded opportunities from childhood through college to receive an education. Having lived in Cambridge from the time he was ten years old, Greener was somewhat insulated from problems others of his race were experiencing. Furthermore, his future in Washington looked promising. A professorship at the University of South Carolina, which was being overhauled by the radical faction of the state's Republican Party, was not as inviting to Greener as it was to black leaders in the South and white sympathizers in the North.[34]

The situation Greener encountered when he arrived at the university was a turbulent one. Five years of uneasy cooperation between the Republican state leadership and the antebellum administration and faculty had come to an end a few months before. In February of 1873, a new board of trustees was elected, consisting of four black and three white Republicans.[35] The university was opened to black students in July. Conservative whites proclaimed the university dead and encouraged white students to go to other institutions.[36] Franklin J. Moses, the governor of South Carolina, and Daniel Chamberlain, the state attorney general who was elected governor in 1874, were both on the board of trustees. The fate of the radical university was directly linked to state politics. In his inaugural address in December 1873, Moses specifically mentioned the hiring of Greener to the Republican-controlled legislature: "For the first time in the history of South Carolina one of the literary chairs in her highest institution of learning is worthily and acceptably filled by a colored Professor." The hire of an African American "gentleman of varied attainments, cultivated and refined, and an honored graduate of grand old Harvard," was a sound decision for academic and political reasons.[37]

Greener made the most of the opportunity. He worked with other faculty members to reorganize the curriculum. The previous curriculum had been designed along the lines of the system used at the University of Virginia. Although it radically departed from the Virginia system's stress on the classics, the curriculum had allowed students to choose among several courses of study. The faculty, based on their experiences at elite northern schools such as Harvard and Yale, instituted two definite courses of study requiring that students be well versed in the classics. The first was a classical course leading to an A.B. degree. The second was a philosophic and scientific course leading to a Ph.B.[38]

On December 6, 1873, Greener was appointed to a committee that reestablished the debating societies. Along with Benjamin Babbit, the chairman of the faculty, he organized the "junior exhibition," in which members of the class gave orations on March 11, 1874, ironically, on the same day that Charles Sumner died. In addition to instructing in philosophy, Latin, Greek, and law, Greener taught in the preparatory school, which was especially important because most of the students enrolling at the university could pass English and mathematics exams, but had trouble with Latin and Greek. In February of 1874 the state legislature provided scholarship money for 124 new students. With only about 30 students enrolled, the faculty looked forward to bringing in the scholarship winners. Greener chaired the committee that prepared questions for their entrance exams. When most of the new students did not pass, he urged the faculty to institute a sub-freshman class. They decided that "all those who have been recommended to the faculty by the State Board of Examiners for scholarships, and who did not qualify for the freshman class, be assigned to the sub-freshman class."[39]

Although this measure did raise enrollment to 166 by 1875, 79 students were in the preparatory school with 24 in the sub-freshman and 29 in the freshman class. There were only two seniors, four juniors, and five sophomores. J. K. Jillson, the state superintendent of education and secretary of the board of trustees, charged in his annual report that the administration of the act was a "miserable farce" and had brought in a "motley crowd of youngsters." He claimed that the new students had been matriculated even though they "were not entitled, either by reason of poverty, merit, or scholarly attainments."[40] The chairman of the faculty, B. B. Babbitt, claimed that Jillson had only been to two classes at the university, had not been present at a single examination, nor, as far as the faculty knew, had he reviewed the semiannual examination questions or the papers presented in reply.[41]

Jillson's attack on the university was designed to raise entrance requirements and defuse criticism from the conservative white press. He did not believe the sub-freshman class should be continued. Greener, who had benefited from an extra year of freshman study at Harvard, supported it. In a spirited defense of the sub-freshman class, Greener reported that teaching these students was "at once a light duty and a source of gratification, performed, it is true, at an expense of leisure for other studies and more attention to the advanced classes but one that ha[d] amply recompensed [him] in the progress of the students." He took the liberty of inviting "those members of the Freshman Modern, and such students of the Preparatory School, as [he] deemed fitted." These students recited in Latin and Greek five times per week, including "the *Orations of Cicero* and the *Aeneid of Virgil*." According to Greener, "Not only the deep interest of the students and their friendly rivalry; but the daily recitations and the actual work done in the examinations give sufficient, indubitable evidence of the good already accomplished by the organization" of the sub-freshman class. Furthermore, "These young men, by their studious habits and gentlemanly behavior, have proved themselves worthy of the bounty of the State."[42]

Greener argued that the State Board of Examiners was justified in retaining them at the university, "rather than to dismiss them to the several Counties where absolutely no opportunity for higher instruction lay open to them." Greener cited the grades of these students to further justify the need to keep them at the university. Of the nearly forty members of the sub-freshman class, "twenty attained an average of seventy per cent or over, and ten reached eighty-five per cent or over." He invited the board of trustees to judge from the questions he asked whether or not they felt the examinations were rigid.[43] Jillson, however, convinced the board of trustees to discontinue the sub-freshman class in June of 1875. The faculty felt "constrained to be very easy on terms of admission to the Freshman class" as they struggled to raise the university's standards without losing large numbers of students.[44]

After the death of Charles Sumner in March of 1874, Greener was asked by the other members of the faculty to give an oration in honor of his deceased friend at the "Public Day," where commencement exercises were held on June 19, 1874. Greener spoke of the time he had spent at Sumner's bedside during the senator's last days, assuring him of the support of black South Carolinians for the Civil Rights Bill. He recounted a conversation in which Sumner told him, "I am in favor of Imperialism—the IMPERIALISM OF HUMAN RIGHTS; and he who accepts less than this is the enemy of his country."[45] More importantly, with government officials, legislators, and the board of trustees in attendance, Greener told the audience, "[T]he record of the school year, just finished, furnishes much material for reflection, and presents many causes for congratulations to the Legislature, the board of trustees and the friends of impartial and universal education throughout the State." He credited Sumner with leaving a legacy of a life of toil and usefulness in public affairs. Greener said that he and his colleagues at the university, as educators and scholars, were "legatees, executors and promoters of that policy of Equality in Matters of Education to whose successful vindication he [Sumner] devoted his rising talent."[46]

Greener cited the history of South Carolina College written by Maximilian La Borde, who resigned from the university in anguish only days before Greener was hired, in defense of the current state of affairs. In his history, LaBorde applauded the state leaders, who in 1801 established a college in Columbia that would "'contribute greatly to the prosperity of society.'" Moreover, "'the establishment of a College in the central part of the State, where all its youth may be educated, will highly promote the instruction, the good order and the harmony of the whole community.'" According to Greener, "for the first time in the history of the college," the board of trustees had brought the university "back to the original design of the founders, in harmony with the theory of education abroad and the foremost institutions of our country." He told the audience that they "stood at the summit of the educational power of the State, resting upon the common school system, firmly impressed with the importance of the work we have to do and certain of its success." He believed that the work to be done would "redound to the lasting welfare of every true citizen, and [would] reflect credit upon the Trustees of the University."[47]

Since Greener had only been at the university for eight months, this speech signified a sort of "coming out party" for him. With the full attention of the governor, legislators, and other state officials, not to mention the students he worked with tirelessly, he demonstrated his talent and refinement as a public speaker. Not surprisingly, other faculty members requested a copy of the address for publication.[48] To those radical Republicans who supported the effort to integrate the university, Greener was an example of what they hoped it could do for its black students.

Equally important to his experience in the state and his future as an African American leader was Greener's marriage to Genevieve Ida Fleet, the daughter of music teacher J. H. Fleet of Washington, D.C., in September of 1874. The Fleets were a well-known elite black family in Washington. The 1845 wedding of Genevieve Fleet's parents was recorded in a registry of *Blacks in the Marriage Records of the District of Columbia.* The Fleet family was listed in the 1850 Washington census as mulattoes. Greener, whose family had always had to struggle to pay for the necessities of life, had come a long way. His marriage to Fleet testified to his rising stature in the African American community. She moved into the Lieber House, where Greener lived on campus at the university.

In February of 1875 Greener sent a letter to the Boston *Commonwealth* in which he commented on Governor Chamberlain's administration and the Republican Party in South Carolina. Franklin J. Moses, Chamberlain's predecessor, had been maligned in the press for corruption that dated back to previous administrations. During Chamberlain's inaugural address, Greener noticed that when the governor called for reform "the applause from the Democratic side was emphatic and hearty." The radical Republicans feared "that 'reform,'" meant "to take power from the hands of the negro." Although a radical himself, Greener believed that Chamberlain was committed to preserving "impartial liberty, equal and exact justice."[49]

During his tenure at the university, Greener was active as a speaker around the state, as well as a participant in community affairs in Columbia. In addition to his oration on Charles Sumner, in March of 1874 he gave a lecture entitled "The Public Life and Political Writings of John Milton" at a meeting in Charleston.[50] In support of the ambitious common school system established by the state during Reconstruction, he spoke at a teachers' meeting in Chester in April of that year.[51] He was a speaker at a local church's lecture series in March of 1875.[52] He delivered a Masonic address at the laying of the cornerstone of Calvary Baptist Church in Columbia in December.[53] He gave an oration at the celebration of St. John the Baptist in June of 1876 at Savannah, Georgia.[54] On April 4, 1876, he spoke at Winnsboro, South Carolina.[55] He served on the Richland County Board of Health from 1875 to 1876 and was appointed by the general assembly in 1875 to serve on a commission charged with revising the state's common school system. In April of 1876 he "presided at the meeting of citizens irrespective of party which nominated and afterward secured the election of Mayor John Agnew, who," according to Greener, "proved to be the best mayor of the city since Reconstruction."[56] The local papers also kept track of Greener's activities. When his carriage wrecked in Washington, D.C., in August of 1876, for example, the Republican paper in Columbia printed an account of the incident, reporting that Greener and his wife "were both slightly injured."[57]

A favorite of the student body for his attention to the sub-freshman class and preparatory school, Greener often used his influence to smooth over discipline problems in other professors' classes. He worked with professors Henry J. Fox and T. N. Roberts, who found the students difficult to handle, to instill "manners, discipline, and a sense of industry" in their studies.[58] When the financial situation at the university worsened in late 1875 and 1876, money for scholarships was not reaching students. Greener received letters from students eager to come to the university on such scholarships. Many of his most promising students returned home to teach in common schools while they waited to see if the scholarship money would be paid. One student told him, "I am very anxious to return to school, but unless I am assured that the scholarship will be paid . . . I must remain until circumstances assume a brighter aspect."[59]

Although many whites deplored the presence of a black faculty member, they had no reason to complain about the quality of Greener's work. In 1875 and 1876, he was teaching metaphysics, Latin, Greek, and constitutional history.[60] He earned a law degree from the university in December of 1876.[61] When Erastus Everson, the school's librarian, left the university in 1875, Greener filled in until a permanent replacement could be found. For six months, Greener was left in charge of a library recognized as one of the best in the South. He continued the work of Everson in cataloging the twenty-seven thousand books in the library collection and sent a report of its contents to the U.S. Bureau of Education. The *Charleston News and Courier* praised his work at the university, especially his cataloging methods and the improvements he made to the interior of the library building.[62] In 1875, he was the first African American elected to the American Philological Association.[63] He was admitted to practice law in the South Carolina Supreme Court on December 20, 1876.[64] Despite these accomplishments, Greener knew his career as a college professor at the University of South Carolina would be over if the Democrats won the election in 1876.

On a personal level, Greener's wife, Genevieve, gave birth to their first child, Horace Kempton, on September 21, 1875. The Lieber House, like many of the buildings on campus, had sustained damage during the Civil War. Greener had repeatedly asked the board of trustees for funds he needed to make repairs to the building. In October of 1875, Greener sent a letter to the board of trustees, imploring them to provide him with the funds. He called the board's attention to the claim of $150, "which I have presented nearly a year ago for repairs of the house now occupied by me—repairs which I have been compelled to make at my own expense because they had not been made when I first took possession." He explained, "It would really conduce to the health as well as comfort of my family, if the board would settle the claim in time to have me make urgent and necessary repairs before the approach of winter." The board did not grant the request, leaving Greener and his family to do the best they could.[65] Greener must have wondered if the board's refusal to help him with the repairs played a part in the death of his infant son on May 11, 1876.[66]

Republicans continued to fight among themselves in 1875 and 1876. Governor Chamberlain began working with Democrats to build a political alliance. In 1875 he removed Republican officeholders in several counties and replaced them with Democrats. Francis W. Dawson, a Democrat and editor of the *News and Courier,* became a key advisor to Chamberlain on appointments and political strategy. Many of Chamberlain's fellow Republicans believed that he would do anything to gain the support of Democrats. Chamberlain claimed he was only trying to put a stop to corruption in the state government.[67] On November 23, 1875, in his annual message, Chamberlain told legislators that state expenditures "should be greatly reduced."[68] On January 29, 1876, in a *News and Courier* column, he proposed cutting the appropriation for the university from $43,000 to $30,000 and replacing professors with northern schoolteachers.[69] On February 2, he told the House Committee of Ways and Means that "keeping the hollow shell of an ancient institution" should give way to a "practical high school." Greener and his colleagues knew the university would be closed if the Democrats won the November election. With Chamberlain proposing to turn it into a "practical high school," they would have to count on a Republican majority in the house and senate to keep their jobs.[70]

The governor's efforts to build a coalition of Democrats and Republicans were successful through the first half of 1876. By July, the Republican Party had split over Chamberlain's strategy.[71] The Hamburg massacre on July 8, in which several blacks and one white man were killed in an armed confrontation between white civilians and black militiamen, polarized the Democratic and Republican parties. Republican leaders across the state closed ranks, believing that Democrats aimed to regain control of state politics by force and intimidation. The Democratic leaders saw the arraignment of several whites who had participated in the riot as a chance to take the party on a more conservative course in the upcoming election.[72] They seized the initiative and nominated Confederate war hero General Wade Hampton for governor. The *News and Courier,* which had supported Chamberlain through July of 1876, endorsed Hampton on August 10.[73]

The Republican Party was left with little time to rebuild its support for Chamberlain. Greener, who unsuccessfully sought the Republican nomination for state superintendent of education, was an active political speaker on behalf of Republicans.[74] In one instance he was invited to address a Democratic ward meeting.[75] Republican Party leaders asked Greener to speak at campaign rallies in the Third Congressional District. Although he had "forcefully opposed" the nomination of Chamberlain and supported House Speaker Robert Brown Elliott's failed attempt to select an alternative candidate at the Republican State Convention of 1876, Greener agreed to speak on behalf of the Republican ticket at Newberry, Abbeville, Anderson, Walhalla, Greenville, Pickens, Laurens, Columbia, and Lexington.[76]

At every stop along the way Greener and his colleagues were harassed by Democrats and their army of mounted men known as "Red Shirts." Once the schedule for the rallies was published by state newspapers, the Democratic Party organized in force to challenge Republican speakers. The Democrats claimed that a "joint discussion" had been arranged by local party leaders. In some cases, such as the rally in Newberry, local Republican leaders agreed to a "joint discussion" to avoid trouble. When Republican speakers tried to address the crowd, they were bombarded with cries of "that was a damn radical lie." Greener was repeatedly called a "God-damned nigger" by some Red Shirts. Lewis Cass Carpenter, a fellow speaker who testified before the House Select Committee on the Recent Election in South Carolina on December 26, 1876, recalled that Greener "persevered and tried to talk for, I should think, thirty or forty minutes." Standing on the same platform, he could not hear Greener's speech "because of the noise and commotion below." After his speech, Democrats surrounded Greener on the platform. Soon he realized that his colleagues had fled for fear that a riot would break out. Two of his university students, who lived in Newberry, finally reached him on the platform and "begged him to go away." He made his way "down the steps amid the jeers of the men on horseback." Democrats accused him of breaking the arrangement they had made with local Republican leaders. If there was such an agreement, local leaders did not tell the incoming speakers. Greener and his colleagues had been told by state party leaders not to engage Democrats in any type of "joint discussion."[77]

The Walhalla rally followed the established pattern of white Democrats riding in with Red Shirts to demand a joint discussion. The "rather opprobrious epithets, jeers, and interruptions" prevented Greener from finishing his speech. While he was speaking, one of the men who had interrupted him went around to the back of the courthouse and drew a pistol to shoot him. Only the quick action of the local postmaster, who had helped arrange the meeting and was inside the building at the time, prevented the gunman from shooting Greener.

The meeting was hastily ended and the Republican speakers made their way to the postmaster's house to spend the night before heading to the Pickens County courthouse. The house was up a hill about a quarter of a mile away. On his way to the house, Greener was separated from his friends by "a large number of the cavalry of democrats." His friends called to him and said that they were "rather fearful for [him] and thought [he] had better not go in among them [the cavalry of democrats]." Greener told his friends that he "was not afraid," but kept his hand in his overcoat pocket on his revolver for the entire time, as he tried "to talk pleasantly." Although the men asked him "a great many pointed questions," Greener finally reached the top of the hill, where his friends were waiting, without incident.[78]

The 1876 election was contested on the state and federal levels. A Republican-controlled house of representatives occupied the statehouse, protected by federal troops, and inaugurated Chamberlain. A Democrat-controlled house inaugurated Wade Hampton and met elsewhere. As part of a compromise, which gave the state's electoral votes to Rutherford B. Hayes in the presidential election, federal troops were ordered to withdraw from South Carolina on April 10, 1877. On that same day, Chamberlain abdicated and several black legislators resigned, leaving Wade Hampton as governor with the Democrats in control of the legislature.[79] Although Greener gave testimony in the official inquiry into election misconduct, he had to resign himself to the fact that his days as a professor at the University of South Carolina were over. The university was closed on June 7, 1877, by a joint resolution of the state legislature. A special commission was set up to plan for an all-white university and a separate school for African Americans.[80] The professors were allowed to resign "with no damage to their reputations."[81]

Greener had accomplished a great deal during his tenure at the university. He was especially proud of Johnson Chestnut Whittaker, a scholarship student who enrolled in the fall of 1874. After taking the entrance exam in July of 1874, Whittaker was found insufficiently prepared and placed in the sub-freshman class.[82] Whittaker worked diligently and within a few months was placed in the full classical course. By 1875 he ranked at the head of his class, keeping an 86 percent average in 1875 and 1876 and scoring 100 percent on his January 1875 examinations. In the spring of 1876, Greener was asked to recommend the student most capable of receiving an appointment to the U.S. Military Academy at West Point. Congressman Solomon Lafayette Hoge, acting on Greener's recommendation, nominated Whittaker for the appointment. With Greener's help, Whittaker passed the entrance exam and entered West Point in the fall of 1876.[83]

Greener left South Carolina in the spring of 1877 a much different man than he was in 1873. He had a law degree that he thought would advance his career. Returning to Washington, Greener needed to find employment to support his wife and infant daughter, Mary Louise, who was born on January 27, 1877. His tenure in South Carolina was a success from an individual standpoint. It was Wade Hampton's conservative white regime, which opposed black participation in the university, that forced Greener to resign. Greener hoped that in Washington the success or failure of his career would depend more on his individual ability than on the position of his race as a whole in American society. He was bitter about the events that caused him to leave South Carolina. He viewed his tenure at the university as a chance, as he put it when he graduated from Harvard, to "do good."[84] By educating young black and white men at the university, Greener hoped to foster cooperation between the races and elevate the political and economic status of the freedmen. He blamed Rutherford B. Hayes for the loss of South Carolina to the Democrats.[85] His affinity for the state continued, however, even though he recognized that the election battle was lost.

In April 1877, he was admitted to the bar in the District of Columbia. John F. Cook, "the best colored lawyer here," offered Greener a partnership in his law firm. Greener needed some money to get settled in Washington. He asked Isaiah Wears, an old family friend and the leading black Republican in Philadelphia, for financial help. He told Wears that the state of South Carolina still had not paid him a substantial portion of his salary for 1876 and 1877. He also claimed that an act had been passed in 1877, specifically mentioning that the state owed him twenty thousand dollars for land he owned in Columbia. According to Greener, his name was omitted from the act and Johnson Hagood, the Comptroller General of South Carolina, refused to pay the claim.[86] Wears helped Greener and his family get settled in Washington. The family moved into a house next to his mother-in-law's home. Hermione Fleet helped her daughter take care of Mary Louise.

Greener accepted a position as an instructor at the Howard University Law School and in 1879 was elected dean. He instructed "in *Kent's Commentaries on the American Law*" and "lectured on the 'Civil Law.'"[87] Howard University was in financial trouble during his tenure and rendered little financial assistance to the Law Department. Law faculty worked as part-time instructors. Greener worked as a clerk at the U.S. Treasury. Howard's executive committee closed the law school on July 7, 1880, because of low enrollment.[88] Greener continued to work at the U.S. Treasury until February 28, 1882, when he started a law practice.[89]

Greener was active in a number of areas while living in Washington. He was a regular contributor to John Wesley Cromwell's newspaper, the Washington *People's Advocate;* his contributions included a sentimental poem, "Les Hirondellas" (The Swallows), about a captured medieval warrior.[90] He was in high demand as a speaker, not only as a campaign orator, but at the meetings of literary clubs and Masonic gatherings and before student societies at Howard.[91] On January 22, 1879, Greener led a delegation of "prominent colored men," who met with Senator William Windom to discuss ways of helping freedmen migrating from the South to Kansas. With the migration already underway, Windom and the delegation were anxious to get information to the freedmen regarding "the character of the soil, the temperature, and prospects held out to them" in the West.[92] In February, he and Francis Lewis Cardozo, the former treasurer of South Carolina during the 1870s, attended a meeting of black leaders in Cincinnati at which meeting Nashville was agreed upon as the site for the National Convention of Colored Men of the United States held in May.[93]

On April 12, 1879, Greener set up a meeting between Charlton H. Tandy, a black leader in St. Louis who initiated relief efforts for African Americans leaving the South, and President Rutherford B. Hayes. Greener and Tandy subsequently traveled throughout the Northeast soliciting funds for the relief of refugees in St. Louis.[94] Greener served as secretary of the National Emigration Aid Society that raised money to buy land in the West for African Americans who wished to leave the South. In an interview after one of its meetings, Greener, drawing on his study of land tenure in Ireland, offered a "material reason" for the exodus, not just a political one: "He [the black tenant] is completely at the mercy of his landlord and the local storekeeper—the one rents him land at exorbitant rates, attempts to dictate his political opinions and evicts in the most approved Irish landlord fashion if the Negro does not acquiesce."[95] At the Social Science Congress at Saratoga in 1879 he was scheduled to debate the wisdom of the exodus with Frederick Douglass. Douglass pulled out of the commitment three days before the scheduled session but sent his paper with permission that it could be read and published.[96] Greener refuted Douglass's arguments with unexpected courtesy and was praised by the press.[97]

In 1879 he was involved in the establishment of the Black Episcopalian St. Mary's Boys' Academy in Washington and was a member of its board of trustees.[98] He was particularly proud of his membership in a club organized by Frederick Douglass for black Republicans supporting James A. Garfield in the 1880 presidential election.[99] He was president of the South Carolina Republican Club in Washington from 1876 to 1880 and represented the state in the Union League of America from 1875 to 1881.[100] In 1882, he received a doctor of letters degree from Monrovia College in Liberia.[101] He was one of the black leaders who signed a letter asking Madame Selika, a famous black concert and operatic soprano, to give a concert in Washington in May of 1882 before she left to study music in Europe.[102] In July of 1883 he started and served as president of an insurance company, the National Benefit and Relief Association.[103] Booker T. Washington began a friendship with him in the 1880s and brought him to Tuskegee to give the commencement address in 1884.[104]

Although he was popular as a speaker and a noted asset to the Republican Party, Greener's experiences in Washington were not gratifying. For example, he acted as associate counsel to former South Carolina governor Daniel Chamberlain in the defense of Johnson Whittaker, the former University of South Carolina student that Greener had recommended for an appointment to West Point. At six in the morning on April 6, 1880, Whittaker was found tied to his bedstead with his ears mutilated. After interviewing each member of the Cadet Corps, General John M. Schofield, the superintendent of West Point, told reporters that "it had been thoroughly demonstrated that not a cadet had any hand in the matter," and suggested that Whittaker had "committed the act on himself." Whittaker "emphatically and persistently denied this" and "asked for a court of inquiry." Schofield ordered the court of inquiry to begin that Friday morning."[105]

Whittaker asked Greener to come to West Point, calling the affair a "heinous plot engaged in by no others than cadets" and, it seemed, "sanctioned by the authorities."[106] Greener attended the trial with the blessing of Secretary of War Alexander Ramsey. Although the purpose of the court of inquiry was only to ascertain the facts of the situation, Whittaker was the focal point of the investigation. Captain Clinton B. Sears, the court recorder, searched through the personal belongings in Whittaker's room, including his personal letters. Sears concluded that a note of warning sent to Whittaker by his assailants the evening before the attack was written by the black cadet himself. Whittaker's personal letters were admitted into evidence. Sears called several handwriting experts to the stand who testified that Whittaker had written the note. The court of inquiry concluded that Whittaker faked the assault to avoid taking his spring examinations.[107]

After the decision was announced, Greener went back to Washington and met with Secretary of War Ramsey. Ramsey assured him, "[H]e shall be heard in reply to the argument of Recorder Sears before final action is taken on the findings of the court of inquiry." Greener advised Whittaker to demand a leave of absence from West Point and a trial by court–martial. He objected to the general conduct of the court of inquiry, believing Whittaker had been treated as the guilty party from the beginning. On firm legal grounds, Greener argued that Whittaker's personal letters should never have been admitted into evidence.[108] According to the rules of evidence, "Evidence of handwriting, by comparison of hands, is inadmissible," except in those instances "where the writing, acknowledged to be genuine, is already in evidence in the case."[109]

Whittaker took his oral examinations in early June 1880. On June 11, he was examined in philosophy, his problem subject, by Captain Sears and Professor Peter S. Michie, who during the inquiry had written an article for the *North American Review* in which he claimed that Whittaker's story was "far from the

truth."[110] Although observers felt that Whittaker had done well given the circumstances, the Academic Board ruled that he failed the exam. He was suspended pending a decision on whether to proceed with a court–martial.[111]
Greener wrote to Secretary of War Ramsey on August 14 arguing that Whittaker should be "given a furlough and a trial by court–martial."[112] It is unclear
whether President Rutherford B. Hayes saw the letter, but within days he
granted Whittaker a leave of absence, "until further notice."[113] On December
13, Whittaker wrote to Hayes asking the president to grant him an immediate
court–martial or an appointment in some "branch of our country's service."[114]
Hayes, impressed by Whittaker's letter and the advice of Schofield's recently
appointed replacement, General O. O. Howard, ordered the court–martial at a
cabinet meeting on December 20.[115] According to the U.S. statutes in force, the
president had the authority to order a court–martial for army officers but not for
cadets. General Howard should have ordered the court–martial himself, or dismissed Whittaker for academic reasons, as the law required. Greener thought a
precedent had been set for West Point cadets to be considered army officers, but
the president's decision amounted to a procedural mistake. In a case dealing with
the longevity pay of army officers decided in 1881, the U.S. Supreme Court
upheld an 1880 court of claims ruling that cadets were not considered officers or
enlisted men.[116]

Greener assisted Daniel Chamberlain, then an attorney in New York, in
Whittaker's defense. The trial began on February 3, 1881. After initial testimony
from the cadets who had reported the incident, the trial became mired in expert
testimony of the same handwriting samples that had been used in the court of
inquiry. After nearly four months of sparring between attorneys and experts,
Chamberlain called his co-counsel to testify.[117] Greener told the court that he
had recommended Whittaker for the appointment from a list of two hundred
applicants. He also testified that he and a New York *Tribune* reporter had noticed
"thirteen to fifteen big blotches of blood" on the floor when they visited Whittaker's room before the trial. His testimony contradicted the doctor at West
Point who claimed there were only a few drops of blood. On cross-examination,
Judge Advocate of the Court Martial Asa Bird Gardiner challenged it as hearsay
evidence. Greener astutely replied that in a regular trial his testimony would not
be admissible but in a court–martial, "which has more latitude," it should be
admitted.[118]

After a lengthy trial, in which Chamberlain and Greener disagreed over
whether to make race an issue, Whittaker was found guilty of mutilating himself.[119] Before the decision was reached, Greener tried to present a note to the
court signed by himself and Chamberlain protesting the absence, due to health
reasons, of one of the judges, Colonel Henry A. Morrow, who throughout the
trial had been skeptical of the prosecution's argument.[120] An orderly at the door

refused to let Greener take the letter to the judges. Afraid the orderly had not delivered the note, Greener sent a copy of it to D. G. Swaim, the judge advocate general.[121] Swaim then told the newly appointed secretary of war, Robert T. Lincoln, that President Hayes should never have convened the court–martial. Swaim was amazed that the handwriting samples had been admitted into evidence.[122] Benjamin Brewster, the attorney general of the United States, issued an opinion on March 17, 1882, in which he concurred with Swaim that such evidence was inadmissible.[123]

On March 22, nine months after the court–martial decision was reached, President Chester Arthur disapproved the findings, citing the inadmissibility of handwriting samples.[124] Whittaker was found not guilty on a technicality. The day before, Secretary of War Lincoln ordered the adjutant general to "prepare [the] usual order discharging Cadet Whittaker by reason of failure to pass, &c."[125] President Arthur had no authority to overrule Lincoln, nor could he reappoint Whittaker.[126] Although Whittaker avoided the one-year sentence of hard labor prescribed by the court–martial order, he was sent home from the academy. Greener, disgusted with the turn of events, returned to the practice of law disillusioned with Washington politics.

Greener earned the reputation among blacks and whites of being "exceedingly hard to get along with."[127] In the paper he presented before the Social Science Congress in 1879, he severely criticized President Rutherford B. Hayes's southern policy. He was criticized in the *New York Times* for acting "very foolishly" during a lecture he gave in Philadelphia on January 4, 1881. According to reports, Greener "bewailed the fact that the negroes in the South had in recent political campaigns been influenced by white carpet-baggers, who had taken most of the offices and all the plunder, leaving the blacks to take all the odium for their misdeeds." Greener reportedly said that he "regretted that the Negroes had not stolen more than they did, and advised that hereafter they look more to the substantial rewards and less to the tinsel of politics."[128]

Although Greener wrote a letter to the editor of the *New York Times* claiming that his remarks had been neither "adequately or correctly reported," he did not dispute the general tenor of the speech.[129] In a lengthy defense, Greener wrote:

> Those who know me will not accuse me of building up a race wall in politics or otherwise. All my efforts have tended to destroy the one which now exists. Never have I countenanced any attempt to array one race against the other. My solution of all the political and social problems is the union and co-operation of blacks and whites on the basis of manhood and fitness. All I am I owe to privileges and advantages enjoyed from free association with the better class of white people. That

> which has inured to my benefit I certainly would not desire to take away
> from less fortunate members of my race.

Although he was mindful of the debt he owed to white Republicans for the opportunities they had provided him, Greener told the editor:

> My work is to look at politics from the negro's point of view, to see that his rights are maintained, not cringingly, but manfully, to defend him when attacked, and to answer his defamers with the facts which they usually ignore. In doing this I cannot hope to be always considerate of my opponent's feelings, nor even to meet the approval of so good a friend as *The New York Times*. The negro has received so many hard knocks, and experienced so little consideration, charity, or justice from those who criticize him, that he has no quarter to give. For myself, I hope always to be grateful for the great strides that have been made in this country toward real equality and mindful of what the friends of humanity are striving to accomplish against heavy odds, and yet to be as severe as honest in my criticisms and as courageous as accurate in my defense.[130]

In this letter, Greener revealed the precariousness of his situation. On the one hand, his "free association" with some influential whites had furthered his career. On the other hand, his association with whites could, and later in his life did, draw criticism from other African Americans. As a result, Greener defended the rights of blacks more arduously in order to emphasize that, while he appreciated the gains he had made with the help of white friends, his ultimate concern was improving the condition of African Americans. Nonetheless, his strong language angered many whites and made black leaders nervous, especially Frederick Douglass, who considered him a rival with considerable talent.

Despite their differences, Greener and Douglass remained cordial on a personal level. On January 1, 1883, the twentieth anniversary of the issuance of the Emancipation Proclamation, Greener was invited to a banquet to honor Douglass.[131] In April, Greener's temper got the better of him again when his name appeared in newspapers, without his authorization, on the call for a national colored convention to meet in Louisville, Kentucky. Douglass agreed to attend the highly controversial meeting. Greener angrily denounced the convention's organizers as office seekers. According to several newspapers, the intense debate boiled down to generational differences. The Philadelphia *Christian Recorder* urged Greener and other younger men to let the veterans of the antislavery movement have their say.[132] Greener backed down, but once more had angered black leaders such as Douglass with his zest for arguing what he saw as a principle in the public eye. Greener continued to be invited to gatherings of prominent African Americans in Washington, such as the memorial for Wendell Phillips held at the First Congregational Church on February 22, 1884.[133] When Douglass was criticized by some black leaders for marrying a white woman in 1884, Greener was one of the leaders who rushed to his defense.[134] Although he joined other African Americans in campaigning for Republican candidates in the 1884 national elections, Greener had been reduced to playing a minor role in the affairs of his race.[135]

Greener, in his capacity as a "well-known colored lawyer" in Washington, was asked by the New York *Evening Post* in October of 1883 to publish his views on the United States Supreme Court's decision to strike down the Civil Rights Act of 1875. The Civil Rights Act, which Charles Sumner had fought hard to have passed, ensured "That all persons within the jurisdiction of the United States shall be entitled to the full and equal enjoyment of the accommodations, advantages, facilities, and privileges of inns, public conveyances on land or water, theaters, and other places of public amusement." The act was "applicable alike to citizens of every race and color, regardless of any previous condition of servitude." Greener considered the court's opinion "the most startling decision" since the *Dred Scott* decision of 1857, in which the court held, simply put, that a black man had no rights that a white man was bound to respect.[136]

In the summer of 1884, Greener went on an extended tour of the South. He found "more pride of race, more independence of character, greater neatness of dress, a stronger desire to enter business, and increasing thirst for education." Although he "was greatly encouraged as to the future of the race," Greener reported that he "was four times ordered out of 'first class' cars," and "in each case refused to go." William Henry Crogman, a friend of Greener's who spoke to a predominantly white audience at the National Education Association convention in Madison, Wisconsin, on July 16, 1884, offered insight into the reasons for Greener's dilemma where race matters were concerned. Referring to Greener as "very little tinged" and "nearer your color than mine," Crogman asked, "What does society care about a Harvard graduate, if his complexion is tinged with the hated color?"[137]

By 1885 Greener had grown tired of fighting the small battles for his race in Washington. Whites in Washington became increasingly critical of their black neighbors.[138] When he and Robert Terrell were denied admission to the Harvard Club, Greener was criticized by William Calvin Chase's black newspaper, the Washington *Bee*. Chase claimed Greener and Terrell were typical examples of "fair-complexioned, well-educated blacks" who were always in search of a way to abandon their race for white society.[139] Reacting to the deteriorating situation, Greener left to accept an appointment as secretary of the Grant Monument Association in New York City.[140] Timothy Thomas Fortune speculated in an 1892 article that Greener left Washington because, "he may have been soured by the repeated failures he met with from successive Administrations he had helped to elect," or "he may have felt that the race had failed to sustain him as it should have done."[141]

Greener was disappointed with the Republican Party. In an open letter sent to the Associated Press on June 28, 1885, he angrily denounced the Republican Party in Ohio for nominating Joseph Benson Foraker for governor. Foraker had represented an old college friend, William J. White, the Springfield, Ohio, superintendent of schools, in an integration case in 1882. The attorneys who represented Eva Gazzaway, the black girl who had been denied access to school facilities in Springfield, said publicly that Foraker had simply helped an old friend and did not defend White because of any racist sentiment. Still, black leaders in Ohio were divided over whether to support Foraker. In the letter addressed to John P. Green, one of the leaders who opposed Foraker, Greener claimed that the Republican Party had "been courting and inviting defeat for eight years by its arrant cowardice, truculency, and exaltation of little men with big ambition, no heart, and a contempt for principles." He confessed that he had "held some [sl]ack allegiance [to the Republican Party] since 1877, but I have smothered my personal feelings for the sake of the interests of the race, hoping we should get better and truer men nominated to carry our banner in the State and nation." Greener was "disgusted" with the decision to nominate Foraker and said, "I shall pray earnestly for a crushing defeat of the republican ticket."[142]

His disillusionment with the Republican Party was only part of the reason Greener left Washington. His poor financial situation also played a part in his decision to move to New York. His wife, Genevieve, had given birth to three children between 1878 and 1880: Russell Lowell on February 2, 1878, Belle Marion on November 26, 1879, and Ethel Alice on December 20, 1880.[143] By 1885, he had little savings from his meager income and was so busy with outside activities that he was not able to spend much time with his children. After living in New York for several months, he told his old friend Isaiah Wears, "I am like the fellow in the boat, I must pull like the devil or drown, and I have come so near drowning that I am determined to get on dry land, this time if possible." With the $200 per month salary from the Grant Monument Association, Greener was able to pay off "a good amount of debts," and hoped that "by Jan. or Feb. [he would] be in the clear." After seven frustrating years in Washington, he said, "[F]or the first time in my life, I seem to be about something big enough for me to handle."[144]

Ulysses S. Grant had befriended Greener during an 1868 visit to Harvard and later received "delegations of Republicans and colored men" headed by him in 1871, 1873, 1875, and 1876.[145] Greener, who was invited to participate in the

Grant Monument Association due to Mayor William R. Grace's desire to have a representative of the black community involved in the project, became the association's "key administrative official." He ran the office at 146 Broadway, conducted all correspondence and served as the association's principal spokesman. Under his direction a nationwide fund-raising campaign was launched that raised $160,000 of the total $600,000 gathered from some ninety thousand Americans, including significant contributions from African Americans. In addition to his other duties, Greener served as the association's artistic adviser. Greener reviewed the design proposed by John Hemenway Duncan, before it was commissioned by the association, and helped get it approved. A squabble between two factions of the association's members, in which a majority decided that its officers should henceforth work as volunteers, caused Mayor Grace, Hamilton Fish, Seth Low, and Governor of New York Roswell P. Flower to resign late in 1891. With most of his friends gone, Greener was forced out in February 1892 and lost the $200 monthly salary. After six years as secretary of the association, Greener was presented with a "highly complimentary testimonial, signed by General Horace Porter, General Dodge, Elihu Root and James Reed, in behalf of the association." He continued to serve as a trustee until his death in 1922.[146]

Greener was appointed an examiner for the New York City civil service by Mayor Grace in 1885.[147] He worked with the Irish Parliamentary Fund Association to raise $150,000 for Charles Stewart Parnell and the fight for home rule in Ireland. In a "pertinent and interesting" speech on March 1, 1886, before the association, Greener told the members that "his travels in and study of Ireland had resulted in making him not only a pro-Irishman, but one of the most radical of Irishmen."[148] During the late 1880s, his family lost contact with African Americans. On February 22, 1886, Genevieve gave birth to another daughter, Theodora Genevieve. On August 10, 1887, she gave birth to a son, Charles Woodson, who died on November 11 of that year. Despite the death of another son in infancy, Greener embarked on a literary career and seemed happy to be freed from the burden of his race. He joined the Commonwealth Club of New York City; the club included among its members Theodore Roosevelt and Elihu Root. According to its constitution, the Commonwealth Club was "committed to the principles of Civil Service Reform" and asserted "the right of individual action in politics." The main activity of the club was "the discussion of political and economic questions."[149] In 1889, probably because of the "Tammany Crowd," Greener was removed from the civil service board. His work for the Grant Monument Association ended with his resignation in 1892. His family was hard pressed to make ends meet.[150]

Greener sent a letter to Booker T. Washington on May 26, 1894, rekindling their old relationship. He told Washington, "I am doing my work in my

152 Michael Robert Mounter

own way, since there is no chance for me to do it in the way I should prefer for the race."[151] This remark revealed a bitterness that had been building in Greener since his days in South Carolina. His second attempt at a career in Washington had confirmed his belief that most white Republicans would do only what was necessary to get a majority of black votes in an election year. With the exception of an article published in 1894, he had not been successful as a writer.[152] This lack of success in literary pursuits did not mean that Greener was a subpar writer. In an address delivered at the First Conference of Colored Women of the United States in 1895, Victoria Earle Matthews singled out her "friend, Professor Greener," as "a metaphysician, logician, orator, and prize essayist" who "holds an undisputed position in the annals of our literature second to none." Matthews gave Greener special praise for an article he wrote in 1880 entitled "The Intellectual Position of the Negro." Matthews noted that Greener's article, written in response to James Parton's "Antipathy to the Negro," in which Parton argued that the "cruelest stroke ever dealt the negro" was "hurling him all unprepared into politics," had been cited in publications in both the United States and England.[153]

From 1892 to 1895, Greener earned a living as a tutor in New York City. Still, he struggled to support his wife and five children. He remained active in politics, campaigning for Republicans in 1892 and 1894 in New York, New Jersey, and Connecticut. In 1894 he was an alternate to the Republican State Convention in New York. In that same year, he served as a delegate to the American Unitarian Association meeting in Saratoga, New York, and to the American Missionary Association, of which he was a life member, at Lowell, Massachusetts.[154]

As a freelance reporter, Greener attended the First National Conference of Colored Women, which convened on July 29, 1895. The conference was called by Josephine St. Pierre Ruffin, a member of the largely white New England Women's Club and founder of the black Women's Era Club, in response to a letter, written by John Jacks, a newspaper editor and president of the Missouri Historical Association, in which Jacks defended the white South and maligned black women for their "immorality."[155] In his account of the meeting, Greener praised African American women for successfully planning and carrying through a convention "with all the dignity, decorum and thorough knowledge of all that is essential in parliamentary law." In praising the delegates, he concluded, "Here was seen again on this arena that combination of qualities so rare in the world in man or woman."[156]

Greener echoed the sentiments of many of the women present, women who believed that black men had failed to make progress on civil rights issues in the late nineteenth century. He noted that "there was not one hastily read paper" and that "it was here that the women appeared in healthy contrast with some of

the 'distinguished men' of their race whom they courteously invited to speak."
According to Greener, "with two exceptions the men were painfully at sea, evidently conscious of the crudity of their platitudenous [*sic*] advice and dogmatis-
ing [*sic*] in the presence of well-shod and practical enthusiasts." Other reporters
were equally impressed by how professionally the conference was run. One
reporter remarked to Greener, "'I'll tell you frankly they [black women] were
more orderly in their crudity than the better trained white women'" and "'were
more deferential in manner to each other and there was less clashing.'" The
reporter recognized them as "'natural tacticians'" who "'were superior to any
similar organization I have attended.'" They gained the reporter's respect
because "they spent no time on trifles and would allow no long discussions of
grievances but addressed themselves vigorously to the points under discussion,
the work cut out for them with admirable directness and celerity."[157]

Greener left the conference with a renewed hope for the prospects of
African Americans. His long absence from race affairs, while he lived in New
York City, was due in part to his disgust with the failure of other black men to
present a united front in the struggle for civil rights. The delegates of the
National Conference of Colored Women had convinced him, with their leadership skills and professionalism, that black women could initiate such a united
effort on the part of the race to secure civil rights. He shared the black women's
lack of confidence in their male counterparts and recognized what Deborah
Gray White identified, in her recent book, *Too Heavy a Load*, "the sum of their
[black women's] equation was the superiority of women in matters of the moral
welfare of black people, and the equality of black men and women in everything
else."[158]

In August of 1895, Greener was asked to "sketch a plan of work, and the
points of an address to the country, and the resolutions" for the National Conference of Colored Men of 1895. Greener sent a letter, along with the official
call for the convention, to John Edward Bruce, a New York friend and leading
black journalist. In the letter, he thanked Bruce for writing an editorial praising
the work he had done for the conference. Greener told Bruce, "[Y]ours is the
first unstinted, not fulsome, fully appreciative praise, I have received from any
colored journalist, for years, and I shall not forget it." He also revealed his frustration at having lost touch with other African Americans: "When other
Negroes passed by my office in Broadway, and went on, saying I didn't wish to
see them, you, and one or two others dared to come and see me, and discover
for themselves whether I had changed." He was anxious to get back into politics
and to take a more active role in the affairs of his race. He had "a message to
deliver, and the Convention and the people of the country will hear from me,
and henceforth I shall be in the political fight."[159]

The National Conference of Colored Men met on December 13, 1895, in

Detroit. Greener stayed with D. Augustus Straker, a leading black attorney in Detroit and former friend of his in South Carolina during Reconstruction. Straker was named president of the National Federation of Colored Men, the organization formed at the conference, but Greener was the pivotal leader. He made sure that the "Women element," which included First National Conference of Colored Women delegates Margaret Murray Washington, Josephine Ruffin, and Victoria Earle Matthews, was "fully and equally recognized." Greener and Straker endured a long and hard fight on that issue, but managed to have the resolution approved.[160] The recognition of Washington, Ruffin, and Matthews revealed the underlying idea of Greener's plans for the men's conference. Taking his cue from the women's conference he had attended a few months before, he was trying to forge a national association of black men that would complement the burgeoning National Association of Colored Women's Clubs. By recognizing these women at the men's conference, he hoped to build a coalition of black men and women. Such a coalition, he believed, would bring more pressure to bear on the Republican Party to go on record as opposing lynchings in the South and would help a host of other issues pertinent to African Americans.

Greener's address was approved by the conference and submitted to the U.S. Senate.[161] The Detroit *Tribune* contrasted the address with Booker T. Washington's Atlanta speech a few months earlier. In the conference address, which was drafted by Greener, the delegates told Congress and the people of the United States, "We do not acquiesce in the dictum that we must trust to time and to the pleasure or disposition of our enemies to grant rights." They aimed "to take on a new form and assume a new attitude among the citizens of this nation," one "which shall resent alike the assumption of any inferiority of our person or any subordination of our claims for rights—and to oppose even the presumption of a denial of any of our privileges." The delegates were clearly, as Herbert Aptheker described them, "opposed to the [Booker T.] Washington policy" and their statement was "in many ways a precursor of the DuBois-founded Niagara Movement to appear a decade later." As Greener put it, after reading the *Tribune* article, "While I do not court antagonism, I cannot skirt the issue."[162]

The National Federation of Colored Men, like the conference itself, was not "national" in the composition of its membership. The vast majority of the delegates were from states such as New York, Michigan, Indiana, Illinois, Minnesota, and Ohio. With Bruce's support, Greener hoped the federation would become national in scope.[163] Only days after the conference had ended, Greener echoed the sentiments of the delegates in a speech entitled "The New Rebellion in South Carolina" at Quinn Hall in Chicago. He reportedly blamed the conservatives of the state "for their squeamishness and timidity in the face of [Benjamin] Tillman's question, 'Will you make common cause with the negroes?'"[164]

On December 20, upon the request of the Boston City Government, Greener spoke in Faneuil Hall, before the city authorities, on the life of Frederick Douglass.[165] By January of 1896, Greener was already losing some interest in the federation. He was still anxious to do the work required of him as the vice president of the northeastern section, but he realized that the federation was getting little publicity. Furthermore, he accepted a job as president, and the only African American employee, of the General Development Company, which mined for gold in Nova Scotia.[166] The venture failed within months and left Greener and his family further in debt.

In the summer of 1896 the Republican National Committee asked him to campaign for their presidential candidate, William McKinley, and take charge of the "department of campaign literature in the colored men's bureau at Chicago."[167] Perhaps the notoriety of being one of the leaders of the 1895 National Conference of Colored Men, along with his lifelong work for the Republican Party, gave Greener the inside track to this job. The National Republican Executive Committee did meet with Straker, Greener, and other members of the National Federation of Colored Men at the June 1896 Republican nominating convention. After the meeting, Straker reported that the Republican Party "unqualifiedly expressed its condemnation of lynching."[168] Greener hoped that through his position he could galvanize support within the party to work for civil rights for black Americans. In any event, he was an asset to the Republicans, as he had been in previous election campaigns. He spoke to audiences in Missouri, Indiana, Illinois, Kentucky, and Tennessee. The crowning achievement of his speaking tour was earned at the National Baptist Convention in Saint Louis, where he "had McKinley & Hobart endorsed by a body representing 1,680,000 Negroes!"[169]

For his efforts, he was nominated by the Republican National Committee for a position in the foreign service. After pursuing a multitude of careers, Greener and his family were steeped in debt. He succumbed to the reality that he would need the support of Booker T. Washington. Greener asked Washington "to say a good word for [him]" at a meeting with President William McKinley in April of 1897.[170] On May 13, 1897, McKinley sent the endorsement papers to the State Department.[171] In January of 1898 President McKinley appointed Greener to the post of consul in Bombay, India. After learning that a severe epidemic of the plague had broken out in Bombay, he declined the appointment. While on indefinite delay from that appointment, he unsuccessfully sought a naval appointment in the Spanish-American War. In June of 1898, he accepted an appointment as consul in Vladivostok, Russia.[172]

Greener's eagerness to accept the appointment can be understood by taking into account his thought on the place of African Americans in society. He had always been an advocate for full civil rights for African Americans and noted the need for leaders of the race. Greener, however, did not want to become an African American leader. In the early 1880s his Harvard ties had been strengthened, while his ties to African Americans were dissolving amidst his frustration with the Republican Party and Washington politics. In the early 1880s, in a speech at the Harvard Club in New York, he applauded "Harvard's impartiality" toward race, describing his alma mater as "the prototype of that ideal America."[173] Ever since his tenure at the University of South Carolina had ended, Greener had looked for a place where he could continue his career in an environment that resembled his Harvard College days. After seven years in Washington and twelve years in New York, he had still not found such a place. Responding to criticism from Thomas McCants Stewart, an attorney and former student of Greener's at the University of South Carolina, Greener wrote in 1896, "I have never aspired to be a leader" and "I am only ambitious to be a full fledged American citizen, demanding all my rights at all times and yielding none of them."[174] He was confident that the appointment in Vladivostok would give him the opportunity to show his abilities as an individual without being hindered by the racial divisions in American society.

One of his contemporaries could not understand why Greener, who was thought by some members of his race to be the most brilliant of possible African American leaders, did not take on the challenge of being a national spokesman for their rights.[175] Even Greener's friends wondered why the government did not call his new post a sentence rather than an appointment.[176] Some African Americans leveled accusations of his "passing" in New York when the American Negro Academy elected new members on March 5, 1897. Alexander Crummell, a venerable black minister who led a group that blocked Greener's membership, charged, "[F]or years he has been a white man in New York and turned his back upon all his colored acquaintance." Crummell objected to Greener "coming back to our ranks, and then getting on my Negro shoulders, to hoist himself, as a Negro, into some political office." Greener claimed that Crummell opposed admitting any mulattoes to the academy. The confrontation with Crummell only served to strengthen Greener's desire to take the diplomatic appointment.[177]

Furthermore, Greener and his wife had separated by the time Greener was appointed to the consular post. Between his activities with the National Federation of Colored Men and his work for the Republican Party, Greener had spent little time with his family in 1896 and 1897. He and Genevieve separated at some point in late 1896 or early 1897. The New York City street directories until 1897 list Richard T. Greener as a lawyer with an office at 27 Chambers Street and a home at 29 West Ninety-ninth Street. In the 1897–98 directory, he is listed as living at the office address, while Genevieve I. Greener is listed at 29 West Ninety-ninth Street.[178] During 1897 and 1898, Greener spent most of his time with friends in Washington, where he made several public speeches.[179] In the first half of 1898, while waiting for the foreign service appointment, Greener was driven out of the dialogue on race affairs. When Greener announced his candidacy for the post of superintendent of the colored schools in Washington in the spring of 1898, W. Calvin Chase, in a Washington *Bee* editorial, advised him "to take his baggage and go to Russia."[180] He blamed his wife's social interaction with whites in New York City as the reason for his loss of standing in the black community.[181] He wrote to Isaiah Wears from Vladivostok in early January 1899, "She has ample grounds now, on which to secure a divorce and I should interpose no objections." He promised to support his children financially, but was glad to be leaving the tension of a bad marriage behind.[182]

While preparing to leave, Greener learned that the Russian government did not accept consuls in Vladivostok. His rank was reduced to commercial agent, which the Russians accepted. He proceeded to Seattle to catch a steamer headed for Japan.[183] He arrived in Japan in late August and toured nearly twelve hundred miles of the Japanese mainland in about a month's time, as he put it, "eating, sleeping and living, á la japonaise, all the time."[184] A local paper in Vladivostok noted Greener's presence on December 23, 1898: "for the first time in our city, and, in fact, in all of Siberia, the National American flag was raised over the house of the new American commercial agent, Mr. Greener."[185] He quickly settled into his new surroundings, learning the Russian language well enough to translate Alexander Pushkin's poem "My Portrait."[186] On July 1, 1900, Greener sent the first report from a U.S. official of Russian troops preparing to invade Manchuria and prevent the spread of the Boxer Rebellion to that province. The Chinese commercial agent asked Greener to serve as secretary of a committee raising funds for victims of the war in China. While his colleague was away from the city late in 1900, Greener represented Chinese interests. For his efforts, he was awarded the Order of the Double Dragon by the Chinese government in 1902.[187]

After three years of service, Greener had the support of Americans in Vladivostok, a good relationship with Russian authorities, and strong ties with the influential Chinese commercial agent. He worked with other U.S. officials in East Asia to ensure that the wave of American travelers there in the late 1890s and early 1900s was given all of the information necessary to guide themselves on tours of Siberia. Nicholas Senn, the surgeon general of Illinois who toured Russia and East Asia in 1901, praised Greener's service: "It is fortunate that our country is represented by such a loyal, capable, enthusiastic, and obliging official as Mr. Greener."[188] It seemed to Greener that only white Americans at home found his race important. He understood that his appointment was considered special because he was an African American and was vulnerable to termination. He reflected these sentiments in a private letter to a friend in 1902: "There is a move to edge 'the brother' out, except at certain undesirable points."[189]

Upon the request of the Japanese commercial agent, who was away from Vladivostok, Greener was asked in March of 1903 to represent two Japanese and three Americans who had been sentenced to sixteen months in prison by the Russians in the fall of 1902 for seal poaching on Robben Island. Greener went to the Russian court to appeal the sentences. He argued that they had gone to the island by mistake and with no hostile intent, as they were not carrying any weapons. Greener reminded the court that the prisoners had been given the highest punishment possible for the offense, "whereas by recent law, American and Japanese, poachers are liable only to imprisonment for 3 months, and confiscated cargo." Since the men had already been imprisoned for nearly six months, he asked the court to at least grant leniency and release them. The sentences for all five men were reduced from sixteen to six months. Greener provided the prisoners with small sums of money throughout their imprisonment for "tobacco, stamps, etc." and upon their release arranged transit for all five back to Japan.[190]

On February 12, 1904, the Japanese declared war on Russia after feeble diplomatic efforts failed to resolve their differences concerning spheres of influence in Manchuria and Korea. The United States agreed to the Japanese request that American representatives take charge of Japanese interests in Russia.[191] Both the white and black press took note of Greener's valuable service. *The Colored American* and the Boston *Globe* agreed that the United States was lucky to have a man of his ability in Vladivostok at such a crucial time.[192] The Japanese government gave Greener an account to cover the costs of housing, feeding, and arranging the departure of its citizens. On March 9, 1904, the Japanese government sent a note to Secretary of State John Hay asking him to express their "cordial thanks for the steps taken by the United States Commercial Agent at Vladivostok." Since the British had no representative in Vladivostok, Greener was asked by the State Department to represent their interests as well.[193]

On October 28, 1904, Greener sent an angry letter to the State Department. Because other consuls and consuls general had received raises since the outbreak of the war, Greener felt he should be given one as well. He informed Second Assistant Secretary of State Francis Loomis that the cost of living had gone up at least 50 percent and would probably rise by twice that amount in the coming months. Greener's assessment of the situation included bitter remarks: "I respectfully call the attention of the Department to the increasing responsibilities and importance of this post, a point which I have not failed, in six years of service, to impress. The additional duties which have been placed upon the Consul [officially Greener was still only a commercial agent], not only at the present time; but during the Boxer war, I venture to say have not been duly appreciated hitherto by the Department." Greener blamed the department for the low wages he was paying his assistants, wages which he claimed were substantially lower than what the staffs at other offices in Russia were paid.[194]

Possibly because of the bombardment of Vladivostok, in May of 1905, Greener stayed for five months with friends in a nearby city. His absence gave rise to rumors that he was neglecting his post. Assistant Secretary of State Herbert Peirce made an inspection tour of Russia in 1905, and although he did not go to Vladivostok, he filed a report describing Greener's "bad habits and neglect of duty." When Greener claimed that there was a man in Vladivostok with a similar name to whom the "bad habits" could be attributed and asked to be retained as commercial agent, the State Department denied his request and appointed Roger Greene to replace him in November of 1905. Greener's complaint against the charges triggered a special investigation by Greene. Although Greene found that Greener had kept a Japanese mistress, charges that he associated with prostitutes were found to be groundless. To add insult to injury, Greener was not rewarded for his service in the Russo-Japanese War. In October 1905, the Emperor of Japan asked President Theodore Roosevelt to honor U.S. diplomats, consular officers, and commercial agents for representing Japanese interests. When the State Department submitted the names of officers who were to receive decorations, Roger Greene was on the list in place of Greener, in spite of the fact that Greene arrived after the war had ended. Senator Henry Cabot Lodge, who had known Greener since their days as students at Harvard in the late 1860s, sent a letter to Secretary of State Elihu Root protesting the absence of Greener's name. Root claimed the mistake was made by the Japanese and refused to correct the error.[195]

Greener returned to the United States early in 1906 only to learn that Booker T. Washington had spread among their friends the official reasons for his dismissal. He convinced Washington that the State Department version was incorrect. In July, he asked for Washington's help again in regard to an overseas post. Greener was in Harper's Ferry preparing to attend the Niagara meeting planned by W. E. B. DuBois. An open break appeared imminent between Washington and DuBois. In a notation on this letter, Washington's assistant E. J. Scott wrote, "Here is a good chance to get a good friend into the inner portals of the Niagara meeting." Greener was asked to "spare no pains to get on the inside of everything." At the National Negro Business League meeting in Atlanta in September 1906, Greener passed on to Washington what information he had gathered at Harper's Ferry.[196]

At the meeting, Greener gave a speech that was clearly designed to cement his relationship with Washington. He told the audience, "I believe in standing up for all our rights when necessary; but there are times and places when you cannot stand up for them without losing power and hope of eventually obtaining them." Greener was a little embarrassed when he left the platform after finishing his speech by saying, "It is better to bend than to break," and saw Mary White Ovington, a white activist who later helped in the founding of the NAACP. Ovington, who was taking notes for reports she planned to publish, had also attended the Harper's Ferry meeting. At Harper's Ferry, Greener spoke of John Brown and antislavery days in a much different tone: "Who would be free himself must strike the blow."[197] Despite Greener's effort to ingratiate himself to Washington, the black leader did little to help him. Although Greener had been exonerated of the State Department's charges, Root told him that he was not in the class of officers who had a right to have cause given for dismissal. Greener asked Washington to arrange a meeting for him with President Roosevelt. When he arrived for the appointment in August of 1907, Greener was told that Roosevelt was on vacation.[198] Greener ended his correspondence with Washington and went into semi-retirement in Chicago until his death in 1922.[199]

In late June of 1906, Archibald, Francis, and Angelina Grimké accompanied Greener, Kelly Miller, and Whitefield McKinlay, a former student of Greener's at the University of South Carolina, on a visit to Charleston, South Carolina. During the trip, Archibald Grimké addressed the graduating class of the Hospital and Training School for Nurses, an institution founded for black women by A. C. McClennan in response to the exclusion of blacks from South Carolina's state institutions. Afterwards, the five native South Carolinians visited the tomb of John C. Calhoun. They "surrounded the tomb and stood, in silence, with uncovered heads," admiring and appreciating "greatness and renown wherever found." They each gave a speech and "read the inscriptions on his tomb with intense interest."[200] In November of 1907 Greener went on an extended tour of South Carolina. While in Columbia he attended classes in psychology and metaphysics at Allen University and Benedict College. He also went to Orangeburg to address the "State Boys" with Johnson Whittaker, his former student and the young man he had defended at West Point, presiding over the class. *The State* recorded his visit to the University of South Carolina library. A black man who once had worked with him in the library noticed him as "Mr. Greener from the radical university." The article praised Greener's lifelong achievements: "A Negro who has done well." "Richard Theodore Greener, who has received a fine education—Has made fine use of his training." Greener also found that the curriculum at the university was similar to the one he helped to implement from 1873 to 1877.[201]

After his visit to South Carolina, Greener traveled to New Orleans, where he stayed with a Mr. Maxwell and family. He attended a meeting of the Phillis Wheatley Club, "a social ladies club, as an invited guest, and got [his] name in the paper." He celebrated the New Year with his New Orleans friends, firing "off roman candles, the Chinese crackers, the squibs, etc.," and drank to the beginning of 1908. As for 1907, Greener was "glad to see him go." The year "had been mixed with all sorts of disasters, social, political, and at last, financial." He explained to Francis J. Grimké, "Hope, buoyant as ever, as expectant, drives away the dull cares, the disappointments, the unfulfilled ambitions, and renews her eternal youth." After a few months of touring the South, Greener's notebook was "filling up, with many facts," and his blood kindled "every day, [at] this persistent, petty degradation of race, while all the American praters of liberty and freedom, are walking by on the other side."[202]

In 1909 Greener helped a man named Elbert R. Robinson, who had been battling the Chicago City Railway Company in court over alleged patent violations since 1902. Robinson had represented himself for six years without success. His most recent suit, alleging that the company had infringed on two of his patents, had been dismissed in 1908 on technical grounds. Robinson asked Greener to help him file an appeal. Greener argued that the circuit court should not have dismissed Robinson's bill in equity without a hearing on the defendant's motion for dismissal, which the circuit court had treated as a demurrer. The court of appeals agreed that the motion should not have been "summarily dispensed with" but treated "with the formality of a demurrer, setting it down for argument on a future day." Robinson was granted a new opportunity to frame "a suitable bill based on either of his letters patent, and thus obviate the numerous technical objections which now confront[ed] him." After the decision, the two men parted ways.[203]

After 1908 Greener finally seems to have accepted that his fate was inescapably tied to the "Negro problem," or, as he termed it, "the White problem." When his old friend Robert H. Terrel, "a favorite pupil at the Sumner High School" in 1873 and an 1884 Harvard graduate, was elected to a municipal judgeship in Washington, D.C., in February of 1909, Greener congratulated him, but was indignant that Terrel was "denominated, as is usual in such Asso.[?] despatches, 'A Negro Judge.'"[204] He went to New York in May of 1909 to attend the National Negro Conference, now considered the unofficial beginning of the NAACP. Greener proposed an amendment, which was unanimously carried, inserting the words "we demand" before resolutions that the conference addressed to the "Congress and the Executive."[205] In February of 1910, he wrote to DuBois, "The White American is not yet freed from his prejudices, cruelties, meanness, hypocrisy!" Greener deplored the "commercial barbarity, and heartlessness, of the so-called superior races."[206] By 1910 he had become fed up with the Republican Party. He talked of writing an indictment against the party for its treatment of African Americans.[207] In November of 1910, Greener's name appeared on the second edition of a leaflet, written by DuBois, that criticized Booker T. Washington, who was on a speaking tour in Great Britain, for "giving the impression abroad that the Negro problem in America is in process of satis-factory solution."[208]

Greener had time to indulge in the "Wears-Greener craze, writing, writ-ing, writing; reading, studying, as hard as if [he] were a young man." He had a gloomy outlook on race relations and the younger men who were taking leading roles in the African American community: "Since, I left College, I seem to have committed the unpardonable sin, and have been cracked at, from Douglass and Bruce [Blanche K.], down to the small fry, who are spirting in the sunlight of today." When he listened to and read "the attitudes of the average Negro lead-ers today," he consoled himself "with Shakespeare[;] 'I'd rather be a dog and bay the moon, than such a roman.'" Although he believed that "the present genera-tion seem[ed] to have a contempt for old men," Greener still gave speeches when asked, including one at the Sumner Memorial Meeting on January 6, 1911.[209] A friend of Booker T. Washington reported to Emmett J. Scott in April of 1912 that Greener was "just a little irritated at Dr. Booker T. Washington."[210] Greener was more than "just a little irritated" and supported the course taken by DuBois. In 1912, he told a friend, "I have a contempt for Taft, Roosevelt's valet for three years; and have analyzed Roosevelt, into an egoist of the first water, and assimilator of any ism that comes up, by which he could gain votes." He called Roosevelt an "ingrate and a coward in his treatment of the Negro." Greener decided, "[I]f I vote at all, I am for the whole Wilson and Marshall, ticket, and shall speak wherever I am needed to talk this time!"[211]

By 1910, Greener's family had severed all ties with him. J. C. Calloway, a mutual friend of the deceased Isaiah Wears, contacted Greener regarding some property that Wears had left to him and his son Russell Lowell. The attorney handling the estate informed Greener that he must contact his son before set-tling the claim. Greener told Calloway, "As to Lowell, I really do not know of his address, and have had so many contradictory stories about him that I pay no attention to them." His "family relations" were "not such, as are pleasant to con-template—much less talk or write about." Greener was reluctant to try and con-tact his wife to find his son's address and obtain a quit claim from him, as he had learned that his son was "well off enough not to need so small an amount."[212]

His family relations had soured further during his time in Vladivostok. His wife, Genevieve, changed her last name to Greene in the 1901–02 New York City street directory. In the 1902–03 directory she listed herself as Genevieve I. Greene, widow. Her name does not appear again until the 1908–09 directory, in which she referred to herself as Genevieve Van Vliet Greene. Her son Russell Lowell lived with her but was listed in the directory as Russell da Costa Greene, a civil engineer. Genevieve and her children claimed their ancestors were of Por-tuguese and Dutch descent and began "passing" as whites in New York. Greener's daughter Belle Marion, who worked as a clerk at the Princeton University Library in 1905 under the name Belle da Costa Greene, was chosen by J. P. Morgan, on the advice of his nephew Junius, to be the director of his personal library late that year. Through her work at Morgan's library Belle worked and socialized with wealthy and influential people, including Bernard Berenson, a prominent expert on Renaissance art.[213] Since Russell da Costa and the rest of the family had severed all of their ties to him, Greener was left to endure a four-year battle with the attorney executing Wears's estate.[214] More importantly, the shame of his wife and children "passing" for whites increased his bitterness and likely influenced the strong opinions he expressed on racial matters in letters to his friends.

In 1913, at the age of sixty-nine, Greener worked in Chicago as an executive and special agent of the Royal Casualty Insurance Company. He joined and lectured at an anthropological society and was the president of a literary club. He joined one of the "leading Democratic Clubs" and in December of 1914 went on a "two weeks lecture tour in Cincinnati and vicinity" in front of "good audiences, speaking on [his] travels in the Far East."[215] On the occasion of his fiftieth class reunion in 1915, Greener returned to Phillips Academy in Andover to give a speech at an alumni dinner. He brought with him and presented to his alma mater, on behalf of the class of 1865, a brass tablet memorializing Ulysses S. Grant and bearing the motto, "If others could not find a way to Richmond he would either find it or make one."[216]

When Roy Nash, the secretary of the NAACP, invited him to the Amenia Conference in July of 1916, Greener "deeply regret[ed]" that he could not go. Greener was "past the stage of active cooperation," or he would "have been more identified with the work."[217] His portrait was featured on the cover of the NAACP's magazine, *The Crisis*, in February of 1917.[218] In the same month, his last published article, in which he reminisced about Frederick Douglass, appeared in *Champion Magazine*.[219] In October of 1917, Greener praised black historian Carter G. Woodson for beginning the *Journal of Negro History*. He asked Woodson to send a copy of the journal to his friend Lewis Hayden Latimer, the black inventor who had worked for many years with Thomas Edison.[220] In June of 1918, Greener told Arthur A. Schomburg, a black bibliophile in New York who was collecting literature written by African Americans, "Business, cares, the long flight to get near the front, and leisure, broke up my literary quests, and I have only been able to applaud 'the new runners' in the race—not victor alone, but those who have remained on 'the run,' for the sake of it, who were 'glad their mission to fulfill.'"[221] In December, he wrote to Francis J. Grimké that he had "no faith in the Roosevelts and the Tafts, who were committed by heredity and training, to true democracy, and have so conspicuously failed, to throw their weight into the breach *when they might have done so.*" He ended the letter optimistically, "I am glad to see the President [Woodrow

Wilson] committing himself more and more to international democracy! I am in hopes, he will later begin *to see the application nearer home. And I really believe he will.*[222]

In the last three years of his life, Greener lived among friends in Chicago, "in a most congenial atmosphere." He retired from his job as an agent for the Royal Casualty Insurance Company, spending his time "in hourly association with works of art, reminiscences of the past, and books." Although he received "tempting invitations" from literary societies to speak at their meetings, Greener's health, which declined rapidly after 1918, prevented him from accepting them. When he died on May 2, 1922, Wendell P. Dabney, the editor of the Cincinnati *Union*, proclaimed, "The last of the old Guard [is] Gone!" Dabney praised Greener's accomplishments and gave an appropriate eulogy: "In the days of Douglass, Bruce, Langston, he was a young man, but ably held his own with those grand old pioneers of the Race."[223]

After his return from Vladivostok, Greener played a negligible role in American politics and race relations. For the most part, his public career came to an end with his dismissal from the foreign service. Greener slipped into obscurity due to his unwillingness to conform to the role that late-nineteenth-century white and black Americans wanted him to play. Instead of becoming a leader for African Americans, he preferred to place value on himself as an individual American. This viewpoint turned out to be unacceptable to members of his own race and, except for his days at Phillips Academy and Harvard, was not acceptable to white Americans. The appointment in Vladivostok could very well have been the pinnacle of a brilliant career. As a result of American political and societal problems in the late nineteenth and early twentieth centuries, however, it led to Greener's demise.

Greener never forgot his times at Harvard. He joined Harvard clubs in every American city where he lived, including the one in Chicago. His views on domestic and foreign affairs were based on the ideals and values that he learned at Harvard. He consistently supported the rights of Irish peasants in Great Britain, women's rights, and the rights of blacks to be treated as equals in American politics and society. His experience as a professor at the University of South Carolina, including his active campaigning for civil rights in the state during Reconstruction, was also an important influence on his life. In an 1879 interview, Greener told the reporter that he was a South Carolinian.[224] He visited South Carolina in 1884, 1906, and 1907 and commonly referred to the state, both negatively and positively, in his speeches and lectures. When Nicholas Senn met him in Vladivostok and asked the U.S. commercial agent where he was from, Greener replied that he was from South Carolina.[225] He had fond memories of the state during Reconstruction, and, at least in one respect, his time in South Carolina was similar to his Harvard College days. In both instances, Greener enjoyed a measure of equality that most members of his race would never experience. As a student at Harvard from 1865 to 1870, and as a professor at the University of South Carolina from 1873 to 1877, Greener exercised his individualistic spirit, professing and practicing an uncompromising stance on the issue of civil rights, a stance that was reminiscent of his friend, Charles Sumner, the "Idealist, statesman, and scholar." The end of Reconstruction brought with it an end to the circumstances that had contributed to Greener's successes. As the federal government pulled back from enforcing civil rights for blacks in the South and the North, Greener struggled to make a place for himself in "public life."

When he asked Booker T. Washington for help in 1897 and 1906 to obtain political appointments, Greener compromised his belief in the individual. In fact, he did not end his association with Washington until the black leader's feeble attempts to help him proved useless. This necessary contradiction between his thought and action, after twelve years of "doing [his] work in [his] own way" in New York and eight years as the U.S. commercial agent in Vladivostok, frustrated Greener and drove him to withdraw from public life.[226] As a result, Richard Theodore Greener's career ended with his return from Vladivostok amid controversy that left him bitter in old age, an obscure figure in American history remembered for little more than his distinction as the first black graduate of Harvard.

7

South Carolina's Black Elected Officials during Reconstruction

ERIC FONER

Today, I want to talk about some of the other black political leaders of the Reconstruction period in South Carolina.[1] Given the success of the film *Titanic*, I hope you won't mind my saying that Jonathan J. Wright was just the tip of the iceberg. There were many, many others. None reached quite so high an office as he did, but there were many other prominent and obscure officeholders— African American political officeholders—in this state during Reconstruction. Most of them are completely unknown today. What I want to do today is to make some general remarks about black leaders during Reconstruction in general and then introduce you to some of the particular figures of South Carolina's history. Some of them we've heard about already today. But there are a whole amazing cast of characters and I can introduce you to a few of them.

As Randall Kennedy pointed out this morning, the advent of African Americans into positions of political leadership and political power in this country was really a remarkable transformation, and we ought to step back for a minute and realize how remarkable that was. Just a few years after the end of slavery you had hundreds, thousands of black men throughout the South occupying positions of real political power, at all levels. In some ways it was as amazing that you'd have a former slave assessing property for taxation purposes on the local level as that a black man [Jonathan Jasper Wright] sat on the Supreme

---

This speech, titled "Jonathan Jasper Wright and the Early African American Bar in South Carolina—A Retrospective," was delivered to the South Carolina Supreme Court Historical Society, first annual colloquium, Feb. 27, 1998; moderators were the Honorable Jean H. Toal and Richard M. Gergel.

Court of South Carolina. Before the Civil War, only a handful of states in the North even allowed blacks to vote, and I have only been able to find two black Americans who held any public office before the Civil War, in the whole country. One we heard briefly mentioned this morning. Macon Allen, the first black lawyer in American history, held a justice of the peace position in Massachusetts in the 1850s. The other was John Langston, later a congressman from Virginia, who held a minor position in Ohio. So black office holding was unprecedented in American history, North as well as South, when Reconstruction came along. By 1877, when Reconstruction ended, my estimate is that about two thousand black men held some position. I'm talking about official positions. There were other important figures—political organizers, newspaper editors—but I'm talking about people who actually held office.

Black office holding did not end entirely when Reconstruction ended. After Reconstruction in the South, in South Carolina some black men continued to hold one office or another until around the turn of the century. Then, it pretty much ended. The next significant group of black officials emerged in the North in the 1920s and '30s as a result of the migration and beginnings of black political power there. It was not until after the passage of the Voting Rights Act of 1965 that we again saw the rise of African American office holding in any significant numbers in the South.

To the critics of Reconstruction, the fact that black men were in office was one of the great horrors of that period. The Democratic press called these legislatures and constitutional conventions—they used language which I find even offensive to read, but these are in the documents and this was the political language of the time. They called them menageries, monkey houses. They ridiculed former slaves who thought themselves competent to frame a code of laws. They said that these officials were ignorant, illiterate, propertyless. They lacked education. They lacked the economic wherewithal to take part intelligently in government. Their criticisms were echoed as Reconstruction retreated by many northerners. James S. Pike, a northern journalist who came to South Carolina and wrote the famous book, *The Prostrate State*, in the 1870s said after visiting the South Carolina state legislature, "It is impossible not to recognize the immense proportion of ignorance and vice that permeates this body."

Some opponents of Reconstruction tried to erase black officials from the historical record altogether. We saw what happened to the memory of Jonathan J. Wright. In Georgia, after the Democrats regained control of Georgia's government, Alexander Abrams, who compiled the legislative manual each year, announced that he was going to omit black lawmakers from the biographical sketches. Every year in that manual, they give a little sketch of each of the members of the legislature. He wrote, "I am not going to include these Black legislators because it would be absurd to record the lives of men who were but yesterday our slaves and whose past careers embrace such occupations as boot blacking, shaving, table waiting, and the like." A quote like that reveals the combination of racism and class prejudice that went into the opposition to Reconstruction. It wasn't just that these men were black but that they were poor that seemed to mark them as being somehow ineligible to be part of the public world. Historians echoed these charges. And you can find in the film *Birth of a Nation*, for example, a scene in the South Carolina legislature with black members taking off their shoes and putting their bare feet up on the table to show how ridiculous and incompetent they supposedly were. *Gone with the Wind* has similar scenes.

Historians all through the century distorted the historical record. For example, E. Merton Coulter, who wrote about black officials in Georgia, wrote that of the thirty-seven black men who served in the Georgia Constitutional Convention in 1868, "most of them could not read and write." Now, I have become very annoyed at historians who misrepresent the facts. I don't mind historians with whom you disagree. That's the nature of historical writing. But we, as a profession, hope that we can rely on the information in previous books. But here's a case where this is a total falsehood. "Most of the thirty-seven delegates could not read." He just made this up instead of going to the record. It's tedious, but if you go the 1870 manuscript census you can find these people and you will find that the great majority of them were not illiterate. And if Mr. Coulter, instead of just sitting in his study thinking of things to say about black legislators, had actually gone out and done a little work, he would have found that this was not correct. Or again, scholars of South Carolina history would always repeat a charge which the Democratic Party leveled at the black delegates to the Constitutional Convention of 1868 here. The Democratic Party issued a document in 1868 saying of the seventy-one black delegates only fourteen were on the tax list.

Now if you go to the manuscript census, you'll discover that it's just not true. Most of them did own property. Thirty-one of them owned more than a thousand dollars worth of property, which in those days was a fairly substantial sum. And again, this is just bad history. If I dwell on this it's because it's more annoying to me as a historian to find outright falsehood masquerading as history than to find differences of point of view, which is how historical scholarship moves forward.

There were historians who challenged these myths. The first ones were black historians writing in the *Journal of Negro History*. Some of them were survivors of Reconstruction, like John R. Lynch. Some of them were the early generation of scholars like W. B. DuBois or Luther P. Jackson, or others. Today, we know a great deal more about these black officials than ever before. Much of what I say today comes out of a book that I put together called *Freedom's*

Lawmakers, where I gathered biographical information on about 1,500 black officials from Reconstruction. Sometimes we know just one or two sentences about somebody. Sometimes we know a lot. I list 1,510 black officials, of whom 315 were from South Carolina. South Carolina had more than any other state. The next were Mississippi and Louisiana. South Carolina had more because South Carolina had the largest black population, at least in percentage terms. About 57 to 58 percent of the population of the state was African American in Reconstruction. Mississippi and Louisiana had about 50 percent and then it trailed off a little in other states. These 315 served in every kind of position—at the federal level, the state level, and the local level. Six black men served in Congress from South Carolina during Reconstruction. And I hope that one of these days we can have portraits of those six men put up somewhere in the state. I doubt if any state has had six black congressmen at a time since Reconstruction.

But there were also others. There were U.S. tax assessors, pension agents, postmasters, customs officials. There were numerous African Americans who served at the state level. In South Carolina, about 72, according to my calculation, served in the Constitutional Convention of 1868. As we heard this morning from Professor Kennedy, the constitution of 1868 is a very progressive and remarkable document. Last night at dinner I was remarking to Chief Justice Ernest Finney, "Why don't you just proclaim that South Carolina is going back to the constitution of 1868? Forget about the constitution of 1895." He said, "I don't think I have the power to do that." He's a very scrupulous person according to the law. According to my calculation, during the course of Reconstruction, 210 African Americans served in the lower house of the state legislature and 29 in the state senate. So that's a very hefty representation in the legislature. And South Carolina is the only state that had a black majority in the legislature during Reconstruction. And then at the top of the state level there were two black lieutenant governors, the state treasurer, secretary of state, and some other state officials in this state. Then there were numerous local officials ranging from justice of the peace to sheriff, school board officials, etc.

Another thing I tried to figure out is, What was the status of these men before the Civil War? Were they free or slave? South Carolina had a substantial free black population, mostly centered around Charleston before the war; and many of these people were well educated and skilled workers of one kind or another, and they were well positioned to move into posts of political power during Reconstruction. Of those whose status I could find, 88 had been free before the Civil War and 131 had been slaves. So even in South Carolina a majority had been slaves before the Civil War. But at the upper levels, the congressmen, the senators, the Speakers of the House, etc., tended to be free before the Civil War. They were free either in South Carolina or, like Jonathan J. Wright, were northern free blacks who moved to South Carolina during the Civil War in order to make a living or seek political office. But it is interesting that even in South Carolina, a majority of those who held office were slaves.

What I'd like to do for the next bit of my talk is to tell you about a few of these people. One of the interesting things is it shows the diversity of the black experience in the nineteenth century. You know, so often we think of all African Americans before the Civil War as slaves, even though there were half a million free blacks in this country in 1860. We think of all slaves as ignorant field hands, whereas, in fact, there was a great diversity of experience among slaves. There were urban slaves, industrial slaves, educated slaves, skilled slaves. Even though it was against the law to teach slaves to read and write, many slaves did somehow "steal" an education, as one of them said.

I'm also interested in what happened to them after Reconstruction. What did they do? You'll see what I mean as I talk about some of these people.

Let's look first at the congressmen. One who we've heard mention of this morning was Robert Brown Elliott. Now, Elliott was a brilliant political organizer. His background is obscure. But according to the most recent study, he actually was born in England in Liverpool. He later claimed to have been born in Boston, but that was to establish American citizenship when he was first elected to the South Carolina Constitutional Convention. But the best information we have is that he was born in England and came to the United States shortly after the Civil War. He worked in Boston and then he came to South Carolina. He became an editor of the *South Carolina Leader*, a short-lived black newspaper, and he established a law practice, as we heard, and according to his law partner, Daniel A. Straker, "Elliott knew the political condition of every nook and corner of the state. He knew every important person in every county, village, or town. He knew the history of the entire State as it related to politics." Some think, said another newspaper, that "he is the ablest Negro intellectually in the South." He served in a number of offices. He was in the constitutional convention, state legislature, county commissioner in Barnwell County, Board of Regents of State Asylums, and he served two terms in the U.S. House of Representatives, starting in 1870. And he served as Speaker of the house here in the legislature, 1874–76.

Elliott was most famous for a couple of speeches in Congress. In 1870, he spoke on the Ku Klux Klan Bill and he talked about the depredations of the Klan in a very pointed remark. He said, "Every Southern gentlemen should blush with shame at this pitiless and cowardly persecution of the Negro. It is the custom of democratic journals to stigmatize the Negroes of the South as being barbarous. But gentlemen, tell me, who is the barbarian here?" Is it more of a barbarian to be illiterate because you have been a slave, or to go out and murder people because they are in an opposition political party? Elliott gave a famous speech on the Civil Rights Bill of 1874 in Congress. Now, I will take the liberty here of inviting you all to go up to Mr. Gergel's office, because on the wall there he has a wonderful lithograph from the 1870s called "The Shackle Broken—By the Genius of Freedom," which shows at the center Robert Elliott giving this famous speech in the House of Representatives on the Civil Rights Bill. Another thing about Elliott is that he ran for the U.S. Senate in 1872. We hear a lot about corruption during Reconstruction. There was some corruption, no question about it. Elliott's opponent was a white northerner called, ironically, Honest John Patterson. Patterson distributed bribes to the legislature. He offered Elliott fifteen thousand dollars to withdraw from the race. Elliott refused. Fifteen thousand dollars was a lot of money. Elliott was rather poor at the time. He turned down Honest John Patterson's bribe, but didn't win the election. After Reconstruction, Elliott, like so many others, found it hard to make a living. There was not much financial wherewithal being a black lawyer in South Carolina. The prospect of political office was gone after Reconstruction was over. He eventually got a job with the Treasury Department, moved to New Orleans, tried to practice law there, and died in the early 1880s penniless. So here is a man who had been at the peak of influence as a congressman, but once Reconstruction was over, there was no prospect for him, and he faded off into oblivion. I gather there may be a portrait of Elliott in the works, too, and I certainly hope so because he was a very, very important member of Congress from this state.

More briefly, I'll mention the other congressmen and some of their backgrounds. One was Joseph H. Rainey, who had been born a slave but acquired his freedom before the Civil War. He was born in Georgetown, the son of a barber and a fairly successful barber himself. In fact, by 1860 Rainey himself owned a slave. There were free black slave owners in South Carolina and other states. He was drafted to work on Confederate fortifications during the Civil War and ran away with his wife to Bermuda to escape having to assist the Confederacy. And indeed, if you've ever been in Hamilton, Bermuda, there is a place called Barber's Alley, named for Joseph Rainey because he was a barber there during the Civil War. He came back to South Carolina when the war was over, served in a series of official positions in the state senate, constitutional convention, etc., and was elected to Congress. In fact, he became the first African American seated in the U.S. House of Representatives in 1870. He served throughout the whole Reconstruction period down to 1879, and in his farewell address in March 1879 he compared the new government, the new Democratic Party government of South Carolina under Governor Wade Hampton, to the Reconstruction government. He said that the Redeemers, as they called themselves, had emphasized that they were spending less money than the Reconstruction government. Rainey said, "As compared with Governor Hampton's, doubtless the Republican Government of Reconstruction was more extravagant. But can the saving of a few thousand dollars compensate for the loss of the political heritage of

American citizens?" Like many black officials after the end of Reconstruction, Rainey survived on federal patronage jobs. Rainey moved to Washington and served in various positions and came back eventually to Georgetown and that's how he survived.

Of the other black congressmen, Alonzo Ransier had been born free in South Carolina in Charleston. Before the Civil War he was a clerk in a shipping house. After the war he was a newspaper editor, served in a whole series of positions, and was lieutenant governor of South Carolina in 1868 through '72, and then was elected to the U.S. House of Representatives and served for one term. Ransier was one of those who, after Reconstruction was over, could not really make a living. Once the possibility of political office was gone, the best he could do was to get a job as a night watchman at the Charleston Customs House. And, when he died in the early 1880s, he was listed as simply a day laborer for the city of Charleston. So you see how the end of Reconstruction closed off opportunities for a whole generation of talented and ambitious black men.

Perhaps the most famous of all the South Carolina congressmen was Robert Smalls, who was a slave raised in Beaufort County and well known for stealing a Confederate ship, the *Planter*, on which he worked as a pilot during the war. He dressed himself up as the captain and under cover of night piloted the ship out of the harbor and surrendered it to U.S. Naval forces. He became a hero. He joined the navy and was later placed in command of the *Planter*. And after the war, he came back to the Sea Islands and set up a very long-lived political machine. He was about the closest thing to a long-term political boss that Reconstruction produced. He served in many local offices here and then in the Congress long after the end of Reconstruction. He served in the 1880s in Congress from the Low Country. And then, he served as collector of customs at Beaufort all the way down to 1913. He was probably the last black official in the state of South Carolina. Why 1913? Because that's when Woodrow Wilson was inaugurated as president, and Wilson, as some of you know, cleaned out all the remaining black officeholders. Wilson instituted rigid segregation in federal offices in Washington and basically got rid of all the remaining black patronage officials.

Another congressman was Richard H. Cain, who served for two terms. He had been born free in Virginia and educated in Ohio. And then he became a preacher for the Methodist Episcopal Church and he came to the South after the Civil War as a minister. He established the Emmanuel Church, in Charleston, which became the largest AME congregation in the city and a basis for his political power. Again, he served in a whole series of offices including the Congress during the Reconstruction period. He was one of those who was a very strong advocate of distributing land among the former slaves. "Let them have homesteads," he said in 1875. "Then we will see the cotton fields and rice plantations produce as never before. Universal prosperity will reign supreme." And he also became involved in private efforts. He was the head of a project to buy thousands of acres of land and then resell it in small plots to freedmen. That went bankrupt because the former slaves just didn't have the money to purchase land. After the end of Reconstruction, Cain devoted himself to church work. He became a bishop in the AME Church. He became president of Paul Quinn College in Waco, Texas. And, at the end of his life he was an AME bishop in Washington, D.C. So his talent flowed out of politics into the church and education.

One other interesting figure, less known, but maybe we ought to have a portrait of him, too, was Richard H. Gleaves, the first black lieutenant governor of South Carolina. He was a free man, before the war, who had been born in Philadelphia, the son of a free black immigrant from Haiti. He was educated there and before the war he worked as a steward on Mississippi River boats. He also was a very active member of the Prince Hall Masons. He used the Masonic lodges as a stepping stone to political organization. After the Civil War he came to Beaufort where he went into business with Robert Smalls. He helped organize the Republican Party. As I say, he served as lieutenant governor as well as several other positions. But again, look what happened to Gleaves after Reconstruction. There was nothing more for him here. He moved to Washington, D.C., and to the end of his life, 1907, he worked as a waiter in a private club in Washington, D.C.

There were other men who we ought to try to memorialize in one way or another. One was Francis L. Cardozo. He was born free in Charleston, the son of a prominent Jewish figure, Isaac Cardozo, and a free black woman. He had as much education as any official. He went to the University of Glasgow and got a degree there in the 1850s. He became a minister in the North, a Congregational minister. And he came back to South Carolina in 1865 for the American Missionary Association to establish schools, and he became the director of their educational activities in Charleston. He established what became Avery Normal Institute to train black teachers and, against his will—he didn't have political ambitions—he was chosen to serve in the constitutional convention, and then other positions: state treasurer, secretary of state, head of the land commission where he tried to assist former slaves in getting land. He later moved to Washington, D.C., after Reconstruction, where he held a number of positions in the Treasury Department. He later became principal of a black high school. Francis L. Cardozo's granddaughter, Eslanda Cardozo Goode, was the wife of Paul Robeson. So through that family you somehow have this link between Reconstruction and the black struggle in the twentieth century, a struggle which Robeson did so much to push forward.

There's a whole other cadre of people who served in the Union army. One of the most famous of them was Prince Rivers, who was a slave in the Low

Country in the Beaufort area. When Thomas Wentworth Higginson was sent down there to organize the first unit of black soldiers in 1862, Rivers became a sergeant and a leader of that unit. After the war, after being discharged from the army, he went into politics, not in Beaufort but in Edgefield County in the up country. And I just want to read you one thing about Rivers. He was appointed to be a magistrate in 1869 and a group of white residents of Edgefield petitioned the governor to remove him, saying that he was not competent to be a magistrate. One hundred nine black residents of Hamburg, South Carolina, opposed efforts to remove Rivers in a petition to the governor. And they said, "While we are not disposed to argue that Prince Rivers is the very best man that might have been appointed to fill the office of magistrate, he is able to rise above existing prejudices and to administer justice under the law with an even hand and for that reason he draws down upon his shoulders the wrath of those perhaps more learned in law than himself." In other words, for these people it wasn't about how learned in law you were, it was whether you were willing to administer the law fairly and evenhandedly. Their experience was that the very learned were not willing to administer the law fairly when it came to African Americans, so they would rather have someone with less background but more sense of justice.

There was a whole series of what sometimes are called black carpetbaggers, blacks who came down from the North. One was Macon Allen, a native of Indiana who was the first black American ever admitted to the bar in the United States in 1844. He was later the first African American appointed as a municipal judge in Charleston.

Another man whom I find very interesting is Martin Becker. Becker was another one of these black carpetbaggers who actually had been born in Surinam in South America, had immigrated to the United States before the Civil War, lived in Massachusetts, and he was a pretty vigorous guy. He served in both the Union army and navy—rather unusual. He later came to South Carolina and served as a trial justice here. One of his sons in the 1890s organized Becker's Orchestra, which toured the country as a musical troupe.

One other official was Benjamin Boseman, who, I think, must be the first black American to practice medicine, that is, to be licensed to practice medicine in the state of South Carolina. Boseman was born in New York City but grew up in Troy, New York. He had been one of the very few black physicians in the North. He had studied at the Medical School of Maine. He worked in the Union army as a surgeon during the Civil War, and he came to South Carolina and established a medical practice in Charleston in September 1865. I can't prove it but I have a strong suspicion that Boseman was the first practicing black physician in this state, and he later was elected to the house of representatives here and also served as the postmaster of Charleston. That was a very lucrative position back then to be the postmaster of Charleston. Now there are charges that some of these black officials were corrupt. As we heard this morning, most of those charges are without foundation. There were a few, though, who did line their pockets, as happened in other parts of the country at that time. Remember, this is the period of whiskey rings, the Tweed Ring, the internal revenue scandals, the Indian frauds. Public morality was not at as high a level as we claim it is today. But one of those who did seem to have sticky fingers was William J. Whipper, a northern antislavery person who had studied law in Detroit before the Civil War and practiced law in the North and served in the Union army and came down here. He had legal and political battles with Robert Smalls. He answered the charge that civil rights and other efforts to uplift African Americans somehow discriminated against whites and became reverse discrimination. The term they used was what they called "class legislation." That is legislation meant to benefit one group as opposed to others. And when some effort on behalf of former slaves was denounced as class legislation, Whipper got up in the legislature and said, "You know white people have had the advantage of class legislation for about 250 years. So why is it suddenly class legislation when you try and do something for former slaves?" Whipper somehow acquired a great deal of money, and I'm sure it wasn't just his salary in the legislature. According to one account I saw, he lost thirty thousand dollars in one night of poker in 1875, including about half of that on one hand in which his four aces were defeated by a straight flush held by another member of the legislature. My experience at poker suggests that both of them were cheating but Whipper came out second best. Four aces is usually enough.

We should also remember a more obscure person, Benjamin Randolph, a native of Kentucky, a minister, a chaplain in the Union army, who came to South Carolina with the Freedmen's Bureau, was an educator, a religious leader, and became in 1868 the head of the state Republican Party, and was serving in the Constitutional Convention of 1868. While campaigning in 1868 for the Republicans, he was assassinated by the Ku Klux Klan in Abbeville County. This is a good example of the dangers these people faced and the courage it took to go out there and stand up for what you believed.

Let us remember these men and many, many others who were much more obscure. Some of them were very successful. Some of them were not that successful. Some of them were very heroic. Some of them were not that heroic. Some of them were very radical. Some of them were not so radical. But, for all of them, I like to quote an Alabama leader, James Greene, a former slave who became a legislator in Alabama and said, "When I was a slave, I didn't know anything except to obey my master. But the tocsin of freedom sounded and I walked out like a man and shouldered my responsibilities." And I think that's how we should remember these people. They walked out of slavery and tried to shoulder their responsibilities.

Notes

1: AFRICAN AMERICAN FOUNDING FATHERS
The Making of the South Carolina Constitution of 1868

1. Dr. Albert G. Mackey, president of the 1868 convention, noted that this was the first South Carolina constitutional convention which had been called pursuant to a vote that had not excluded a large segment of the population because of slavery. He observed, "Manhood suffrage has for the first time been invoked to convene a body which is to make the fundamental law for all." See *Proceedings of the Constitutional Convention of South Carolina, 1868* (Charleston: Denny and Perry, 1868), 16 (hereafter cited as *1868 Proceedings*). Mackey, a white delegate representing Charleston, was known for his Unionist views and as a scholarly writer on Masonic lore. See Francis Butler Simkins and Robert Hilliard Woody, *South Carolina during Reconstruction* (Chapel Hill: University of North Carolina Press, 1932), 93. See also Alrutheus Ambush Taylor, *The Negro in South Carolina during the Reconstruction* (Washington, D.C.: Association for the Study of Negro Life and History, 1924), 127 (argues that the 1868 Constitutional Convention "was the first experiment in this country of working out a government based on the cooperation of the two races").

2. Compare S.C. Constitution of 1790, art. 2 and 6 (showing legislative dominance in the provisions providing for the election of most major officials by the legislature), and S.C. Constitution of 1790, art. 1, sec. 16 (absence of executive veto), with S.C. Constitution of 1868, art. 3, sec. 2 (showing greater executive independence from the legislature in the provision providing for the popular election of the governor). See S.C. Constitution of 1868, art. 3, sec. 22, which is similar to the presidential veto power in U.S. Constitution, art. 1, sec. 7, cl. 2 (an executive veto that can be overridden only by two-thirds vote in both houses).

3. See S.C. Constitution of 1868, art. 4, sec. 19. For an account of the old system of providing local service through specialized commissions authorized by the legislature to perform specific tasks, see James Lowell Underwood, *The Constitution of South Carolina*, vol. 2, *The Journey toward Local Self-Government* (Columbia: University of South Carolina Press, 1989), 13–17, also 48–50 (describing how comprehensive councils replaced specialized commissions under the constitution of 1868).

4. See S.C. Constitution of 1868, art. 1 (Declaration of Rights), especially sec. 1 (equality of all men), sec. 10 (prohibiting establishment of religion), sec. 31 (equal access to political process), sec. 39 (prohibiting distinctions based on race, color, or class), and art. 3, sec. 3 (Supreme Being belief).

5. S.C. Constitution of 1868, art. 10, sec. 3 (public schools) and sec. 4 (compulsory attendance).

6. S.C. Constitution of 1868, art. 11, sec. 5 (aid to needy).

7. See S.C. Constitution of 1868, art. 9, sec. 7 (state debt can be increased only by two-thirds of both houses of the legislature); see also *1868 Proceedings*, 656–60 (debate on whether

limitations should be placed on the legislature's spending power). These minimal restraints proved to be inadequate. An 1873 amendment added Article 16, which prohibited an increase of state debt unless approved by the electorate by two-thirds of those voting. See Act No. 9 of 1873, 15 *S.C. Statutes* 466.

8. For examples of black delegates using comparative government and historical perspectives in the debates, see *1868 Proceedings*, 685 (H. E. Hayne states the compulsory education "system has worked well in Germany and Massachusetts"), 689 (B. F. Randolph citing New Hampshire as an example of a successful compulsory education system), 705–8 (F. L. Cardozo cites practices in Prussia and Massachusetts in support of compulsory education), 563–65 (B. F. Randolph uses comparative religion arguments and references to the early constitutions of other states to support the proposal that no one who denies the existence of a Supreme Being can be governor), 645–46 (A. J. Ransier uses the constitutions of other states and the life of John Quincy Adams to support his arguments in favor of 85 rather than 70 as the age at which one should be disqualified from being elected a judge), 665 (B. Byas discusses international trade in rice), and also 698 (J. J. Wright denies that Massachusetts has a compulsory education system).

9. In a letter to Rev. E. P. Smith of the American Missionary Association, Cardozo noted that friends had asked him to be a candidate for delegate to the constitutional convention, and he considered it his duty to serve. So that he could begin to prepare himself, Cardozo asked Smith to "send [him] for that purpose a copy of the book containing the Constitutions of *all the states*" (emphasis in original). Letter from F. L. Cardozo, to Rev. E. P. Smith, General Field Agent, American Missionary Association, Nov. 4, 1867, on file with the American Missionary Association Archives, Amistad Center, Tulane University. In a follow-up letter, Cardozo reminded Smith of his request for the book of constitutions. A note written on this letter, apparently by a member of Smith's staff, indicated that the book had been sent on Nov. 11, 1867. Letter from F. L. Cardozo, to Rev. E. P. Smith, General Field Agent, American Missionary Association, Dec. 7, 1867, American Missionary Association Archives. Smith observed that Cardozo was "noted for his scholarship, culture, & gentlemanly deportment." William H. Armstrong, *A Friend to God's Poor, Edward Parmelee Smith* (Athens and London: University of Georgia Press, 1993), 157. Also see Joe M. Richardson, "Francis L. Cardozo: Black Educator during Reconstruction," in *African American Life in the Post-Emancipation South, 1861–1900: African Americans and Education in the South, 1865–1900*, ed. Donald G. Nieman (New York and London: Garland, 1994), 343, 352.

10. See Walter Edgar, *South Carolina, A History* (Columbia: University of South Carolina Press, 1998), 386 [concluding that 73 of 124 delegates "were black (closely reflecting the percentage of the black population)"]; Richard Zuczek, *State of Rebellion: Reconstruction in South Carolina* (Columbia: University of South Carolina Press, 1996), 48 (placing black membership at 73 out of 124 delegates); see also W. E. Burghardt DuBois, *Black Reconstruction in America* (New York: Russell and Russell, 1935; reprint, 1963), 389 (placing black membership at 76 out of 124); Eric Foner, *Reconstruction: America's Unfinished Revolution, 1863–1877* (New York: Harper and Row, 1988), 318 n.70 (placing the black membership at 71); Richard L. Hume, "Negro Delegates to the State Constitutional Conventions of 1867–69," in *Southern Black Leaders of the Reconstruction Era*, ed. Howard N. Rabinowitz (Urbana: University of Illinois Press, 1982), 129, 133 (placing the membership of "Negroes" at 71); John S. Reynolds, *Reconstruction in South Carolina 1865–1877* (Columbia, S.C.: The State Co., 1905), 78 (placing black membership at 76 out of 124 delegates); Simkins and Woody, *South Carolina during Reconstruction*, 91 (placing black membership at 76 out of 124); Joel Williamson, *After Slavery: The Negro in South Carolina during Reconstruction, 1861–1877* (Chapel Hill: University of North Carolina Press, 1965), 367 (stating that 74 black delegates "attended" the convention); John Porter Hollis,

"The Early Period of Reconstruction in South Carolina," *John Hopkins University Studies in Historical and Political Science* 23 (1905): 83 (placing black membership at 73).

11. See Richard L. Hume, "Negro Delegates to the State Constitutional Conventions of 1867–69," in *Southern Black Leaders of the Reconstruction Era.* ed. Howard N. Rabinowitz (Urbana: University of Illinois Press, 1982), 129, 130.

12. William Archibald Dunning, *Reconstruction, Political and Economic, 1865–1877,* ed. Albert Bushnell Hart (New York: Harper & Brothers, 1907), 112.

13. Ibid.

14. See "South Carolina, The Reconstruction Convention—Its Tone and Temper—The Colored Delegates the Ablest and Most Respectable," *New York Times,* Jan. 21, 1868, 2–3.

15. See *Charleston Mercury,* Jan. 15, 1868 ("It is, therefore, not as burlesque, but to give a correct impression of the appearance and character of the convention, that we style it the great ring—streaked and striped. It is composed of men of every hue, from jet-black to a pure white, there being two or three men among its members who might even by some possibility be mistaken for gentlemen."). For a sampling of other depictions of the black delegates in the media, see "The Convention, Held by Authority of the Reconstruction Laws of Congress, to Frame a State Constitution for South Carolina," *Charleston Daily News,* Jan. 17, 1868 ("disposition on the part of the colored delegates far more moderate and impartial than was exhibited by many of the whites"); *Charleston Daily News,* Jan. 24, 1868 ("the Negroes are likely to form a compact, solid body of voters in one direction"); *Charleston Daily News,* Jan. 31, 1868 ("Beyond all question the best men in the convention . . . are the colored members. Considering the influences under which they were called together, and their imperfect acquaintance with parliamentary usage, they have displayed for the most part, a remarkable moderation and dignity; and have produced some of the best speeches of the convention."); *Charleston Daily News,* Feb. 17, 1868 ("you might as well attempt to compromise with [the colored delegates] as to make an oyster walk"); *Charleston Daily News,* Mar. 5, 1868 ("in all questions which concern the colored race, the colored leaders upon the floor have only to make a sign, and opposition dwindles into insignificance"); *New York Times,* Jan. 31, 1868, 5 ("blacks, who but a little while ago filled with the most bitter and hateful prejudices, are now the moderate and conservative men of this Convention").

16. See John S. Reynolds, *Reconstruction in South Carolina, 1865–1877* (1905), 79; see also Yates Snowden, *History of South Carolina* vol. 2 (Chicago and New York: Lewis Publications, 1920), 885 (contending that "there was not one really prominent man in the convention," that most were "without character" or sufficient financial resources, and that most were not taxpayers).

17. See W. E. B. DuBois, *Black Reconstruction in America,* 390–91.

18. See Simkins and Woody, *South Carolina during Reconstruction,* 91 (estimating that the proportion of former slaves among the black delegates could have been as high as two-thirds and that "illiteracy was one of their most distinguishing characteristics"); see also Eric Foner, *Freedom's Lawmakers: A Directory of Black Officeholders during Reconstruction* (New York: Oxford University Press, 1993), (an examination of the delegates' biographies confirms that most ex-slave delegates had attained basic literacy); Thomas Holt, *Black over White: Negro Leadership in South Carolina during Reconstruction* (Urbana: University of Illinois Press, 1977), 54 (concluding that many black leaders who had been slaves had been able to "attain a basic literacy and sometimes more"). But see Williamson, *After Slavery,* 377, who cautiously states that "thirty-eight of the [74 black] delegates were clearly former slaves" and "the degree of education possessed by these freedmen was not high. However, nearly all appeared to be literate in some degree."

19. See Richard L. Hume, "Negro Delegates to the State Constitutional Conventions

of 1867–69," in *Southern Black Leaders of the Reconstruction Era*, ed. Howard N. Rabinowitz (1982), 129, 139.

20. See John Hope Franklin, *Reconstruction after the Civil War* (Chicago: University of Chicago Press, 1961), 88–89. The importance of the practical skills acquired by Smalls should not be underestimated. He gained on-the-job knowledge of navigation and seamanship that enabled him to make a daring escape to Union lines in the ship *Planter*, which he later commanded for the federal forces. How he learned reading and writing is still the subject of some debate, but his son William believed that he was helped by a Beaufort schoolteacher after the war. Perhaps it was his own struggle to gain an education that made Smalls a leading figure in developing educational opportunities for blacks and in organizing South Carolina's public schools. See Okon Edet Uya, *From Slavery to Public Service: Robert Smalls, 1839–1915* (New York: Oxford University Press, 1971), 7–10 (developing practical skills), 11–15 (describing his escape with the *Planter* and his Civil War naval career), 25–26 (assistance from schoolteacher in learning to read and write), 35–36 (working for education of blacks), 52–54 (discussing Smalls's contribution to developing the public education system in the 1868 Constitutional Convention); *1868 Proceedings*, 100 (Smalls introduces resolution for a system of compulsory education in common schools open to all classes); see also Edward A. Miller Jr., *Gullah Statesman: Robert Smalls from Slavery to Congress, 1839–1915* (Columbia: University of South Carolina Press, 1995), 44–45, 49 (discussing Smalls's contribution to the development of public education in the convention and his contribution to the education of blacks in Beaufort).

21. Foner, *Reconstruction: America's Unfinished Revolution*, 319, also see 318–19 (where Foner notes that South Carolina and Louisiana had the "longest history" of black "political organizing" which was "led by the free urban elite"). The fact that leading black delegates to the constitutional convention displayed parliamentary skills should not be surprising since several had honed their abilities in an earlier state conclave, the 1865 Colored People's Convention of the State of South Carolina. These included Jonathan J. Wright, Robert C. DeLarge, Alonzo J. Ransier, W. B. Nash, Rev. R. H. Cain, F. L. Cardozo, John Chestnut, John Bonum, and H. D. Edwards. See *Proceedings of the Black State Conventions, 1840–1865*, vol. 2, ed. Philip S. Foner and George E. Walker (Philadelphia: Temple University Press, 1980), 287–88. Eric Foner found that there were twelve delegates to the 1865 Colored People's Convention who served as delegates to the 1868 Constitutional Convention (*Reconstruction: America's Unfinished Revolution*, 112). In addition, black leaders sharpened their political and parliamentary skills in various Republican conventions and meetings prior to the 1868 Constitutional Convention. Miller, *Gullah Statesman*, 45–46.

22. See Foner, *Freedom's Lawmakers*, 39 (biography of Cardozo) and 175–176 (biography of Randolph).

23. See Richard Zuczek, *State of Rebellion, Reconstruction in South Carolina* (1996), 13–14 (describing the intransigent attitude of the white power structure controlling the 1865 convention). In an address to the 1865 convention, Governor B. F. Perry recommended that the convention recognize the elimination of slavery but only because it was "unavoidable" as an act necessary for South Carolina to regain the right to participate in the federal government. See *Journal of the Convention of the People of South Carolina, Held in Columbia, S.C., September 1865* (Columbia, S.C.: I. A. Selby), 12–15 (available on microfilm at the University of South Carolina School of Law Library, Columbia).

24. See S.C. Constitution of 1865, art. 4 (containing no property qualifications for voters except that they not be paupers but requiring that they be white males) and art. 9, sec. 11 (prohibiting slavery).

25. See S.C. Constitution of 1790, art. I, sec. 4 (property holding qualifications),

amended by amendment of 1810, 1 *S.C. Statutes* 193 (Cooper 1836) (providing for alternative property holding or residency requirements for voting in a district), amended by amendment of 1856, 12 *S.C. Statutes* 471 (generally continuing the 1810 approach); S.C. Constitution of 1861, art. I, sec. 13 (this Civil War–era constitution continued the alternative property holding/residency approach). The 1865 constitution finally completely removed references to property in the voter standards. See S.C. Constitution of 1865, art. 4 (containing no property qualifications for voters except that they not be paupers, but requiring that they be white males). For further information on the 1810 amendment see *The Papers of John C. Calhoun, 1801–1817*, vol. 1, ed. Robert L. Meriwether (Columbia: University of South Carolina Press, 1959), 40. See *Journals of the House of Representatives of the State of South Carolina*, Dec. 9, 1809, 73 (Calhoun is listed first [as chairman?] of the committee to whom the suffrage bill was referred). See also *Charleston Times*, Dec. 19, 1810, 2 (reporting the amendment to art. 1, sec.4). See also Lacy K. Ford Jr., *Origins of Southern Radicalism: The South Carolina Upcountry, 1800–1860* (New York: Oxford University Press, 1988), 108 (noting how Calhoun's political career benefited from his role "as a champion of white manhood suffrage"). See Edgar, *South Carolina*, 261–62 (discussing changes in apportionment and the 1810 amendment removing property qualifications).

26. See "Extracts from the Message of His Excellency the Governour Delivered to the Legislature of This State on Tuesday, the 29th ult.," *Carolina Messenger*, Dec. 13, 1808, 1. Pinckney argued that property qualifications for voters led to "invidious distinctions" among citizens. *Charleston City Gazette and Daily Advertiser*, Dec. 7, 1808. These remarks were made in the context of a speech praising President Thomas Jefferson for his high regard for civil rights. Earlier in his career, while debating the federal constitution, Pinckney held more elitist views. See Edgar, *South Carolina*, 249. His later democratic views led to charges that he had betrayed his aristocratic origins. David Duncan Wallace, *The History of South Carolina*, vol. 2 (New York: American Historical Society, 1934), 357–58.

27. *Carolina Messenger*, Dec. 13, 1808, 1. With regard to the question of whether South Carolina was the first state to dispense with property-holding requirements for voting, it is notable that the gubernatorial message stated that "it [no property-holding requirement] is the case in several of the other states, and is the true principle of republicanism." For legislative activity relating to the governor's message and passage of the amendment, see *Journals of the House of Representatives of the State of South Carolina*, Nov. 29, 1808, 7 [4] (message from governor), Nov. 30, 1808, 25 (Major Miles announced intent to move to amend art. 1, sec. 4, "to do away [sic] all pecuniary qualifications of voters for members to the legislature"), and Dec. 2, 1808, 37–38 (no motion from Miles is found but the house referred the matter to a committee consisting of Major Miles and others). See *Journals of the House of Representatives of the State of South Carolina*, Dec. 6, 1810, 61–63 (bill to amend art. 1, sec. 4, passes house); See also *Journals of the Senate, State of South Carolina*, Dec. 8, 1810, 86 (amendment to art. 1, sec. 4, passes senate). The message of Nov. 29, 1808, was delivered toward the end of the term of Charles Pinckney. *Journal of the Senate of South Carolina*, Dec. 9, 1806, 117 (Charles Pinckney elected governor for constitutional term of two years). John Drayton was elected governor on Dec. 7, 1808, and sworn in on Dec. 10, 1808. *Journals of the House of Representatives of the State of South Carolina*, 1808, 60, 84. See also *Journal of the Senate of South Carolina*, Nov. 29, 1808, 6 (governor's message). *Senate Journal*, Dec. 7, 1808, 75–76 (Drayton elected), and Dec. 10, 1808, 98–99 (Drayton sworn in). See J. Harold Easterby, "Charles Pinckney," in *Dictionary of American Biography*, vol. 14, ed. Dumas Malone (New York: Scribners, 1934), 611–14 (describing Charles Pinckney's support of universal white male suffrage in 1808). See Helen Kohn Hennig, *Great South Carolinians* (Chapel Hill: University of North Carolina Press, 1940), 209 (biographical material describing Pinckney's support of removal of pecuniary qualifications).

28. David Duncan Wallace concluded that after vigorous protests against double voting, a custom developed under which a person voted in more than one district only for local offices. See Wallace, *The History of South Carolina*, vol. 2, 375. See William A. Schaper, *Sectionalism and Representation in South Carolina* (New York: Da Capo Press, 1901; reprint, 1968), 188–89 (describing double voting by the landed gentry under 1790 constitution) and 202 (noting that plural voting by the propertied class was accepted by some election officials and rejected as illegal by others). The laws were ambiguous. For example, see Act 2551 of 1831, 6 *S.C. Statutes* 442–44 at III (providing for separate qualification oaths for those who voted as residents and those who voted as property holders in the district but prohibiting voting more than once in the same election). See Act 4414 of 1858, 12 *S.C. Statutes* 624–25 at II (prohibiting voting more than once for the same office). The Resolution of Dec. 10, 1833, directed election officials interpreting art. I, sec. 4, to give an oath to voters which required them to swear that they had not voted in any other district in that election. 1 *S.C. Statutes* 199.

29. S.C. Constitution of 1790, art. 1, sec. 6 (property qualifications for house members) and sec. 8 (property qualifications for the senate); see also S.C. Constitution of 1790, art. 2, sec. 2 (property qualifications for governor).

30. See S.C. Constitution of 1861, art. 1, sec. 13 (continuing alternative property holder–residency standards for voting in a district); see also S.C. Constitution of 1861, art. 1, sec. 15 (continuing property-holding requirements for house members), sec. 16 (continuing property-holding requirements for senate members), and art. 2, sec. 2 (continuing property qualifications for governor).

31. See S.C. Constitution of 1865, art. 4 (suffrage). The capitation tax referred to in art. 10, although to be imposed "upon each poll" whenever land was taxed, was not textually linked to voting. The term "poll" was used in the older sense as a tax on each head rather than in reference to voting. No link to voting is found in implementing statutes either. See Act 4728 of 1865, 13 *S.C. Statutes* 236 (levying a $2 tax on all males between 21 and 60), and Act 4776 of 1865, 13 *S.C. Statutes* 366[30] (levying a $1 tax on each male between 21 and 50). Although not entirely clear, the former appears to have been designed for gathering by the regular tax collector, not election officials, and the latter for collection, at least in part, by employers (Act 4776 of 1865, 13 *S.C. Statutes* 366[30], at 369). Walter Edgar notes that a capitation tax was used as a means of keeping track of free persons of color in the antebellum period (*South Carolina*, 308).

32. Earlier South Carolina Constitutions provided for the election of the governor by the general assembly. S.C. Constitution of 1776, art. 3 (selection of President by General Assembly and legislative council); S.C. Constitution of 1778, art. 3 (legislative election of governor); S.C. Constitution of 1790, art. 2, sec. 1 (legislative selection of governor); S.C. Constitution of 1861, art. 2, sec. 1 (legislative selection of governor). Under the constitution of 1865 the governor was elected by the people. S.C. Constitution of 1865, art. 2, sec. 2 (providing for the popular election of the governor). The earliest South Carolina state constitution, that of 1776, gave the governor an absolute veto power. S.C. Constitution of 1776, art. 7 (absolute veto power of the president). This was abolished by the Constitution of 1778, and the governor had no veto authority until the 1865 document reintroduced a weak veto power that could be overridden by a simple majority vote of both houses of the legislature. S.C. Constitution of 1778, art. 16 (no requirement for governor's signature on legislation); S.C. Constitution of 1790, art. 1, sec. 16 (no requirement for governor's signature); S.C. Constitution of 1861, art. 1, sec. 24 (no requirement for governor's signature); S.C. Constitution of 1865, art. 2, sec. 21 (restores veto but it can be overridden by majority vote in both houses). It remained for the constitution of 1868 to grant the governor a strong veto power that could be reversed only by a two-thirds vote in both houses. S.C. Constitution of 1868, art. 3, sec. 22 (veto can be overridden by two-

thirds vote of both houses). The refinement of the veto power continued with the constitution of 1895, which provided the governor power to veto individual items in appropriations bills. S.C. Constitution of 1895, art. 4, sec. 23 (item veto).

33. S.C. Constitution of 1865, art. 1, sec. 13–14 (containing no property qualifications for house and senate membership), art. 2, sec. 3 (containing no property qualifications for governor), and art. 4 (containing no property qualifications for voters); see also S.C. Constitution of 1868, art. 1, sec. 32 (no property qualifications for any office).

34. See S.C. Constitution of 1865, art. 1, sec. 11 (not using parishes as the basis of apportionment and providing for one senator from each district except for the election district of Charleston which was given two). Governor Perry's address to the constitutional convention recommended abolition of the parish system and adoption of a more equal representation plan for the senate. See *Journal of the Convention of the People of South Carolina Held in Columbia, S.C., September, 1865*, 13. See the description of the debate on this issue and other electoral issues in "The Restoration Problem," *New York Times*, Oct. 2, 1865, 1. The 1865 S.C. Constitution did make some references to the "late parishes" in defining the new election districts in the transitional phase from the old to the new system. See art. 1, sec. 3 and 5 and compare those provisions with S.C. Constitution of 1861 art. 1, sec. 3 and 11 making extensive use of parishes to define election districts.

35. See S.C. Constitution of 1865, art. 1, sec. 5 and 7 (continuing the formula giving equal weight to property and population in House apportionment); Wallace, *South Carolina: A Short History*, 573 (1868 constitution was the first to base representation on population alone); compare S.C. Constitution of 1790, art. 1, sec. 3, 7, 9, amended by amend. of 1808, 1 *S.C. Statutes* 193–95 (Cooper 1836), with S.C. Constitution of 1868, art. 1, sec. 34 (representation based on population). See *1868 Proceedings*, 813 (adopting what became art. 2, sec. 4 (apportionment of house based on "number of inhabitants contained in each [county]" with no reference to taxes). But see S.C. Constitution of 1868, art. 2, sec. 8 (each county has one senator, except Charleston has two). In defense of the system of basing apportionment equally on taxable property and population, John C. Calhoun argued that it promoted harmony between the upper and lower parts of the state and checked the power abuses that would occur if either population or property were dominant alone. See John C. Calhoun, "A Discourse on the Constitution and Government of the United States," in *Works of John C. Calhoun*, vol. 1, ed. Richard K. Cralle (New York: Appleton, 1851), 405. See also Lacy K. Ford, *Origins of Southern Radicalism: The South Carolina Upcountry, 1800–1860* (1988), 108. Although there is some language in Wallace, *The History of South Carolina*, vol. 2, 374, that seems to suggest that the system of basing representation equally on property and white population was abolished in 1865, Wallace makes clear that the system was retained in the 1865 constitution, 375 n.40. He was probably referring to the abandonment in 1865 of the administrative division of the state into upper and lower divisions for the conduct of certain key offices. Compare S.C. Constitution of 1861, art. 10 (administration of treasury and secretary of state departments in both Columbia and Charleston) with S.C. Constitution of 1865, art. 7 (no reference to such system in providing for treasurer and secretary of state) and art. 11 (one treasurer; and the secretary of state's office was at the seat of government).

36. S.C. Constitution of 1865, art. 4 (voter qualifications) and art. 1, sec. 13 (qualifications for house membership) and sec. 14 (senate membership). All of these provisions required that the political system participant be a white man.

37. Reconstruction Act of 1867, ch. 153, sec. 5, 14 Statutes 428, 429 (1867) (requiring state constitutions in former rebel states to grant universal male suffrage without regard to race).

38. *Journal of the Convention of the People of South Carolina, Held in Columbia, S.C. September 1865,* 14 (address of Governor B. F. Perry opposing giving freedmen the vote) (available on microfilm at the University of South Carolina School of Law Library, Columbia). Perry later claimed that he had originally contemplated recommending to the convention that intelligent property-holding freedmen be given the vote but that he had been persuaded not to do so. He later thought that if such a moderate measure had been adopted that it could have helped preempt more radical plans. See Benjamin Franklin Perry, *Reminiscences of Public Men with Speeches and Addresses* (Greenville, S.C.: Shannon and Company, 1889), 275. Perry urged whites to vote against calling the constitutional convention that met in 1868 because he thought it would adopt a plan that would permit universal black male suffrage which in turn would lead to black political dominance and confiscation of property. See Lillian Adele Kibler, *Benjamin F. Perry, South Carolina Unionist* (Durham, N.C.: Duke University Press, 1946), 451–55.

39. *Charleston Daily Courier,* Sept. 26, 1865, 2. The *Columbia Daily Phoenix* reported that a large gathering of freedmen on St. Helena Island had passed a resolution petitioning the convention to grant the vote to all men who were at least twenty-one and asking that no racial qualifications be imposed. *Columbia Daily Phoenix,* Sept. 23, 1865, 2. Although the convention seems to have avoided extensive debate directly dealing with black suffrage, there was a vigorous debate on whether the word "white" should be deleted from the constitutional provisions basing house apportionment on a formula giving equal weight to the white population and taxable property. This debate does not seem to have contemplated giving the vote to blacks but merely to have considered all inhabitants, regardless of race, when considering the population part of the formula. Ironically, this merely would have increased the power of white voters in areas with heavy black populations without giving black citizens a more direct role as voters. See *Charleston Daily Courier,* Sept. 25, 1865, 2, reporting on September 23 debates. See letter to the editor from delegate John A. Inglis (commenting that the debate over deleting "white" from the apportionment formula did not involve extending the vote to blacks). *Columbia Daily Phoenix,* Sept. 24, 1865, 4. See *Journal of the Convention of the People of South Carolina, Held in Columbia, S.C., September 1865,* 79–80 (proposal to delete word "white" fails). "White" was retained in the apportionment formula in S.C. Constitution of 1865, art. 1, sec. 7.

40. See Resolution of Nov. 24, 1865, Colored People's Convention of the State of South Carolina, Held in Zion Church, Charleston, November 1865, in Foner and Walker, *Proceedings of the Black State Conventions,* vol. 2, p. 297. The quotation is from S.C. Constitution of 1865, art. 9, sec. 1. The emphasis is found in the resolution.

41. Act No. 4730 of 1865, 13 *S.C. Statutes* 245. The statute defined a white person as one who had seven-eights or more of Caucasian blood.

42. S.C. Constitution of 1865, art. 3, sec. 1.

43. Act No. 4732 of 1865, 13 *S.C. Statutes* 254, 256, 263; see James Lowell Underwood, *The Constitution of South Carolina,* vol 4, *The Struggle for Political Equality* (1994), 7–9 (providing the basis for this discussion of the Black Codes); see also Act. No. 4733 of 1865, 13 *S.C. Statutes* 269 (guaranteeing certain marital and family rights for persons of color); Theodore Brantner Wilson, *The Black Codes of the South* (Tuscaloosa: University of Alabama Press, 1965), 73–74 (contending that the Black Codes had some positive features, such as guaranteeing the legality of black marriages).

44. Act No. 4732 of 1865, 13 *S.C. Statutes* 254, 263.

45. Act No. 4731 of 1865, 13 *S.C. Statutes* 246, 251.

46. Act No. 4733 of 1865, 13 *S.C. Statutes* 269, 275.

47. Ibid., 276.

48. Ibid.

49. Ibid., 279.

50. Ibid.

51. See General Orders, No. 1, Jan. 1, 1866, Major General D. E. Sickles, HQ, Dept. of S.C., printed in *Charleston Daily Courier*, Jan. 23, 1866, 2; Act No. 4798 of 1866, 13 *S.C. Statutes* 366[29] (purporting to grant blacks improved rights as witnesses, property owners, and criminal defendants being sentenced); see also Simkins and Woody, *South Carolina during Reconstruction*, 58–60 (describing General Sickles's order). The federal Civil Rights Act of April 9, 1866, 14 Statutes 27, established the equal right to contract, hold property, to sue and be sued, give evidence, and receive the same punishment for crimes as white people.

52. Sickles's credibility as a fount of fundamental law may have been undermined by his checkered prewar career as a congressman, including the trial and acquittal on temporary insanity grounds for the murder of his wife's lover. See Nat Brandt, *The Congressman Who Got Away with Murder* (Syracuse, N.Y.: Syracuse University Press, 1991), 162–89.

53. Reconstruction Act of 1867, ch. 153, sec. 5, 14 Statutes 428, 429 (1867).

54. See Carol K. Rothrock Bleser, *The Promised Land: The History of the South Carolina Land Commission, 1869–1890* (Columbia, S.C.: University of South Carolina Press, 1969), xv–xvi.

55. See *1868 Proceedings*, 437–39, for the final debate and passage of Cain's motion to petition the federal government for a million dollar loan for land purchases. See also Bleser, *The Promised Land*, 19–22.

56. See Bleser, *The Promised Land*, 22; see also *1868 Proceedings*, 507–9 (introduction and text of land commission ordinance), 651 (committee report on land commission ordinance), and 788 (final passage of land commission ordinance). For the statute implementing the commission ordinance, see Act No. 186 of 1869, 14 *S.C. Statutes* 275–77. The statute sought to discourage speculation by requiring that the commission sell the land to "actual settlers," that one-half of the of a purchaser's land "be placed under cultivation within five years from the date of such purchase," and that no person could "purchase, in his own name, or for his own use, more than one hundred acres," sec. 6; easy terms for the nonaffluent purchaser were 6 percent annual interest and postponement of payment on the principal until after the third anniversary of purchase. See also Act No. 678 of 1878, 16 *S.C. Statutes* 811 (Sinking Fund taking over responsibility for sale of land that had been purchased by the Land Commission); Act No. 43 of 1872, 15 *S.C. Statutes* 49 (repealing the 1869 act and assigning the duties of land commissioner to the secretary of state); Act No. 278 of 1870, 14 *S.C. Statutes* 385–86, sec. 1 (treasurer to issue bonds to fund commission land purchases), sec. 2 (land sales and purchases by commissioner not valid unless made with advice and consent of Advisory Board).

57. See "Report of House Special Committee to Investigate Charge of Breach of Trust, Etc., Against C. P. Leslie, ex-Land Commissioner," 1157–64, reprinted in *S.C. Reports and Resolutions* (1875–76), which found that Leslie kept such poor records that it was sometimes impossible to trace the disposition of the state's money. The committee found evidence that substantial sums had ended up in Leslie's hands, that he took bribes in return for facilitating transactions, and that he agreed to leave office only if the state purchased stock he owned in the Greenville and Columbia Railroad.

Earlier, concerns about Land Commission operations prompted passage of legislation designed to curb corruption and abuse of power. See Act No. 182 of 1872, 15 *S.C. Statutes* 239, sec. 1 (providing that fees collected by the land commissioner from "actual purchasers or settlers upon the State lands" be deducted from the commissioner's salary if he appropriated the fees to "his own use" or profit); see also Act No. 48 of 1877, 16 *S.C. Statutes* 637 (directing the secretary of state to fill in the gaps in the records concerning price, the ultimate disposition of the land, and whether the state had obtained title); Bleser, *The Promised Land*, 47–65; Williamson, *After Slavery*, 143–48.

The Land Commission often paid inflated prices for the land it sold to settlers. According to the secretary of state, "many tracts of land were purchased at prices far above their actual value," and many people "were unable and unwilling to pay two and three times the value of the land, notwithstanding the terms of sale were easy." "Report of the Secretary of State to the General Assembly of S.C., at the Regular Session, 1872–73," reprinted in *S.C. Reports and Resolutions* (1872–73), 43, 49.

58. See Williamson, *After Slavery*, 148 (concluding that "by the early 1890's approximately 2,000 families had obtained titles to farms through the agency of the Land Commission"); see also Bleser, *The Promised Land*, 157–59 (discussing the estimate that "14,000 Negro families, or 70,000 persons, had participated in the redistribution program").

People who obtained land from the Land Commission often had trouble holding onto it. For example, a statement by the Land Commission Department in 1872 described land in Lancaster as "lying idle" because threats and intimidation by the Ku Klux Klan drove the settlers away. See "Report of the Secretary of State to the General Assembly of S.C., at the Regular Session, 1872–73," reprinted in *S.C. Reports and Resolutions* (1872–73), 43, 149. The Land Commission had difficulty in ousting settlers who had either forfeited their certificate of purchase or who had not made their payments. In fact, the secretary of state suggested that the general assembly take action to enable the Land Commission "to eject parties from the lands of the State when they have clearly forfeited their certificates of purchase." The secretary of state noted, "This will relieve my office of a great deal of petty annoyance and expense of trying titles before the Courts when the parties holding the lands have scarcely a shadow of title." "Annual Report of the Secretary of State to the General Assembly of S.C., at the Regular Session Commencing Nov. 26, 1878," reprinted in *S.C. Reports and Resolutions* (1878), 383, 386. In 1879, Secretary of State R. M. Sims stated that he had "difficulty in ousting parties" who had "forfeited all rights by reason of non-payment." He said that he had "no authority to employ a lawyer to defend the State's interest" when the land owners go to court to prevent ejectment. "Annual Report of the Secretary of State to the General Assembly of S.C., at the Regular Session Commencing Nov. 25, 1879," reprinted in *S.C. Reports and Resolutions* (1879), 421, 422.

59. See S.C. Constitution of 1868, art. 2, sec. 32 (homestead exemption); see also *1868 Proceedings*, 137 (black delegate R. H. Cain contending that he favored "securing to every man, white or black, rebel or union, the right to maintain himself and family from executions of law") and 887–89 (final debate and passage of the homestead exemption).

60. See Foner, *Reconstruction: America's Unfinished Revolution*, 327 n.85 (Foner describes the convention's action on the debt collection stay as follows: "The breakdown of South Carolina votes on the motion (which passed 57–52) calling upon the Army to suspend the collection of debts was carpetbaggers 6–4, scalawags 27–6, Northern blacks 6–8, freedmen 13–22, Southern free blacks 4–11, unidentified 1–1."). See also *1868 Proceedings*, 107–10 (R. H. Cain opposes the resolution on the grounds that rebel landowners should be forced to pay their honest debts, and if this requires them to sell their land, the poor will benefit from redistribution of the estates), 115–18 (F. L. Cardozo argues that stay laws are unconstitutional and debts should be enforced as a means of breaking up the plantations to create a system of independent farmers), and 148 (final passage of resolution). South Carolina courts had in the two years preceding the convention already struck down earlier stay laws as unconstitutionally impairing the obligation of contracts. See *Wood v. Wood*, 48 S.C.L. (14 Rich.) 148 (1867) (interpreting U.S. Constitution, art. 1, sec. 10, and S.C. Constitution of 1790 and 1865, art. 9, sec. 2); *State v. Carew*, 47 S.C.L. (13 Rich.) 498 (1866).

61. S.C. Constitution of 1868, art. 4, sec. 34 (contracts for the purchase of slaves are void).

62. Compare S.C. Constitution of 1868, art. 8, sec. 2 (universal male suffrage), with S.C. Constitution of 1865, art. 4 (restricting the vote to white males), and S.C. Constitution of 1895, art. 2, sec. 4(c) (temporary literacy test with alternative "understand and explain" provision), 4(d) (permanent literacy test with taxable property ownership alternate), 4(e) (poll tax), and art. 2, sec. 6 (disqualification for any of a long list of criminal convictions).

63. S.C. Constitution of 1868, art. 8, sec. 2 (the durational residency requirement was reduced to one year but even this did not apply to those who were residents at the time of the adoption of the constitution). See also the political equality standard in the S.C. Constitution of 1868, art. 1 (Declaration of Rights), sec. 1 ("all men are born free and equal"), sec. 3 ("all political power is vested in and derived from the people only"), sec. 31 (all elections are free and open), sec. 32 (no property qualifications for holding public office), and sec. 39 (distinction on account of race or color is prohibited).

64. *1868 Proceedings*, 824.

65. *1868 Proceedings*, 826. Cardozo argued that the literacy test should be rejected entirely, but if it were adopted, its implementation should be postponed until 1890. In John Belton O'Neall, *The Negro Law of South Carolina Collected and Digested* (Columbia, S.C.: J. G. Bowman, 1848), 23, sec. 41–42, the author describes the law prohibiting the teaching of slaves to read and write and criticizes it as being contrary to Christian doctrine because it prevented slaves from being able to read the Bible. See Janet Duitsman Cornelius, *"When I Can Read My Title Clear": Literacy, Slavery, and Religion in the Antebellum South* (Columbia: University of South Carolina Press, 1991), 39–58 (discussing the legal and social pressure, as well as mob violence, directed at those who sought to educate blacks in pre–Civil War South Carolina, especially noting the Charleston violence of the mid-1830s); see also Act No. 670 of 1740, 7 *S.C. Statutes* 397, 413 sec. 45 (McCord 1840) (prohibiting teaching slaves to write); Act No. 2639 of 1834, 7 *S.C. Statutes* 468, sec. 1 (McCord 1840) (prohibiting free persons of color or slaves from teaching free persons of color to read or write); Episcopal Bishop Nathaniel Bowen, Pastoral Letter on the Religious Instruction of the Slaves, 1835 (criticizing slaveholders who denied "Christian knowledge" to their slaves as consigning them to a "condition by a moral hopelessness" but not suggesting that slaves be taught to read so that they could gain religious knowledge on their own) (available in the South Caroliniana Library, University of South Carolina, Columbia); *Bullwhip Days: The Slaves Remember, An Oral History*, ed. James Mellon (New York: Weidenfield & Nicholson, 1988), 197–200 (including anecdotal accounts of brutal punishment imposed on slaves who attempted to learn to read, noting that some succeeded despite such treatment).

66. See Foner, *Freedom's Lawmakers*, 69–70; see also J. Clay Smith Jr., *Emancipation: The Making of the Black Lawyer, 1844–1944* (Philadelphia: University of Pennsylvania Press, 1993), 209–14, for a brief description of Elliott's career. Elliott's role in the literacy test and poll-tax debates is discussed in Peggy Lamson, *The Glorious Failure: Black Congressman Robert Brown Elliott and the Reconstruction in South Carolina* (New York: W. W. Norton & Company, 1973), 57–60.

67. *1868 Proceedings*, 826; see also Reconstruction Act of 1867, ch. 153, sec. 5, 14 Statutes 428, 429 (1867).

68. *1868 Proceedings*, 830.

69. *1868 Proceedings*, 830–31.

70. *1868 Proceedings*, 832.

71. *1868 Proceedings*, 828; see also Foner, *Freedom's Lawmakers*, 145 (stating that "McKinlay owned $14,388 in real estate according to the 1870 census").

72. S.C. Constitution of 1868, art. 10, sec. 3 (mandating a uniform system of free public schools throughout the state); *1868 Proceedings*, 835.

73. *1868 Proceedings*, 835 (views of B. F. Randolph on the literacy test for voters); see also S.C. Constitution of 1868, art. 10, sec. 4 (compulsory attendance at public or private school by all children ages 6–16). In the final vote, B. F. Randolph voted to remove the literacy test. *1868 Proceedings*, 834.

74. *1868 Proceedings*, 834–35 (W. J. McKinlay, who supported the literacy test, was absent from voting). The vote was on R. B. Elliott's proposal to delete the literacy test from the voter qualifications proposed by the Committee on Franchise and Elections. *1868 Proceedings*, 824–27.

75. The Fourteenth Amendment was probably ratified on July 9, 1868. See *The Constitution of the United States: Analysis and Interpretation*, ed. Johnny H. Killian and George A. Costello (Washington: GPO, 1996), 30–1 n. 6.

76. U.S. Constitution, amend. 14, sec. 2.

77. S.C. Constitution of 1868, art. 8, sec. 8. After the return of white rule, an amendment was passed that added to the list of offenses that disqualified a voter the crimes of "burglary, larceny, perjury, forgery or any other infamous crime." Act No. 3 of 1882, 18 *S.C. Statutes* 3 (ratifying the amendment to art. 8, sec. 8).

78. S.C. Constitution of 1868, art. 10, sec. 3 (mandating a system of public schools which were to be financed by a statewide property tax and the poll tax) and sec. 5 (property and poll taxes finance public schools but failure to pay poll tax cannot disqualify voter).

79. *1868 Proceedings*, 712.

80. *1868 Proceedings*, 730.

81. *1868 Proceedings*, 713. Cardozo studied at the University of Glasgow, became a minister, and had a long career in education. See Foner, *Freedom's Lawmakers*, 39–40.

82. *1868 Proceedings*, 713 and also see 719 (L. S. Langley argues in favor of making payment of the poll tax a prerequisite to voting, declaring that the "Legislature should have the power to enforce the collection of taxes").

83. *1868 Proceedings*, 725 and see also 737–38 (Wright voted to disqualify voters for nonpayment of the poll tax). Wright became a controversial figure in South Carolina government. He served as a justice of the South Carolina Supreme Court from 1870 to 1877. See R. H. Woody, "Jonathan Jasper Wright: Associate Justice of the Supreme Court of South Carolina, 1870–77," in *Journal of Negro History*, vol. 18, ed. Carter G. Woodson (1933), 114–31. Wright was educated at Lancasterian Academy in New York. He studied in a Pennsylvania law office and was admitted to that state's bar in 1866 and the South Carolina bar in 1868. Woody, "Jonathan Jasper Wright," 115, 121. Woody, a Duke University historian, reviewed all of Wright's judicial opinions and concluded that although he was not a legal giant "his written opinions were clearly expressed and judicious in tone." Woody, "Jonathan Jasper Wright," 121. However, Ulysses R. Brooks, *South Carolina Bench and Bar* (Columbia, S.C.: The State Company, 1908), 68–69, contended that Wright did not author his own opinions but "had the help of some capable lawyer in preparing his opinions." Brooks offered no proof of this assertion. A careful analysis of Justice Wright's decision-making technique on the Supreme Court of South Carolina is found in a chapter in this volume by J. Clay Smith entitled "The Reconstruction of Justice Jonathan Jasper Wright." Smith concludes that Wright made skillful use of the jurisprudential approach known as "formalism."

Wright resigned in 1877, having come under fire for reversing himself in an important case involving the Dual Government Controversy in South Carolina during which both Democrat Wade Hampton and Republican D. H. Chamberlain claimed to have been elected governor in the disputed 1876 election. Wright at first agreed to sustain a pardon issued by Hampton and then reversed himself. See *Ex Parte Norris*, 8 S.C. 408, 459 (1876); see also Woody, "Jonathan Jasper Wright," 122–27. Intense pressure to resign was put on Wright by impeachment articles approved by the state house of representatives. The articles charged Wright with bringing discredit on the judiciary by drunkenness. Before the case could be tried in the senate, Wright resigned. In their chapter (in this book) entitled "'To Vindicate the Cause of the Downtrodden': Associate Justice Jonathan Jasper Wright and Reconstruction in South Carolina," Richard Gergel and Belinda Gergel conclude that the charges were unproven and politically motivated. See Edgar, *South Carolina*, 409.

Charges were made that Wright accepted a bribe in *Whaley v. Bank of Charleston*, 5 S.C. 189 (1873), rev. denied 5 S.C. 262 (1874). Woody concluded that the charges were false and politically motivated. Indeed, a joint legislative investigating committee concluded that money to influence the case had passed from D. H. Chamberlain to F. L. Moses Jr. but that there was no proof that money had been given to Wright. See Woody, "Jonathan Jasper Wright," 127–28; see also "Bribery by D. H. Chamberlain in the Whaley Case before the Supreme Court," in "Report of the Joint Investigating Committee on Public Frauds and Election of Hon. J. J. Patterson to the United States Senate, Made to the General Assembly of South Carolina at the Regular Session of 1877–78," (1878), 109–15, South Carolina State Archives, Columbia, S.C.

84. *1868 Proceedings*, 737–38 and also see 709 (original poll tax proposal) and 712, 720 (Robert Elliot amendment providing that nonpayment not disqualify voters).

85. This vote passed the provision to a third reading.

86. *1868 Proceedings*, 838. Whipper became a controversial figure in South Carolina politics. He was elected a circuit judge in 1874 but Governor D. H. Chamberlain refused to deliver the commission of office to Whipper and F. L. Moses Jr., who had also been elected. See Wallace, *The History of South Carolina*, vol. 3, 301. Whipper brought a lawsuit against the incumbent judge to gain the office but the state supreme court ruled against him, finding that at the time of the election there was no vacancy in the position. See *Whipper v. Reed*, 9 S.C. 5 (1877). Later he served as a probate judge from 1885 to 1888, but he was defeated for reelection as the result of a fraudulent vote count. See Foner, *Freedom's Lawmakers*, 226–27. When Whipper refused to turn over the records of office to his successor, he was confined under court order pending compliance. When Whipper sought his release by habeas corpus, the state supreme court held that his confinement was valid. *In re Whipper*, 10 S.E.2d 579 (S.C. 1890).

87. See Proceedings of the American Equal Rights Association Convention in Cooper Institute, New York, May 14, 1868, in *Frederick Douglass on Women's Rights*, ed. Philip S. Foner (Westport, Conn.: Greenwood, 1976), 84 (Frederick Douglass asserted that though he had "always championed woman's right to the vote," the "present claim of the negro is one of the most urgent necessity" since "the negro needs suffrage to protect his life and property, and to ensure him respect and education."). See also the Proceedings of the American Equal Rights Association Convention, Steinway Hall, New York City, May 12, 1869, in which Susan B. Anthony and Elizabeth Cady Stanton opposed giving priority to obtaining the vote for black men. Anthony argued that the greater need was for woman suffrage so that women would no longer eat the "bread of dependence," in Foner, *Frederick Douglass on Women's Rights*, 86–89. The minutes describe Stanton as contending that "she did not believe in allowing ignorant negroes and foreigners to make laws for her to obey," in Foner, *Frederick Douglass on Women's Rights*, 90. A historian of the woman suffrage movement quotes Stanton as arguing that the ballot should be open to women because only the "feminine element . . . can hold the masculine in check." Ellen Carol DuBois, *Woman Suffrage and Women's Rights* (New York: New York University Press, 1998), 95. Women's rights advocates were also bitterly disappointed in the Four-

teenth and Fifteenth Amendments since sec. 2 of the former reduced a state's congressional representation only for denying the vote to "male citizens" and the latter forbade federal and state denial of the right to vote "on account of race, color, or previous condition of servitude" but did not prohibit sexual discrimination. See Foner, *Frederick Douglass on Women's Rights*, 93–98. See also Eric Foner, *Reconstruction: America's Unfinished Revolution*, 447–48. Douglass later conceded the force of Stanton's arguments when he noted that society could not afford to deny itself "one-half of the moral and intellectual power of the government of the world." "Frederick Douglass, Life and Times" in *Douglass Autobiographies*, ed. Henry Louis Gates Jr. (1881, 1893; reprint, New York: Library of America, 1994), 907. See also Philip S. Foner, "Frederick Douglass" in *The Life and Writings of Frederick Douglass*, vol. 4, ed. Philip S. Foner (New York: International Publications, 1955), 43 (describing the Equal Rights Association debates). See also *Elizabeth Cady Stanton, Susan B. Anthony, Correspondence, Writings, Speeches*, ed. Ellen Carol DuBois (New York: Schocken Books, 1981), 152–65, containing an 1872 speech by Anthony in which she argued that despite their disappointing wording, the Fourteenth and Fifteenth Amendments could be used to support woman suffrage. She contended that under the Fourteenth Amendment, sec. 1, women were citizens of the United States as persons born or naturalized there and subject to its jurisdiction, and under sec. 2 they had the right to vote as one of the privileges and immunities due all citizens. When the Fifteenth Amendment prohibited denial of the vote "on account of race, color or previous condition of servitude" women got the vote because the legal disabilities imposed on them amounted to servitude.

88. *1868 Proceedings*, 838.

89. S.C. Constitution of 1868, art. 14, sec. 8.

90. *1868 Proceedings*, 786–87 (remarks of B. F. Randolph in behalf of married women's separate property rights).

91. S.C. Constitution of 1868, art. 17, sec. 5; see Foner, *Reconstruction: America's Unfinished Revolution*, 320 (concluding this was the first time that divorce was permitted in South Carolina). S.C. Constitution of 1895, art. 14, sec. 3, abolished divorce and it was not permitted again until a 1949 amendment. See Act No. 95, 1949, S.C. Acts 137–38, sec. 1 (ratifying an amendment to art. 17, sec. 3). Unlike its 1895 successor, the S.C. Constitution of 1868 did not prohibit interracial marriage. See S.C. Constitution of 1895, art. 3, sec. 33 (prohibiting interracial marriage); Wallace, *The History of South Carolina*, vol. 3, 255 (no anti-miscegenation provision in the S.C. Constitution of 1868).

92. See Underwood, *The Constitution of South Carolina*, vol. 4, *The Struggle for Political Equality*, 34–43.

93. See Act No. 717 of 1882, 17 *S.C. Statutes* 1110.

94. Ibid.

95. See Act No. 542 of 1894, S.C. Acts 802, 804–05 (especially sec. 7). The 1882 and 1894 laws were challenged in federal court as violating the equal protection clause of the Fourteenth Amendment and the Fifteenth Amendment's prohibition of racial discrimination with respect to voting rights. The trial court enjoined implementation of the laws but it was reversed by higher courts. See *Miller v. Green*, 67 F. 818 (C.C.D.S.C. 1895)(enjoining the laws as unconstitutional); *Green v. Mills*, 69 F. 852, 859 (4th Cir. 1895) (dissolving the trial court's order and dismissing the case as beyond the court's equity power); *Mills v. Green*, 159 U.S. 651 (1895) (dismissing the appeal from the court of appeals as moot); *Gowdy v. Green*, 69 F. 865 (C.C.D.S.C. 1895) (trial judge disagrees with but follows the decision of the court of appeals).

96. See S.C. Constitution of 1895, art. 2, sec. 4(c)–(d) (literacy test), sec. 4(a) and (e) (poll tax), and sec. 6 (disqualification for conviction of listed crimes).

97. See Underwood, *The Constitution of South Carolina*, vol. 4, *The Struggle for Political*

Equality, 64; see also *Journal of the Constitutional Convention of the State of South Carolina* (1895), 111–12.

98. S.C. Constitution of 1895, art. 2, sec. 4(c) (literacy requirement with "understand and explain" alternate) (emphasis added).

99. S.C. Constitution of 1895, art. 2, sec. 4(d) (post-1898 literacy test with property tax alternate)(emphasis added).

100. Tillman's remarks are reported in the *Journal of the Constitutional Convention of the State of South Carolina* (1895), 469. For another account of a Tillman speech supporting his suffrage proposal, see *The State* (Columbia, S.C.), Nov. 1, 1895, 4–5.

101. *The State*, Oct. 26, 1895, 2. Since most of the 1895 debates were not reported verbatim, resort must be made to press accounts.

102. *Journal of the Constitutional Convention of the State of South Carolina* (1895), 411–12 (suffrage plan proposed by James Wigg).

103. Ibid., 411–12 (Wigg proposals), sec. 4 (protection against having to travel more than eight miles to register to vote) and sec. 8 (prohibition on eight-box system). Wigg also sought to protect against official manipulation of the selection of registrars and vote tabulators by making those positions elective. Ibid., 411–12, sec. 11.

104. *Journal of the Constitutional Convention of the State of South Carolina* (1895), 412–13.

105. The alternate suffrage plan proposed by W. J. Whipper received only 6 affirmative votes versus 130 against. Those voting for it were all black: R. B. Anderson, Thomas E. Miller, Isaiah R. Reed, Robert Smalls, James Wigg, and W. J. Whipper. See *Journal of the Constitutional Convention of the State of South Carolina* (1895), 420. See George Tindall, *South Carolina Negroes, 1877–1900* (Columbia: University of South Carolina Press, 1952), 81.

106. See S.C. Constitution of 1895, art. 2, sec. 4(c)–(d) (literacy test and alternative) and sec. 6 (disqualifications for certain criminal convictions). For a general discussion of the disqualifications for criminal convictions, see Underwood, *The Constitution of South Carolina*, vol. 4, *The Struggle for Political Equality*, 109–19.

107. S.C. Constitution of 1895, art. 2, sec. 6(1). The full list of disqualifying crimes included "burglary, arson, obtaining goods or money under false pretenses, perjury, forgery, robbery, bribery, adultery, bigamy, wife-beating, house-breaking, receiving stolen goods, breach of trust with fraudulent intent, fornication, sodomy, incest, assault with intent to ravish, miscegenation, larceny, or crimes against the election laws."

108. See William Preston Vaughn, *Schools for All: The Blacks and Public Education in the South, 1865–1877*, (Lexington: University of Kentucky Press, 1974), 65.

109. See Foner and Walker, *Proceedings of the Black State Conventions*, vol. 2, pp. 286, 289–90. See also *1868 Proceedings*, 724–26 (remarks of J. J. Wright).

110. Frederick Douglass, *Narrative of the Life of Frederick Douglass*, ed. Stanley Appelbaum (1845; reprint, New York: Dover, 1995), 20. See also Janet Duitsman Cornelius, *"When I Can Read My Title Clear": Literacy, Slavery, and Religion in the Antebellum South* (1991), 1–10, 150 (discussing the value of literacy as a component of a sense of self-worth as well as a route toward political and economic freedom, and emphasizing the importance given by blacks to public education during Reconstruction).

111. Underwood, *The Constitution of South Carolina*, vol. 2, *The Journey toward Local Self-Government*, 27–32.

112. See Act No. 1980 of 1811, 5 *S.C. Statutes* 639, sec. 1 (Cooper 1839).

113. See S.C. Constitution of 1790, amended by amend. of 1808, 1 *S.C. Statutes* 193–94 (Cooper 1836); Wallace, *South Carolina: A Short History*, 359.

114. Act No. 1980 of 1811, 5 *S.C. Statutes* 639, sec. 3 (Cooper 1839).

115. See Stephen Elliot Jr. and J. H. Thornwell, Reports on the Free School System to the General Assembly of South Carolina, Regular Session, 1839, South Caroliniana Library, University of South Carolina, Columbia.

116. Ibid., 7–8.

117. S.C. Constitution of 1868, art. 10, sec. 1.

118. Ibid., art. 10, sec. 3.

119. Ibid., art. 10, sec. 4.

120. Ibid, art. 10, sec. 10 (schools and colleges open to all regardless of race).

121. *1868 Proceedings*, 100 (resolution by Robert Smalls referred to Committee on Education).

122. See Okon Edet Uya, *From Slavery to Public Service: Robert Smalls, 1839–1919* (1971), 25–26, 52–53. See also Miller, *Gullah Statesman*, 44, 49.

123. Foner, *Reconstruction: America's Unfinished Revolution*, 321–22 (interpreting the provision as requiring integration).

124. *1868 Proceedings*, 889–93.

125. *1868 Proceedings*, 893.

126. *1868 Proceedings*, 894 (in response to a question from black delegate R. C. DeLarge, Wright stated that he was against compelling children of the two races to go to schools together).

127. *1868 Proceedings*, 705–08 (F. L. Cardozo argues in behalf of compulsory education). Cardozo's experience as an educator in Charleston during 1865 through 1867 is described in Joe M. Richardson's "Francis L. Cardozo: Black Educator during Reconstruction," in *African American Life in the Post-Emancipation South, 1861–1900*, vol. 10, *African Americans and Education in the South, 1865–1900*, ed. Donald G. Nieman (New York: Garland, 1994), 343.

128. *1868 Proceedings*, 707.

129. *1868 Proceedings*, 706. Although he did not think the education article required integrated schools, Cardozo believed that mingling of the races at an early age in school was the best means to prevent the formation of prejudiced attitudes. *1868 Proceedings*, 900–01.

130. *1868 Proceedings*, 899, 901–02.

131. *New York Times*, July 3, 1874, 2. Walter Edgar concluded that "With the exception of one integrated school in Kershaw County and several in Richland County the remainder of the state's public schools were segregated" (*South Carolina*, 390). See also John Hammond Moore, *Columbia and Richland County: A South Carolina Community, 1740–1990* (Columbia: University of South Carolina Press, 1993), 257 (estimating that one-fifth of the schools in Columbia and Richland County had "both black and white pupils"). Higher education presented a complex picture. An 1869 statute prohibited racial discrimination in admission to the University of South Carolina, and blacks were admitted from 1873 to 1877. Act No. 125 of 1869, 14 *S.C. Statutes* 203, sec. 1. For a description of the tumultuous conditions at the university during Radical rule, see Daniel Walker Hollis, *University of South Carolina*, vol. 2, *College to University* (Columbia: University of South Carolina Press, 1956), 61–79. Hollis states that "[by] 1876 the University student body appears to have been predominantly Negro," 76. Shortly after the return of white rule, a law was passed requiring separate colleges for white and black students. See Act No. 37 of 1877, 16 *S.C. Statutes* 315, sec. 2. During this reorganization period, the university was closed from 1877 to 1880. Hollis, *University of South Carolina*, vol. 2, *College to University*, 81–82. See also the chapter in this volume by W. Lewis Burke Jr. entitled "The Radical Law School."

132. See Act No. 238 of 1870, 14 *S.C. Statutes* 339–48 (law implementing the education provisions of the S.C. Constitution of 1868); see also Henry T. Thompson, *The Establishment*

of the Public School System of South Carolina (Columbia, S.C.: R. L. Bryan, 1927), 20 (arguing that many county school commissioners of the time could not write an intelligible letter themselves much less administer schools efficiently); Williamson, *After Slavery*, 223–29. George Brown Tindall, in his *South Carolina Negroes, 1877–1900* (Columbia: University of South Carolina Press, 1952), 209–16, describes education under the constitution of 1868. He notes that the schools were segregated, 211. Progress was retarded by a belief among some whites that their tax funds should be used only to support white schools, 212.

133. See Walter Allen, *Governor Chamberlain's Administration in South Carolina* (New York: G. P. Putnam's Sons, 1888), 55. Chamberlain apparently relied on statistics provided by the superintendent of education. 6th Annual Report of the State Superintendent of Education of the State of South Carolina, reprinted in *S.C. Reports and Resolutions* (1874–75), 313, 461.

134. Williamson, *After Slavery*, 228–29.

135. See S.C. Constitution of 1868, art. 4, sec. 2 (providing for the election of supreme court judges by joint vote of the houses of the general assembly for the term of six years) and sec. 13 (providing for the election of circuit judges by joint vote of the houses of the general assembly for four-year terms).

136. See S.C. Constitution of 1776, art. 20; S.C. Constitution of 1778, art. 27; S.C. Constitution of 1790, art. 3, sec. 1 (providing for service of judges during good behavior), and art. 6, sec. 1 (providing for the election of judges and certain other officers by joint ballot of the two houses); S.C. Constitution of 1861, art. 3, sec. 1 (tenure during good behavior), and art. 6, sec. 1 (election of judges by joint ballot of both houses); S.C. Constitution of 1865, art. 3, sec. 1 (providing for the election of judges by the general assembly and service during good behavior).

137. The resentment of South Carolinians toward this royal practice is described in Josiah Quincy, *Memoir of the Life of Josiah Quincy, Junior, of Massachusetts, 1744–1775: By His Son, Josiah Quincy* (Boston: John Wilson, 1874), 106–07. See also Jack P. Greene, *The Quest for Power: The Lower Houses of Assembly in the Southern Royal Colonies, 1689–1776* (Chapel Hill: University of North Carolina Press, 1963), 400–402.

138. See Act No. 980 of 1768, 7 *S.C. Statutes* 197 (McCord 1840) (providing for tenure during good behavior); 32 *British Public Records Office Transcript*, 51–53 (disallowance by the Privy Council on Oct. 15, 1768), S.C. State Archives; John Faucheraud Grimké, *The Public Laws of the State of South Carolina* (Philadelphia: R. Aitken and Son, 1790), 268 (abstracting the finally approved version, Act No. 1095, July 29, 1769). Greene, *The Quest for Power*, 402 n. 4, documents the resentment of the South Carolina Commons House of Assembly. See letter from S.C. Committee of Correspondence to Charles Garth, Provincial Agent, July 29, 1769, in *S.C. Historical and Genealogical Mag.* 31 (1930): 61–62; letter from Charles Garth, Provincial Agent, to S.C. Committee of Correspondence, in *S.C. Historical and Genealogical Mag.* 31 (1930): 137–38; letter from the Board of Trade to the King, in 32 *British Public Records Office Transcript*, 113–17, S.C. State Archives.

139. See James Lowell Underwood, *The Constitution of South Carolina*, vol. 1, *The Relationship of the Legislative, Executive, and Judicial Branches* (1986), 22 n.3, 68–71.

140. See *1868 Proceedings*, 598 (B. F. Randolph argues for executive appointment of judges with the advice and consent of the senate after the model afforded by U.S. Constitution, art. 2, sec. 2, cl. 2).

141. *1868 Proceedings*, 601 (J. D. Bell argues for executive appointment of judges).

142. See U.S. Constitution, art. 3, sec. 1.

143. *Scott v. Sandford (Dred Scott)*, 60 U.S. 393 (1857), 404 (descendants of slaves cannot be citizens), 452 (federal government cannot forbid holding slaves as property in the territories

and the status of slavery is defined by the law of the state in which the person is found); *The Oxford Companion to the Supreme Court of the United States*, ed. Kermit L. Hall (New York: Oxford University Press, 1992), 857–59 (essay on Chief Justice Taney); Walker Lewis, *Without Fear or Favor: a Biography of Chief Justice Roger Brooke Taney* (Boston: Houghton Mifflin, 1964), 398–411 (discussing Taney's opinion in *Scott v. Sandford*). Although Wright seems to attribute life-term sentiments to Randolph, that delegate actually supported a six-year term. *1868 Proceedings*, 598.

144. *1868 Proceedings*, 599 (J. J. Wright prefers legislative election of supreme court justices).

145. See *1868 Proceedings*, 617 (J. J. Wright prefers popular election of judges below the supreme court), 621–22 (Wright voted against C. M. Wilder's amendment to retain legislative selection of circuit judges, the major trial judges).

146. See Woody, "Jonathan Jasper Wright," 114, 119–20

147. For an account of Chamberlain's governorship, see Walter Allen, *Governor Chamberlain's Administration in South Carolina* (1888); see also Wallace, *The History of South Carolina*, vol. 3, 293–302.

148. *1868 Proceedings*, 601–02 (D. H. Chamberlain argues for popular election of judges but compromises and supports legislative selection), 617 (C. M. Wilder proposes an amendment requiring judges to be elected "by joint vote of the General Assembly" rather than by "qualified electors").

149. *1868 Proceedings*, 602–03.

150. Ibid.

151. *1868 Proceedings*, 610 (A. J. Ransier prefers popular election of judges but concludes that the people are not yet ready to play that role), 619 (W. B. Nash asserts that the "people will not be so well qualified to choose who shall be Judges as the Legislature of the State will be").

152. *1868 Proceedings*, 621–22 (the vote was on black delegate C. M. Wilder's proposal to continue election of circuit judges by the general assembly), 617 (Wilder makes proposal).

153. *1868 Proceedings*, 610 and see also 611 (B. Byas also supports limiting the term of office for judges to 6 years).

154. Foner, *Freedom's Lawmakers*, 176–77.

155. See *1868 Proceedings*, 640–46 (see especially the remarks of B. F. Randolph), 641 (against the age limit for judges), 641 (R. H. Cain in favor of the age limit), 643–44 (R. C. DeLarge against the age limit).

156. See S.C. Constitution of 1868, art. 4, sec. 10 (placing a minimum age of 30 for judges of the supreme and circuit courts but setting no upper age limit).

157. See Julius Goebel Jr., *History of the Supreme Court of the United States*, vol. 1, *Antecedents and Beginnings to 1801* (New York: Macmillan, 1971), 241 (describing the debates in the federal convention).

158. See U.S. Constitution, art. 3, sec. 2, cl. 1; see also *Muskrat v. United States*, 219 U.S. 346 (1911) (federal courts may not render advisory opinions). For a discussion of the requirement that federal courts take only cases that are ripe for litigation, brought by parties with an actual injury or threat of injury and that focus upon concrete issues that are not better handled by the political branches, see *The Constitution of the United States: Analysis and Interpretation*, ed. Johnny H. Killian and George A. Costello (1996), 647–98.

159. See *Warth v. Seldin*, 422 U.S. 490 (1975) (discussing the limitation of federal jurisdiction to cases and controversies, especially the requirement that the party bringing the case have standing).

160. See *1868 Proceedings*, 611 (proposal of J. M. Rutland that courts have power to render advisory opinions on constitutional issues "upon special occasions").

161. Goebel, *History of the Supreme Court of the United States*, vol. 1, *Antecedents and Beginnings to 1801*, 104–5 (discussing advisory opinion procedures under the Mass. Constitution of 1780, ch. 3, art. 2).

162. *1868 Proceedings*, 612 (J. J. Wright argues against giving the judiciary power to render advisory opinions). For a general discussion of the traditional role of the South Carolina Judiciary in constitutional litigation, see Underwood, *The Constitution of South Carolina*, vol. 1, *The Relationship of the Legislative, Executive, and Judicial Branches*, 27–58.

163. S.C. Constitution of 1868, art. 4, sec. 16 (granting the court of common pleas equity jurisdiction and providing for the expiration of the courts of equity after Jan. 1, 1869) and sec. 17 (providing that equity court records will be transferred to the court of common pleas); see also *1868 Proceedings*, 674–682 (debates on the consolidation of law and equity jurisdiction).

164. *1868 Proceedings*, 680.

165. Killian and Costello, *The Constitution of the United States*, 1273; see also Wayne L. Morse, "A Survey of the Grand Jury System," *Oregon Law Review* 10 (1931): 101.

166. Bernard Schwartz, *The Bill of Rights*, vol. 1, *A Documentary History* (New York: Chelsea House, 1971), 162, 166; see also Killian and Costello, *The Constitution of the United States*, 1273.

167. See *Costello v. United States*, 350 U.S. 359, 362 (1956) (describing the historic role of the grand jury); see also *United States v. Mandujano*, 425 U.S. 564, 571 (1976) (plurality opinion) (describing the grand jury as "a shield against arbitrary or oppressive action" because it was composed of "a representative body of citizens").

168. *1868 Proceedings*, 304–5 (remarks of C. C. Bowen).

169. *1868 Proceedings*, 305 (W. J. Whipper arguing in favor of the grand jury system).

170. S.C. Constitution of 1868, art. 1, sec. 19. N. G. Parker, the proponent of the version finally adopted, stated that it was based on a provision in the Bill of Rights of the state of Iowa. See *1868 Proceedings*, 315. A similar provision was retained in the S.C. Constitution of 1895, art. 1, sec. 17.

171. S.C. Constitution of 1868, art. 4, sec. 19 (powers of county commissions). County voters also elected school commissioners. See S.C. Constitution of 1868, art. 10, sec. 2.

172. The road commission system is described in Underwood, *The Constitution of South Carolina*, vol. 2, *The Journey toward Local Self-Government*, 13–15 and see also 252–56 n. 28 (where a detailed description and citation of road commission statutes is found). An example of the road commission system at its maturity is found in Act. No. 2372 of 1825, 9 *S.C. Statutes* 558 (McCord 1841). For a general description of the early road commissions, see M. Eugene Sirmans, *Colonial South Carolina* (Chapel Hill: University of North Carolina Press, 1966), 143; see also Thomas Pope, *The History of Newberry County* (Columbia: University of South Carolina Press, 1973), 163 (road commissioners in that county were initially elective but became self-perpetuating).

173. *1868 Proceedings*, 630 (William McKinlay criticizing the local government system as ripe for abuse of power and promiscuous spending). The reader will note in the convention records that the provision finally numbered art. 4, sec. 19, then was numbered sec. 21. For a discussion of McKinlay's considerable property holding and taxpaying, see Simkins and Woody, *South Carolina during Reconstruction*, 95; see also Foner, *Freedom's Lawmakers*, 145–46 (noting that William McKinlay owned $23,820 in real property in 1859, owned slaves prior to the Civil War, and "favored disenfranchising illiterates and those who did not pay a poll tax").

174. *1868 Proceedings*, 630.

175. See Act No. 66 of 1868, 14 *S.C. Statutes* 128, 134 sec. 34.

176. Senate, *Report of the Joint Select Committee to Inquire into the Condition of Affairs in*

the Late Insurrectionary States, 42d Cong., 2d sess., 1872, S. Rept. no. 41, pt. 3, see especially 472, 516–17 (complaints about the tax burden).

177. See House, *Report of the Joint Select Committee to Inquire into the Condition of Affairs in the Late Insurrectionary States,* 42d Cong., 2d sess., 1872, H. Rept. no. 22, pt. 4, 997; Act. No. 66 of 1868, 14 *S.C. Statutes* 128, 134, sec. 34 (requiring general assembly approval for certain local government expenditures).

178. See House, *Report of the Joint Select Committee to Inquire into the Condition of Affairs in the Late Insurrectionary States,* 42d Cong., 2d sess., 1872, H. Rept. no. 22, pt. 4, 987–88; see also *Remarks of Judge Hugh L. Bond in Proceedings in the Ku Klux Trials at Columbia, S.C. in the United States Circuit Court, November Term, 1871* (1872; reprint, 1969), 789–91; Allen W. Trelease, *White Terror: The Ku Klux Klan Conspiracy and Southern Reconstruction* (New York: Harper and Row, 1971), 351–63. Ku Klux Klan interference in the governmental and voting processes is discussed in Underwood, *The Constitution of South Carolina,* vol. 2, *The Journey toward Local Self-Government,* 53, and vol. 4, *The Struggle for Political Equality,* 28–34.

179. Jonathan P. Thomas Jr., *The Formation of Judicial and Political Subdivisions in South Carolina, Read before the South Carolina Bar Association, December 12, 1889,* 23, South Caroliniana Library, University of South Carolina, Columbia. An early twentieth-century commentator looking back on the local government system under the constitution of 1868 said it almost turned each local government into a "separate sovereignty." See S. J. Simpson, "The Constitution of South Carolina," *Bulletin of South Carolina College,* vol. 3 (Sept. 1905): 92, available in the South Caroliniana Library.

180. 1886 S.C. House J. 50 (message from Governor J. C. Sheppard to the general assembly).

181. See 1889 S.C. House J. 363 (for the introduction of amendment); Act No. 433 of 1890, 20 *S.C. Statutes* 649–50.

182. S.C. Constitution of 1895, art. 10, sec. 6 (listing permissible county taxing and bonding purposes).

183. S.C. Constitution of 1895, art. 7; see also *Gaud v. Walker,* 214 S.C. 451, 464, 53 S.E.2d 316, 321 (1949) (concluding that concerns about alleged local government power abuse under the constitution of 1868 had led to the omission of detailed local government provisions in the constitution of 1895).

184. The legislative delegation system is described in Underwood, *The Constitution of South Carolina,* vol. 2, *The Journey toward Local Self-Government,* 92–104.

185. See *Berry v. Milliken,* 234 S.C. 518, 109 S.E.2d 354 (1959); *Evatte v. Cass,* 217 S.C. 62, 59 S.E.2d 638 (1950); Underwood, *The Constitution of South Carolina,* vol. 2, *The Journey toward Local Self-Government,* 90–92, 188 (indicating that special purpose districts were not limited by the narrow list of county purposes in S.C. Constitution of 1895, art. 10, sec. 6).

186. See current S.C. Constitution, art. 8, sec. 7 (directing the general assembly to provide up to five alternate forms of county government); Act No. 283, 1975 S.C. Acts 692 (codified as amended at S.C. Code Ann. sec. 4–9–10 to 4–9–1230 [Law. Co-op 1976]).

187. S.C. Constitution of 1868, art. 3, sec. 3 (no person who denies the existence of the Supreme Being is eligible to be governor); see S.C. Constitution of 1868, art. 14, sec. 6 (applying a similar requirement to other offices); *1868 Proceedings,* 547 (L. S. Langley supports extending the proposed "Supreme Being" requirement to all office holders).

188. S.C. Constitution of 1868, art. 1, sec. 9 (guaranteeing religious freedom by providing that "no person shall be deprived of the right to worship God according to the dictates of his own conscience" but that this does not condone "practices inconsistent with the peace and moral safety of society") and sec. 10 (providing "no form of religion shall be established by

law"). Compare S.C. Constitution of 1868, art. 1, sec. 9–10, with U.S. Constitution, amend. 1 (stating in part, "Congress shall make no law respecting an establishment of religion, or prohibiting the free exercise thereof").

189. See Act No. 225 of 1704, 2 S.C. Stat 236, 237 (Cooper 1837) (example of early colonial South Carolina legislation establishing the Church of England); see also James Lowell Underwood, *The Constitution of South Carolina*, vol.3, *Church and State, Morality and Free Expression* (1992), 19–28 (describing the administrative machinery of the Church of England establishment).

190. S.C. Constitution of 1778, art. 38.

191. S.C. Constitution of 1790, art. 8, sec. 1 (guaranteeing religious freedom "without discrimination or preference"). This approach was continued in S.C. Constitution of 1861, art. 8, sec. 1, and S.C. Constitution of 1865, art. 9, sec. 8. See Underwood, *The Constitution of South Carolina*, vol.3, *Church and State, Morality and Free Expression*, 56–89 (describing the demise of the established church).

192. S.C. Constitution of 1868, art. 1, sec. 10 (antiestablishment language).

193. S.C. Constitution of 1868, Preamble (expressing gratitude to God).

194. S.C. Constitution of 1778, art. 38 (specifying beliefs that must be subscribed to in order to become an established church).

195. See Act No. 885 of 1759, 4 *S.C. Statutes* 98, 99, par. 1–3 (Cooper 1838).

196. S.C. Constitution of 1778, art. 3 (governor, lieutenant governor, and privy council must be "of the Protestant religion"), art. 12 (senators must be "of the Protestant religion"), and art. 13 (members of the house of representatives must be "of the Protestant religion").

197. See U.S. Constitution, art. 6, sec. 3 (stating "no religious test shall ever be required as a qualification to any office or public trust under the United States"). On August 20, 1787, Charles Pinckney proposed to the federal convention a provision that stated "no religious test or qualification shall ever be annexed to any oath or office under the authority of the U.S." See Max Farrand, *The Records of the Federal Convention of 1787*, vol. 2 (New Haven: Yale University Press, 1911):342 and see also vol. 2, p. 468 (on August 30, he revised the language to a form that was close to that which was finally adopted).

198. Amendment of Dec. 6, 1834, to art. 4 of 1790 S.C. Constitution (includes "so help me God" in oath for officeholders). See also S.C. Constitution of 1861, art. 4 ("So help me God" in oath for officeholders). See S.C. Constitution of 1865, art. 5 ("So help me God" in oath for officeholders"). The oath in art. 4 of the original constitution of 1790 did not contain this phrase.

199. *1868 Proceedings*, 568–69 (R. H. Cain argues that belief in a Supreme Being is essential to a civilized society). A brief biography of Cain is found in Foner, *Freedom's Lawmakers*, 35–36.

200. *1868 Proceedings*, 526 (B. F. Randolph argues for a requirement that no one can be eligible to be governor who denies the existence of the Supreme Being. Randolph believed that the requirement was merely an adoption of majoritarian Christian beliefs.). Randolph was educated at Oberlin College and served as a minister in both the Presbyterian and Methodist churches. See Foner, *Freedom's Lawmakers*, 175–76 (noting that Randolph was killed by the Ku Klux Klan in October 1868 while participating in a Republican campaign).

201. *1868 Proceedings*, 562 (R. C. DeLarge opposes placing a religious test in the constitution even though he would not support an unbeliever for governor). DeLarge ended up voting for the final version of the religious test that was less likely to provoke a state inquisition than the version that was originally proposed. *1868 Proceedings*, 569–70. The original version would have disqualified any candidate "who does not profess a belief in the existence of the

Supreme Being." *1868 Proceedings,* 525; see also Underwood, *The Constitution of South Carolina,* vol. 3, *Church and State, Morality and Free Expression,* 44–45. The final version disqualified only a person "who denies the existence of the Supreme Being." S.C. Constitution of 1868, art. 3, sec. 3. This provision was embodied in a motion made by B. F. Whittemore. *1868 Proceedings,* 559, 569.

202. *1868 Proceedings,* 560–61 (J. J. Wright criticizes the religious qualifications for governor on the grounds that they violate the federal constitutional prohibition against religious tests for officeholders).

203. See *Silverman v. Campbell,* 486 S.E.2d 1 (S.C. 1997) (striking down S.C. Constitution, art. 6, sec. 2, and art. 17, sec. 4).

204. See S.C. Constitution, art. 4, sec. 2 (no one can be governor who denies the existence of the Supreme Being).

205. See *Torcaso v. Watkins,* 367 U.S. 488 (1961). The court did not reach the question whether U.S. Constitution, art. 6, sec. 3, applied to state offices.

206. *1868 Proceedings,* 569–70. A substitute motion of B. F. Whittemore replaced the original version that prohibited a person from being governor if he "does not profess a belief in the existence of the Supreme Being" (*1868 Proceedings,* 525), with the final version that said "No person shall be eligible to the office of Governor who denies the existence of the Supreme Being" (559). The Whittemore (final) version was somewhat less intrusive on the candidate's personal liberty because it did not require an affirmative avowal of belief or create as strong a likelihood of an inquisition into the candidate's beliefs.

207. See Reconstruction Act of 1867, ch. 153, sec. 5, 14 Statutes 428, 429 (1867).

208. Ratification of the new constitution by the people was made a requirement for regaining representation in Congress by the Reconstruction Act of 1867, ch. 153, sec. 5, 14 Statutes 428, 429 (1867). See also Yates Snowden, *History of South Carolina,* vol. 2 (1920), 887. A 1951 study noted that "[i]n South Carolina only the 1868 Constitution was submitted to the voters for their approval. All of the others, including the present one [1895] have been proclaimed by the convention." Raymond Uhl et al., *Constitutional Conventions, Organizations, Powers, Functions, and Procedures* (Columbia: Bureau of Public Administration, University of South Carolina, 1951), 32.

209. Compare S.C. Constitution of 1868, art. 10, with S.C. Const of 1895, art. 11, and current S.C. Constitution, art. 11.

210. See also Underwood, *The Constitution of South Carolina,* vol. 2, *The Journey toward Local Self-Government,* 116–214 (describing the twentieth-century home rule movement). Compare S.C. Constitution of 1868, art. 4, sec. 19 (broad power for county board of commissioners), with S.C. Constitution of 1895, art. 7 (focusing on merging and forming new counties but making no provision for county government), and current S.C. Constitution, art. 8 (restoring broad county government power).

211. Compare S.C. Constitution of 1868, art. 3, sec. 22 (gubernatorial veto can be overridden only by two-thirds vote of both houses), with U.S. Constitution, art. 1, sec. 7 (presidential veto can be overridden by two-thirds vote of both houses), and S.C. Constitution of 1776, art. 7 (providing for an absolute veto). Although this document can be described as the first South Carolina state constitution, it still uses the term "colony."

212. Compare S.C. Constitution of 1868, art. 8 (universal male suffrage but incorporating disqualifications in the U.S. Constitution, amend. 14), with S.C. Constitution of 1895, art. 2, sec. 4(c)-(d) (literacy requirement with "understand and explain" and property holding alternatives) and sec. 4(e) (poll tax).

213. Act No. 23, 1951 S.C. Acts 24–25 (repealing the South Carolina poll tax); see also

U.S. Constitution, amend. 24 (forbidding the state and federal governments from imposing poll taxes in federal elections); *Harper v. Virginia Board of Elections*, 383 U.S. 663 (1966) (striking down poll taxes in state elections as a form of wealth discrimination impinging on the fundamental right to vote).

214. See Voting Rights Act of 1965, Pub. L. No. 89–110, 79 Statutes 437–38, sec. 4(a) (suspending literacy tests and other discriminatory devices); see also *South Carolina v. Katzenbach*, 383 U.S. 301 (1966) (upholding the Voting Rights Act).

215. See Act of June 22, 1970, Pub. L. No. 91–285, Title II—Supplemental Provisions, sec. 201(a)-(b), 84 Statutes 314–15.

216. See *State v. Gathers, State v. Smalls*, 15 S.C. 370 (1881) (S. J. Lee obtains reversal of conviction obtained contrary to the Article 1, sec. 18, rule against double jeopardy); See also *State v. Williams*, 40 S.C. 373 (1893) (S. J. Lee fails to convince the court to reverse a conviction for a minor offense obtained before a trial justice on the grounds that the right to a jury trial was violated but succeeds in obtaining a reduction in the sentence as unconstitutionally exceeding the authority of an inferior court). See also S.C.Constitution of 1868, art. 1, sec. 11, 13, and 14 (relating to the right to a trial by jury), and art. 1, sec. 19 (limiting the sentencing power of trial justices). See the discussion of Lee's career as a lawyer in the chapter in this book by John Oldfield entitled "The African American Bar in South Carolina, 1877–1915." See also Smith, *Emancipation*, 217–218 (discussing Lee's legal and political careers).

217. See Simkins and Woody, *South Carolina during Reconstruction*, 94.

2: "To Vindicate the Cause of the Downtrodden"
Associate Justice Jonathan Jasper Wright and the Reconstruction of South Carolina

1. Letter from Jonathan Jasper Wright (hereafter cited as Wright) to Rev. S. Hunt (hereafter cited as Hunt), Dec. 4, 1866, American Missionary Association Papers (hereafter cited as AMA Papers), doc. H5833, microfilm, South Caroliniana Library, University of South Carolina, Columbia, S.C.

2. Ibid.

3. Debra Adleman, *Waiting for the Lord: Nineteenth-Century Black Communities in Susquehanna County, Pennsylvania* (Camden, Maine: Picton Press, 1997), 107–8; *Columbia Register*, Aug. 20, 1878; Susquehanna County Tax Books, Susquehanna County Courthouse, Montrose, Pennsylvania; Springville Presbyterian Church Records, file "CR," Susquehanna County Historical Society. The authors are deeply indebted to the assistance of Debra Adleman, author of the above referenced history of the nineteenth-century black community of Susquehanna County and executive director of the Susquehanna County Historical Society, who has pieced together the family history of Jonathan Jasper Wright in Springfield, Pennsylvania, by a meticulous search of local tax, property, and church records and local newspapers. Additionally, all historians seeking an understanding of the early African American lawyers and judges are indebted to the pioneering work of J. Clay Smith Jr., who compiled a record of the earliest black attorneys state by state in his notable work *Emancipation: The Making of the Black Lawyer* (Philadelphia: University of Pennsylvania Press, 1993). All serious study of the early members of the African American Bar must necessarily begin with *Emancipation*.

4. Adleman, *Waiting for the Lord*, 39, 107; *Columbia Register*, Aug. 20, 1878.

5. R. H. Woody, "Jonathan Jasper Wright, Associate Justice of the Supreme Court of South Carolina, 1870–77," *Journal of Negro History* 18 (1933): 114–15; Eric Foner, *Freedom's*

Lawmakers: A Directory of Black Officeholders during Reconstruction, (Baton Rouge: Louisiana State University Press, 1996), 236; N. Louise Bailey, ed., *Biographical Directory of the South Carolina Senate*, vol. 3 (Columbia: University of South Carolina Press, 1986):1785–86; *Columbia Register*, Aug. 20, 1878.

6. Eric Foner, *Reconstruction: America's Unfinished Revolution* (New York: Harper and Row, 1989), 27; *Proceedings of the State Equal Rights Convention of the Colored People of Pennsylvania* (1865; reprint, Wilmington, Del.: Scholarly Resources, 1970), 4; Foner, *Freedom's Lawmakers*, 236; *Christian Recorder*, June 10, 1865; Adleman, *Waiting for the Lord*, 107.

7. *Columbia Register*, Aug. 20, 1878; R. M. Stocker, *History of Susquehanna County, Pennsylvania* (Philadelphia: R. T. Peck & Company, 1887), 94–95.

8. Adleman, *Waiting for the Lord*, 108; *Montrose (Pa.) Independent Republican*, Apr. 18, 1865.

9. Letter from Wright to Hunt, Sept. 23, 1865, AMA Papers, doc. H5746; Oct. 1865 Monthly Report, AMA Papers, doc. 5784; letter from Wright to Hunt, Dec. 4, 1865, AMA Papers, doc. H5833; Dec. 1865 Monthly Report, AMA Papers, doc. H5879; letter from Wright to Hunt, Jan. 2, 1866, AMA Papers, doc. H5895; letter from Wright to Hunt, Feb. 5, 1866, AMA Papers, doc. 5960; letter from Wright to Hunt, Mar. 2, 1866, AMA Papers, doc. 6017.

10. AMA Papers, docs. H5833, 5895, 5960; Thomas Holt, *Black over White: Negro Political Leadership in South Carolina during Reconstruction* (Urbana: University of Illinois Press, 1977), 82–83.

11. AMA Papers, doc. H5960. This reference to work as a bootblack and waiter is interesting because while studying law and preparing for admission to the bar, Wright apparently worked part-time at a local inn, where he "blacked boots and did all kinds of porter work for thirteen dollars a month." Stocker, *History of Susquehanna County*, 94.

12. Susquehanna County Common Pleas Docket No. 29, Susquehanna County Courthouse, 29. Stocker, *History of Susquehanna County*, 95; *Columbia Register*, Aug. 20, 1878; letter from Wright to Hunt, Mar. 2, 1866, AMA Papers, doc. H6017; Adleman, *Waiting for the Lord*, 108; *Montrose Democrat*, Oct. 16, 1866. There has been some scholarly dispute regarding the exact date of Wright's admission to the Pennsylvania Bar. *See*, Smith, *Emancipation*, 185, n. 256. The official court record in the Susquehanna County Courthouse, indicating admission on Aug. 13, 1866, would presumably settle the matter.

13. *Columbia Register*, Aug. 20, 1878; Adleman, *Waiting for the Lord*, 108; *Montrose Democrat*, Oct. 16, 1866; Freedmen's Bureau Records, Mar. 1867 Roster, microfilm, roll 43, South Carolina Department of Archives and History, Columbia, South Carolina (hereafter cited as SCDAH).

14. Walter Edgar, *South Carolina: A History* (Columbia: University of South Carolina Press, 1998), 385–86; Foner, *Reconstruction*, 228–71; *Columbia Register* Aug. 20, 1878.

15. Freedmen's Bureau Records, *United States v. William T. Bennett*, microfilm, roll 15.

16. *Charleston Mercury*, July 29, 1867; *Charleston Daily Courier*, July 29, 1867.

17. *Charleston Mercury*, Dec. 30, 1867; *Proceedings of the Constitutional Convention of South Carolina, 1868* (Charleston: Denny and Perry, 1868), 36 (hereafter cited as *Proceedings*).

18. *Proceedings*, 699, 724, 726.

19. *Proceedings*, 692–93; Joel Williamson, *After Slavery: The Negro in South Carolina during Reconstruction* (Chapel Hill: University of North Carolina Press, 1965), 221–22; Alrutheus Ambush Taylor, *The Negro in South Carolina During Reconstruction* (Washington, D.C.: Association for the Study of Negro Life and History, 1924), 137–38.

20. *Proceedings*, 724, 726. A poll tax was adopted in art. 10, sec. 5, of the 1868 S.C. Constitution, along with a property tax for the support of the schools; but a proviso stipulated that

no one be disqualified from voting because of nonpayment. See also James Lowell Underwood, *The Constitution of South Carolina*, vol 4, *The Struggle for Political Equality* (Columbia: University of South Carolina Press, 1994), 18–24. However, these funding sources proved to be inadequate.

21. *Proceedings*, 139, 465–66.

22. *Proceedings*, 217–19, 319, 912; Taylor, 131. See *Grier v. Wallace*, 7 S.C. 182 (1875); *Bailey v. Greenville and Columbia Railroad*, 2 S.C. 312 (1870).

23. *Proceedings*, 599.

24. *Proceedings*, 182, 561–62, 660, 787.

25. *Charleston Daily News*, Mar. 9, 1866.

26. Peggy Lamson, *The Glorious Failure: Black Congressman Robert Brown Elliott and the Reconstruction in South Carolina* (New York: W. W. Norton, 1973), 67.

27. Bernard E. Powers Jr., *Black Charlestonians: A Social History, 1822–1885* (Fayetteville: University of Arkansas Press, 1994), 93; *Charleston Daily Courier*, Feb. 20, 1885; Williamson, *After Slavery*, 330; *New York Times*, July 27, 1868.

28. *Charleston Daily News*, Feb. 3, 1870; *Charleston Daily Courier*, Feb. 3, 1870.

29. *Charleston Daily Courier*, Feb. 2 and 3, 1870; *Charleston Daily News*, Feb. 2 and 3, 1870.

30. *Charleston Daily Courier*, Feb. 3, 1870; *Charleston Daily News*, Feb. 2, 1870.

31. *Charleston Daily News*, Feb. 3, 1870; *South Carolina House Journal* (1869–70), 315–17. SCDAH.

32. *Charleston Daily Courier*, Feb. 2, 1870; *Charleston News and Courier*, Feb. 20, 1885, citing references from the *Nation* (New York) and the *Charleston Daily News*.

33. *Charleston Daily Courier*, Feb. 4, 1870; *Charleston Daily News*, Feb. 4, 1870.

34. George B. Tindall, *South Carolina Negroes, 1877–1900* (Columbia: University of South Carolina Press, 1952), 330; J. H. Cornish Diary, Apr. 14, 1870, University of North Carolina Library, Chapel Hill, N.C.; Stocker, *History of Susquehanna County*, 94–95. *South Carolina House Journal* (1870–71), 76. Wright was reelected with 97 votes. The three other candidates in the race received a total of 37 votes.

35. Stocker, *History of Susquehanna County*, 95. Mercur later served as associate justics and chief justice of the Pennsylvania Supreme Court.

36. Francis Butler Simkins and Robert Hilliard Woody, *South Carolina during Reconstruction*, (Chapel Hill: University of North Carolina Press, 1932), 143–44; Woody, "Jonathan Jasper Wright," 118–20; Barry Edmond Hambright, "The South Carolina Supreme Court" (Ph.D. diss., University of South Carolina, 1981), 44–46.

37. *Burgess v. Carpenter*, 2 S.C. 7, 10 (1870).

38. *Redding v. South Carolina Railroad Company*, 3 S.C. 1 (1871).

39. Ibid., 7.

40. *Charleston News and Courier*, Apr. 13, 1871; Foner, *Freedom's Lawmakers*, 236.

41. "Speech Delivered by Hon. J. J. Wright at Liberty Hall, Charleston, S.C., May 31, 1872" (Columbia, 1872), South Caroliniana Library, University of South Carolina, Columbia.

42. *Grier v. Wallace*, 7 S.C. 182 (1875).

43. *Bailey v. Greenville and Columbia Railroad Company*, 2 S.C. 312 (1870).

44. *Russell v. Cantwell*, 5 S.C. 477 (1874).

45. Ibid., 477.

46. *Chicora Company v. Crews*, 6 S.C. 243 (1874).

47. Ibid., 279.

48. *Creighton v. Pringle*, 3 S.C. 77 (1870).

49. Ibid., 98.

50. *Brewster v. Williams*, 2 S.C. 455 (1871).

51. Ibid., 458.

52. *Detheridge v. Earle*, 3 S.C. 396 (1871).

53. Ibid., 400.

54. *Ex Parte Hewett*, 5 S.C. 409 (1874).

55. *Kibler v. Bridges*, 3 S.C. 44 (1871).

56. Richard Zuczek, *State of Rebellion: Reconstruction in South Carolina* (Columbia: University of South Carolina Press, 1996), 167; Edgar, *South Carolina*, 402; Martin Witherspoon Gary Papers, South Caroliniana Library; Richard Mark Gergel, "Wade Hampton and the Rise of One Party Racial Orthodoxy in South Carolina," *Proceedings of the South Carolina Historical Association* (1976), 7–8.

57. Zuczek, *State of Rebellion*, 163–64; Edgar, *South Carolina*, 403; Lamson, *The Glorious Failure*, 234–37; Foner, *Reconstruction*, 574–75; Gergel, "Wade Hampton," 8.

58. Zuczek, *State of Rebellion*, 176–78.

59. Ibid., 190–93; Foner, *Reconstruction*, 575; Lamson, *The Glorious Failure*, 250–52; *New York Times*, Nov. 10, 1876; Gergel, "Wade Hampton," 8.

60. *Statutes at Large of South Carolina*, no. 284 (1870); S.C. Constitution of 1868, art. 2, sec. 14; *New York Times*, Nov. 13, 14, 16, and 17, 1876.

61. *Charleston News and Courier*, Nov. 13, 1876; *New York Times*, Nov. 13, 1876; Zuczek, *State of Rebellion*, 193; Lamson, *The Glorious Failure*, 252.

62. *New York Times*, Nov. 15 and 20, 1876; *Charleston News and Courier*, Nov. 15, 1876.

63. *New York Times*, Nov. 15, 20, and 25, 1876; Lamson, *The Glorious Failure*, 252.

64. *New York Times*, Nov. 18, and 22, 1876; *Charleston News and Courier*, Nov. 18, 1876; *Columbia Union Herald*, Nov. 17, 1876. Several orders issued by the South Carolina Supreme Court concerning the 1876 election disputes, including the one directing the Board of Canvassers to deliver the election results to the court before a decision on the scope of the board's authority was made, were never published, and water damage to the court's archives many years ago has apparently lost the official orders to history. The authors have relied on secondary sources, primarily newspapers, to reconstruct the litigation history of these important cases.

65. *News and Courier*, Nov. 22, 1876. Wright's dissent was no casual matter. This was apparently his first dissenting opinion in his seven years on the South Carolina Supreme Court.

66. *New York Times*, Nov. 20, 1876; *Charleston News and Courier*, Nov. 21 and 22, 1876; Lamson, *The Glorious Failure*, 252–53

67. *New York Times*, Nov. 23, 24, and 25, 1876; *Charleston News and Courier*, Nov. 23, 1876; *Columbia Union Herald*, Nov. 24, 1876; Lamson, *The Glorious Failure*, 254. The supreme court's order to the Board of Canvassers, as well as Wright's dissent, were not officially published, and the substance of these opinions has been reconstructed from secondary sources. See discussion at footnote 64.

68. *Charleston News and Courier*, Nov. 23 and 24, 1876; *New York Times*, Nov. 23 and 25, 1876.

69. *New York Times*, Nov. 25, 1876; *Charleston News and Courier*, Nov. 25, 1876. The National Republican leadership watched the legal proceedings in South Carolina with increasing alarm and concern since the fate of the South Carolina presidential electors could determine the outcome of the Hayes-Tilden election dispute. Reflecting the importance of the South Carolina election dispute litigation, the *New York Times*, a major Republican newspaper, had a reporter on the scene and provided virtually daily coverage of South Carolina events. After the supreme court moved to enforce its order against the Board of Canvassers, articles in

the *New York Times* referred to the court's majority of Willard and Moses as "mercenary func-
tionaries who happen to have at their command the formalities of the Supreme Court" and
"reckless partisans [acting] under the thin cover of judicial authority." Nov. 26, 1876.

70. *Charleston News and Courier*, Nov. 25, 1876.

71. *New York Times*, Nov. 25 and 27, 1876.

72. *New York Times*, Nov. 26, 1876; *Charleston News and Courier*, Nov. 27, 1876.

73. *New York Times*, Nov. 26 and 27, 1876.

74. *Charleston News and Courier*, Nov. 27, 1876; *New York Times*, Nov. 26 and 27, 1876;
Frank Leslie's Illustrated Newspaper (New York), Dec. 16, 1876.

75. *Columbia Union Herald*, Nov. 27, 1876. Wright claimed that he visited the jail at the
request of one of the imprisoned members of the Board of Canvassers, Henry Hayne, to relay
a message to a very ill mutual friend. *Columbia Register*, Nov. 30, 1876. This was an apparent
reference to Walter R. Jones, a black attorney who was reported to be gravely ill on Nov. 22,
1876, and died on Nov. 29, 1876. *Columbia Union Herald*, Nov. 22 and Dec. 1, 1876. Hayne,
however, denied that he requested that Wright visit him while he was in the Richland County
Jail. *Columbia Register*, Dec. 12, 1876. The authors are indebted to the meticulous research of
Dean Lewis Burke of the University of South Carolina School of Law regarding Wright's visit
to the Richland County Jail, research which he gathered in the course of his work on the first
black graduates of the university's law school, graduates who included Walter Jones.

76. *Charleston News and Courier*, Nov. 28 and 29, 1876; *New York Times*, Nov. 29 and Dec.
1, 1876. The members of the Board of Canvassers technically remained under the control of
the U.S. marshal but were allowed to move freely pending the court's decision. The presence
of a number of the board members at the State House upon the convening of the general
assembly on Nov. 29, 1876, particularly angered the Democrats. The Democrats were also
upset by the alleged pro-Republican bias of Judge Bond, who, according to local news reports,
was staying with Governor Chamberlain while holding court in Columbia. *Charleston News and
Courier*, Nov. 21, 1876. Judge Bond publicly denied the report that he was staying in Chamberlain's home, but there could be little doubt that as an early abolitionist in his home state of
Maryland his sentiments were with the Republican Party. *New York Times*, Nov. 27, 1876;
Foner, *Reconstruction*, 40; Richard P. Fuke, "Hugh Lennox Bond and Radical Republican Ideology," *Journal of Southern History* 45 (1979): 569–86.

77. *Charleston News and Courier*, Nov. 29, 1876; *New York Times*, Nov. 27 and 30, 1876;
Zuczek, *State of Rebellion*, 194; Lamson, *The Glorious Failure*, 254–55.

78. *New York Times*, Nov. 30, 1876; Zuczek, *State of Rebellion*, 194.

79. *New York Times*, Dec. 1, 1876.

80. *New York Times*, Dec. 2 and 3, 1876; Lamson, *The Glorious Failure*, 255–56; Zuczek,
State of Rebellion, 195.

81. *New York Times*, Dec. 2 and 3, 1876; Zuczek, *State of Rebellion*, 195–96; Lamson, *The
Glorious Failure*, 256–57.

82. *New York Times*, Dec. 3 and 4, 1876; *Charleston News and Courier*, Dec. 4, 1876.

83. *Charleston News and Courier*, Dec. 5, 1876; *New York Times*, Dec. 5, 1876.

84. *Wallace v. Hayne*, 8 S.C. 367 (1876).

85. Ibid., 381.

86. *New York Times*, Dec. 8 and 11, 1876; *Charleston News and Courier*, Dec. 6, 1876; Zuczek,
State of Rebellion, 196–97; Lamson, *The Glorious Failure*, 257; Edgar, *South Carolina*, 404–05.

87. *New York Times*, Dec. 12, 1876.

88. *New York Times*, Dec. 4 and 5, 1876; *Wallace v. Hayne*, 381. The South Carolina
Supreme Court did later issue an order refusing to dismiss the presidential elector case brought

by the Democrats for lack of jurisdiction, which suggested an intention by the court to address this question. However, the court subsequently reversed itself on the jurisdiction issue, holding that the proper parties were not before the court. *Barker v. Bowen,* 8 S.C. 382 (1876) and 8 S.C. 400 (1877).

89. *Charleston News and Courier,* Dec. 9, 1876; *New York Times,* Dec. 9 and 12, 1876; Zuczek, *State of Rebellion,* 197–98; *Columbia Register,* Mar. 2, 1877.

90. *New York Tribune,* Feb. 18, 1877; Zuczek, *State of Rebellion,* 198.

91. *Charleston News and Courier,* Jan. 29 and 30, 1877; *New York Times,* Jan. 29, 1877; Woody, "Jonathan Jasper Wright," 122; Simkins and Woody, *South Carolina during Reconstruction,* 532–33.

92. *New York Times,* Mar. 2, 1877; *Ex Parte Norris,* 8 S. C. 408, 460 (1877); Woody, "Jonathan Jasper Wright," 123.

93. *New York Times,* Feb. 28, 1877, Mar. 2, 1877.

94. *New York Times,* Feb. 28 and Mar. 2, 1877; *Columbia Union Herald,* Mar. 2, 1877; *Ex Parte Norris,* 459, 469. The Democrats claimed that Wright's change of mind was the result of a "system of espionage, persuasion, intimidation and cajoling" by Chamberlain supporters. The *Charleston News and Courier,* Mar. 2, 1877.

95. *Ex Parte Norris,* 460–68; *New York Times,* Mar. 2, 1877.

96. *Ex Parte Norris,* 468.

97. Ibid.

98. *Columbia Union Herald,* Mar. 2, 1877; *Ex Parte Norris,* 469–71.

99. *Columbia Register,* Mar. 2, 3, and 4, 1877.

100. Foner, *Reconstruction,* 579–82.

101. *New York Times,* Mar. 10, 1877; Zulczek, *State of Rebellion,* 199–201.

102. Tindall, *South Carolina Negroes,* 17–18; *Columbia Register,* Aug. 20, 1878; *South Carolina House Journal* (1877), 31, 39, 92, 211.

103. *South Carolina House Journal* (1877), 137, 159, 182.

104. Tindall, *South Carolina Negroes,* 7–18; Holt, *Black over White,* 210; *Columbia Register,* Aug. 20, 1878; *South Carolina House Journal* (1877), 31, 39, 92, 98, 101, 106, 137, 158–59, 164–65, 179, 182, 193–94, 197–99, 210–11, 222, 225–27, 233–36, 239, 241.

105. Tindall, *South Carolina Negroes,* 17–18; *Charleston News and Courier,* Feb. 20, 1885; *Columbia Register,* Aug. 20, 1878.

106. Holt, *Black over White,* 210; Tindall, *South Carolina Negroes,* 17; Edgar, *South Carolina,* 408–9. Historian Walter Edgar, in expressing skepticism regarding the charges against Wright, noted that the allegation of drunkenness was "a test . . . few legislators could have passed."

107. "Bribery of D. H. Chamberlain in the Whaley Case" (1878), 757–63. *General Assembly Reports of Joint Investigating Committee on Public Frauds* (hereafter cited as *Report of Joint Committee*), SCDAH.

108. *Whaley v. Bank of Charleston,* 5 S.C. 189 (1873).

109. *Report of the Joint Committee,* 761–62.

110. *Report of Joint Committee,* 757–62.

111. *Report of Joint Committee,* 757.

112. *Report of Joint Committee,* 762–63; *South Carolina House Journal* (1878), 559.

113. Woody, "Jonathan Jasper Wright," 128–29. After carefully analyzing the allegations against Wright, Woody concluded that the charges of taking a bribe in the *Whaley* case were meritless.

114. *Columbia Register,* Aug. 20, 1878.

115. Tindall, *South Carolina Negroes*, 31; David Duncan Wallace, *The History of South Carolina*, vol. 3 (New York: American Historical Society, 1934):329, n. 19.

116. Tindall, *South Carolina Negroes*, 25, *Columbia Register*, Aug. 20, 1878; Edgar, *South Carolina*, 412.

117. E. Horace Fitchett, "The Role of Claflin College in Negro Life in South Carolina," *Journal of Negro Education* 12 (winter 1943): 43, 49; Bailey, *Biographical Directory of the South Carolina Senate*, 1786; Tindall, *South Carolina Negroes*, 145. Wright had seven known students who studied law with him, George Marshall, Robert L. Smith, Thomas A. McLean, John Wragg, Dr. William F. Holmes, Joe McKnight, and Joseph C. Berry. Of these, Holmes, Smith, and Marshall became members of the South Carolina Bar. See Oldfield-Burke appendix ("African American Lawyers in South Carolina, 1868–1900") following chapter 5.

118. See John Oldfield, "The African American Bar in South Carolina, 1877–1915," chapter 5 in this volume.

119. Charleston County Bar Docket, 1882–85, South Carolina Archives; *Charleston News and Courier*, Feb. 20, 1885. For further information on Samuel Lee, see Oldfield's chapter in this volume and "A High and Honorable Calling: Black Lawyers in South Carolina, 1868–1915," *Journal of American Studies* 23 (1989): 395, 400–404.

120. *State v. August Gibbes*, Charleston County Bar Docket, June 1882, SCDAH.

121. *State v. Bill Brown*, Charleston County Bar Docket, Feb.1883, SCDAH.

122. *State v. Ben Scott and August Gibbes*, Charleston County Bar Docket, June 1882, *State v. Bill Brown*, Charleston County Bar Docket, Feb. 1883.

123. Charleston County Bar Docket, *State v. Merriman DeVeaux* (Nov. 1884); Charleston County Indictment File No. 6008, South Carolina Archives.

124. Charleston County Probate Records of Jonathan Jasper Wright, Charleston County Courthouse, box 298, no. 11 (Noncupative will); death certificate of Jonathan Jasper Wright, Feb. 19, 1885, Charleston County Courthouse (hereafter cited as Wright's death certificate).

125. *Charleston News and Courier*, Feb. 20, 1885.

126. Ibid.

127. *Charleston News and Courier*, Feb. 22, 1885; *Charleston City Directory* (1881, 1882, 1883); Wright's death certificate; Calvary Episcopal Church Burial Records, Calvary Episcopal Church, Charleston, S.C.

128. Examples include Foner, *Reconstruction*, Powers, *Black Charlestonians;* Zuczek, *State of Rebellion;* Lamson, *The Glorious Failure;* and Edgar, *South Carolina*.

129 *Columbia State Newspaper*, Feb. 20 and 23, 1997; *Greenville News*, Feb. 20, 1997; *Charleston Post and Courier*, Feb. 20 and 21, 1997; *Orangeburg Times and Democrat*, Feb. 21, 1997; *Susquehanna County Independent*, Feb. 3, 1999. The Wright homestead is situated in the town of Springville, Pennsylvania, and is presently owned by Ms. Judy Wilmarth.

130. *Columbia Register*, Aug. 20, 1878.

131. "Speech Delivered by Hon. J. J. Wright at Liberty Hall, Charleston S.C., May 31, 1872" (Columbia, 1872), South Caroliniana Library.

3: THE RECONSTRUCTION OF JUSTICE JONATHAN JASPER WRIGHT

1. R. H. Woody, "Jonathan Jasper Wright, Associate Justice of the Superior Court of South Carolina," *Journal of Negro History* 18 (1933): 114. The son of free parents, Wright was born on Feb. 11, 1840, in Luzerne County, Pennsylvania. He attended Lancasterian University

in Ithaca, New York, and began his legal education as an apprentice in the law offices of Bently, Fith, and Bently in Montrose, Pennsylvania; he also interned for Judge O. Collins in Wilkes-Barre, Pennsylvania. Woody, "Jonathan Jasper Wright," 114–15. While it is unknown if Wright received a degree from Lancasterian, he was awarded the degree of LL.D. from Avery College in Pittsburgh, Pennsylvania, shortly after he was elected to the South Carolina bench on Dec. 9, 1870. Woody, "Jonathan Jasper Wright." 120.

According to one author, Wright came from a rather well-to-do family. His father owned a farm during the 1850s in Pennsylvania valued at $800. Debra Adelman, *Waiting for the Lord: Nineteenth-Century Black Communities in Susquehanna County, Pennsylvania* (Rockport, Maine: Picton Press, 1997), 107.

Shortly after the Civil War, Jonathan Jasper Wright went South and settled in South Carolina to teach. This was a religious mission for him. His object was to assist in "the elevation of [his] race" and to protect the newly freed slaves from the "wolves in sheep's clothing." Letter from J. J. Wright to Mr. M. E. Strieby, Feb. 15, 1865 (from author's files; hereafter cited as Strieby letter); letter from J. J. Wright to Rev. S. Hunter, Sept. 23, 1868, (from author's files; hereafter cited as Hunter letter). During this period, Wright appears to have little faith that whites would ever accord blacks the respect due them even when educated. See Strieby letter. Wright's determination as a black man shows through in a letter in which he affirms to be "a friend to myself, my race and the cause in which I am engaged." See Hunter letter. Shortly thereafter, writing from Beaufort, South Carolina, he explained the meaning of that cause: "as one who is a laborer in the cause of human freedom and progress . . . particularly among my own class." Letter from J. J. Wright to Dear Sir, Nov. 14, 1868 (from author's files). These words help to explain the quality of Wright's struggle as a justice on the South Carolina Supreme Court: that of enlarging "human freedom" for all against the "wolves in sheep's" clothing to whom he and other educated black men and women eventually fell victim.

2. J. Clay Smith Jr., *Emancipation: The Making of the Black Lawyer, 1844–1944* (Philadelphia: University of Pennsylvania Press, 1993), 209.

3. *Proceedings of the Constitutional Convention of South Carolina*, vol. 1 (Charleston, S.C.: Denny & Perry, 1868), 56 (hereafter cited as *Proceedings*, volume 1 or 2). See generally, the chapter in this volume written by James Lowell Underwood, entitled "African American Founding Fathers: The Making of the South Carolina Constitution of 1868" (listing black delegates and discussing their contributions to the constitutional convention). See also James Lowell Underwood, *The Constitution of South Carolina*, vol. 4, *The Struggle for Political Equality* (1994), 11–23 (discussing the contribution of black delegates to the 1868 convention's debate on the right to vote).

4. Woody, "Jonathan Jasper Wright," 116–17.

5. John Belton O'Neall, *Biographical Sketches of the Bench and Bar of South Carolina*, vol. 2 (Charleston: S. G. Courtney & Co., 1859):4.

6. Ibid., 63, 64.

7. Ibid., 378, 381.

8. See, e.g., *The State v. Claiborne*, 19 Tenn. 331 (1838).

9. The black members of the convention believed that within the definition of the common good was a representative government that allowed for rule of black people as well as white people. See, e.g., Mark Seidenfeld, "A Civic Republican Justification for the Bureaucratic State," *Harvard Law Review* 105 (1992): 1511, 1528 (explaining that civic republicanism embraces ongoing deliberative process, embracing all cultures, values, needs, and interests to achieve public good).

10. See, e.g., Seidenfeld, "A Civic Republican Justification," 1511, 1528.

11. Ibid.

12. Ibid.

13. *Proceedings*, vol. 2, p. 593.

14. Ibid., 661.

15. Ibid.,. 578.

16. Ibid., 465.

17. *Proceedings*, vol. 2, p. 465.

18. Ibid., 680.

19. Ibid., 599.

20. Ibid.

21. Wright was concerned that life terms for justices would exclude able members of the bar from serving their state. However, Wright had another reason for opposing life terms: He said, "We have in our ranks but few men of legal experience, capable of discharging the high duties incumbent upon a Judge, to acquit themselves in a manner acceptable to the people. There are men in the legal profession, men of ability and experience, liberal men, who are now ready to get upon the reconstruction train, and acknowledge the principles of progress and civilization, were it not for the fear of the prejudice of that public opinion which is opposed to our plan of reconstruction." *Proceedings*, vol. 2, p. 599–600.

22. Ibid., 617.

23. See appendix preceeding notes, "Opinions by Justice Jonathan Wright, South Carolina Supreme Court, 1870–1877." Other sources have cited a fewer number of opinions decided by the court as a whole, as well as by Justice Wright individually, during Justice Wright's tenure; however, no list of cases is provided to determine which cases were excluded. See, e.g., Woody, "Jonathan Jasper Wright," 121 (stating the total number of cases decided by the court as 425 and the total number of majority opinions by Wright as 87).

24. Volume eight (included in table 3.1) may not represent an accurate account of cases decided during that term because 1877 was a year of transition for the court; Chief Justice Moses died, Associate Justice Willard assumed the position of chief justice, Justice Wright retired, and two new justices were appointed to the bench.

25. The following represents the numbers used to generate the chart: total cases, 441; Moses, 175; Willard, 162; Wright, 90.

26. See Eric Foner, *Reconstruction: America's Unfinished Revolution*, 1863–1877 (New York: Harper and Row, 1988).

27. Smith, *Emancipation*, 217. The racially charged atmosphere facing Wright is exemplified in the following excerpt: "The most bitter attack upon Wright was that of Edward McCrady, in a pamphlet which the Charleston newspapers refused to print. He stated that had Wright been a white man he could never have attained the position he then held; that he had been nominally a lawyer for only four years; and that he had never been engaged in any case before the court in which he then sat, or indeed in any other court." Woody, "Jonathan Jasper Wright," 121.

28. Bailey Kuklin and Jeffrey W. Stempel, *Foundations of Law* (St. Paul, Minn.: West Publishing, 1994).

29. Ibid., 143.

30. Ibid.

31. Ironically, the year before Justice Wright took office Harvard Law School graduated its first black student. See J. Clay Smith Jr., "In Freedom's Birthplace: The Making of George Lewis Ruffin, the First Black Law Graduate of Harvard Law School," *Howard Law Journal* 39 (1995): 201, 214.

32. Kuklin and Stempel, *Foundations of Law*, 147.

33. Ibid., 145.

34. In addition to the cases discussed at length in this section, the following cases are exemplary of Justice Wright's formalistic approach to judicial review: *Redding v. South Carolina R.R. Co.*, 3 S.C. 1 (1871) (holding a master liable for the intentional acts of his servants); *Roof v. Railroad Co.*, 4 S.C. 61 (1872) (holding that the death of cattle by a railroad company is prima facie evidence of negligence on the part of the railroad); *Rowe v. Railroad Co.*, 7 S.C. 167 (1876) (holding the owner of cattle not contributorily negligent in the cattle's death because no duty to contain the cattle existed).

35. *Russell v. Cantwell*, 5 S.C. 477 (1875).

36. Ibid., 478.

37. Ibid.

38. A. E. Keir Nash, "Negro Rights, Unionism, and Greatness on the South Carolina Court of Appeals: The Extraordinary Chief Justice John Belton O'Neall," *South Carolina Law Review* 21 (1969): 141, 167.

39. A. E. Keir Nash, "Fairness and Formalism in the Trials of Blacks in the State Supreme Courts of the Old South," *Virginia Law Review* 56 (1970): 64, 67 (quoting *State v. Manner*, 22 S.C.L. 453.454–55 [1834], prior to emancipation slaves were "'not generally regarded as legally capable of being within the peace of the State'"), and 81 (referring to Judge Nathan Green's decision in *Wesely v. State*, 30 Tenn. 502 [1851]).

40. Walter Allen, *Governor Chamberlain's Administration in South Carolina: A Chapter of Reconstruction in the Southern States* (New York: G. P. Putnam's Sons, 1888; reprint, New York: Negro Universities Press, 1969), 430.

41. *Chicora Co. v. Crews*, 6 S.C. 243 (1875).

42. Ibid., 277.

43. Ibid., 276 (citing *Horn v. Lockhart*, 84 U.S. [17 Wall] 570, 575 [1873]). Justice Wright's rationale appears justified under the doctrine first established by the U.S. Supreme Court in the Prize Cases; i.e., that in an insurrection "insurgents who have risen in rebellion against their sovereign, expelled her Courts." Prize Cases, 67 U.S. (2 Black) 635, 670 (1862).

Although the majority, this was not a unanimous decision from the court. Associate Justice Willard argued that the issue was whether or not the corporation had been duly incorporated. As the certificate of incorporation had been issued by the state, it was of no moment that some of the corporation's stated purposes were in conflict with the U.S. Constitution. *Chicora Co. v. Crews*, 278 (Willard, J., dissenting).

44. In addition to the cases discussed in this section, the following cases show an exceptional adherence to precedent: *Hammond v. North East R.R. Co.*, 6 S.C. 130 (1875); *Davis v. Vaughn*, 7 S.C. 342 (1876); *Wolf v. Haneburg*, 8 S.C. 82 (1876).

45. *Roof v. Railroad Co.*, 4 S.C. 61 (1872).

46. Ibid.

47. Ibid., 62 (citing *Murray v. South Carolina R.R. Co.*, 10 Rich. 227; *Wilson v. Wilmington and Manchester R.R. Co.*, 10 Rich. 52; *Morse v. Adams*, 2 S.C. 56).

48. *Rowe v. Railroad Co.*, 7 S.C. 167, 170 (1876) (citing the holding in *Roof v. Railroad Co.* in addition to the rule in Danner's Case, *Danner v. Railroad Co.*, 4 Rich. 329).

49. *Rowe v. Railroad Co.*, 64 (Willard, J., dissenting) (arguing that a legal principle which has outlived its usefulness should be abandoned as opposed to enforced without respect to its intrinsic fairness).

50. *Grier v. Wallace*, 7 S.C. 182 (1876).

51. Ibid., 182. One interesting fact of this case is that defendant had resold all of the

slaves for an amount over and above the amount he purchased them for, thereby realizing a profit on the "unsound" slaves!

52. *Grier v. Wallace*, 184 (citing *Chastain v. Johnson*, 2 Bail. 574; *Dogan v. Ashby*, 1 Rich. 37; *Gardner v. Hust*, 2 Rich. 608).

53. *Gilliland, Howell, and Co. v. Gasque*, 6 S.C. 406 (1875).

54. Ibid., 409.

55. Ibid. (citing *Abrahams and Son v. Kelly and Barnett*, 2 S.C. 235 [1870]; *Byrd v. Small*, 2 S.C. 388 [1871]; *Meyer v. Blease*, 4 S.C. 10 [1872]).

56. In addition to the cases discussed in this section, the following cases involved statutory interpretation and construction: *Cureton v. Gilmore*, 3 S.C. 46 (1871); *Hunter v. Wardlaw*, 6 S.C. 74 (1875); *Rhodes v. Railroad Co.*, 6 S.C. 385 (1875); *Loyns v. Tedder*, 7 S.C. 69 (1876); *Prince v. Nance*, 7 S.C. 351 (1876); *Hair v. Blease*, 8 S.C. 63 (1876); *Tinsley v. Kirby*, 8 S.C. 113 (1877).

57. *Boykin v. Watts*, 6 S.C. 76 (1876).

58. Ibid., 77.

59. Ibid., 83.

60. *Sullivan v. Hellams*, 6 S.C. 184 (1875).

61. Ibid.

62. Ibid., 185.

63. Ibid., 184.

64. Ibid.

65. See Statement of Political Cases, 8 S.C. 365 (1876) (provides an extraordinary summary of the background of the political cases).

66. See Hampton M. Jarrell, *Wade Hampton and the Negro* (Columbia: University of South Carolina Press, 1950), 41–45, 60.

67. "How Voting Was Done in Edgefield," *New York Times*, Nov. 23, 1876, 1.

68. Ibid.

69. Allen, Governor Chamberlain's Administration, 430 (quoting sections 26 and 27 of an act approved Mar. 1, 1870). The statute limited the powers of the board only in cases where such power resided elsewhere, such as in the legislature. Ibid.

70. Allen, *Governor Chamberlain's Administration in South Carolina*, 428.

71. "The Situation in South Carolina," *New York Times*, Nov. 22, 1876, 1.

72. "South Carolina," *New York Times*, Nov. 18, 1876, 1.

73. G. N., "South Carolina," *New York Times*, Nov. 23, 1876, 1 (reporting on whites intimidating blacks at voting polls).

74. Ibid.

75. "The Situation in South Carolina," *New York Times*, Nov. 22, 1876, 1.

76. "South Carolina, Canvassers," *New York Times*, Nov. 28, 1876, 1.

77. Allen, *Governor Chamberlain's Administration* 434 ("The court avenged itself for its mortification by consigning all the members of the Board to prison for contempt"). For a further account of the election dispute, see ibid. 436–67.

78. *State ex rel. Wallace v. Hayne and Mackey*, 8 S.C. 367 (1876).

79. Ibid., 380 (Justice Willard concurring). He states: "The Court commanded that specific ministerial act to be performed. After the judgment was rendered from the bench, and before the writ of mandamus was issued, it appears from the proceedings in that case, which are before us, that the Board undertook to make certain declarations in violation of their duty under the judgment of this Court. Under familiar principles, that action was null and void and could give no legal foundation to any legal action whatever." *State ex rel. Wallace v. Hayne and Mackey*.

80. *State ex rel. Wallace v. Hayne and Mackey*, 380–81.

81. Tim Smith, "State Supreme Court to Honor Nation's First Black Appellate Judge," *Greenville News*, Feb. 20, 1997, D-1. (Wright died of tuberculosis in 1885). Wright, a state senator, was elected to the post of justice by the South Carolina legislature by a vote of 72 to 52. Sid Gaulden, "S.C. Court Honors Pioneering Justice," Charleston *Post and Courier*, Feb. 21, 1997, A-6.

82. See note 21.

83. See Hunter letter.

84. *Whaley v. Bank of Charleston*, 5 S.C. 189 (1873) (Willard, J., dissenting).

85. See, e.g., John S. Reynolds, *Reconstruction in South Carolina, 1865–1877* (Columbia, S.C.: The State Company, 1905; reprint, New York: Negro Universities Press, 1969). Originally published in 1905, ten years after the 1895 South Carolina Constitution had been enacted and blacks had fallen from political power, Reynolds's book's depiction of black leaders during the Reconstruction would be remembered only "as 'stench in the nostrils of decent people' and a disgrace to the country." Reynolds, *Reconstruction in South Carolina*, 514.

86. Smith, *Emancipation*, 217 (citing Peggy Lamson, *The Glorious Failure: Black Congressman Robert Brown Elliott and the Reconstruction in South Carolina* [New York: W. W. Norton, 1973], 271).

87. Woody, "Jonathan Jasper Wright," 117.

88. Ibid., 121.

4: THE RADICAL LAW SCHOOL
The University of South Carolina School of Law and Its African American Graduates, 1873–1877

1. *University of South Carolina School of Law Alumni Directory* (White Plains, NY: Harris, 1989), vi.

2. Edwin L. Green, *A History of the University of South Carolina*, vol. 95 (Columbia, S.C.: The State Company, 1916), 409–15

3. *Charleston News and Courier*, Oct. 13, 1873.

4. *Edgefield Advertiser*, Oct. 16, 1873.

5. Quoted in the *Edgefield Advertiser*, Oct. 23, 1873.

6. *Columbia Daily Union Herald*, Feb. 9, 1875, quoting the *Charleston News and Courier*.

7. Green, *A History of the University of South Carolina*, 90.

8. See *Columbia Daily Union Herald*, Feb. 11, 1875, and *Register of South Carolina College*, 1874–75, South Caroliniana Library, University of South Carolina (hereafter cited as SCL). One historian says that the university had 231 students in 1875. See David Duncan Wallace, *South Carolina: A Short History* (Chapel Hill: University of North Carolina Press, 1951), 590. Green, in his *A History of the University of South Carolina*, refused to list any enrollments for the "Radical" period. But if Wallace is right about the figure of 231, according to Green's enrollment figures, the university had not had such a large enrollment since 1858 and did not exceed that number again until 1886. Ibid., 437–38.

9. *Columbia Daily Union Herald*, Feb. 10, 1875.

10. Green, *A History of the University of South Carolina*, 413, quoting John S. Reynolds, *Reconstruction in South Carolina* (Columbia, S.C.: The State Company, 1905).

11. *Abbeville Medium*, Oct. 15, 1873.

12. Ibid.

13. Daniel Walker Hollis, "College to University," in *University of South Carolina*, vol. 2 (Columbia: University of South Carolina Press, 1956):72

14. Senate, *Miscellaneous Documents of the Senate of the United States for the 2nd Session of the Forty-Fourth Congress: South Carolina in 1876 Testimony as to the Denial of the Elective Franchise in South Carolina at the Elections of 1875 and 1876*, 44th Cong., 2nd sess., 1877, vol. 1, p. 238 (hereafter cited as *South Carolina in 1876*).

15. Professor Fisk Brewer's written statement dated 1876, Papers of Fisk Brewer, SCL.

16. Racial identification of students cannot be exact. However, it appears from university records, census records, city directories, and secondary sources that all of these law school classes were integrated. See the appendix at the end of this chapter which lists 19 African American students and 17 white students who were enrolled in the law school between 1873 and 1877.

17. By comparison in the first eight years of its "real beginning," 1883–1891, the law school had 53 graduates. See *Roll of Students, 1805–1905—South Carolina College*, University of South Carolina Archives, Columbia (hereafter cited as USC Archives).

18. Walter B. Edgar, ed., *Biographical Directory of the South Carolina House of Representatives*, vol. 1 (Columbia: University of South Carolina Press, 1974), 13.

19. See *Columbia Directory*, 1875–76, *Columbia, So. Ca., Directory*, 1879–80, and *Columbia City Directory*, 1885.

20. Under an 1868 statute, the circuit courts of the state were authorized to admit any male citizen who had read law for two years or graduated from any law school in the United States to practice in the circuit or probate courts. See No. 46, *An Act to Regulate the Admission of Persons to Practice As Attorneys, Solicitors and Counselors in the Courts of the State*, in *The Statutes at Large of South Carolina*, vol. 14 (1873). Reports of such admissions are fairly common. For example, the *Columbia Daily Union* on May 20, 1874, reported that Henry Sparnick of Aiken was admitted to practice by the circuit court. The *Columbia Daily Union Herald* on July 9, 1875, carried a similar report that C. C. Puffer and J. G. Thompson were admitted to the circuit and probate court. None of these names appear on the Roll of Attorneys of the South Carolina Supreme Court. There are numerous such admissions. While I have not found any newspaper reports that mention any USC graduates as being admitted through the circuit court procedure, it is logical to assume that since city directories and other such sources report these individuals as practicing law they were admitted to practice by the circuit courts.

On Mar. 12, 1878, the legislature repealed the provision that allowed admissions by practice by the circuit court. Act No. 442, *Acts and Joint Resolutions of the General Assembly of the State of South Carolina* (1876).

21. See Hollis, *University of South Carolina*, vol. 2, p. 61. Hollis used the term "Radical" to describe the university during the period of 1873 to 1877. The term was commonly used to describe Republicans during Reconstruction. One Democrat during the period told a congressional committee, "I do not say republicans. It is radicals here and not republicans." *South Carolina in 1876*, vol. 1, p. 603.

22. See letter of C. C. Scott, *The State* (Columbia, S.C.), May 8, 1911 (hereafter cited as the Scott letter).

23. According to the Scott letter to *The State* newspaper in May of 1911, there were 17 "colored" in the law school in 1874 and 1875. Unfortunately, Scott did not identify all of them in his letter. Based on those identified by Scott and other sources, I have actually identified 19 African Americans. These include the 11 who graduated with LL.B.'s between 1874 and 1877 and who are the main focus of this article. Of the African American students who did not receive a degree, I have identified 8. These are Thomas E. Miller, William F. Myers, Arthur

O'Hear, C. M. Wilder, Joseph Boston, Edward James Sawyer, Charles H. Sperry, and Paul J. Mishow.

O'Hear was from a prominent Charleston family and had attended Avery Institute and Oberlin College. He died of tuberculosis on Aug. 3, 1876. See Willard B. Gatewood, "Alonzo Clifton McClennan: Black Midshipman from South Carolina, 1873–1874," *South Carolina Historical Magazine* 89 (1988): 24, 30 n. 18; and Edmund Drago, *Initiative Paternalism and Race Relations: Charleston's Avery Normal Institute* (Athens: University of Georgia Press, 1990), 54. Wilder had been a delegate to the constitutional convention in 1868, served one term in the legislature, and was postmaster in Columbia for many years. See Michael E. Thompson, "Blacks, Carpetbaggers, and Scalawags: A Study of the Membership of the South Carolina Legislature, 1868–1870" (Ph.D. diss., Washington State University, 1975), 194; and *The Columbia City Directory* (1885), 105. A brief biographical sketch of Wilder can be found in Eric Foner, *Freedom's Lawmakers: A Directory of Black Officeholders during Reconstruction* (New York: Oxford University Press, 1993), 229–30. Boston represented Newberry County in the state house of representatives from 1868 to 1876. Boston was born free in Virginia and was an educator. Walter B. Edgar, ed., *Biographical Directory of the South Carolina House of Representatives*, vol. 1 (Columbia: University of South Carolina Press, 1986); and Thompson, *Blacks, Carpetbaggers, and Scalawags.* Also see Foner, *Freedom's Lawmakers*, 21. Edward James Sawyer was enrolled in 1874 and 1875. He was admitted to the bar in 1885. See Roll of Attorneys of the South Carolina Supreme Court. According to Scott, Sawyer was a very successful businessman and lawyer in Bennetsville, S.C. Charles H. Sperry was from Georgetown and was a teacher before he enrolled in the law school in January 1874. See Bureau of the Census, U.S. Manuscript Census, 1870 for Georgetown, S.C. (Washington, D.C., National Archives; hereafter, all census records will be cited as U.S. Manuscript Census, with appropriate date and location. All S.C. census records may be located at the South Carolina Department of Archives and History, hereafter cited as SCDAH); and *Register of South Carolina College, 1873,* USC Archives. In 1880 Sperry was again living in Georgetown and employed as a carpenter. See *Manuscript U.S. Census, 1880 for Georgetown, S.C.*

The Register of South Carolina College for the Reorganization of the University, 1873 (SCL) lists Mishow only as an undergraduate and does not list Miller or Myers as students. Miller and Myers are mentioned in the Scott letter. While Myers is not listed in the register, he is listed as a student in the university's catalogue for 1876. Mishow is listed as a law student in the *Report of the Chairman of the Faculty of the University of South Carolina* (1875). He was a student at Howard University and probably was persuaded to attend USC by F. L. Cardozo. See John E. Farley, "Francis L. Cardozo" (B.A. thesis, Princeton University, 1949), 75. Mishow was a free person of color whose father, Joshua Mishow, supported the family as a carpenter. See U.S. Manuscript Census, 1860, for Charleston, S.C. Mishow had attended Avery Institute in Charleston and after leaving USC moved to Washington, D.C., and became a physician. Edmund Drago, *Initiative, Paternalism, and Race Relations: Charleston's Avery Normal Institute* (1990), 98. Miller and Myers both became lawyers and were admitted to practice by the state supreme court. See Roll of Attorneys. Miller became a U.S. congressman, a state senator, a college president, and a delegate to the 1895 Constitutional Convention. Miller died in 1938. See *Biographical Directory of the South Carolina Senate*, vol. 2 (Columbia: University of South Carolina Press, 1974), 1114; William C. Hine, "Thomas E. Miller and the Early Years of South Carolina State University," *Carologue* 12 (1996): 8; and James Lowell Underwood, *The Constitution of South Carolina*, vol. 4, *The Struggle for Political Equality* (Columbia: University of South Carolina Press, 1994), 36–37. Myers served in the state senate from Colleton County from 1874 to 1878. He remained active in Republican politics until the 1890s and died in Columbia in 1917. *Biographical Directory of the South Carolina Senate*, vol. 2, p. 1185. Also see Foner, *Freedom's Lawmakers*, 157.

24. Avery Institute was begun by the American Missionary Society in Charleston to educate the freedmen at the conclusion of the Civil War. For a history of Avery Institute see Drago, *Initiative, Paternalism, and Race Relations*.

25. See letter dated Dec. 23, 1873, from Prof. R. W. Mitchell of Howard University informing the university: "Mr. T. MCcants Stuart [*sic*], at his own request, has been granted an honorable dismission from this University. Mr. Stuart has been for a long time under my personal instruction. He has always deported himself as a gentleman and has the confidence and respect of all with whom he has come in contact during his stay here." USC Archives. Stewart was enrolled by January 1874 as it was reported that he had achieved "a satisfactory in Latin and Greek, Mathematics and History." Report to Faculty, Jan. 7, 1874, USC Archives.

26. Dorothy Sterling, ed., *The Trouble They Seen* (Garden City, N.Y.: Doubleday, 1976), 346.

27. William J. Cooper, *The Conservative Regime: South Carolina, 1877–1890* (Baltimore, Md.: The Johns Hopkins University Press, 1968), 40–41.

28. See Robert Stevens, "Two Cheers for 1870: The American Law School," in *Law in American History*, ed. Donald Fleming and Bernard Bailyn (Boston: Little, Brown, 1971). Also see Lawrence M. Friedman, *A History of American Law* (New York: Simon and Schuster, 1973), 525–38; and Dennis R. Nolan, *Readings in the History of the American Legal Profession* (Charlottesville, Va.: Michie Company, 1980), 197–258.

29. George C. Rogers Jr., in *Generations of Lawyers* (Columbia: South Carolina Bar Foundation, 1992), 56, reports that Dean Melton in 1872 "had reported that only four out of the ten students in the law school submitted to daily recitations and examinations."

30. See Lou Falkner Williams, *The Great South Carolina Ku Klux Klan Trials, 1871–1872* (Athens: University of Georgia Press, 1996), 89.

31. South Carolina College, chartered in 1801, became the University of South Carolina in 1865. See Hollis, *University of South Carolina*, vol. 2, for a discussion of the various permutations of the university's name from 1801 forward.

32. *Columbia Directory*, 1875–76.

33. *Catalogue, University of South Carolina* (1873) 11, USC Archives.

34. Ibid., 5.

35. *Catalogue of the University of South Carolina* (1869) 38, USC Archives.

36. *Catalogue, University of South Carolina, 1875–76*, 16–17, USC Archives.

37. William Shepard McAninch, "Petigru College," *South Carolina Law Review* 49 (1998): 531.

38. See U.S. Manuscript Census of Slaves, 1800, for Sumter, South Carolina, SCDAH.

39. *Catalogue, University of South Carolina, 1875–76*.

40. Jones's admission appears to have only been noted by one of the state's newspapers. See the *Yorkville Enquirer*, Oct. 23, 1873.

41. See J. Clay Smith Jr., *Emancipation: The Making of the Black Lawyer, 1844–1944* (Philadelphia: University of Pennsylvania Press, 1993), 35. Harvard and Howard Universities both had African American law school graduates before the University of South Carolina, but neither is a state-supported school. The University of Michigan followed in 1877 and the University of Iowa in 1879.

42. Septima Jones paid capitation tax in Charleston as a "free Negro" starting in 1848. See Judith M. Brimelow and Michael F. Stevens, *State Free Negro Capitation Tax Books, Charleston, S.C., ca. 1811–1860* (1983). Evidence of their relationship is found in the Estate of Walter B.[*sic*] Jones, box 105, package no. 2605 (Dec. 15, 1876), Estate records of Richland County, SCDAH. According to the 1870 census Septima A. Jones was a 40-year-old mulatto. U.S. Manuscript Census, 1870, for Charleston, S.C., SCDAH.

43. See Scott letter.

44. Alumni Records, Archives of Oberlin College, Oberlin, Ohio.

45. "Report of the Secretary of State," *Reports and Resolutions of the General Assembly of the State of South Carolina* (1872–73), 50.

46. Carol K. Bleser, *The Promised Land* (Columbia: University of South Carolina Press, 1963), 92.

47. Diary of Josephus Woodruff, Nov. 1873, 111, SCDAH.

48. See clippings dated Dec. 22, 1873, and Feb. 8, 1874, from the Scrapbook of Fisk P. Brewer, Caroliniana. The Clariosophic Society was a student literary society that dated from 1806. See Green, *A History of the University of South Carolina,* 264.

49. Gatewood, "Alonzo Clifton McClennan," 24. This description by Alonzo McClennan was in part the result of the successful efforts by Jones and Arthur O'Hear to tutor McClennan to pass the Naval Academy entrance exam.

50. *Columbia Daily Union,* Apr. 22, 1874. It is interesting to note that on the day Jones was elected city clerk, the *Columbia Daily Union* reported that Professor John Ellis from Jones's alma mater, Oberlin College, was in town and visited the state house, the university, and other public buildings. Had Ellis been one of Jones's professors?

51. *Catalogue, University of South Carolina* (1876), Caroliniana.

52. See Roll of Attorneys.

53. See letter dated Dec. 2, 1874, from D. H. Chamberlain, Governor, to W. R. Jones, Private Secretary, Correspondence of D. H. Chamberlain, SCDAH.

54. *Columbia Union Herald,* Aug. 28, 1876 (Jones debates Col. Thomas Taylor in Gadsden); *Columbia Union Herald,* Sept. 8, 1876 (Jones participated in ward meetings); *Columbia Union Herald,* Sept. 11, 1876 (Jones elected secretary of the Richland County Republican convention).

55. Foner, *Freedom's Lawmakers,* 123.

56. *Columbia Daily Union,* May 12, 1874.

57. Correspondence of Gov. D. H. Chamberlain, no. 2548, Jan. 1, 1876, SCDAH.

58. *Columbia Union Herald,* Nov. 13, 1876 (Jones defeated Andrew Crawford: 3,845 votes to 2,403); *Columbia Union Herald,* Dec. 1, 1876 ("Death of Walter R. Jones"). Jones's illness led to a display of the infighting among Republicans after the 1876 election. Apparently, Justice Jonathan Jasper Wright visited Jones on his deathbed to deliver a message from Secretary of State Henry E. Hayne, who had been jailed for contempt by the supreme court for failure to certify election results from Edgefield and Laurens Counties. The propriety of Wright's visit to someone in jail was questioned in the press and Hayne denied he had sent for Wright. See *Columbia Register,* Nov. 30, 1876, and Dec. 12, 1876. For another account of this jailhouse visit see Richard Gergel's chapter on the life of Jonathan Jasper Wright, in this volume.

And even in death, Jones was involved in the struggle with the Redshirts. Richard Greener testified before a U.S. Senate subcommittee that when he and the Jones family were accompanying the body to Charleston for burial they were verbally assaulted by Hampton supporters and that he feared they were going to be physically attacked. *South Carolina in 1876,* vol. 1, p. 238.

59. See Estate of Jones.

60. Foner, *Freedom's Lawmakers,* 123.

61. See Report of the Joint Investigating Committee on Public Frauds, *1877–78 Reports and Resolutions of the General Assembly,* 677.

62. C. L. Anderson served for a time as a revenue collector. See *Columbia Directory* (1875–76), 27. Charles W. Cummings's father was on the faculty of the university. Nothing is

known of Edgar Caypless, who enrolled in 1873 and graduated in 1874. None of these three were admitted to practice before the S.C. Supreme Court, but it is possible that any of them could have practiced law in the state by being admitted to the circuit court.

63. See *Columbia Daily Union Herald*, July 11, 1875.

64. See the Scott letter.

65. Ibid.

66. *Columbia Register*, Oct. 27, 1876 (describing a Henry Johnson as a member of "a motley crew" at a Republican rally from which "Every decent white republican was absent").

67. See Appointments of D. H. Chamberlain, Mar. 24, 1876, and Sept. 7, 1876, SCDAH.

68. *Columbia Daily Union Herald*, Feb. 24, 1877.

69. See *Biographical Directory of the South Carolina Senate, 1776–1985*, vol. 2, p. 702. Also see Foner, *Freedom's Lawmakers*, 100.

70. *The (Washington) Peoples' Advocate*, Dec. 13, 1879, and Aug. 14, 1880.

71. *Columbia Daily Union*, Mar. 13, 1874.

72. For more complete biographical information on Stewart, see Albert S. Broussard, *African-American Odyssey: The Stewarts, 1853–1963* (Lawrence: University Press of Kansas, 1998); and Robert J. Swan, "Thomas McCants Stewart and the Failure of the Mission of the Talented Tenth in Black America, 1880–1923" (Ph.D. diss., New York University, 1990).

73. William J. Simmons, *Men of Mark: Eminent, Progressive, and Rising* (Cleveland, G. M. Bewell & Co., 1887), 1052.

74. U. S. Manuscript Census, 1860, for Ward 5, Charleston, S.C., SCDAH.

75. Swan, "Thomas McCants Stewart," 6.

76. *Columbia Daily Union Herald*, May 20, 1875, June 30, 1875, and July 27, 1875. Handbill of the Clariosophic Society, dated Dec. 18, 1874, in Scrapbook of Fisk P. Brewer, Caroliniana.

77. See Student Petitions file, 1873, USC Archives.

78. USC Order of Exercises at the Commencement, Tuesday, Dec. 21, 1875, "Oration 'The Relation of Capital to Labor' with the Valedictory Address by T. McCants Stewart, Sumter, S.C.," USC Archives. However, Stewart did not excel in his examinations. In February of 1875 Professor Melton gave him a 60 on an intermediate examination while the three other students' reported grades ranged from 94 to 97. Professor Melton reported, "The average stand of Mr. T. McCants Stewart has been better than that exhibited by his answers to the examination paper." See *Report of the Chairman of the Faculty of the University of South Carolina* (1875), 52, Caroliniana. This same report also records Professor Richard Greener giving Stewart a 66 for a final grade, 49.

79. Columbia *Register*, Dec. 12, 1876.

80. *Columbia Union Herald*, Aug. 23, 1876. Other long speeches were given in Williamsburg (*Columbia Union Herald*, Nov. 11, 1876), Bishopville, and Sumter (*Columbia Union Herald*, July 18, 1876). He also spoke in Horry County, Marion, and Manning. Alfred Williams, *Hampton and His Red Shirts* (Charleston, S.C.: Evans & Cogswell, 1935), 109,318, 366.

81. *Columbia Union Herald*, Dec. 28, 1876. Stewart's prominence is borne out by the guests at his wedding. State Treasurer F. L. Cardozo and supreme court justice Jonathan J. Wright were in attendance.

In 1872 the college had been established by the general assembly for African Americans. See Hollis, *University of South Carolina*, vol. 2, p. 62.

82. Swan, "Thomas McCants Stewart," 38–39.

83. See Gov. Hampton's *Letterbooks*, vol. 3, 345, SCDAH.

84. Swan, "Thomas McCants Stewart," 39.

85. Ibid., 42.

86. Broussard, *African-American Odyssey*, 37.

87. In one case Stewart represented T. Thomas Fortune in a civil rights case against a New York saloon and received a jury verdict of $1,000. See the *Washington Bee*, June 18, 1892.

88. George B. Tindall, *South Carolina Negroes, 1877–1890* (Columbia: University of South Carolina Press, 1952), 305, quoting from a letter of Stewart's published in *New York Age*, Sept. 6, 1890.

89. Underwood, *The Constitution of South Carolina*, vol. 4, *The Struggle for Political Equality*, 58–59. Underwood says that the goal of the suffrage provisions of the 1895 constitution were to "cripple the black vote" without incurring the wrath of the federal government, 58. The adopted measures included literary and property requirements, durational residency provisions applicable to state, county, and precinct levels, and disqualification for conviction of certain crimes, 58. The criminal disqualification provision includes a list of crimes that were considered more likely to be commited by African Americans. But murder was not a disqualifying crime. Could this crime have been excluded because so many white politicians had committed murders. See Fox Butterfield, *All God's Children* (New York: Knopf, 1995), for an interesting telling of the murderous instincts of the eighteenth- and nineteenth-century South Carolina politicians.

90. Swan, "Thomas McCants Stewart," 158.

91. In the fall of 1887 it was reported that he was offering to canvass the state of New York for the Democratic Party. *Washington Bee*, Oct. 15, 1887.

92. *Washington Bee*, Nov. 19, 1887.

93. See *Washington Bee*, Jan. 7, 1893, Apr. 22, 1893, May 6, 1893, May 27, 1893, and Sept. 15, 1894.

94. *Washington Bee*, May 13, 1893.

95. *Washington Bee*, Apr. 6, 1895.

96. See *Indianapolis Freeman*, Jan. 25, 1896, where Greener makes a vicious attack on Stewart. It is unclear how Stewart responded to Greener's attacks. However, the two men may not have been the best of friends from their South Carolina days. At one point Professor Greener had given student Stewart a failing grade. See *Report of the Chairman of the Faculty*.

97. *Plessy v. Ferguson*, 163 U.S. 537 (1896).

98. Smith, *Emancipation*, 492.

99. Swan, "Thomas McCants Stewart," 254–55.

100. Ibid., 268.

101. Ibid., 269–71.

102. Ibid., 272–74.

103. Charles Wynes, "T. McCants Stewart: Peripatetic Black," *South Carolina Historical Magazine* 80 (1979): 311.

104. Rayford W. Logan and Michael R. Winston, eds., *Dictionary of American Negro Biography* (New York: Norton, 1982), 572.

105. See Roll of Attorneys.

106. Various clippings dated Oct. 1875, in Scrapbook of Fisk P. Brewer, Caroliniana.

107. *Columbia Daily Union Herald*, July 9, 1875. Students today might not be happy having their examination grades published in the press.

108. See handbill in Scrapbook of Fisk P. Brewer, Caroliniana.

109. USC Order of Exercises at the Commencement, Tuesday, Dec. 21, 1875: "6. Oration 'Reflections on International Law' by Joseph H. Stewart, Camden, S.C." and "8. Oration

'The Relation of Capital to Labor' with the Valedictory Address by T. McCants Stewart, Sumter, S.C.," USC Archives.

110. Scott letter.

111. *Charleston News and Courier,* Feb. 11, 1879.

112. See Smith, *Emancipation,* 497.

113. Louis R. Harlan, ed., *The Booker T. Washington Papers,* vol. 6 (Urbana: University of Illinois Press, 1977), 332.

114. *Denver Post,* Apr. 5, 1910.

115. See *Register of the South Carolina College* (1873).

116. *Columbia Directory* (1875–76), 48.

117. See Scott letter.

118. See Correspondence of Gov. Chamberlain, Jan. 10, 1877, C. J. Babbitt listed as private secretary, SCDAH.

119. See *Columbia, So.Ca., Directory,* 1879–80. Babbitt was admitted to the bar in Nov. of 1878. See Roll of Attorneys.

120. Letterbook of D. H. Chamberlain, Aug. 15, 1874, appointing Thomas M. Canton as trial justice, SCDAH.

121. O. Vernon Burton, "Edgefield Reconstruction Political Black Leaders," *Proceedings of the South Carolina Historical Association* 27 (1988).

122. *Columbia Daily Union,* Mar. 17, 1874 (speech on the death of Charles Sumner); *Columbia Daily Union Herald,* Feb. 10, 1875 (bill to establish a commission on forfeited lands); *Columbia Union Herald,* Sept. 14, 1876 (speech endorsing Chamberlain at Republican State Convention).

123. *Columbia Daily Union Herald,* Jan. 28, 1875.

124. Cooper, *The Conservative Regime,* 22.

125. See Richard Mark Gergel, "Wade Hampton and the Rise of One Party Racial Orthodoxy in South Carolina," *Proceedings of the South Carolina Historical Association* 5 (1977).

126. In the S.C. Census of 1875 Edgefield had 2,722 white males over 21 and 4,400 blacks over 21. Secretary of State Records, State Population Schedules of 1875, SCDAH.

127. See House, *Miscellaneous Documents of the House of Representatives for the second session of the 44th Congress: Testimony Taken by the Select Committee on the Recent Election in South Carolina,* 44th Cong, 2nd sess., 1876–77, App. 101 (hereafter cited as *Recent Election in South Carolina*).

128. *South Carolina in 1876,* vol. 2, pp. 544–50.

129. *Biographical Directory of the South Carolina Senate, 1776–1885,* vol. 1 (1986), 246.

130. See *Register of the South Carolina College.*

131. *Proceedings of National Convention of Colored Men Held in the City of Syracuse, New York* (1864l; reprint, Wilmington, Del.: Scholarly Resources, 1970).

132. *Proceedings of the Colored People's Convention of the State of South Carolina Held in Zion Church, Charleston, November 1865* (Charleston: S.C. Leader Office, 1865), 9–10.

133. See the chapter by James Lowell Underwood entitled "African American Founding Fathers: The Making of the South Carolina Constitution of 1868" in this volume.

134. Farley, "Francis L. Cardozo," 64.

135. John S. Reynolds, *Reconstruction in South Carolina* (1905), 86–87. Reynolds notes that Cardozo was the only "colored" on the Republican ticket for statewide office. Reynolds somehow neglects to point out the actual election of constitutional officers in the election of 1868. Their election is recorded by Francis Butler Simkins and Robert Hilliard Woody, *South Carolina during Reconstruction* (Chapel Hill: University of North Carolina Press, 1932), 109.

136. Simkins and Woody, *South Carolina during Reconstruction*, 77. See also "Address before the Grand Council of the Union Leagues at the Annual Meeting held July 27, 1870, by Hon. F. L. Cardozo, President," 1870, Caroliniana.

137. See Peggy Lamson, *The Glorious Failure* (New York: Norton, 1973), 215.

138. Cardozo is a very well known figure. Also see Logan and Winston, *Dictionary of American Negro Biography*, 89; Joe Richardson, "Francis L. Cardozo: Black Educator during Reconstruction," *Journal of Negro Education* 48 (1979): 73; Edward F. Sweat, "Francis L. Cardoza—Profile of Integrity in Reconstruction Politics," *Journal of Negro History* 46 (1961): 217; Simmons, *Men of Mark*; and Bertram W. Korn, *Jews and Negro Slavery in the Old South, 1789–1865* (Elkins Park, Pa.: Reform Congregation Kenesith Israel, 1961), 51–52.

139. Some historians identify his father as Jacob Cardozo, an economist. See e.g., Leon Litwack, *Been in the Storm So Long* (New York: Knopf, 1979), 495. The records of Glasgow University from 1858 indicate that Cardozo's father was Isaac. See letter dated Nov. 10, 1930, from the secretary to the principal, the University, Glasgow, Manuscripts Division, Library of Congress.

140. The family tree was provided to the author by Elise Taylor Goins. No Lydia Williams is found in the census or capitation records for Charleston.

141. The records of the University of Glasgow indicate that Cardozo was a student in the faculty of arts during sessions of 1858–59 and 1859–60. See letter dated Nov. 10, 1930, from the secretary of the Glasgow principal, the University, Glasgow, Manuscripts Division, Library of Congress.

142. See Euline W. Brock, "Thomas W. Cardozo: Fallible Reconstruction Leader," *Journal of Southern History* 47:183, reprinted in *The Politics of Freedom*, ed. Donald G. Nieman (New York: Garland, 1994), 63.

143. For the role of Cardozo in the convention see the chapter by Underwood in this volume. It is presumed by some sources that Cardozo was chairman of the education committee since his name is listed first in the listing of committee members in the convention proceedings. See Edward F. Sweat, "Public Career of Francis Louis Cardozo" (M.A. thesis, Indiana University, 1948), 24, citing p. 56 of the proceedings (Proceedings of the Constitutional Convention of South Carolina [Charleston: Denny & Perry, 1868]).

144. Eric Foner and Olivia Mahoney, *America's Reconstruction* (New York: HarperPerennial, 1995), 43.

145. Report of the Secretary of State, *Reports and Resolution of the General Assembly 1871–72*, SCDAH.

146. He owned at least $5,000 worth of property. See Loren Schweninger, *Black Property Owners in the South, 1790–1915* (Urbana: University of Illinois Press, 1990), 224.

147. Lamson, *The Glorious Failure*, 250–270. Also see the chapter in this volume by Richard Gergel on the life of Jonathan Jasper Wright. As Gergel notes, Cardozo was one of the election commissioners who tried to throw out the returns and was jailed for contempt of the supreme court for not reporting all of the returns.

148. Gov. Hampton's Misc. Letters, Apr. 14, 1877, SCDAH.

149. South Carolina General Assembly, *Report of the Attorney General to the General Assembly* (Columbia, Oct. 31, 1877), 318.

150. Edgar, *South Carolina*, 409.

151. Cooper, *The Conservative Regime* 30.

152. Simkins and Woody, *South Carolina during Reconstruction*, 448. Cardozo declined the nomination and remained loyal to the Republican Party in the 1870 election.

153. Bleser, *The Promised Land*, 89.

154. See Eric Foner, *Reconstruction: America's Unfinished Revolution, 1863–1877* (New York: Harper and Row, 1988), 375.

155. These appraisals run from W. E. B. DuBois, *Black Reconstruction* (New York: Harcourt, Brace, 1935), 413; to David Duncan Wallace, *The History of South Carolina*, vol. 3, 89.

156. *Columbia Daily Union Herald*, Feb. 21, 1875 (reprinting an editorial from the Democratic *Charleston News and Courier*). Also see *Columbia Daily Union Herald*, Feb. 5, 1875.

157. See Victor Ullman, *Martin R. Delany: The Beginnings of Black Nationalism* (Boston: Beacon Press, 1971), 435.

158. Walter Allen, *Governor Chamberlain's Administration in South Carolina* (New York: G. P. Putnam's Sons, 1888), 8.

159. Ibid., 80.

160. Ibid., 86.

161. Ibid., 269.

162. Most of these charges were for neglect of duty and not for specific acts of corruption. See South Carolina, *Report of the Attorney General to the General Assembly* (Oct. 31, 1877), 321–23.

163. *Charleston News and Courier*, Nov. 2, 1877.

164. Ironically, Conner was one of a group of native whites who had benefited from the work of the infamous "Railroad Ring" in early years of Reconstruction. The S.C. legislative investigation of Reconstruction-era fraud named a number of Republicans in its report on this fraud but neglected to name Conner, M. C. Butler, and M. W. Gary. Of course, at the time of the investigation these native whites were in power. See Lamson, *The Glorious Failure*, 139–40.

165. Lee, Congressman Robert Smalls, Senate Clerk Josephus Woodruff, House Clerk A. O. Jones, and Lieutenant Governor R. H. Gleaves were all indicted together, but only Smalls and Cardozo were tried. See the Papers of Charles Richardson Miles, Caroliniana.

166. See Joel Williamson, *After Slavery: The Negro in South Carolina during Reconstruction* (Chapel Hill: University of North Carolina Press, 1965), 415–16.

167. Thomas Holt, *Black over White, Negro Leadership in South Carolina during Reconstruction* (Urbana: University of Illinois Press, 1977), 210; Tindall, *South Carolina Negroes*, 19; Cooper, *The Conservative Regime*, 32; Edgar, *South Carolina*, 409.

168. See Hon. William D. Simpson Papers, Petitions for Pardon, 1879, SCDAH.

169. Letter from Samuel Shellabarger to John Sherman, Nov. 24, 1878, quoted in Farley, "Francis L. Cardozo," 143.

170. For example, see the letter of D. H. Chamberlain to Secretary of Treasury, C. J. Folger, Apr. 24, 1882, quoted in Farley, "Francis L. Cardozo," 144.

171. See *The Peoples' Advocate*, May 17, 1879, and Oct. 6, 1883.

172. *The People's Advocate*, Nov. 12, 1881 (Cardozo not participating in the S.C. Association in D.C.), Dec. 8, 1883 (speaking favorably that the North was more favorable to the African American than the South), and Dec. 15, 1883 (speaking favorably of the greater inducements offered by the North).

173. *The People's Advocate*, Jan. 1, 1884.

174. *The People's Advocate*, Mar. 1, 1884.

175. Simmons, *Men of Mark*, 430.

176. South Carolina General Assembly, "Report of the Secretary of State," *Reports and Resolutions of the General Assembly of the State of South Carolina* (1871–72), 193.

177. *Washington Bee*, Oct. 13, 1888, and Nov. 17, 1888.

178. See, for example, *Washington Bee*, July 14, 1888 (first attack noted), and July 4, 1896 (Cardozo removed). A review of the newspaper during this period reveals that Chase called for Cardozo's removal or the advancement of Hugh M. Brown to be principal in virtually every issue of the weekly newspaper.

179. *The (Washington, D.C.) Colored American*, Feb. 17, 1894.

180. Louise Daniel Hutchinson, *Anna J. Cooper* (Washington, D.C.: Smithsonian Institute Press, 1981), 47, 67.

181. See letter in possession of author from Anatol Steck of the Charles Sumner School Museum and Archives, Washington, D.C., Feb. 27, 1998.

182. See autobiographical sketch by Richard Theodore Greener, May 19, 1870, Harvard Archives. For a more complete biography of Greener see the chapter by Michael Mounter, "Richard Theodore Greener and the African American Individual in a Black and White World," in this volume.

183. See autobiographical sketch by Richard Theodore Greener.

184. Werner Sollors, Caldwell Titcomb, and Thomas A. Underwood, eds., *Blacks at Harvard*, vol. 2 (New York: New York University Press, 1993). In 1869 Harvard University graduated African Americans in medicine, law, and dentistry.

185. See *Catalogue, University of South Carolina, 1873*, USC Archives.

186. See autobiographical sketch by Richard Theodore Greener, May 19, 1870, Harvard Archives.

187. *Columbia Daily Union*, Apr. 13, 1874.

188. *Columbia Daily Union Herald*, Mar. 11, 1875.

189. Clipping dated Mar. 10, 1875, in Brewer Scrapbook.

190. See letter from Greener to Ficken dated May 2, 1878, Harvard Archives.

191. *Columbia Daily Union Herald*, July 20, 1875.

192. *Columbia Union Herald*, Aug. 19, 1876. Greener and his wife, Genevieve Ida Fleet, were only slightly injured. His wife was a native of Washington. They had married on Sept. 24, 1874. See *Harvard Alumni Bulletin* (1875).

193. See letter from Greener to Ficken dated May 2, 1878, Harvard Archives.

194. *Columbia Union Herald*, Sept. 20, 1876.

195. See letter from Greener to Ficken dated May 2, 1878, Harvard Archives.

196. Ibid.

197. See *Columbia Union Herald*, Sept. 8, 1876 (activities in ward meetings); *Columbia Union Herald*, Nov. 6, 1876 (speech in Lexington); and *Recent Election in South Carolina*, 459.

198. See Greener's letter of resignation dated June 29, 1877, USC Archives. In this letter Greener notes that there were "no charges of inefficiency or lack of duty having been alleged, to my knowledge against me during the nearly four years of my commitment with the University." Signed by "Richard T. Greener, Second Auditors, Treasury Dept. Washington D.C."

Greener was not paid for his last year of employment because he had campaigned for Chamberlain. In fact, he asserted that he had "been cheated out of some $1,500." See letter from Greener to Ficken dated May 2, 1878, Harvard Archives.

199. See letter from Greener to Ficken dated May 2, 1878, Harvard Archives.

200. Letter from Greener to Ficken, June 3, 1878, Harvard Archives.

201. John F. Marszalek, *Court-Martial* (New York: Scribner, 1972), 176.

202. *Washington Bee*, Mar. 20, 1897, and Apr. 3, 1897.

203. See U.S. Department of State, Despatches from United States Consuls in Vladivostok, 1898–1906, National Archives.

204. Dispatch from Vladivostock, dated Sept. 16, 1903 (Greener was allowed to appear on behalf of the poachers after presentation of his "passport, [his] law diploma, and certificate as a lawyer"), Despatches from U.S. Consuls.

205. Logan and Winston, *Dictionary of American Negro Biography*, 267–268.

206. See *Robinson v. Chicago Rys. Co.*, 174 Fed. 40 (1909).

207. Logan and Winston, *Dictionary of American Negro Biography*, 268.

208. J. Bliss White, comp., *Biography and Achievements of the Colored Citizens of Chattanooga* (n.p., 1904), 3. This biography of Hutchins probably was based on an account provided by Hutchins to White.

209. Donald L. Grant, *The Way It Was in the South: The Black Experience in Georgia* (Secanus, N.J.: Carol, 1993), 226.

210. *Recent Election in South Carolina*, 417–22.

211. *South Carolina in 1876*, vol. 1, pp. 604–8.

212. One record indicates that an S. L. Hutchins married a Talulah Milner in Barton, Georgia, on Mar. 20, 1873. He subsequently married Cora B. Martin on May 25, 1887, in Hamilton, Tennessee. *See International Genealogical Index for North America*, www.Familysearch.org. The second Mrs. Hutchins died on Nov. 14, 1895, and was buried in Chattanooga, Tennessee. See Robert M. McBride, ed., *Biographical Directory of the Tennessee General Assembly* (Nashville: Tennessee Historical Commission, 1979), 448.

213. *Register of the South Carolina College.* This register lists Hutchins twice and the only date of admission is listed as April 1876. He graduated on Dec. 13, 1876. See USC Order of Exercises at the Commencement, Wednesday, Dec. 13, 1876, USC Archives.

214. *Columbia Union Herald*, Mar. 9, 1877.

215. It was not so unusual for blacks to be affiliated with the Democratic Party. William Hine found that there were as many as 39 black Democratic politicians in Charleston alone. William C. Hine, "Black Politicians in Reconstruction Charleston, South Carolina: A Collective Study," *Journal of Southern History* 49 (1983): 187, 198.

216. *Columbia Union Herald*, Sept. 4, 1876, reported an incident at Macedonia Church in Richland. A. C. Haskell, the chairman of the state Democratic Party, led a group of Democrats who insisted on the right to of Hutchins to speak at a Republican meeting. The incident was reported as follows:

[Hutchins] would not be allowed to speak and was threatened with death. [Haskell] was prepared to defend the Indiana negro with the blood of his "braves." The leading [Republican] assured him that this man was a harmless fellow and he couldn't injure the Republican Party and whether he could or not he would be given a peaceful hearing. . . . The democratic brought this man Hutchin forward and told him to do his best. He launched out into a tirade of abuse of everything, generally extolled the Confederate congress, advised the colored people to vote for Tilden and Hampton as true friends and denied he was bought by the democracy for $100. He could get thousands, but didn't want it. The audience smiled, the convert retired and the hostiles saw that the fellow was not a "big catch" after all. Professor Greener completely demolished him.

217. See *Recent Election in South Carolina*, 417–22.

218. See Papers of Governor Wade Hampton, Appointments of County Officials, May 7, 1877, SCDAH,

219. See Governor Hampton, *Letterbooks*, vol. 1, June 13, 187, SCDAH.

220. It seems unlikely that Hutchins was the first African American admitted in Georgia. For example, Edwin T. Belcher and E. R. B. Belcher, Howard graduates, were admitted to the South Carolina Bar in November 1871 and listed their hometown as Augusta, Georgia. J. Clay Smith describes James M. Simms as Georgia's first known black lawyer. Simms was appointed to a judgeship in 1871. See Smith, *Emancipation*, 242.

221. See Smith, *Emancipation*, 342. Also see Mark Curriden and LeRoy Phillips, Jr., *Contempt of Court* (New York: Faber and Faber, 1999), for a full reconstruction of Hutchins's role in the case of Ed Johnson, the lynching victim.

222. Allen B. Ballard, *One More Day's Journey* (New York: McGraw-Hill, 1984), 62.

223. W. E. B. DuBois, *The Philadelphia Negro* (Philadelphia: University of Pennsylvania Press, 1899), 32, 34–35. DuBois identifies Henry Minton as a caterer in Philadelphia.

224. Roger Lane, *William Dorsey's Philadelphia and Ours*, (New York: Oxford University Press, 1991), 44, 174. Lane identifies Minton as the son of a prominent caterer but does not name the father as Henry.

225. See *Recent Election in South Carolina*, 463.

226. *Columbia Register*, Nov. 2, 1876.

227. *Columbia Daily Union Herald*, July 11, 1875.

228. *Charleston News and Courier*, Nov. 5, 1877.

229. Lane, *William Dorsey's Philadelphia and Ours*, 45.

230. See for example, *The People's Advocate*, Dec. 18, 1880, and Jan. 26, 1884.

231. *The People's Advocate*, Feb. 7, 1880.

232. *Washington Bee*, July 10, 1888.

233. See the Minton correspondence in the Whitefield McKinlay Papers, Carter Woodson Collection, Library of Congress.

234. See American Negro Historical Society Papers, Leon Gardiner Collection, Historical Society of Pennsylvania, Philadelphia.

235. Ibid.

236. Theophilus J. Minton, "Robert Brown Elliott," *African Methodist Episcopal Church Review* 8 (1892): 363, Ohio State Historical Society, Columbus.

237. For example, see correspondence in Whitfield McKinlay Papers, Carter Woodson Collection.

238. *Charleston Tax Collector, Free Negro Tax Book: 1862–1864*, SCDAH.

239. Larry Koger, *Black Slaveowners: Free Black Slaveowners in South Carolina, 1790–1860* (Jefferson, N.C.: McFarland, 1985), 9.

240. Ibid.

241. John Belton O'Neall, *The Negro Law: South Carolina* (Columbia, S.C.: J. G. Bowman, 1848), sec. 37, 11.

242. Drago, *Initiative, Paternalism, and Race Relations*, 55.

243. Simmons, *Men of Mark*, 162–63.

244. *Allen University Catalog* (1911), xvi, Caroliniana.

245. See chapter by Oldfield in this volume.

246. Ibid.

247. *Allen University Catalog* (1912), Caroliniana.

248. *Walsh's Columbia, South Carolina, City Directory for 1913*.

249. Morris was listed in the 1913 city directory but was not listed in the 1914 directory. His wife, Ella, was listed as living alone at their home at 1500 Harden Street in the 1915 directory. *Walsh's Columbia, South Carolina, City Directory for 1915*.

250. "Honorable Paris Simkins," by Francis Frederick; and "A Brief Narrative of the Life of Paris Simkins" by Edwin Booth Simkins and other children. Undated manuscripts provided by the Simkins family to Orville Vernon Burton and graciously supplied to the author by Dr. Burton.

251. Letters dated Feb. 17, 1874, and Mar. 7, 1874, Letterbook of D. H. Chamberlain, SCDAH.

252. *Columbia Daily Union Herald*, Feb. 26, 1875, quoting the *Charleston News and Courier.*

253. *Columbia Daily Union Herald*, Feb. 25, 1875, and see also Feb. 10, 1875.

254. *Columbia Daily Union Herald*, Feb. 2 and 26, 1875 (both stories quoting the *New York Evening Post*).

255. *Columbia Daily Union Herald*, Apr. 22, 1875.

256. *Columbia Union Herald*, Aug. 10, 1876.

257. See *Recent Election in South Carolina*, 237–40.

258. *South Carolina in 1876*, vol. 2, pp. 631–32.

259. *Recent Election in South Carolina*, appendix, 100.

260. Interview by author with C. B. Bailey, Nov. 11, 1997.

261. Ibid.

262. In the *Letterbook of Gov. J. C. Sheppard*, Henry T. Thompson signed all of the correspondence as private secretary to Sheppard, SCDAH.

263. See Gov. Hampton, *Abstracts of Letter* (1877), 265, SCDAH, noting the receipt of a letter from W. A. Warren notifying the governor of the closing of the university and the disposition of the keys and books.

264. See the chapter by Richard Gergel and Belinda Gergel in this volume.

265. See Simmons, *Men of Mark*. Simmons included J. W. Morris, F. L. Cardozo, T. McCants Stewart, and Richard T. Greener.

266. See Cooper, *The Conservative Regime*, 84–115.

267. See chapter by John Oldfield in this volume.

268. Smith, *Emancipation*, 223.

269. *The State*, Aug. 23, 1938.

270. *The State*, Aug. 23, 1938, quoting the *Charleston News and Courier.*

271. Ibid., Aug. 29, 1938.

272. Interview with C. B. Bailey on Nov. 11, 1997. The first descendant of Simkins to obtain a University of South Carolina degree was Mr. Bailey's son, C. B. Bailey Jr., who earned a master's degree in music education in 1971.

273. Bernard E. Powers Jr., *Black Charlestonians: A Social History, 1822–1885* (Fayetteville: University of Arkansas Press, 1994), 141.

5: THE AFRICAN AMERICAN BAR IN SOUTH CAROLINA, 1877–1915

1. Eric Foner, *Freedom's Lawyers: A Directory of Black Officeholders during Reconstruction* (New York: Oxford University Press, 1993), 227 (entry for William Whipper), 236 (entry for Jonathan J. Wright); Peggy Lamson, *The Glorious Failure: Black Congressman Robert Brown Elliott and the Reconstruction in South Carolina* (New York: W. W. Norton, 1973).

2. George B. Tindall, *South Carolina Negroes, 1877–1900* (Columbia: University of South Carolina Press, 1952), 144.

3. Thomas Holt, *Black over White: Negro Political Leadership in South Carolina during Reconstruction* (Urbana: University of Illinois Press, 1977), 76–77, 82–83, 90; Lamson, *The Glorious Failure*, 21–23, 76; Joel Williamson, *After Slavery: The Negro in South Carolina during Reconstruction, 1861–1877* (New York: W. W. Norton, 1975), 233, 330–33, 349. For Reconstruction see Eric Foner, *Reconstruction: America's Unfinished Revolution, 1863–1877* (New York: Harper and Row, 1988).

4. See Oldfield-Burke appendix, "African American Lawyers in South Carolina, 1868–1900," following chapter 5 in this volume.

5. Tindall, *South Carolina Negroes*, 145; Emily Reynolds and Joan Faunt, eds., *Biographical Directory of the Senate of South Carolina* (Columbia, S.C.: Archives Department, 1964), entry for Thomas J. Reynolds; *Charleston News and Courier*, Dec. 14, 1881; *Charleston City Directory*, 1886 and 1895.

6. *Aiken Tribune*, Dec. 6, 1873.

7. See chapter by W. Lewis Burke Jr. in this volume.

8. Williamson, *After Slavery*, 223, 233; Holt, *Black over White*, 299–41; Emma Lou Thornborough, *T. Thomas Fortune: Militant Journalist* (Chicago: University of Chicago Press, 1972), 100; Louis Harlan, ed., *The Booker T. Washington Papers, 1860–1889*, vol. 2 (Urbana: University of Illinois Press, 1972), 255.

9. John Hammond Moore, *Columbia and Richland County: A South Carolina Community, 1740–1990* (Columbia: University of South Carolina Press, 1993), 245; *Catalogue of Allen University, 1890 and 1891* (Columbia, 1891), 4.

10. Asa H. Gordon, *Sketches of Negro Life and History in South Carolina*, (1929; reprint, Columbia: University of South Carolina Press, 1971), 94–95; *Catalogue of Allen University, 1890 and 1891*, 31–32.

11. Gordon, *Sketches of Negro Life*, 95; Louis Harlan, ed., *The Booker T. Washington Papers, 1895–1898*, vol. 4 (Urbana: University of Illinois Press, 1975), 236–37. Straker later went on to become one of Detroit's leading black lawyers.

12. *Catalogue of Allen University*, 1890 and 1891, 40; *Catalogue of Allen University, 1911–1912* (Columbia, 1912), 59–69.

13. *Catalogue of Allen University, 1890 and 1891*, 34.

14. Ibid., 31–32.

15. *Charleston News and Courier*, May 14, 1887.

16. *Catalogue of Allen University, 1911–1912*, 59–69.

17. *Charleston News and Courier*, Apr. 2, 1895.

18. Lamson, *The Glorious Failure*, 271, 273.

19. *Columbia Daily Register*, July 24, 1887.

20. John F. Marszalek, *Court-Martial: A Black Man in America* (New York: Charles Scribner's Sons, 1972), 257–61.

21. Tindall, *South Carolina Negroes*, 147; Marszalek, *Court-Martial*, 260–63. Whittaker later moved to Oklahoma before returning to Orangeburg in 1925.

22. W. T. Andrews to Whitfield McKinlay, Mar. 9, Sept. 13 and 27, 1903, Carter G. Woodson Papers, Library of Congress, Washington, D.C.

23. Lamson, *The Glorious Failure*, 75–76; Tindall, *South Carolina Negroes*, 145.

24. *Charleston City Directory*, 1879–1920.

25. *Aiken Tribune*, Dec. 6, 1873; Record of Admissions, Supreme Court, Columbia, S.C., Mar. 6, 1872; Lawrence C. Bryant, *Negro Legislators in South Carolina* (Orangeburg: South Carolina State College, 1967), 7–12; Lamson, *The Glorious Failure*, 199–200.

26. Quoted in *Aiken Tribune*, July 26, 1873.

27. *Aiken Tribune*, Dec. 6, 1873.

28. *Aiken Tribune*, June 19, 26, July 3, 10, Sept. 4, 1875; Oct. 2, 16, 1876. Clyde was admitted to the bar in November 1873.

29. *Aiken Courier Journal*, Dec. 13, 1875; Reports and Resolutions of the Assembly of South Carolina, *Report of the Attorney General* (Columbia, 1878), 323; Alrutheus Ambush Taylor, *The Negro in South Carolina during Reconstruction* (Washington, D.C.: Association for the Study of Negro Life and History, 1924), 278, 284.

30. Copybook of Matthew Buswell and R. W. Seymour, 1867–83, South Carolina Historical Society, Charleson; *Charleston City Directory,* 1882.

31. In 1882 black lawyers were handling 33 percent of all cases in the court of general sessions. By 1886 this figure had fallen to 28 percent. Over the same period, however, the number of cases where there was no lawyer involved at all increased from 30 percent to 63 percent. These figures are based on an analysis of the Bar Dockets, Court of General Sessions, Charleston County, 1882–93, State Archives, Columbia, S.C..

32. Bar Dockets, Court of General Sessions, Charleson County, 1885 and 1890.

33. Session Rolls, Court of General Sessions, Charleston County, 1882–1893, State Archives, Columbia.

34. Bar Calendar Number 1 (1881–85), Number 2 (1881–88, 1892–99), Number 3 (1876–85, 1892–1900), Number 4 (1878–82), Court of Common Pleas, Charleston County, State Archives, Columbia.

35. *Reports of Cases Argued and Determined in the Supreme Court of South Carolina* (hereafter cited as *Supreme Court Reports*), vol. 22 (Nov. 1884), 298–301; vol. 23 (Apr. 1885), 209–12; vol. 26 (Nov. 1886), 296–300; vol. 41 (Apr. 1894), 526–31. For Whipper see the Leigh Whipper Papers, Box 1, Record Group 114 (folders 45–60), Moorland-Spingarn Research Center, Howard University, Washington, D.C.

36. See, e.g., *State v. Bright,* 14 S.C. 7 (1880) (Lee brought an action by a mother of three illegitimate children to recover under the bond promised by the father; the court affirmed the judgment for father because the bond was not contemplated by the statute); *State v. Collins,* 15 S.C. 373 (1881) (court upheld conviction of murder based on error in admitting witness's testimony); *Brown v. Buttz,* 15 S.C. 488 (1881) (Lee won a trespass case where the court held that a jury was not necessary to a hearing on a demurrer); *State v. Bowen,* 17 S.C. 58 (1881) (Lee appealed an indictment on the grounds that resisting an officer without process was not indictable; the court upheld the indictment); *State v. Beaden,* 17 S.C. 55 (1881) (appealed conviction of assault and battery with a shovel on grounds that indictment did not allege an assault of an "aggravated nature"; the court upheld the conviction); *State v. Gathers, State v. Smalls,* 15 S.C. 370 (1881) (State appealed indictment of assault and battery with a barrel stave; Lee won the case on a double-jeopardy argument because the court held that an appeal could not be taken from a judgment of acquittal.); *Sanders v. Etwian Phospate Co.,* 19 S.C. 510 (1883) (appealed grant of nonsuit for plaintiff on basis that the defendant was negligent by not providing a safe work environment for his employees; court held that witness's testimony did not support an inference of negligence); *Jones v. Columbia and Greenville R. R. Co.,* 20 S.C. 249 (1883) (affirmed judgment for plaintiff who recovered value of livestock that was killed on the railroad); *State v. Huckie,* 22 S.C. 298 (1884) (the usual right of the defendant to make the final argument, if he offered no evidence, did not apply if another defendant, charged with the same offense, offered evidence); *State v. Hines,* 23 S.C. 170 (1885) (conviction reversed on grounds that the circuit judge misled the jury by contending that there were two false pretenses when only one false pretense was alleged in the indictment); *State v. Brown,* 24 S.C. 224 (1885) (conviction of burglary overturned on basis of insufficient indictment where the indictment did not allege the specific day of the burglary); *Whipper v. Talbird,* 32 S.C. 1 (1889) (Lee represented a candidate for the office of probate judge who appealed and the court held that there was no right of appeal from an action by the Board of Canvassers); *Ex parte Whipper,* 32 S.C. 6 (1889) (writ of habeas corpus to discharge a candidate for probate judge from jail was not allowed where the candidate was held in contempt for not handing over court records); *State v. Ezekiel,* 33 S.C. 15 (1890) (conviction for forgery was overturned where it was found that the handwriting samples were not properly admitted into evidence); *Connor v. Edwards,* 36 S.C. 563 (1892) (Lee lost an appeal to recover real property); *State v. Talbert,* 41 S.C. 526 (1894)

(conviction of murder appealed on basis of wrongful admission of a dying declaration; Lee lost because the declaration was made under oath and the statements were not objected to at trial); *State v. Williams,* 40 S.C. 373 (1893) (Lee represented the defendant, who was sentenced to pay $25 or work on the chain gang for 30 days for carrying a concealed weapon. Lee appealed on grounds that the defendant could not be punished except by a jury of 12 men. The court held that defendant was not entitled to a trial by a jury of 12 men. The court also held that the sentence to work on the chain gang was null and void because the statute did not authorize a sentence of hard labor for a misdemeanor.).

This list does not include all supreme court cases argued by Lee in this period. Neither does it include cases decided during this period but not reported in full. For example, in *Dingle v. Mitchell,* 20 S.C. 202 (1883), Lee represented the nephew of a former slave who was trying to inherit title to a house in Charleston. Lee argued that the widow who owned the house was never freed by her husband and was, therefore, unable to transfer title to the plaintiff. Lee also argued that there was no evidence that the widow was ever married to her husband. The South Carolina Supreme Court disagreed with Lee and held that it was not error for the trial court to let the jury determine if the widow was a slave or had been freed by her husband who had purchased her.

In another interesting case, *State v. Evans,* 23 S.C. 209 (1885), Lee appealed a conviction of larceny of livestock. Lee contended that the conviction was improper because of a fatal variance between the charge and the proof. The charge contended that the defendant stole three hogs belonging to one person but the evidence proved that only one of the hogs was the property solely of the person named as victim. The court concluded that so long as any one of the hogs stolen by the defendant was proven to be the separate property of the named victim, the conviction was valid.

37. *Whipper v. Talbird,* 32 S.C. 1 (1889); *Supreme Court Reports,* vol. 32 (Nov. 1889), 1–5. See also the companion case, *Ex Parte Whipper,* 5–13.

38. *Charleston News and Courier,* Apr. 2, 1895.

39. All these figures are compiled from the Bar Dockets, Court of General Sessions, 1882–93.

40. Charleston County Court House, Charleston Register of Mesne Conveyance, B22, 169, D20 757; E22 150; F23 30; G19 319; H19 163; J19 21; M20 33, 355; Q20 46, 185, 207, U18 631; Y18 235, 236.

41. *Charleston News and Courier,* Apr. 2, 1895.

42. *Catalogue of Allen University, 1890 and 1891,* 40; *Columbia Daily Register,* Feb. 24, 1887; *Charleston City Directory,* 1895–1913.

43. Record of Admissions, Supreme Court, Columbia, May 12, 1897, and Dec. 19, 1900.

44. *Charleston City Directory,* 1910–15.

45. *Columbia City Directory,* 1918; *Catalogue of Allen University, 1911–1912,* 59–69; "Butler W. Nance," vertical file, South Caroliniana Library, University of South Carolina, Columbia; Moore, *Columbia and Richland County,* 380–81.

46. Moore, *Columbia and Richland County,* 380–81.

47. *Charleston City Directory,* 1895–1912.

48. "Butler W. Nance," vertical file, South Caroliniana Library.

49. A. W. Dozier to Richard Dozier, Mar. 23, 1870, Southern Historical Collection, University of North Carolina at Chapel Hill.

50. Cornelius Scott, a black graduate of the University of South Carolina, recalled in 1911 that Lee "enjoyed the confidence of some of the most prominent white lawyers in the

state, and particularly in Charleston, and was retained by them in cases." *The (Columbia) State,* May 8, 1911.

51. *Charleston News and Courier,* Apr. 2, 1895.

52. Report of the Inquiry into the Contested-Election of (Samuel J.) Lee v. (John S.) Richardson, n.d., Special Collections, University Library, College of Charleston, Charleston, S.C.; Lamson, *The Glorious Failure,* 280.

53. *Charleston News and Courier,* Apr. 2, 1895; *The State,* Apr. 2, 1895.

54. *Charleston News and Courier,* Apr. 3, 4, 1895.

55. *Charleston News and Courier,* Oct. 18, 1885.

56. Charleston County Court House, Charleston, Probate Records, 298–0011 (Wright), 397–27 (Lee), 586–0024 (Smith).

57. W. T. Andrews to Whitfield McKinlay, Mar. 9, 1903, Carter G. Woodson Papers.

58. U.S. Manuscript Census, 1900, for Charleston, South Carolina, vol. 13, E.D. 110, sheet 12 and E.D. 13, sheet 19; vol. 14, E.D. 114, sheet 6 (Washington, D.C., National Archives).

59. See J. R. Oldfield, *Blacks on Charleston's Police Force, 1868–1915* (forthcoming).

60. *Palmetto Leader,* Nov. 20, 1926.

6: Richard Theodore Greener and the African American Individual in a Black and White World

1. *Cincinnati Union,* Nov. 13, 1920.

2. W. E. B. DuBois, "Talented Tenth," *The Negro Problem* (New York: J. Pott & Company, 1903), 34–35. Greener was prominent enough to warrant a biographical sketch in *Who's Who in America* from 1899 to 1911, in *Appletons' Cyclopedia of American Biography* in 1898, and later in the *Dictionary of American Biography.* See "Greener, Richard Theodore," in *Who's Who in America* (1899–1911); in *Appletons' Cyclopedia of American Biography* (1898); and in *Dictionary of American Biography* (1931).

3. Allison Blakely, "Richard T. Greener and the 'Talented Tenth's' Dilemma," *Journal of Negro History* 59 (Oct. 1974): 305–21.

4. C. C. Harper to R. R. Gurley, Dec. 13, 1826, Letters Received, American Colonization Society Papers, Library of Congress; *New York Freedom's Journal,* May 18, 1827; Ira Berlin, *Slaves without Masters: The Free Negro in the Antebellum South* (New York: Pantheon, 1974), 204–5; Christopher Phillips, *Freedom's Port: The African American Community of Baltimore, 1790–1860* (Urbana: University of Illinois Press, 1997), 223; John L. Thomas, *The Liberator: William Lloyd Garrison* (Boston: Little, Brown, 1963), 101, 105.

5. Richard T. Greener, "Richard T. Greener," autobiographical sketch, dated May 19, 1870, Harvard University Archives, Cambridge, Mass.; no author cited, "For Good Government and Urban Politics: The Career of R. T. Greener, '70," *Harvard Alumni Bulletin* 67 (Dec. 12, 1964): 266–68.

6. "For Good Government and Urban Politics," 266–7; Richard T. Greener to Caroline Langston, Nov. 16, 1897, John Mercer Langston Papers, Fisk University, Nashville, Tenn.

7. *Boston Commonwealth,* May 27, 1864; Linda M. Perkins, *Fanny Jackson Coppin and the Institute for Colored Youth, 1865–1902* (New York: Garland, 1987), 40–41.

8. Frances Marchant, "Richard Theodore Greener: A Story of a Busy Man, 1882," Biographical sketch of Greener sent to the *Gloucester Bulletin* in Mar. 1882, South Caroliniana Library, University of South Carolina, Columbia (hereafter cited as SCL).

9. Phillips *Bulletin*, July 1922, Phillips Academy Archives, Oliver Wendell Holmes Library, Phillips Academy, Andover, Mass.; Ruth Ann Stewart, Guest Curator, and David M. Kahn, Curator, General Grant N.M., "Richard T. Greener: His Life and Work," an exhibit and tribute sponsored by the National Park Service and the National Park Foundation, the General Grant National Memorial, Riverside Drive at 122nd Street, June 4, 1980–Oct. 31, 1980, 2., Schomburg Center for Research in Black Culture, New York.

10. August E. Batchelder to President Hill, Feb. 2, 1866, Harvard University Archives, Cambridge, Mass.; Harvard College, Faculty Minutes, Jan. 31, 1866.

11. Harvard College, Minutes of the Meetings of the President and Fellows of Harvard College, July 16, 1868; *Philadelphia Press*, Aug. 12, 1869, and *Philadelphia Evening Bulletin*, Aug. 12, 1869, clippings in the Richard T. Greener File, William Dorsey Collection, Cheyney University, Cheyney, Penn..

12. Richard T. Greener, "The Tenure of Land in Ireland" (senior diss., Harvard College, 1870); Minutes of the Meetings of the President and Fellows of Harvard College, June 29, 1870.

13. Seymour Martin Lipset and David Riesman, *Education and Politics at Harvard* (New York: McGraw-Hill, 1975), 110; Marchant, "Richard Theodore Greener: A Story of a Busy Man"; Stewart and Kahn, "Richard T. Greener," 2.

14. Dorothy Sterling, ed., *We Are Your Sisters: Black Women in the Nineteenth Century* (New York: W. W. Norton, 1984), 453–55, 459.

15. *Philadelphia Press*, Aug. 12, 1869, *Philadelphia Evening Bulletin*, Aug. 12 and 13, 1869, clippings in Richard T. Greener File, William Dorsey Collection.

16. *Boston Commonwealth*, May 14, 1870, notes undated articles from the *Troy Whig*.

17. Greener, "Richard T. Greener," autobiographical sketch.

18. Institute for Colored Youth, *Minutes of the Board of Managers*, RS 515, 1866–1884, Oct. 11 and 18, Nov. 15, 1870, Cheyney University; Board of Trustees of Colored Schools of Washington and Georgetown, D.C., *Report of the Board of Trustees of Colored Schools of Washington and Georgetown, D.C.* (1871), 4, 42–53, Daniel Murray Pamphlet Collection, Manuscripts Division, Library of Congress.

19. Institute for Colored Youth, *Minutes of the Board of Managers*, RS 515, 1866–1884, Dec. 20, 1870, Cheyney University.

20. Fanny Jackson Coppin, *Reminiscences of School Life, and Hints on Teaching*, ed. Henry Louis Gates Jr. and Jennifer Burton (New York: G. K. Hall, 1995), 22.

21. Institute for Colored Youth, *Minutes of the Committee on Discipline and Instruction*, RS 514-b, 1871–1884, Oct. 17 and 24, 1871, Cheyney University.

22. Richard T. Greener to [?], Dec. 19, 1871, Richard T. Greener File, William Dorsey Collection.

23. Richard T. Greener to Charles Sumner, Jan. 15, 1872, Charles Sumner Papers, Houghton Library, Harvard University; *Washington New National Era*, Jan. 18, 1872; *Congressional Globe*, 42nd Cong., 2nd sess., Jan. 31, 1872, 727; Charles Sumner, *Charles Sumner: His Complete Works* (1902; reprint, New York: Negro Universities Press, 1968), 270–72.

24. Institute for Colored Youth, *Minutes of the Committee on Discipline and Instruction*, Jan. 22, Feb. 20, May 19, June 3, 1872; Perkins, *Fanny Jackson Coppin*, 100–102, 108, 110–13.

25. Richard T. Greener to Charles Sumner, Mar. 18, 1872, Charles Sumner Papers.

26. Institute for Colored Youth, *Minutes of the Committee on Discipline and Instruction*, Sept. 30, Dec. 14 and 17, 1872; Darlene Clark Hine and Kathleen Thompson, eds., *Facts on File Encyclopedia of Black Women in America: The Early Years, 1619–1899* (New York: Facts on File, 1997), 102; Louise Daniel Hutchinson, *Anna J. Cooper: A Voice from the South* (Washington,

D.C.: Anacostia Neighborhood Museum/Smithsonian Institute Press, 1981), 48; *School Building Survey, District of Columbia,* Perry School (M Street High School), D.C. Public Schools, D.C. Historic Preservation Division, 1986, the Charles Sumner School Museum and Archives, Washington, D.C; *New National Era,* Oct. 9, 1873; Constance McLaughlin Green, *The Secret City: A History of Race Relations in the Nation's Capital* (Princeton, N.J.: Princeton University Press, 1967), 110.

27. William J. Simmons, *Men of Mark: Eminent, Progressive, and Rising* (Cleveland, Ohio: G. M. Revell, 1887), 332; "John F. Cook, Grand Master, and Carter A. Stewart, Grand Secretary, to the National Grand Lodge," Washington City, D.C, Oct. 6, 1869, Official Records, National Grand Lodge, printed in William H. Grimshaw, *Official History of Freemasonry among the Colored People in North America* (1902; reprint, New York: Negro Universities Press, 1968), 195–99, 347.

28. Dorothy Sterling, ed., *The Trouble They Seen: Black People Tell the Story of Reconstruction* (Garden City, N.J.: Doubleday, 1976), 295–96; *New York World,* Oct. 21, 1889; Werner Sollors, Caldwell Titcomb, and Thomas A. Underwood, eds., *Blacks at Harvard* (New York: New York University Press, 1993), 59–68.

29. *Washington Republican,* July 17, 1873, clipping in scrapbook 28, 11–12, William Dorsey Collection.

30. Greener was an editor of the *New National Era* from April to September of 1873. See *Washington New National Era,* April through September of 1873.

31. *New National Era,* Apr. 17 and 24, 1873.

32. Marchant, "Richard Theodore Greener: A Story of a Busy Man."

33. Faculty Minutes, Oct. 28, 1873, with attached letters, "J. K. Jillson to Richard T. Greener," Oct. 10, 28, 1873, in Records of the University of South Carolina from the Reorganization of the University, Nov. 1, 1873 to Oct. 30, 1875, SCL.

34. Marchant, "Richard T. Greener: A Story of a Busy Man."

35. South Carolina General Assembly, *Journal of the House of Representatives of the State of South Carolina, 1872–1873* (Columbia, 1873), 460–67, 475–79.

36. *Columbia Daily Phoenix,* Aug. 17 and 20, 1873; Thomas G. Clemson to A. L. Burt, Nov. 16, 1873, Thomas Green Clemson Papers, Duke University Library, Durham, N.C.

37. South Carolina General Assembly, *Journal of the House of Representatives of the State of South Carolina, 1873–1874* (Columbia, 1874), 91.

38. Fisk P. Brewer, "South Carolina University, 1876," Fisk P. Brewer Papers, SCL; USC Faculty Minutes, Feb. 21, 1874, SCL.

39. USC Faculty Minutes, Dec. 8, 13, 1873, Feb. 28, Mar. 7, Apr. 2, 1874, SCL; *Catalogue, University of South Carolina, 1873,* 11, SCL; South Carolina, *Statutes at Large,* vol. 15, 555 (1874).

40. South Carolina, *Reports and Resolutions, 1874–75, Sixth Annual Report of the State Superintendent of Education of the State of South Carolina* (Columbia, 1874), 329.

41. South Carolina, *Reports and Resolutions, 1874–75,* appendix, *Report of the Chairman of the Faculty of the University of South Carolina, 1874,* 6, 55; Daniel Walker Hollis, *University of South Carolina,* vol. 2, *College to University* (1956), 71.

42. South Carolina, *Reports and Resolutions, 1874–75,* appendix, *Report of the Professor of Mental and Moral Science, &c., 1874,* 42; Pamela Mercedes White, "'Free and Open': The Radical University of South Carolina, 1873–1877" (MA thesis, University of South Carolina, 1975), 21.

43. South Carolina, *Reports and Resolutions, 1874–75,* appendix, *Report of the Professor of Mental and Moral Science, &c., 1874,* 42.

44. USC Faculty Minutes, Feb. 15, 1875, SCL; USC Board of Trustees' Minutes, Nov. 1, 1875, SCL; Fisk P. Brewer, "South Carolina University, 1876," Fisk P. Brewer Papers.

45. Richard T. Greener, *Charles Sumner: the Idealist, Statesman, and Scholar* (Columbia, S.C.: Republican Printing Company, 1874), 9, 41.

46. Ibid., 7, 9.

47. Ibid., 38–39.

48. Benj. B. Babbitt, A. W. Cummings, Henry J. Fox, Fisk P. Brewer, T. N. Roberts, William Main, Rudolph Vamphill, E. W. Everson, to Richard T. Greener, July 7, 1874, in Greener, *Charles Sumner,* 3.

49. *Boston Commonwealth*, Feb. 27, 1875.

50. Simmons, *Men of Mark*, 334.

51. *Columbia Daily Union*, Apr. 13, 1874.

52. Clipping dated Mar. 10, 1875, in the Scrapbook of Fisk P. Brewer, Fisk P. Brewer Papers.

53. Simmons, *Men of Mark*, 335.

54. Ibid., 334.

55. Richard T. Greener to [?] Ticknor, Washington, D.C., May 2, 1878, Harvard University Archives.

56. Harvard College, Sixth Report of the Secretary of the Class of 1870 of Harvard College (Cambridge, Mass.: Riverside Press, 1895), 26–27; Richard T. Greener to [?] Ticknor, Washington, D.C., May 2, 1878, Harvard University Archives; John Hammond Moore, *Columbia and Richland County: A South Carolina Community, 1740–1990* (Columbia: University of South Carolina Press, 1993), 223.

57. *Columbia Union Herald*, Aug. 19, 1876.

58. John Herbert Roper, "A Reconsideration: The University of South Carolina during the Reconstruction," *The Proceedings of the South Carolina Historical Association, 1974,* 49; Henry J. Fox, "Our Work at the South," *Methodist Quarterly Review* 4 (Jan. 1874): 29–45.

59. E. R. Roberts to R. T. Greener, Sept. 27, 1876, Miscellaneous Files, SCL; Josh Boston to Prof. Greener, Newberry, S.C., Oct. 2, 1876, and [?] Dickson to Prof. Greener, Orangeburg, S.C., Sept. 27, 1876, Richard T. Greener File, SCL.

60. *Reports and Resolutions, 1875–76, Annual Report of the Board of Trustees of the University of South Carolina Together with Examination Papers, Catalogue, &c., for the Year 1875,* 774–5.

61. USC Faculty Minutes, Dec. 7, 1876, SCL.

62. B. F. Whittemore to Richard T. Greener, East Woburn, Mass., June 11, 1875, *Records of the University of South Carolina;* Board of Trustees' Minutes, Oct. 25, 30, 1875, with attached letter, Richard T. Greener to the Board of Trustees, Oct. 30, 1875; U.S. Bureau of Education, *Public Libraries in the United States of America: Their History, Condition, and Management* (Washington, D.C.: GPO, 1876); *Charleston News and Courier,* Nov. 1, 1875. For more information on Greener as a librarian, see Dale F. Herter, "For the Love of Books: Richard T. Greener's Brief Career as the University of South Carolina's First African-American University Librarian," *Proceedings of the South Carolina Historical Association, 1997,* 54–60; Henry G. Fulmer, "Richard T. Greener and the Radical University Library," *Ex Libris* (1995): 34–37; Robert H. McDonald, "Richard T. Greener: Portrait of a Librarian," 25th Anniversary Historical Papers Presentation at the College of Library and Information Science at the University of South Carolina, Apr. 4, 1998.

63. American Philological Association, *Transactions of the American Philological Association, 1876,* vol. 12 (reprint, New York: Kraus, 1964), 49; *Columbia Daily Union Herald,* July 20, 1875.

64. Simmons, *Men of Mark*, 329, 334.

65. Board of Trustees' Minutes, Oct. 30, 1875, with attached letter, Richard T. Greener to the Board of Trustees, Oct. 30, 1875, SCL.

66. Richard T. Greener to [?] Ticknor, Washington, D.C., May 2, 1878, Harvard University Archives, Cambridge, Mass.

67. Daniel H. Chamberlain to Francis W. Dawson, Jan. 27, June 9 and 24, 1875, and May 22, 1876, Francis Dawson Papers, Duke University, Durham, N.C.; Albert Dial to Daniel H. Chamberlain, Jan. 3, 1876, and Stephen A. Swails to Daniel H. Chamberlain, Jan. 8, 1876, Governor Daniel Chamberlain Papers, South Carolina Department of Archives, Columbia, S.C.

68. South Carolina House, *Journal of the House of Representatives of the State of South Carolina, 1875–76* (Columbia, 1876), 8, 18.

69. *Charleston News and Courier*, Jan. 29, 1876.

70. *Columbia Union-Herald*, Feb. 3, 1876.

71. U.S. Department of Justice, *Letters Received by the Department of Justice from the State of South Carolina, 1871–1884* (Washington, D.C.: National Archives, 1974), R. M. Wallace, U.S. Marshall, to A. Taft, Attorney General, Charleston, S.C., July 26, 1876, with enclosed copy of *Charleston Journal of Commerce*, July 25, 1876.

72. Walter Allen, *Governor Chamberlain's Administration in South Carolina: A Chapter of Reconstruction in the Southern States* (New York: G. P. Putnam's Sons, 1888), 307–30; Joel Williamson, *After Slavery: The Negro in South Carolina during Reconstruction, 1861–1877* (Chapel Hill: University of North Carolina Press, 1965), 267–73.

73. *Charleston News and Courier*, Aug. 10, 1876.

74. Richard T. Greener to [?] Ticknor, Washington, D.C., May 2, 1878, Harvard University Archives.

75. *Columbia Union-Herald*, Sept. 4, 8, 20, 1876.

76. Robert Joseph Swan, "Thomas McCants Stewart and the Failure of the Mission of the Talented Tenth in Black America, 1880–1923" (Ph.D. diss., New York University, 1990), 35; U.S. House of Representatives, *Testimony Taken by the Select Committee on the Recent Election in South Carolina*, 44th Cong., 2d sess., Jan. 22, 1877, 459; *Columbia Union-Herald*, Nov. 6, 1876.

77. U.S. House, *Testimony Taken by the Select Committee on the Recent Election in South Carolina*, 44th Cong., 2d sess., 459–60; U.S. Senate, *South Carolina in 1876*, Dec. 19, 1876, 224–26.

78. U.S. House, *Testimony Taken by the Select Committee on the Recent Election in South Carolina*, 44th Cong., 2d sess., 249, 462; U.S. Senate, *South Carolina in 1876*, 229.

79. Allen, *Governor Chamberlain's Administration in South Carolina*, 480.

80. South Carolina, *Statutes at Large*, vol. 15, 314–15.

81. Richard T. Greener to the USC Board of Trustees, June 29, 1877, Miscellaneous Files, SCL.

82. USC Faculty Minutes, Oct. 5, 1874, SCL.

83. Depositions of Fisk Brewer, Henry J. Fox, A. W. Cummings, B. B. Babbitt, with grades supplied by Cummings, Exhibit Box, The Proceedings of the General Court Martial of Johnson C. Whittaker, United States Military Academy, Records of the Judge Advocate General (Army), RG 153, QQ 2774, National Archives; Testimony of Richard Greener, The Proceedings of the General Court Martial of Johnson C. Whittaker, vol. 62, 25; S. L. Hoge to Secretary of War, May 26, 1876, J. C. Whittaker to Secretary of War, June 2, 1876, Johnson C. Whittaker Acceptance Papers, 395–1876, RG 94, National Archives; *Columbia Union Herald*, Sept. 7, 1876.

84. Greener, "Richard T. Greener," autobiographical sketch, May 19, 1870.

85. Richard T. Greener, "Emigration of Colored Citizens from the Southern States,"

Journal of Social Science (May 1880): 23–35; Greener, "The Intellectual Position of the Negro," *National Quarterly Review* (July 1880): 164–89: *New York Times*, Jan. 23, 1879.

86. Richard T. Greener to Isaiah Wears, Washington, D.C., Apr. 6, 1878, Jacob C. White Papers, Moorland-Spingarn Research Center, Howard University, Washington, D.C.; Richard T. Greener to Nathaniel B. Barnwell, Washington, D.C., Aug. 14 and 30, 1877, Miscellaneous Files, SCL. The treasurer of South Carolina listed the unpaid balance of Greener's salary at $543.36. See *Reports and Resolutions, 1877–78, Report of the Treasurer of the State of South Carolina for the Fiscal Year Ending Oct. 31, 1877*, 21.

87. Richard T. Greener to Isaiah Wears, Washington, D.C., Apr. 6, 10, 25, 1878, Jacob C. White Papers.

88. Rayford Logan, *Howard University: The First Hundred Years, 1867–1967* (New York: New York University Press, 1969), 86. Although the official reason for closing the law school was low enrollment, some have speculated that the predominantly white board of trustees, which included Frederick Douglass as its only black member, used that excuse as "a device to rid of Greener" because of his involvement in the black exodus of 1879. See, J. Clay Smith, *Emancipation: The Making of the Black Lawyer, 1844–1944* (Philadelphia: University of Pennsylvania Press, 1993), 46.

89. Simmons, *Men of Mark*, 330.

90. Emma Lou Thornbrough, *T. Thomas Fortune: Militant Journalist* (Chicago: University of Chicago Press, 1972), 29; *The (Washington) People's Advocate*, Nov. [?], 1878, clipping in scrapbook 58, 37, William Dorsey Collection.

91. Richard T. Greener, "The Academic Life," an address delivered before the students of the Alpha Phi Society, Howard University, Nov. 26, 1878, and "Socrates as a Teacher," a lecture delivered at Washington, D.C., Apr. 5, 1880, Richard T. Greener Papers, Schomburg Center for Research in Black Culture, New York. A list of Greener's speeches and writings can be found in Simmons, *Men of Mark*, 334.

92. *New York Times*, Jan. 23, 1879. Although Greener was criticized by some African Americans for supporting the exodus and charged with being one of its "original promoters," he was simply reacting to the migration that was already underway. He did not consider himself a leader of the exodus, but supported it in the belief that the West offered the freedmen a better chance to make a decent living. See *New York Herald*, Apr. 5, 1879; and U.S. Senate, *Report and Testimony of the Select Committee of the United States Senate to Investigate the Causes of Removal of the Negroes from the Southern States to the Northern States*, 46th Cong., 2d sess., Jan. 24, 1880, 106–7.

93. *Nashville Weekly American*, Feb. 20 and Mar. 13, 1879; Nell Irvin Painter, *Exodusters: Black Migration to Kansas after Reconstruction* (New York: Knopf, 1977), 221–22; National Conference of Colored Men of the United States, *Proceedings of the National Conference of Colored Men of the United States, held in the State Capitol at Nashville, Tennessee, May 6–9, 1879* (Washington, D.C.: n.p., 1879).

94. Charlton H. Tandy to Rev. Moses Dickson, Washington, D.C., Apr. 15, 1879, printed in unidentified newspaper clipping, Charlton H. Tandy Papers, Western Historical Manuscript Collection, Thomas Jefferson Library, University of Missouri-St. Louis, St. Louis, Mo.; Walter M. Merrill and Louis Ruchames, eds., *The Letters of William Lloyd Garrison*, vol. 6, *To Rouse the Slumbering Land, 1868–1879* 586 (Cambridge, Mass.: The Belknap Press of Harvard University Press, 1981); *St. Louis Missouri Republican*, Apr. 19, 1879, May 16, 1879; *St. Louis Globe-Democrat*, May 16, 1879; Robert G. Athearn, *In Search of Canaan: Black Migration to Kansas, 1879–80* (Lawrence: The Regents Press of Kansas, 1978), 34, 114, 118, 253.

95. William Windom and Richard T. Greener to James A. Garfield, Apr. 2, 1879, James A. Garfield Papers, Library of Congress; Richard T. Greener, Secretary, "Official Statement of

Purpose of the National Executive Committee of the National Emigration Aid Society," Apr. 12, 1879, Scrapbook 8, 120, and clipping from *Philadelphia Record*, Apr. 30, 1879, Scrapbook 8, 157, William Dorsey Collection; *New York Herald*, Apr. 5, 1879.

96. Frederick Douglass to Franklin B. Sanborn, Sept. 4 and 9, 1879, Alfred Williams Anthony Collection, New York Public Library. These letters are published in Joseph A. Borome, "Some Additional Light on Frederick Douglass," *Journal of Negro History* 38 (Apr. 1953): 218–19.

97. Frederick Douglass, "The Negro Exodus from the Gulf States," and Richard T. Greener, "The Emigration of Colored Citizens from the Southern States," *Journal of Social Science* (May 1880): 1–35; John Blassingame and John McKivigan, eds., *The Frederick Douglass Papers, Series One: Speeches, Debates and Interviews*, vol. 4, *1864–1880* (New Haven, Conn.: Yale University Press, 1991), 510.

98. *The People's Advocate*, June 7, 1879; Willard B. Gatewood, *Aristocrats of Color: The Black Elite, 1880–1920* (Bloominton: Indiana University Press, 1990), 263–64.

99. John Mercer Langston to James A. Garfield, Washington, D.C., Aug. 31, 1880, and Greener to Garfield, Nov. 3, 1880, James A. Garfield Papers.

100. *Sixth Report of the Secretary of the Class of 1870 of Harvard College* (1895), 26–27.

101. Edward Wilmot Blyden to William Coppinger, Jan. 20, 1882, American Colonization Society Papers, Library of Congress.

102. Richard T. Greener et al., to Madame M. Selika, Washington, D.C., May 11, 1882, Christian A. Fleetwood Papers, Carter G. Woodson Collection, Library of Congress.

103. *The People's Advocate*, July 21, 1883.

104. Letter to John Mercer Langston, Jan. 14, 1886, in Louis R. Harlan, ed., *The Booker T. Washington Papers*, vol. 2, *1860–1889* (Urbana: University of Illinois Press, 1972), 290; Booker T. Washington, *The Story of My Life and Work* (Toronto: J. L. Nichols & Co., 1900), 108–9.

105. *New York Times*, Apr. 7, 8, 1880.

106. Johnson C. Whittaker to "Dear Friend" [Greener], Apr. 7, 1880, The Proceedings of the General Court Martial of Johnson C. Whittaker.

107. Ibid.; The Proceedings of the Court of Inquiry in the Case of Johnson C. Whittaker, United States Military Academy, Records of the Judge Advocate General (Army), RG 153, QQ 1858, part 10, 2806–17, National Archives; John Marszalek, *Court-Martial: a Black Man in America* (New York: Scribners, 1972), 130.

108. *New York Tribune*, May 31, 1880.

109. U.S. Attorney General, *Official Opinions of the Attorneys-General of the United States*, vol. 17 (Washington, D.C.: GPO, 1890), 310–13.

110. Peter S. Michie, "Caste at West Point," *North American Review* 130 (June 1880): 612.

111. *New York Tribune*, June 12, 1880.

112. Richard T. Greener to Alexander Ramsey, Aug. 14, 1880, The Proceedings of the General Court Martial of Johnson C. Whittaker.

113. Rutherford B. Hayes to Secretary of War, Aug. 17, 1880, Whittaker Appointment and Acceptance Papers.

114. Johnson C. Whittaker to Rutherford B. Hayes, Dec. 13, 1880, The Proceedings of the Court of Inquiry in the Case of Johnson C. Whittaker.

115. Howard University, which offered collegiate training for African Americans, was started and named after General O. O. Howard.

116. *U.S. Revised Statutes* (1873–74), sections 1325, 1326, and 1342, article 72; *United States v. Babbitt*, 104 U.S. 767; *Babbitt v. United States*, 16 Ct. Cl. 202. President Hayes ordered

the replacement of Schofield with Howard as superintendent of West Point on Dec. 13, 1880. Schofield, who was convinced of Whittaker's guilt in the matter, was probably removed from the post to appease protests from white and black Americans who believed that changes were needed at West Point. See John M. Schofield, *Forty-Six Years in the Army* (New York: Century, 1897), 445–48.

117. Two of the handwriting experts, one working for the prosecution and one for the defense, published articles in legal periodicals at the time. A reading of these articles gives a good representation of how tedious and confusing the expert testimony must have been. See "Calligraphy and the Whittaker Case," *Criminal Law Magazine* 2 (Mar. 1881): 139–79; and R. U. Piper, "Expert Testimony–Scientific Testimony in the Examination of Written Documents, Illustrated by the Whittaker Case, &c.," *American Law Register,* n.s. 21, 30 (July–Aug.): 425–42, 489–507.

118. The Proceedings of the General Court Martial of Johnson C. Whittaker, 6046–101. For latitude of court–martial proceedings, see Charles McClure, *A Digest of Opinions of the Judge-Advocates General of the Army* (Washington, D.C.: GPO, 1901), 356, sec. 1285.

119. General Court Martial Order #18, Headquarters of the Army, Mar. 22, 1882, Whittaker Appointment and Acceptance Papers.

120. Richard T. Greener and Daniel H. Chamberlain to Nelson A. Miles, June 10, 1881, Exhibit Box, The Proceedings of the General Court Martial of Johnson C. Whittaker.

121. Greener to D. G. Swaim, not dated, Exhibit Box, The Proceedings of the General Court Martial of Johnson C. Whittaker.

122. D. G. Swaim to Robert T. Lincoln, Dec. 1, 1881, Exhibit Box, The Proceedings of the General Court Martial of Johnson C. Whittaker.

123. U.S. Attorney General, *Official Opinions of the Attorneys-General of the United States,* vol. 17 (1890), 310–13.

124. General Court Martial Order #18, Headquarters of the Army, Mar. 22, 1882, Whittaker Appointment and Acceptance Papers.

125. Robert T. Lincoln to the Adjutant General, Mar. 21, 1882, Whittaker Appointment and Acceptance Papers.

126. U.S. Attorney General, *Official Opinions of the Attorneys-General of the United States,* vol. 17 (1890), 67–69.

127. William S. McFeely, *Frederick Douglass* (New York: Norton, 1990), 301.

128. *Philadelphia Inquirer,* Jan. 5, 1881, *Philadelphia Public Ledger,* Jan. 5, 1881; invitation and ticket to an address by Greener at the Musical Fund Hall in Philadelphia on Jan. 4, "The Educational, Industrial, Mechanical, and Political Progress of the Colored People of the United States," clippings in Richard T. Greener File, William Dorsey Collection; *New York Times,* Jan. 6, 1881.

129. Richard T. Greener to the editor of the *New York Times,* Washington, D.C., Jan. 8, 1881, published in the *New York Times,* Jan. 21, 1881.

130. Ibid.

131. John Blassigame and John McKivigan, eds., *The Frederick Douglass Papers, Series One: Speeches, Debates, Interviews,* vol. 5, *1881–1895* (New Haven, Conn.: Yale University Press, 1992), 80–81.

132. Ibid., 148; *Philadelphia Christian Recorder,* May 24 and 31, 1883, cited in ibid.

133. *Washington Post,* Feb. 23, 1884.

134. *New York Globe,* Feb. 2, 1884.

135. *Baltimore Sun,* June 14, 1884, newspaper clipping in scrapbook 62, 33, William Dorsey Collection.

136. Civil Rights Act of 1875, 18 Statutes 114 (1875); *Dred Scott v. Sandford*, 60 U.S. (19 How.) 393, 407 (1857); *The Civil Rights Cases*, 109 U.S. 3 (1883); *New York Evening Post*, Oct. 16, 1883; Smith, *Emancipation*, 221–22.

137. William Henry Crogman, "Negro Education—Its Helps and Hindrances," speech delivered before the National Educational Association convention in Madison, Wisc., on July 16, 1884, in *Lift Every Voice: African American Oratory, 1787–1900*, ed. Phillip S. Foner and Robert James Branham (Tuscaloosa: University of Alabama Press, Mar. 10, 1998), 623–24, 632.

138. Green, *The Secret City*, 119.

139. *Cleveland Gazette*, Feb. 7, 1885; Gatewood, *Aristocrats of Color*, 163–64.

140. *New York Times*, July 30, 1885; *New York Tribune*, July 31, 1885; Richard T. Greener to John Edward Bruce, New York, Sept. 16, 1885, John Edward Bruce Papers, Schomburg Center for Research in Black Culture, New York.

141. *New York Age*, Feb. 22, 1892, clipping in Richard T. Greener File, William Dorsey Collection.

142. Richard T. Greener to John P. Greener [misprint, should read "John P. Green"], untitled newspaper clipping, July 11, 1885, Richard T. Greener File, William Dorsey Collection; *New York Times*, June 29, 1885; *New York Tribune*, June 30, 1885; Joseph Benson Foraker, *Notes of a Busy Life*, vol. I, 3rd ed. (Cincinnati, Ohio: Stewart & Kidd, 1917), 175–91; David A. Gerber, *Black Ohio and the Color Line, 1860–1915* (Urbana: University of Illinois Press, 1976), 232, 240–41.

143. *Sixth Report of the Secretary of the Class of 1870 of Harvard College*, 28.

144. Richard T. Greener to Isaiah Wears, New York City, Dec. 7, 1885, Jacob C. White Papers.

145. *Sixth Report of the Secretary of the Class of 1870 of Harvard College*, 27.

146. Daniel S. Lawson to Richard T. Greener, Washington, Oct. 8, 1885, Grover Cleveland Papers, Library of Congress; Stewart and Kahn, "Richard T. Greener," 10–15; David M. Kahn, "The Grant Monument," *Journal of the Society of Architectural Historians* 41 (Oct. 1982): 212–31; *New York Age*, Feb. 22, 1892, and untitled newspaper clipping, Nov. 22, 1896, from Richard T. Greener File, William Dorsey Collection; *New York Times*, Oct. 6, Nov. 27, 28, Dec. 1, 8, 22, 1891; *Minute Book*, July 1885–Mar. 1886, Grant Monument Association Archives, General Grant National Memorial, National Park Service, New York City. The minute books from April 1886 to January 1912 were destroyed when the Equitable Life Insurance Company Building caught fire on Jan. 9, 1912. N. Lebrun to R. T. Greener, Dec. 17, 1888, GMAA, box 6, file 7; letters, R. T. Greener to each of the architects competing for the honor of designing the Grant Monument, Apr. 12, 1890, GMAA, box 6, file 9; R. T. Greener to C. Clinton, Apr. 26, 1890, GMAA, box 6, file 9.

147. Richard T. Greener to Isaiah Wears, New York City, Dec. 7, 1885, and Feb. 12, 1886, Jacob C. White Papers; New York City Civil Service Commission, *Annual Reports and Rules and Regulations of the New York City Civil Service Commission, 1884–1896, Second Annual Report of the Supervisory Board of Commissioners of the New York Municipal Civil Service* (New York: Martin B. Brown, 1898), 103; *Third Annual Report*, 15; *Fourth Annual Report*, 13; *Fifth Annual Report*, 21, all ibid.

148. Untitled newspaper clipping, Nov. 22, 1896, Richard T. Greener File, William Dorsey Collection; Sollors, Titcomb, and Underwood, *Blacks at Harvard*, 44; *New York Times*, Mar. 2, 1886. *Blacks at Harvard* and the newspaper clipping in the Dorsey Collection both refer to Greener as the secretary of the Irish Parliamentary Fund. After looking through the reports of the Irish Parliamentary Fund Association's meetings in the *New York Times*, I did not find any listing of Greener as secretary of the association. The one *Times* article I found that described

his speech on Mar. 1, 1886, simply mentioned that he was the secretary of the Grant Monument Association. Greener probably got involved with the Irish Parliamentary Fund as a volunteer. William Russell Grace, the former mayor of New York and president of the Grant Monument Association, more than likely encouraged Greener to get involved with the Irish Fund. Grace was a regular at meetings of the association and two weeks before Greener's speech had given one of his own in Boston. See William Russell Grace, "The Irish in America," a lecture at Boston Theatre, Feb. 21, 1886 (Chicago: McDonnell Brothers, 1916); *New York Times*, Jan 12, 13, Mar. 30, June 15, 1886, June 1–7, July 12, 1887.

149. Commonwealth Club (New York City), *Members, 1891–1892* (New York: A. B. King, 1892), 4, 15, 23.

150. Richard T. Greener to Francis Grimké, New York City, Dec. 27, 1890, in Carter G. Woodson, ed., *The Works of Francis Grimké*, vol. 4, *Letters* (Washington, D.C.: Associated Publishers, 1942), 24–26; letter from Ellen Collins, New York, Aug. 23, 1892, in Harlan, *Booker T. Washington Papers*, vol. 3, p. 258; letter from Thomas Junius Calloway, Washington, D.C., May 2, 1894, ibid., 415.

151. Letter from Greener, 26 May 1894, in Harlan, *Booker T. Washington Papers*, vol. 3, p. 447.

152. Richard T. Greener, "The White Problem," *Lend a Hand: a Record of Progress* 12 (May 1894): 354–67.

153. Richard T. Greener, "The Intellectual Position of the Negro," *National Quarterly Review* (July 1880): 164–89; James Parton, "Antipathy to the Negro," *North American Review* 127 (Nov.–Dec. 1878): 476–91; Shirley Wilson Logan, *With Pen and Voice: A Critical Anthology of Nineteenth-Century African-American Women* (Carbondale, Ill.: Southern Illinois University Press, 1995), 133–34, 138, 139; National Association of Colored Women's Clubs, Records of the National Association of Colored Women's Clubs, 1895–1992, *History of the National Association of Colored Women's Clubs* (1902; reprinted Washington, D.C.: National Association of Colored Women's Clubs, 1978), 7–8; Elizabeth Lindsay Davis, *Lifting as They Climb* (Washington, D.C.: National Association of Colored Women's Clubs, 1933), 16. When visiting Washington, D.C., Greener attended the regular, but informal, gatherings at Francis Grimké's home on Friday nights and Anna Julia Cooper's home on Sunday nights to engage in what Cooper described as "planned, systematic and enlightening but pleasurable and progressive intercourse of a cultural and highly stimulating kind." See Charles Lemert and Esme Bhan, eds., *The Voice of Anna Julia Cooper* (New York: Rowman & Littelfield, 1998), 311.

154. Untitled newspaper clipping, Nov. 22, 1896, Richard T. Greener File, William Dorsey Collection; Richard T. Greener to Isaiah Wears, New York City, Apr. 27, 1894, Jacob C. White Papers.

155. National Association of Colored Women's Clubs, *History of the National Association of Colored Women's Clubs*, 3–5.

156. Richard T. Greener, "Report on the First National Conference of Colored Women, 1895," Rare Book Room, Boston Public Library; Beverly Guy-Sheftall, *Black Women in United States History*, vol. 11, *Daughters of Sorrow: Attitudes toward Black Women, 1880–1920* (Brooklyn, N.Y.: Carlson, 1990), 27–28; Wilson Jeremiah Moses, "Domestic Feminism, Conservatism, Sex Roles, and Black Women's Clubs, 1893–1896," *Journal of Social and Behavioral Sciences* 24 (fall 1978): 172.

157. Richard T. Greener, "Report on the First National Conference of Colored Women, 1895," Rare Book Room, Boston Public Library, 4–7.

158. Deborah Gray White, *Too Heavy a Load: Black Women in Defense of Themselves, 1894–1994* (New York: Norton, 1999), 36–39.

159. R. T. G. to John Edward Bruce, Chicago, Ill., Sept. 10, 1895, with attached "Call for a National Conference," John Edward Bruce Papers, Schomburg Center for Research in Black Culture.

160. R. T. Greener to John Edward Bruce, Detroit, Dec. 13, 1895, John Edward Bruce Papers; Rosalyn Terborg-Penn, *African American Women in the Struggle for the Vote, 1850–1920* (Bloomington: Indiana University Press, 1998), 88–89.

161. R. T. Greener to John Edward Bruce, Detroit, Dec. 13, 1895, John Edward Bruce Papers; unidentified newspaper clipping, Feb. 5, 1896, Richard T. Greener File, William Dorsey Collection; U.S. Senate, *Memorial of the National Association of Colored Men of America Relative to the Status of the Colored Race in the United States*, 54th Cong., 1st sess., Jan. 2, 1896, S. Doc. 61.

162. U.S. Senate, *Memorial of the National Association of Colored Men of America Relative to the Status of the Colored Race in the United States*, 54th Cong., 1st sess., Jan. 2, 1896, S. Doc. 61.; Greener to Bruce, Detroit, Dec. 13, 1895, John Edward Bruce Papers; *Detroit Tribune*, Dec. 14, 1895; *New York Times*, Dec. 14, 1895; Herbert Aptheker, *A Documentary History of the Negro People in the United States*, vol. 2, *From the Reconstruction to the Founding of the N.A.A.C.P.* (1992), 765–68.

163. R. T. G. to John Edward Bruce, Chicago, Sept. 10, 1895, and R. T. Greener to John Edward Bruce, Detroit, Dec. 13, 1895, John Edward Bruce Papers.

164. *Chicago Tribune*, Dec. 18, 1895.

165. R. T. Greener to John Edward Bruce, Detroit, Dec. 13, 1895, John Edward Bruce Papers.

166. Richard T. Greener to John Edward Bruce, New York City, Jan. [?], 1896, John Edward Bruce Papers; Richard T. Greener to Francis J. Grimké, New York City, Jan. 27, 1896, Jacob C. White Papers.

167. Richard T. Greener to George A. Myers, Chicago, Aug. 20 and Sept. 2, 1896, George A. Myers Papers, National Afro-American Museum and Cultural Center, Ohio Historical Society, Columbus.

168. Dorothy Drinkard-Hawkshawe, "Prelude to the Niagara Movement and the NAACP," *The Crisis* 84 (Feb. 1977): 54–55.

169. Richard T. Greener to Isaiah Wears, Chicago, Sept. 27, 1896, Jacob C. White Papers.

170. Letter from Richard Theodore Greener, Washington, D.C., Mar. 26, 1897, in Louis R. Harlan, ed., *The Booker T. Washington Papers*, vol. 4, *1895–1898*, (Urbana: University of Illinois Press), 265–66; letter from Greener, Philadelphia, Apr. 5, 1897, ibid., 269.

171. John Addison Porter to Richard T. Greener, May 13, 1897, William McKinley Papers, Library of Congress.

172. Blakely, "Richard T. Greener and the 'Talented Tenth's' Dilemma," 308.

173. Ibid., 308–10; Sollors, Titcomb, and Underwood, *Blacks at Harvard*, 442–44.

174. *Indianapolis Freeman*, Jan. 25, 1896; Swan, "Thomas McCants Stewart," 298, 300.

175. William Ferris, *The African Abroad*, vol. 2 (New Haven, Conn.: Tuttle, Morehouse, and Taylor, 1913), 773.

176. Paul L. Dunbar, "Representative American Negroes," in *The Negro Problem* (New York: J. Pott & Company, 1903), 202–3.

177. Alexander Crummell to John Edward Bruce, Jan. 21, 1898, John Edward Bruce Papers; Alfred A. Moss, *The American Negro Academy: Voice of the Talented Tenth* (Baton Rouge: Louisiana State University Press, 1981), 31–33, 88–89.

178. Jean Strouse, *Morgan: American Financier* (New York: Random House, 1999), 515.

179. *Report of the Secretary of the Class of 1870 of Harvard College, 1920*, 66. In addition to speaking at the Bethel Literary Society meeting, Greener spoke at the Sumner School in Washington. An introduction to his address is misfiled in the Robert Terrell Papers in a folder that contains an address by Booker T. Washington. Terrell evidently introduced Greener, noting the work he had done in the 1870s at the Institute for Colored Youth in Philadelphia and at the Sumner School, when it was called the Preparatory School for Colored Children in Washington. See Booker T. Washington speech, Robert Terrell Papers, Library of Congress; *Cleveland Gazette*, Dec. 12, 1896.

180. *Washington Bee*, June 18 and 25, 1898.

181. Richard T. Greener to Isaiah Wears, New York City, Apr. 18, 1898, and Richard T. Greener to Isaiah Wears, New York City, Apr. 24, 1898, Jacob C. White Papers. In the Apr. 24, 1898, letter, Greener claimed that he had been driven so far out of the affairs of his race that he was not even notified of the death of Andrew F. Stevens Sr., a prominent black leader Greener had known in Philadelphia. See Roger Lane, *William Dorsey's Philadelphia and Ours: On the Past and Future of the Black City in America* (New York: Oxford University Press, 1991), 113, 114, 168, 206, 213, 222, 287, and 298.

182. Richard T. Greener to Isaiah Wears, Vladivostok, Russia, Jan. 7, 1899, Jacob C. White Papers.

183. Richard T. Greener to Alvey A. Adee, Second Assistant Secretary of State, Chicago, Ill., July 27, 1898., U.S. Department of State, Despatches from United States Consuls in Vladivostok, 1898–1906, National Archives.

184. Ibid., Richard T. Greener to Thomas Wilbur Cridler, Third Assistant Secretary of State, Vladivostok, Russia, Sept. 20, 1898.

185. Ibid., Richard T. Greener to Thomas Wilbur Cridler, Vladivostok, Russia, Dec. 23, 1898; *Dalnii Vostok* (Vladivostok), (Dec. 23) Dec. 11, 1898, enclosure.

186. Richard T. Greener, English translation of the poem, "My Portrait," by Alexander Pushkin, Richard T. Greener Papers, Schomberg Center for Research in Black Culture.

187. U.S. Department of State, *Despatches from United States Consuls in Vladivostok, 1898–1906*, Richard T. Greener to Thomas Wilbur Cridler, Vladivostok, Russia, July 1, 1900, May 21, 1901.

188. Nicholas Senn, *Around the World via Siberia* (Chicago: W. B. Conkey, 1902), 171–72; Norman E. Saul, *Concord and Conflict: The United States and Russia, 1867–1914* (Lawrence: University of Kansas Press, 1996), 435, 448.

189. Richard T. Greener to Whitefield McKinlay, Vladivostok, Russia, Feb. 18, 1902, Whitefield McKinlay Papers, Carter G. Woodson Collection, Manuscripts Division, Library of Congress.

190. U.S. Department of State, *Despatches from United States Consuls in Vladivostok, 1898–1906*, Richard T. Greener to H. H. D. Peirce, Third Assistant Secretary of State, with enclosure of *Vostchni Vestnik* (Vladivostok), (May 12) Apr. 30, 1903.

191. Baron Komura, Japanese Foreign Minister, to John Hay, Feb. 16, 1904, and Takahira, Secretary of Legation, to Hay, Mar. 5, 1904, U.S. Department of State, Notes from the Japanese Legation in the United States to the Department of State, 1858–1906, National Archives.

192. "Colored Diplomats Abroad," *Washington (D.C.) Colored American*, Feb. 27, 1904; *Boston Globe*, Mar. 12, 1904.

193. U.S. Department of State, *Notes from the Japanese Legation in the United States to the Department of State*, Takahira to Hay, Mar. 5, 9, Apr. 20, 1904.

194. U.S. Department of State, *Despatches from United States Consuls in Vladivostok*,

1898–1906, Richard T. Greener to Francis B. Loomis, Assistant Secretary of State, Oct. 28, 1904.

195. Blakely, "Richard T. Greener and the 'Talented Tenth's' Dilemma," 312; ibid., 316; U.S. Department of State, *Notes from the Japanese Legation in the United States to the Department of State, 1858–1906*, Emperor of Japan to the President of the United States, Oct. 19, 1905; Harvard Alumni Association, *Harvard University Directory: A Catalogue of Men Now Living Who Have Been Enrolled as Students in the University* (Cambridge, Mass.: Harvard University Press, 1910), 297, 415.

196. Letter to Samuel Laing Williams, Tuskegee, Ala., Feb. 15, 1905, in Louis R. Harlan and Raymond W. Smock, eds., *The Booker T. Washington Papers*, vol. 8, *1904–1906* (Urbana: University of Illinois Press, 1979), 193–94; letter to John Stevens Durham, Tuskegee, Ala., Apr. 10, 1905, ibid., 253–54; letter to Charles William Anderson, Tuskegee, Ala., Feb. 20, 1906, ibid., 255; 528; letter to Richard Theodore Greener, Tuskegee, Ala., May 18, 1906, in Harlan and Smock, eds., *The Booker T. Washington Papers*, vol. 9, *1906–1908* (Urbana: University of Illinois Press, 1979) ,10; letter from Greener, Storer College, Harper's Ferry, W.Va., July 31, 1906, ibid., 48; letter to Greener, Sioux City, Iowa, Aug. 7, 1906, ibid., 51; letter from Greener, Chicago, Ill., Aug. 11, 1906, and letter to Greener [no location], Aug. 11, 1906, ibid., 55–56; letter from Greener, Washington, D.C., Aug. 2, 1906, ibid., 61; Washington to Elihu Root, Feb. 23, 1906, and Washington to Greener, Aug. 9 and 24, 1906, Booker T. Washington Papers, Library of Congress.

197. Richard T. Greener, "Progress of the Negro Race," *The Colored American Magazine* 12 (Feb. 1907): 117; Carolyn Wedin, *Inheritors of the Spirit: Mary White Ovington and the Founding of the NAACP* (New York: John Wiley & Sons, 1998), 74–75; Mary White Ovington, *Black and White Sat Down Together: The Reminiscences of an NAACP Founder*, ed. Ralph E. Luker (New York: The Feminist Press, 1995), 24–25.

198. Greener to Washington, Oct. 15, 1906; Washington to Greener, Oct. 20, 1906; Greener to Washington, Feb. 23, 1907; Washington to William Loeb Jr., June 12, 1907; Greener to Washington, June 23, 1907; Greener to Washington, Aug. 31, 1907, all in Booker T. Washington Papers, Library of Congress; Washington to Whitefield McKinlay, Feb. 23, 1907, Whitefield McKinlay Papers.

199. *Chicago Daily Tribune*, May 4, 1922.

200. *Charleston (S.C.) Southern Reporter*, June 30, 1906, clipping in the Archibald Grimké Papers, Moorland-Spingarn Research Center; Dickson J. Bruce, *Archibald Grimké: Portrait of a Black Independent* (Baton Rouge, La.: Louisiana State University Press, 1993), 153–54.

201. *Columbia (S.C.) The State*, Nov. 18, 1907; Woodson, ed., *The Works of Francis J. Grimké*, vol. 4, *Letters*, 104–12.

202. R. T. Greener to "Dear Friends" [Grimké's], New Orleans, Jan. 1, 1908, Francis J. Grimké Papers, Moorland-Spingarn Research Center.

203. *Robinson v. Chicago City Ry. Co. et al.*, 118 F. 438 (C.C.N.D.I.L. 1902) (No. 810); *Robinson v. Chicago Rys. Co.*, 174 F. 40 (C.C.N.D.I.L. 1909) (No. 1558).

204. Richard T. Greener to Robert H. Terrell, Chicago, Feb. 18, 1909, Robert Terrell Papers; Richard T. Greener to C. J. Woodson, Esq., Chairman, Committee, "Harvard men," Middle Atlantic States, etc., Chicago, May 16, 1914, Robert Terrell Papers.

205. *Proceedings of the National Negro Conference, 1909* (New York: Arno Press, 1969), 224.

206. R. T. G. to W. E. B. DuBois, Chicago, Feb. 4, 1910, in Herbert Aptheker, ed., *The Correspondence of W. E. B. DuBois*, vol. 1, *Selections, 1877–1934* (Amherst: University of Massachusetts Press, 1973), 168.

207. Richard T. Greener to Whitefield McKinlay, Chicago, Aug. 1, 1910, Whitefield McKinlay Papers.

208. Herbert Aptheker, ed., *The Complete Published Works of W. E. B. DuBois, Pamphlets and Leaflets* (White Plains, N.Y.: Kraus-Thomson,1986), 95–98.

209. Richard T. Greener to J. C. Calloway, Chicago, Dec. 23, 1910, Jacob C. White Papers.

210. Cornelius Bailey Hosmer to Emmett Jay Scott, Milwaukee, Wisc., Apr. 20, 1912, in Louis R. Harlan and Raymond W. Smock, eds., *The Booker T. Washington Papers*, vol. 11, *1911–12* (Urbana: University of Illinois Press, 1981), 524–25. In fact, Greener came to resent Booker T. Washington and his school, referring to it as the "Tuskegee junket" and the "Tuskegee Colossus." See R. T. G. to Archibald Grimké, Chicago, Ill., Apr. 10, 1915, Archibald Grimké Papers, Moorland-Spingarn Research Center.

211. Richard T. Greener to J. C. Calloway, Oct. 4, 1912, Jacob C. White Papers. After the election, Greener wrote a letter to his old friend Archibald Grimké criticizing him for supporting Theodore Roosevelt's unsuccessful bid for a third term as the Progressive party's candidate. Greener supported Robert LaFollette's attempt to get the nomination from the Progressive Party. Once Roosevelt won it, Greener supported Wilson in the election. Greener admitted that he had written some flattering letters to Roosevelt from Vladivostok when the latter was nominated for president by the Republicans in 1904. He told Grimké that Roosevelt was a disappointment as a leader and advocate for black civil rights. Greener also disliked Roosevelt personally, feeling that the president had turned his back on him by refusing to meet with him in 1907 regarding his dismissal from the foreign service. See Greener to Archibald Grimké, Apr. 28, 1913, Archibald Grimké Papers; Bruce, *Archibald Grimké*, 183.

212. Richard T. Greener to J. C. Calloway, Dec. 23, 1910, Jacob C. White Papers.

213. Strouse, *Morgan: American Financier*, 509–20.

214. Richard T. Greener to J. C. Calloway, Oct. 4, 1912, May 14, 1913, and Dec. 18, 1914, Jacob C. White Papers.

215. Ibid.

216. Phillips *Bulletin*, July 1922, Phillips Academy Archives, Oliver Wendell Holmes Library, Phillips Academy; Stewart and Kahn, "Richard T. Greener," 8–9.

217. Richard T. Greener to Roy Nash, Secretary, NAACP, July 20, 1916, Joel S. Spingarn Papers, Moorland-Spingarn Research Center, Howard University.

218. *The Crisis* 13 (Feb. 1917): front cover.

219. Richard T. Greener, "Reminiscences of Frederick Douglass," *Champion Magazine* 1 (Feb. 1917): 291–95.

220. R. T. Greener to Carter G. Woodson, Chicago, Oct. 24, 1917, Carter G. Woodson Papers, Carter G. Woodson Collection, Library of Congress; Dick Russell, *Black Genius and the American Experience* (New York: Carroll & Graf, 1998), 303.

221. Richard T. Greener to Arthur A. Schomburg, Chicago, June 4, 1918, Richard T. Greener Papers, Schomburg Center for Research in Black Culture.

222. Woodson, ed., *The Works of Francis J. Grimké*, vol. 4, *Letters*, 236. The italics in the quote are Greener's.

223. *Cincinnati Union*, Nov. 13, 1920, and May 13, 1922.

224. *New York Herald*, Apr. 5, 1879.

225. Senn, *Around the World via Siberia*, 171–72.

226. Harlan, ed., *Booker T. Washington Papers*, vol. 3 , *1889–1895*, 447.

7: SOUTH CAROLINA'S BLACK ELECTED OFFICIALS DURING RECONSTRUCTION

1. These remarks are based on material found in two books by Eric Foner: *Freedom's Lawmakers: A Directory of Black Officeholders during Reconstruction* (New York: Oxford University Press, 1993); and *Reconstruction: America's Unfinished Revolution, 1863–1877* (New York: Harper and Row, 1988).

Contributors

W. LEWIS BURKE JR. is a Professor of Law in the Department of Clinical Legal Studies at the Law School at the University of South Carolina. He earned his bachelor's degree from Mississippi State University and his J.D. from the University of South Carolina. While he is the author of a book on consumer law and has written other scholarly legal articles, his only prior historical work was "A History of the Opening Statement from Barristers to Corporate Lawyers" in the *American Journal of Legal History* (1993).

ERIC FONER is the DeWitt Clinton Professor of History at Columbia University; he specializes in the Civil War and Reconstruction, slavery, and nineteenth-century America. He earned bachelor's degrees from both Columbia University (1963) and Oriel College, Oxford University (1965), and received his doctorate from Columbia in 1969. Notable among his many publications are *Free Soil, Free Labor, Free Men: The Ideology of the Republican Party before the Civil War* (1970), *Politics and Ideology in the Age of the Civil War* (1980), *Nothing but Freedom: Emancipation and Its Legacy* (1983), *Freedom's Lawmakers: A Directory of Black Officeholders during Reconstruction* (1993), and *Reconstruction: America's Unfinished Revolution, 1863–1877* (1988), which won the Bancroft Prize in American History, the Parkman Prize, and the Los Angeles Times Book Award, among other honors. His latest book, *The Story of American Freedom*, was published in 1998.

BELINDA GERGEL is an Associate Professor of History and Chair of the Department of History and Political Science at Columbia College in Columbia, South Carolina. She received her B.A. from Columbia College in 1972 and earned both a M.Ed. (1974) and a Ph.D. (1976) from Duke University. She has published several works, including "The Israelites of Columbia, South Carolina: The Development of an Antebellum Jewish Community" in *Proceedings of the South Carolina Historical Association* (1996), a book review for the scholarly journal *American Jewish History*, and *In Pursuit of the Tree of Life: A History of the Early Jews of Columbia, South Carolina, and the Tree of Life Congregation* (1996), which she coauthored with her husband, Richard. Dr. Gergel is also extensively involved in the Jewish Historical Society of South Carolina.

RICHARD GERGEL is a partner in the law firm of Gergel Nickles & Solomon, P.A., in Columbia, South Carolina. He earned both his bachelor's and his law degree from Duke University (B.A., 1975; J.D., 1979). His published works include "School Desegregation: A Student's View," in *New South* (1971); "Wade Hampton and the Rise of One Party Racial Orthodoxy in South Carolina," in *Proceedings of the South Carolina Historical Association* (1977); and *In Pursuit of the Tree of Life: A History of the Early Jews of Columbia, South Carolina, and the Tree of Life Congregation* (1996), which he coauthored with his wife, Belinda. Since 1998, he has held positions as president of both the South Carolina Supreme Court Historical Society and the Jewish Historical Society of South Carolina.

MICHAEL ROBERT MOUNTER is a Ph.D. candidate in the Department of History at the University of South Carolina. He received his bachelor's degree in history and Spanish from Queens College in Charlotte, North Carolina, in 1993, and his master's degree in history from the University of South Carolina in 1997. His works include a transcription of "The Tenure of Land in Ireland" by Richard Greener, "The Political-Military Relationship and Austrian State Treaty Negotiations, 1945–1949" (M.A. thesis), and "A Guide to the Robert P. Wilkins Collection on the History of the South Carolina Judiciary, 1965–1985" for the Legal History Collection at the Coleman Karesh Law Library, University of South Carolina. He is currently working on his dissertation, "Richard Theodore Greener and the African American Individual."

JOHN OLDFIELD is a Senior Lecturer in History at the University of Southampton. His focus is on American race relations and slavery and abolition in the Atlantic world, 1750–1870. He earned both his M.A. and his Ph.D. from Cambridge University. He is the author of several works, including *Alexander Crummell (1819–1898) and the Creation of an African-American Church in Liberia* (1990), *Civilization and Black Progress: Selected Writings of Alexander Crummell on the South* (1995), and *Popular Politics and British Anti-Slavery: The Mobilisation of Public Opinion against the Slave Trade, 1787–1807* (1995). Most recently, he has received a research award from the British Academy to write an intellectual biography of John Edward Bruce.

J. CLAY SMITH JR. is Professor of Law at Howard University, teaching in the public law area. His education includes a B.A. from Creighton University

(1964), a J.D. from Howard University (1967), and both an LL.M. and S.J.D. from George Washington University (1970; 1977). He has formerly held positions as a member of the United States Equal Employment Opportunity Commission, the dean of Howard University Law School, and the president of the Washington Bar Association. His publications include two recent works on African American lawyers, *Emancipation: The Making of the Black Lawyer, 1844–1944* (1993) and *Rebels in Law: Voices in History of Black Women Lawyers* (1998), and numerous scholarly articles on law, politics, society, and the arts.

JAMES LOWELL UNDERWOOD is the Strom Thurmond Professor of Law at the University of South Carolina where he has taught since 1966. He received both his bachelor's and his J.D. degrees from Emory University (A.B., 1959; J.D., 1962), and was awarded his LL.M. from Yale University in 1966. He has served as head of the National Institute of Justice and has held a Fulbright professorship at Queen's University in Belfast, Northern Ireland. He has also twice received the University of South Carolona's Outstanding Law Professor Award. Professor Underwood's publications include the four-volume series *The Constitution of South Carolina*, the most recent volume of which, *The Struggle for Political Equality*, was published in 1994; *A Guide to Federal Discovery Rules* (1979); and *Civil Trial Manual* (1974), among other legal publications.

Index

University of Virginia, 135
University of Wisconsin, 123

Vicksburg, Miss., 106
Virgin Islands, 97
Virginia, 167, 172, 212
Vladivostok, Russia, 105, 130, 155, 156,
    157– 59, 162, 164, 165, 240
Voting Rights Act of 1965, 25, 167
voting rights and qualifications, 2, 3, 4,
    5, 7–13, 25, 112, 180–81, 183, 184,
    191, 198, 216; black voter influence,
    demise of, 11–13

Waco, Tex., 173
Walhalla, 141
Wallace, David Duncan, 182, 210
Wallace, William Henry, 58, 59
Wallace v. Hayne (1876), 59–60
Wallace House, 58–64 *passim*
Wardlaw, possible reference to David
    Lewis or Francis Hugh, 124
Warren, Mortimer Alanson, 98, 115
Warren, W. A., 223
Washington, Booker T., 98, 144, 151–
    52, 154, 155, 159–60, 161, 162, 165,
    238
Washington, E. C. C., 128
Washington, George, 73
Washington, Julius I., 128
Washington, Margaret Murray, 154
Washington, D.C., 95, 98, 103–4, 105,
    108, 119, 120, 133–35, 138, 139;
    143–45, 149, 150, 152, 156, 157,
    161, 162, 172, 173, 212
Washington Bee, 103, 149, 157
Watson, A. R., 127
Watson, Benjamin E., 128
Wears, Isaiah, 143, 150, 157, 162, 163
Wempey, John A., 106
West Indies, 131
West Point, 111, 142, 145–47, 160, 234
West Virginia, 118
Whaley v. Bank of Charleston (1874), 66,
    86, 189
Wheeler, Thomas H., 128

Whipper, William, xix, 10, 12, 19, 40,
    43, 44–45, 73, 116, 117, 120, 122,
    127, 175, 189, 191, 195; photograph
    of, following 115
Whipper v. Talbird (1889), 122
White, Deborah Gray, 153
White, John H., in group photograph
    following 71
White, William J., 150
White House, 64, 82
Whittaker, Johnson Chestnut, 120, 128,
    142, 145–47, 160, 224, 234
Whittemore, B. F., 198
Wigg, James, 12, 191
Wigg plan, 12
Wilder, C. M., 92, 114, 194, 212, in
    group photograph following 71
Wilkes, T. M., 115
Wilkes-Barre, Pa., 206
Wilkes-Barre, Pa., school district, 37
Willard, A. J., 45, 46, 53, 54, 55, 56, 62,
    63, 66, 75, 79, 82, 83, 203, 207, 208,
    209
Williams, Lydia, 100, 218
Williams, Mark A., 120, 123, 129
Williams, Walton W., 129
Williamsburg (S.C.), 215
Wilmarth, Judy, 205
Wilson, Woodrow, xxi, 162, 163–64,
    172
Wimbush, Lucius W., in group photo-
    graph following 71
Windon, William, 144
Wingate, John, 115
Winnsboro, 138
Withers, Thomas Jefferson, 124
woman suffrage, 10–11, 189–90
Women's Era Club, 152
women's rights, 10–11, 154, 164,
    189–90
Woodruff, Josephus, 102, 219
Woodson, Carter G., 163
Woodward, C. Vann, xxi
Woody, R. H., 188–89, 204
Wragg, John, 205
Wright, Campfield, 69